**2008** EDITION

# BUYING A HOUSE IN
# France

**André De Vries and
Michael Streeter**

**crimson**

This third edition published in Great Britain in 2008 by:
Crimson Publishing
Westminster House
Kew Road
Richmond
Surrey
TW9 2ND

First published 2003
3rd edition 2008

A catalogue record for this book is available from the British Library.

ISBN: 978-1-85458-377-2

Printed and bound by Mega Printing, Turkey

# Contents

# Acknowledgements

During the writing of this book, many French and foreign residents of France have shared their experiences of life in France with me, and given me hospitality during my travels. As they say in France: *les copains d'abord.* I am particularly indebted to Mark Salik, *un véritable puits de science,* and Frédérique Dalhoum for their generous help, as well as to Christophe Guyon, Sandrine Trillaud, Hélène Audiot and Régis Rousseau. Sarah Woodbridge has been of immense help in answering many of my questions.

In the course of my research, I had the good fortune to stay with (amongst others) Lt-Col. and Mrs Michael Chilcott in Bayeux, Jane and John Edwards in Pauliac, Dordogne, Nick Goldsworthy in the Ariège and Hugo Nuyts in Nice, all of whom were informative and helpful beyond the call of duty. Others who gave me the benefit of their specialist knowledge include: Paul Foulkes on electrics, Gordon Eaton on health insurance, Henry Dyson on property law, Patrick Delas for legal advice, and Islay Currie of Currie French Property Services on building. Sam Crabb, of Sam Crabb Consultants, generously shared his extensive experience of the French property scene with me. For the second edition I would also like to thank Carole Bayliss of Mortgage France, Andy Martin of AS24 Telecommunications and Terry Young of Installapool for their contributions. For the third edition, Michael Streeter would like to add his thanks to Julia Jones of Bright Jones, Marie Slavov of Blake Lapthorn Tarlo Lyons, Georgina Field of Siddalls, Ross Husband of Rent a Place in France, Rachel Loos of www.FrenchEntrée.com, Anne Préveraud of Imo Conseil, Brian Hersee, Céline Anthonioz of Learn French at Home, Ellie Jones, Cathy Davis, David Darling and Katie Ash at VEF.

I owe much to my colleague Victoria Pybus, whose *Live and Work in France* provided a starting point for my own text in many instances, and to David Woodworth. I have also been blessed with entertaining informants, including: Richard Burton, Richard and Christina Coman, Alexandra Connolly, Jane and John Edwards, James Ferguson, Roz and Graham Jefferies, Susan and Derek Pearse, Anne Pilling, Rosemary Rudland, Philip Seabrook, Tim Swannie, Trever Talbert and Tim Weir. Finally, I should like to thank Claire de Vries and Ian Mitchell for obtaining French magazines and newspapers for me, and some expert advice on various aspects of building, and Penny Ainsworth for ongoing support.

Photographs in the colour section are provided courtesy of VEF Agency (www.vefuk. com), MGM Constructeur (www.mgm-constructeur.com) and Alliance Labelisation (www.alliancelabelisation.fr).

# Foreword

It would be no exaggeration to say that there has been a veritable stampede towards French property in recent years. Estate agents and notaries in France reported a 75% rise in enquiries in 2002 compared with 2001. This had much to do with the rise in the UK housing market. Many owners found that their properties had shot up in value and were tempted to remortgage to buy a holiday home in France. During 2004 and 2005 interest cooled off somewhat as prices levelled off in the UK, and this was still the trend in 2006 and the first half of 2007. There are nonetheless many who are considering a permanent move to France, and looking at the less fashionable areas of France, where property is still very cheap.

There is also a more fundamental reason for the move towards France, which is not based on financial considerations, but the widespread belief that quality of life is generally better in France than in the UK. France has excellent public services, trains that run on time, and a more laid-back attitude towards work. Stress, high crime, pollution and the general aggravations of life in an Americanised Britain are driving many to consider moving to a more civilised environment across the Channel. While it is not easy to find work in France, there are many who can carry on their profession there, and for others it is a matter of running a bed and breakfast, or using some ingenuity to offer services to other expats.

Another important factor is the ease with which one can travel to France. There is not only the Eurostar, already running for 14 years, but also a wealth of cheap flights to more and more provincial French destinations. The extension of the French motorway network has also played a large role, opening up many previously remote areas of France to foreign buyers, as is the extension of the high-speed TGV service to new areas.

The French property boom has slowed since the last edition of this book, with prices rising at a more moderate pace. Finding the right property at the right price may mean considering less fashionable areas. With this in mind, we have included sections on up-and-coming areas and the kinds of properties that you might expect to find there.

**André de Vries and Michael Streeter, September 2007**

## France – The Easy Way!

Having spent the past eight years moving other people's treasured possessions, Jon Blades from Eurospeed Removals tells us more about the business.

"We started the business in 1999," says Jon. "We're very much a family concern and initially it was just myself and my dad, Stephen. In the early days, we were actually involved in waste disposal. After a while, people started to ask us to move their furniture from A to B, and we quickly discovered this was preferable to the dirty work we were carrying out on a daily basis. We upgraded the fleet and began to focus on high-quality furniture delivery and household moving and storage. Getting into storage was great. It means we can offer a much more flexible service to our customers when something goes wrong. As part of the European service, customers are offered up to six weeks free storage whilst they locate the perfect property or simply settle in.

"I was at university at the time. I had always known that I could only work for myself; it was just a case of deciding what I would actually do. Luckily, I stumbled upon an industry that I came to love. Only last week, we successfully carried out a quarter-of-a-million-pound antique removal to the Limousin region. Certainly in recent years we have become consummate professionals within the industry. For me, only perfection is good enough, and that's the only level of service I am prepared to offer."

With access to a combined fleet of ten specialist vehicles and 20 staff over two depots, Eurospeed certainly have come a long way in the past eight years. In addition to moving homes within the UK, they now specialise in moves to and from France.

"Being a family business we are very flexible; whatever people need, we will do it," explains Jon with his 'no problem' philosophy. "The way I look at it, if people wanted problems, they'd hire a van and do it themselves. We can do anything: from pianos to Paris through to art and antiques to chateaux in the Dordogne. Whatever the challenge, Eurospeed will carry out the move to the highest possible standard. See you in France!

Jon Blades
Managing Director
Eurospeed *(Eurospeed is a trading name of South Cheshire International Moving & Storage Limited)*

## A Home in France

You may think your A level French, or even an internet translator, will be enough to make the contracts intelligible. However legal French is very technical and what is not there is often as important as what is ….. Notaires, even if they speak some English, are not used to giving advice on purchases – it is not their job to do so - and are forever "in a signature meeting" if you phone them. They do however respond to other professionals, particularly those who speak French and understand the conveyancing system. Philip and Danielle Seabrook have a wide experience of buying and selling property in France (flats, new build/off plans, houses) from having done it themselves and helping hundreds of others to do so in many different areas of France. Because they know both English and French procedures they can explain the differences, help you to decide on the choices you have to make and highlight practical issues on buying and living in France.

# PART ONE
## Getting Started

# 1 Introduction

## France – an Enduring Appeal

FRANCE IS A COUNTRY THAT JUST ABOUT HAS IT ALL. Great food, excellent climate, beautiful scenery, mountains, sea, a relaxed way of life, and a wonderful emphasis on culture and the arts. On top of this there is a rail system that really works and a health system rated one of the best of the world, and all this in a country whose political system is based explicitly on human rights – *Liberté, Égalité, Fraternité.*

Little wonder then, perhaps, that France has consistently remained the world's top tourist destination as foreigners flock to get a taste of the good life. And it's not just the 'traditional' nationalities that make up these tourists. The Russians, for example, have been coming in ever greater numbers in recent years. And in 2006, an estimated 600,000 Chinese tourists came to scale the Eiffel Tower, visit the Louvre and scour Paris' many chic stores. By 2020 that number could reach 2 million, according to French tourism officials. Many French people also adhere to the accepted wisdom that France is not just the best place to live in the world, it is the *only* place to live. Though this is changing, the French have not *en masse* been great travellers; they have preferred to holiday at home rather than travel abroad and be confirmed in their view that no where else on the planet can quite come up to standard.

Many foreigners share this view to the extent that they don't just want to visit France – they want to own a piece of it too. Foreign ownership in France is nothing new. Wealthy Americans have long been attracted to the Côte d'Azur, as have the British and Italians. Historically, the British have had a strong attachment to Biarritz, an upmarket resort town squeezed in the gap between the Pyrenees and the Atlantic Ocean. The French Alps, too, have always held an appeal among lovers of skiing and other winter sports. There have been influxes of neighbouring peoples before as well. Along the borders with Spain, Italy, Germany and Switzerland, there has long been a trend for people to buy second homes across the frontier in France, or even to move there.

However, in the last 10 to 15 years, the number of foreigners buying second homes or permanent residencies in France has increased dramatically. Led by the British, but closely followed by the Irish, Dutch and Germans, thousands of new home owners and residents have flocked to such areas as south-western France, Normandy, Brittany, the centre-west and the south. In Paris, foreign ownership remains high and continues to grow, as it does in the Alps, while newly rich Russians have been snapping up upmarket homes and châteaux across France.

*'great food, excellent climate, beautiful scenery, mountains, sea, a relaxed way of life, and a wonderful emphasis on culture and the arts: on top of this there is a rail system that really works and a health system rated one of the best of the world'*

Precise figures on exactly how many foreigners have bought property in France are hard to come by, partly thanks to the ease of movement allowed by citizens of the European Union (EU). However, the French Interior Ministry believes that as many as 250,000 properties in France may be owned by British subjects, either as second homes or as a place of main residence. Meanwhile, French academic research has suggested that by 2004 there were 130,000 British subjects living in France, as against 75,000 in 1999. It seems reasonable to assume that this figure has grown considerably since then. If one adds in the many other nationalities who have bought in France in recent years – the Irish, Dutch, German, Belgians, Americans, Scandinavians, Spanish, Portuguese, Italians and Swiss for example, one can see that there are hundreds of thousands of overseas property owners in France. So why are people flocking to buy property in France?

# Why Buy in France?

## Climate

The climate is undoubtedly a big pull for overseas home owners. Though the weather in the north of France can be every bit as cold and gloomy as in Holland, Ireland, Britain and Germany, there are large parts of it which boast a wonderful climate. Once you travel below the Loire Valley the average temperatures really start to rise. Obviously the Mediterranean coast and the immediate interior have the best weather, but parts of the south-west – for example the Charente-Maritime – can boast high levels of sunshine too, as well as plenty of green scenery. One thing that does catch out unwary home owners is the winter. Away from the coasts the winters can get very cold indeed, for example in the Limousin and even the Dordogne.

## Public services

The old saying that you get what you pay for in life was never more true than in France. The country has one of the higher overall tax burdens in Europe. But in return for this it has some of the best public services. Many British residents, for example, find the French health service significantly better than the National Health Service in the UK. In fact the World Health Organization (WHO) ranks the French system as the best in the world. The French take medicine and medicines very seriously – to the extent that some accuse them of being a nation of hypochondriacs. The trains too, are impressive, especially the high-speed TGV service that operates between Paris and many of the major cities. The education system, however, seems to be suffering from similar problems faced by those in other Western countries – including growing bad behaviour among pupils, a major concern among French parents.

# Transport

The improvement in French motorways, the extension of the high-speed TGV train service and above all the arrival of low-cost airlines such as Ryanair, EasyJet and FlyBe in regional airports, has made travel to and from France much, much easier – especially for British and Irish buyers. According to David A Todd, owner of the The French Property Shop (www.frenchpropertyshop.com), the fact that it is now far easier for many more people to travel quickly and cheaply to France is the fundamental reason behind the enormous growth of British property buyers there:

> In the late 1980s, Le Tunnel sous la Manche was still under construction, there were still large chunks missing in the French autoroute network (including the A26 dual carriageway stopping half an hour short of the ferries where Townsend Thoresen was boasting about 90 minute crossings), and scheduled air fares were the reserve of the rich and only served Paris and a few large urban centres.
>
> Nowadays Calais to Angoulême can be done in six hours and a previously little-known town like Bergerac can be reached from seven UK airports for little more than a commuter's daily train fare. Suddenly it's quicker and cheaper to get to a weekend home in the Haute Vienne than it is to get to Newquay.
>
> This is the main reason that, whereas 20 years ago an English owner of a French home was likely to be a prosperous upper-middle-class Francophile with time to spare, today that owner is more likely to be your neighbour.

# Culture and arts

Few nations take their culture and the arts as seriously as the French. This means not just large events such as the film festival in Cannes or the annual arts festival in Avignon, but the countless events that take place in towns and villages across the country. The people take great pride in their local culture and the state backs this up with cash. And while it may be an exaggeration to describe France as a country of philosophers, there is no doubt that intellectuals are held in higher regard than they are in many other Western countries. This can of course mean that the French come across as a little pretentious from time to time.

# Food and wine

Is France the gastronomic capital of the world? That's certainly how the French would look at it. A French person may concede many things, but they will never relinquish the conviction that French cooking is the best in the world. At its best – and this can be found across the country in many establishments – there is no doubt that the cuisine can be outstanding, in particular the emphasis on fresh, seasonal ingredients. It must also be added, however, that many French people have not woken up to the fact that the rest of the world have become 'foodies' too, and that some French cooking can sometimes seem tired and lacking in variety in comparison. The markets, however, though declining in number, show French food at its very best. As for the wine … the country produces some wonderful vintages, from the reds of Bordeaux to the whites of Burgundy, and including some excellent wines from many other regions too such as the Loire valley, Alsace and the Rhone Valley, not to mention champagne. In the countryside it can be hard to buy non-French produce, but many people don't mind too much when you can find such good local wine at very reasonable prices readily available.

## Quality of life

Few people have chosen to live in France on the strength of its economy. For years the country has suffered from high unemployment, disappointing economic growth and a decline in spending power. But if the economy may not be anything to write home about, France's quality of life is. Many visitors look with envy at the relaxed French lifestyle, the devotion to leisure time, the emphasis on family and community and the approach to life that states that people should work to live, not live to work. Coupled with rural settings – and many overseas buyers head for the French countryside – this can be an intoxicating combination. Of course

*'the French approach to life states that people should work to live, not live to work'*

there are downsides – shops and offices being closed for much of the weekend or at lunchtime. And in big cities such as Paris, for example, the pace of life and commuting can be every bit as relentless as in other Western countries. But there is little doubt that it is the French small town or rural lifestyle that attracts so many foreign buyers. France is a country with a slightly larger population than Britain but has a larger surface area and a considerably lower population density. In France you really can still get away from it all. For many people in neighbouring countries the slow pace of life and lack of congestion in parts of rural France reminds them of life back home several decades ago.

French academic Marie-Martine Gervais-Aguer of the Université Montesquieu Bordeaux IV recently carried out a study of Britons who were either already living in the Aquitaine region (which includes the Dordogne) or those who were thinking about moving there. In both groups, the main factor why they had chosen France as their home was lifestyle. Among existing British residents, 36.3% picked this as their leading factor, a figure that jumped to 58.2% among future residents. Asked about why they had specifically chosen Aquitaine as the place to buy a house, some 43.6% of current residents cited the 'quality of environment'; property prices came second at 16%. Among those who intended to move to the area, an overwhelming 64.6% gave 'quality of environment' as their main motivation.

Noël Castinel, who runs VIP Real Estate on the Côte d'Azur (www.vip-real-estate.com), points out another aspect of the quality of life that will appeal to some, but not all:

*If you are in a small town or in the countryside and don't speak French it can be hard to integrate, but in the south you have newspapers in English, radio in English, shops that specialise in British food and drink, and so on. All this means that you can have it both ways. You can live both the French and the British lifestyle. And as a Frenchman I think that – whether the French like it or not – we have to accept that English is an international language and we need to learn to speak it better.*

# Cheap property

One factor is common to most people looking to buy in France – the relative cheapness of property prices. Though property prices have increased considerably in recent years in France – it is a constant source of complaint among locals – they have not matched rises and valuations in countries such as Britain and cities such as Dublin. For example, prices in France are on average around 30% to 50% cheaper than those in the UK. In some cases the contrast is even greater. Someone moving from, say, a town in southern England to an area such as Poitou-Charentes or the Limousin may find property prices considerably less than half of what they are used to. In a sense, moving to buy in France has been a natural progression for many British buyers. In the last 15 years, as house prices in the UK have risen, buyers have looked further and further away from the hotspots of London and the south-east to buy cheaper property. Now that the whole of the south has become expensive, Britons have simply carried on looking over the Channel and into France. In that respect the property market in Normandy, Brittany and the south-west of France has become an extension of the UK housing market. Cash from property sales and equity releases in Britain has been pouring into the French market.

# Investment potential

For a number of years most overseas buyers in France were primarily interested in a character holiday home or place of residence where they could spend their time. That has begun to change. Areas such as Paris, the French Alps and the south have always had investment potential. The country's coastlines are now another area where people are looking to invest, as well as large and bustling cities such as Bordeaux. These are the areas where the French themselves are moving, which suggests that the potential for buying property as an investment may be a good idea. The French middle classes have for years bought property as an investment or a form of pension. The most popular way has been through the leaseback system, where the buyer owns the freehold, but leases it to a holiday or lettings company who rent it out. Yields are guaranteed over set periods and there are tax benefits involved too. This system has become popular with overseas buyers too. Tens of thousands of new developments

*'the French tend to think long term when it comes to property investment and overseas buyers might be advised to do the same'*

are being built in France to meet housing demand, and many of these attract investment buyers because they need little or no maintenance. These are often in large cities, along the coastline or attached to leisure facilities such as golf courses. Potential buyers need to be aware that while the French market looks in a healthy condition, they are not necessarily going to see some of the spectacular gains recorded in other property markets. The French tend to think long term when it comes to property investment and overseas buyers might be advised to do the same.

## A rosy future?

It should be noted that the positive picture outlined above is not shared by everyone – nor indeed by every French person. For some foreigners, it is a land of arrogance, haughtiness, self-obsession and self-indulgence. A country where the leaders expect the rest of the world to follow one set of rules while France blithely follows another in its own naked self-interest. This is what is known as the 'French exception'; the idea that when it comes to France, they do things differently and the rest of the world just has to accept it.

And in recent years the French have also come to fear that their country is in terminal decline. They have looked on with a mixture of shock and envy as the rest of the Western world has modernised itself and as the new nations in Asia grow ever stronger. At home, meanwhile, the French have resolutely shunned all efforts to adapt to the changing world, preferring to complain from the sidelines about 'globalisation', which they naturally assume is a plot by the English-speaking peoples – *les Anglo-Saxons* – to undermine the French way of life. In this most philosophical of countries, there is even a popular term for this gloomy frame of mind – *déclinisme*.

*'the number of foreigners buying second homes or permanent residencies in France has increased dramatically'*

Nevertheless, gloomy French introspection has not deterred foreign visitors and buyers, and besides, all this may start to change under the presidency of Nicolas Sarkozy, elected in May 2007, and whose start to his term of office was marked by an energy and positive outlook that was very different from the 12 years under his more languid predecessor Jacques Chirac. Only time will tell.

# Who Buys in France?

The profile of overseas property owners in France is changing. Once it was the reserve of the very wealthy or artists. Then a few brave souls started to buy in the south and the Dordogne on the lookout for a change of life, or in most cases a holiday home in the sun. Others bought chalets in the Alps. Gradually other groups have started to buy too. There are many people who buy a home in France with the aim of retiring here. Typically they will own the house for several years or more before making the move permanent. Another recent growth area has been in young professionals with young families. Some continue to work freelance for UK or Irish businesses, but live full time in France, commuting as and when necessary. Others work full time in France, setting up businesses in tourism or providing services to fellow overseas property owners, for example as builders, plumbers, surveyors, decorators or installers of septic tanks. In some cases, young Britons are buying property in France because they have been priced out of the market back home and France is the nearest area where they can afford to buy. Another relatively new group are the investors.

It is also an attractive country in which to buy because the legal system is robust and secure, where, unlike in some other countries, there are very few horror stories about owners finding they did not have the full title to a property they had bought.

## In the Know

**Trisha Mason is the founder of VEF (www.vefuk.com), a leading estate agency handling property in France. She explains why so many British people are choosing to buy a house in France:**

UK buyers who clearly identify their reasons for purchasing a property in France, who spend time seeking out the right area of France to suit their needs, and who take correct professional advice during the purchase, are certainly likely to make far more of a success of their new way of life than people buying in other countries. The reasons for this are numerous but I would list the following as the most important:

- The French way of life epitomises many things to which the Brits hold dear and which they feel the UK is losing. Traditional family values, good education and healthcare, a pride in one's community and a respect for others are all evident in France. These facilities and values make it easy for the growing number of full-time movers of all ages to settle in France.
- Although many buyers do not have a full grasp of the French language when they buy, most of them know the basics on which they can then build. Speaking to the people you live amongst is a sure way to become integrated into local society.
- Ease of access means that frequent holidays are possible or easy, and cheap travel to and from the UK means that full-time movers do not feel cut off from their old life.
- Property prices, which remain 30% to 50% cheaper than in the UK allow buyers to own a holiday home, move out full time or buy an investment property without over-stretching themselves financially.
- One of the biggest bonuses of buying in France is that the property market is so tightly regulated. Whereas for the wise buyer this can prove to be a huge benefit, for those who rush in without sound advice, it can present problems.

# 2 Thinking It Through

## Things to Consider

MANY, IF NOT MOST, PEOPLE WHO BUY PROPERTY IN FRANCE have done so after going on holiday there and falling in love with an area, a village or a particular house. 'Darling, wouldn't it be lovely if we had a place of our own here…?' is one of the typical questions that often precede a decision to buy somewhere.

This is not a bad reason for buying; after all, an emotional attachment to a place is an important consideration whether you are buying somewhere as a second home or a full-time place to live. The problem arises if this emotional attachment to a place becomes the *only* consideration.

There are all sorts of factors you need to take into account if you are considering buying a property in France, for whatever use. Above all, you have to use reason as well as emotion. When looking to buy abroad you should use your good sense every bit as much as you would if you were buying a property in your own country. Buying property in France is not just about location – it's about research too, and asking the right questions. And the first question is, can you afford it?

## The Price is Right

One of the first casualties when you've formed an emotional attachment to a place abroad is usually rigorous financial planning. Don't get carried away by the apparent cheapness of the property. When looking to buy in France, you need to consider more than just the cost of the house itself or any finance you need to make the transaction. Are the legal fees included (they usually are) and the estate agent's fees? One of the most important factors is how much any necessary repair or renovation work will cost. Many people are wildly unrealistic and optimistic about such costs.

*'don't get carried away by the apparent cheapness of the property'*

Think seriously about getting some professional advice on the likely costs *before* you commit to buy. France is littered with sad stories of people who have started grandiose redevelopment plans on a house and numerous outbuildings, only for the project to be left unfinished because the owners have run out of money. You'll also need to consider the cost of travel to and from the property. Is the local air service running all year round? Will you have to drive sometimes? Another important consideration is upkeep. All properties cost money whether they are occupied or not, older ones more so than newer ones. Tiles can fall off, pipes burst and gardens grow. You need to factor in the cost of dealing with these situations, plus take into account local property taxes and heating bills in winter. These considerations are dealt with in more detail in later chapters.

# Cost of Living

More generally, you'll need to think about the cost of living in France. Some items are undoubtedly cheaper – wine being one good example. But many electrical goods can be more expensive. And even if local supermarkets are cheaper than back home, you may have to travel further to reach them. If you're working, you will also have to consider taxation. The good news is that only about half of workers in France pay income tax. The bad news is that the social charges – the obligatory taxes that go towards your healthcare, pension and social security – are quite high and are payable even if you earn very little. Also the chances of you getting a job if you don't speak good French are remote (except perhaps for some seasonal work). Don't leave the issue of work and earning money until you get to France. It should be at the top of your list before you buy. The rules on self-employment are also less flexible in France than in many countries; if you want to do some work, for example as an IT consultant, but also plan to grow and sell your own vegetables, these are counted as two separate businesses – and you'll be liable for two lots of social charges.

# The Right Property for You

The first thing you need to think about is why you want the property and what you want to do with it. Make a list of what you want from an area and a house and why – and try to stick to that. There are many different ways of looking for property. There is, however, no substitute for driving around properties and checking them out personally, with agents or with the owners if they are private sales. Ideally, take a checklist or wish list with you and tick them off one by one as you go around the property. By visiting areas, you'll soon pick up an idea of where the main roads, noisy or quiet streets, attractive areas and so on are to be found. You'll also get a much better idea of what you are getting for your money and

## Insider Tip

The internet is clearly an excellent starting point and you'll find all kinds of properties on sale there. These will give you an idea of price variations between areas.

be able to compare different styles of house and construction in an area. It's good to be open minded and flexible but be wary about changing your entire wish list just because you've fallen in love with a particular property. French law gives you a brief cooling-off period after you have signed the initial purchase contract – but you should give yourself a cooling-off period before you even put in an offer on a place.

# Permanent Homes

If you are planning to live in your house in France, then clearly there are many other factors you need to consider rather than just whether you like the house. You will need to consider the area you are planning to move to. If you need to work, will you be able to find work in the area? What are communications like: for example, does it have a high-speed internet connection, and do mobile phones work? Is the place deep in the countryside: if so, how many cars will you need, and will you feel isolated, especially in winter? Very few rural communities in France have public transport unless they are on a main route between larger towns. How cold does it get in winter, and will you be cut off if it snows? If you are planning to set up a business or undertake any building work that needs permission from the local mayor, how sympathetic is he or she to your plans? Having the mayor on your side can be crucial. What leisure facilities are there nearby, and which shops? If you have or plan to have children, you'll need to find out in advance about local schools. You'll also need to think about how far the nearest doctors, dentists and hospitals are to you. You should also reflect on how big a building and how much land you really need. Having a few acres sounds a great idea but how will you maintain that land? According to Wouter Haajman, founder of property assessment firm CPA (www.check-property.com), purchasing too much land is a common mistake:

> After looking at property pictures, some people decide on a property with a lot of land. Large plots of land are still for sale in France at a reasonable price. Though they don't need all these hectares, they justify their intended purchase with plans to grow vegetables or keep animals. For many these are unfamiliar activities but their lack of experience in that field seems to be no obstacle.
>
> Later, many of these new owners of large amounts of land will admit that they don't know what to do with the land – and come to see it as a burden.
>
> Buying something because it seems 'nice to have' is not sensible. Purchasing land is one thing; but the consequences of buying the wrong property can be far reaching.
>
> Think too about how many of your fellow countrymen and women there are living in the area where you plan to live. Some people like to have fellow countrymen around them, others don't. Which are you?

You should also remember that a number of the considerations that apply to permanent homes also apply to holiday homes.

# Investment Properties

Emotional attachment is the last thing you need if you are buying a place for investment. Here everything should come down to how much the property can appreciate in value and how much it can earn in the meantime. Obviously location is king here. Who is your market? Is this an area that people will want to come to stay on holiday or to rent permanently? Is the area thriving and attracting new businesses and young families or is it fading? What are transport connections like? Bear in mind that local low-cost air services can stop as well as start up. What are the facilities and amenities like? You also need to think about the tax implications on the income you derive from your rental as well as capital gains tax one day. You will also need to think about who can keep an eye on the property when you are not around and how secure it is. If you plan to let the building out, you will have to find someone to handle this for you if you are not around. And you must declare your earning to your tax authorities, no matter how little it is you earn. If it is not your main place of residence you also need to think that one day you will be liable for capital gains tax when you sell it. Again, large gardens and land sound a great idea but they take up a lot of time – and will cost you money if you have to pay someone to tend them.

# Research

In all the above cases one thing is vital above all else – research. The mayor and mayor's staff are an invaluable source of information about local taxes, transport, schools, planning and the environment. You'll want to found out, for example, whether there are plans to put a new road through the area one day, build an airport, route a new railway line, put up a wind farm, build a housing development or even construct a nuclear power plant. The internet is also a good potential source of local information.

There is no rule that says you have to buy in the first place you think of. If you can't find the right kind of property in an area, maybe the area is wrong for you – try another. France is a big country offering all types of properties, weather, terrain and lifestyles. Take your time, do your homework and the chances are you will be able to find the right place for your needs.

Many Brits aim to be self-employed, and working for oneself is one of the allures of living in France. But being self-employed is more expensive in France than it is in Britain. The famed French bureaucracy is as dreadful as its reputation. But more seriously, the amount you pay to the French state is considerably higher, especially if your income is relatively modest. Before you move, find

## Insider Tip

Don't use the fact that details might be harder to find out in a foreign country where you may not speak the language as an excuse for no research. There is no substitute for local knowledge and it is likely that you will be able to find some fellow countrymen living nearby to where you want to buy to help you. If you can, try to speak to the local mayor even if it means getting someone to act as interpreter.

out what you might need to pay in tax and social charges (*charges sociales* – the equivalent of national insurance), and then do a realistic business plan. Most people recommend having savings for the first three years of payments – on average that's about €12,000. Even doing something as simple as selling home-made jam at a market stall is tricky, as you have to be legally registered as a food-producing business before you are allowed to do it. And that means registering for tax and paying those charges…

The cost of living also comes as a shock to many expats. Yes, property and wine are cheap but other costs are equivalent to or sometimes more expensive than the UK. If you're going to work from home, remember some bills, such as electricity and heating, will be higher, so you need to factor these in when thinking about how much money you will need to live.

In the countryside, where many expats choose to live, very little English is spoken. This is slowly changing in some areas, but the bottom line is that if you do not have a comfortable grasp of French then you are likely to find it difficult and frustrating dealing with the everyday aspects of life. There are many Brits in France who cannot say much more than *bonjour* but they tend to live in a bubble of Britishness, with little interaction with their French neighbours. If you don't want to live like this, start learning the language before you arrive, and continue with lessons once you are here. It does make a huge difference to the enjoyment of your French life.

Finally, the emotional cost of moving to France is very rarely considered, but it is another major issue. For many couples the shock of living and working together 24 hours a day can be too much. If your relationship is rocky, life in France is unlikely to fix it, as you need to be able to work as a team. Leaving friends and especially family behind can also have an impact; women in particular miss seeing children and grandchildren. When planning your new life in France, think about how you can keep the bonds going. Have a spare room or two so people can comfortably visit; include in your budget the cost of regular visits – more trips of a shorter duration are said to be better than one or two longer ones.

If, after reading this, you're feeling a bit doubtful about moving to France, don't be. Tens of thousands of Brits live very happily in France, but in the main they are the ones who planned what they wanted from their life in France and what they needed to do to make it work. Time spent now will make all the different in the future. Good luck!

# In the know

**Rachel Loos has lived in France for several years and is editor of the 'Living in France' section of www.FrenchEntrée.com. Here she describes some of the issues people need to consider when planning to move to France:**

For many people, emigrating to France is about fulfilling a rather romantic notion of what life could be like. It's about escaping the rat race to live in a rambling house in the countryside, surrounded not by roads choked with traffic but fields full of sunflowers. And on balmy summer evenings, with the birds singing in the trees and a cool drink in the hand, this dreamy view of life in France is spot-on. However, it is quite a different story in the middle of February, when the temperature has plummeted to well below freezing, everyone is behind doors and nothing is going on anywhere. Then life in France can feel deeply dull and lonely.

If there is one piece of advice I can give people thinking about moving to France it is this: focus on the reality of what your life in France will be like – and plan carefully for it. Far too many expats come to France hoping to sort things out when they arrive, only to find that they cannot, and so they end up emotionally and financially crippled. For them, the dream turns into a complete nightmare.

One of the biggest issues is employment – or lack of. If you need to work to support yourself and your family, do your research about what you can and cannot do. To be in paid employment, you will need to speak the language well. I have had teachers ask me whether they can work in French schools without speaking the language. Could you teach in Britain without speaking English? Of course not, so why would it be any different in France?

Also, France is a country of high unemployment, so jobs are scarce, even more so in the countryside.

# 3 Practicalities

## Getting There

TRAVELLING TO FRANCE FROM THE UK has never been cheaper or easier than it is now, with the opening of the Channel Tunnel and the revolution in low-priced air travel of recent years. Despite these developments many Britons still prefer to take the ferry, to cut down on the distance they have to drive at the other end.

## Trains

Since 1993 there has been a direct rail link between London and Paris, run by Eurostar. The journey time is approximately 2 hours and 35 minutes and will be cut by 20 minutes once the new London terminal at St Pancras has replaced Waterloo in November 2007. You can also leave the train at Lille, near the Belgian border, and change to a TGV (French high-speed train) which will bypass Paris entirely and take you to Bordeaux, Poitiers, Lyon, Marseille, the ski fields and other destinations. There is also a direct train from London to Avignon once a week. For the Eurostar, call 08705 186 186 in the UK, 0044 1233 617 575 outside the UK or visit www.eurostar.com. You can book a French rail pass or any other rail ticket in France by calling Rail Europe on 08705 848 848 (www.raileurope.co.uk), or by going in person to the French tourist office at 178 Piccadilly, London W1V 0AL. French rail passes have become more and more expensive in recent years. Given the cheapness of rail travel in France, it is not even certain that you will save any money with such a pass.

## By car

Although you cannot actually drive through the Channel Tunnel, you can put your car onto a train, and drive off at the other end. If you want to take a car through

### Insider Tip

If you dislike the idea of driving long distances on the right in France, it is easy enough to put your car on a train in Calais and collect it again at your destination, while you head for your sleeper carriage. The cost is fairly steep, but worth it. This is an overnight service; the destinations are Brive, Avignon, Toulouse, Nice and Narbonne. There are no drinks or refreshments available on the train; breakfast is served at the destination. There is a limit to the vehicle's height. The full details are on www.frenchmotorail.com; ☎ 08702 415 415.

the tunnel, you need the Eurotunnel service, which starts from Cheriton, Folkestone (08705 353 535 from the UK, 0810 63 03 04 from France; www.eurotunnel.com). You can buy your ticket at Folkestone. The journey is short (35 minutes) and spartan. No one-armed bandits or dancing girls.

Route planning within France is easy if you have access to the internet. Several sites give you detailed routes from any street in the UK to any street in France: see www.mappy.fr; www.michelin-travel.com; www.theaa.com or www.rac.co.uk. These sites will also estimate the time and cost of your journey. For a further refinement, you can download maps of larger French towns, and photographs of houses, on www.wanadoo.fr under 'Photos de Ville'.

## French driving

House hunting in France is easiest done with a car. You will need to look around places on your own as well as in the company of an estate agent; public transport is simply not adequate for getting around the countryside. The roads are generally good, especially the motorways or *autoroutes,* which are financed by tolls. The annual road tax has been abolished.

It can be a pleasure driving off the beaten track where there is little traffic. The downside is the driving of the French, who want to prove their non-conformism by ignoring the highway code. One simply has to learn to live with lunatic Gallic drivers. The worst drivers are in the south of the country. Lorries can be a problem on some routes so if you are planning to drive on such a road for any distance, pick a Sunday – only refrigerated lorries are allowed to drive then.

French roads are classified according to three letters:

**A** *Autoroute* (M roads in the UK). These are almost all toll roads – *autoroutes à péage.* The cost of using them is about €5 per 100 km. You will be given a computer card when you join the motorway and you pay on exit. A quicker way of paying is to go to a *télépéage* with your French RIB (bank account number), where you can have a transponder fitted to your windscreen that allows you to pay by direct debit. You should not drive to the *télépéage* if you have no French bank account, and you do not wish to pay by direct debit. You can also pay by using a French debit card. One potential hazard of the computerised cards is that your journey will be timed, and if you have averaged over the speed limit you will receive a hefty fine. See www.autoroutes.fr for more information.

**N** *Route Nationale* (A roads in the UK). These were the main roads before the motorways. They are single or dual carriageway and pass through towns, which makes journeys slower. They often run alongside motorways and are generally best avoided if possible.

**D** *Route Départementale* (B roads in the UK).

## Speed limits

The limit in towns varies between 45 kph (30 mph) and 60 kph (38 mph). The number of speed cameras and mobile police radar traps has increased dramatically in recent years as the government has tried – with some success – to reduce the annual death toll on the roads. The fixed camera points are currently indicated in advance by road signs, but this may change in the future.

## Driving licences

EU citizens including those from the UK can continue to drive with their own country's licences as long as their licence remains valid in their home country. They may also choose to apply for a French licence. US citizens may use their own licences, or a certified translation of an international driving licence for 90 days. If they apply for a *carte de séjour* they may drive for a year on a US licence with a certified translation (but not an international licence). After a year you will either have to take a French driving test, or if your state has an agreement with France, you may exchange your licence for a French one at a *préfecture de police*. Ask for the *service permis de conduire*. For information on importing a car into France, see chapter 13.

## By sea

Many thought that the ferries would go out of business when the Channel Tunnel opened but this did not happen immediately, because the ferry companies have banded together to fight their common competitor and new operators have joined the fray. P&O Ferries gave up the sailing to Caen and Cherbourg from Portsmouth in early 2005, but still runs other routes. The ferries stress the cruise aspect of the journey and offer restaurants and entertainment to try to make things more interesting. Note that routes are subject to change; always check the website first. Sometimes it is easier to take a ferry to Belgium if you are going to northern France.

Brittany Ferries runs a frequent traveller scheme for property owners in France, offering a 33% discount on payment of an annual membership fee. This can be extended to people renting your property. See the website, www.brittany-ferries.com, for details under 'Property Owners Travel Club' and to download an application form. Chez Nous is a well-established agent offering discount bookings for all sea routes to France, plus air and Eurostar bookings if you book a holiday property through them, which is useful if you want to explore a certain region before you go to live there. Eurotunnel has a Frequent Traveller scheme. You can qualify for discounts if you buy at least 5 return or 10 single tickets per year. See the website, www.eurotunnel.com. You can also obtain lower fares by going through Ferry Savers: ☎0870 990 8492; www.ferrysavers.com. A list of ferry companies and their contact details can be found in The Directory.

# By air

The real revolution in travel to France has come about with Ryanair flying to small airports all over France from the UK, and also now from Ireland and Belgium. Other low-cost airlines such as Buzz (now defunct), EasyJet and Flybe then got in on the act. Destinations can change, and new ones are being added. It is important to bear in mind that routes can be axed and

## Insider Tip

The speed limit on all autoroutes is 130 Kph (80 mph); this is reduced to 110 Kph (65 mph) in bad weather. The limit is 110 Kph on non-toll autoroutes. The speed limit on dual carriageways is 110 Kph and 90 Kph (55 mph) on single carriageways, both reduced by 10 Kph in wet weather. A new speed limit of 50 Kph has been introduced for foggy conditions, where visibility is reduced to 50 m. 'Rappel' means the restriction is continued.

fares can rise, if the proximity of an airport has a bearing on where you buy your property. You need to check the websites regularly to see what is on offer. Prices also change from day to day: as planes fill up the price goes up, so you need to try to book as early as possible. Ryanair sometimes offers free flights, but you have to add on something for taxes. Other airlines, such as BA and Air France, are still very expensive (except for the Paris route), but you do get a free meal. If you are determined to take one of the conventional airlines to France then it is worth looking at the websites www.ebookers.com or www.lastminute.com. These do not list budget airlines and are not necessarily any cheaper than a travel agent. An independent booking service for low-cost flights on scheduled and charter services to France is available from www.skybargains.co.uk, who are members of ABTA. Telephone 0800 195 1300 or book online at www.skybargains.co.uk.

Contact details for the main airlines can be found in The Directory.

# Residence and Entry

While France is part of the EU, there are still formalities to be gone through if a citizen of another EU country wants to settle down here. British and Irish citizens are entitled to live and work in France without going through any special formalities. For non-EU citizens the situation is a lot more complicated: in principle, anyone from outside the EU who wants to remain in France other than as a tourist has to arrange their residence permit before going to France.

## Obtaining a residence permit

### EU nationals

Travelling to France is easy enough for British citizens. There are French immigration police at the Eurostar terminal in London looking for undesirables trying to get to France, but British passport holders should have nothing to worry about.

Nationals of the 'older' EU countries (Austria, Belgium, Denmark, Ireland, Finland, Germany, Greece, Italy, Luxembourg, the Netherlands, Portugal, Spain, Sweden and the UK) have the right to settle permanently in France, without preconditions. Of the new EU states, citizens of Cyprus and Malta have the same rights as French residents. Swiss citizens have similar rights. Those from Slovakia, Poland, Hungary, the Czech Republic, Slovenia, Lithuania, Latvia and Estonia do not yet have the right to live and work in France without a residence permit. The restrictions on citizens of these countries may last until 2009. In the case of the two countries that joined the EU in January 2007, Bulgaria and Romania, work permits may be required for their citizens until 2013. In the case of the UK, your passport must state that you are a 'British Citizen', meaning you have the right of abode in the UK. If you have another type of British passport, contact a French consulate in your home country to find out whether you can move to France.

France reformed its immigration laws in 2003, coming to the conclusion that the time and money expended on issuing residence permits to EU citizens would be better directed at keeping out illegal immigrants. France was in any case breaking EU law by placing restrictions on the rights of EU citizens on its territory. This is not the end of the matter, because all French citizens are expected to place themselves on the population register (*état civil*) and to have an official principal address. It is therefore logical that British and other foreign residents should do the same thing, if they want to enjoy the same rights as French citizens, such as the right to vote in local and European elections.

## Applying for a residence permit voluntarily

After you have registered for social security and the tax office, you may want to apply voluntarily for a *carte de séjour*, a sort of identity card that shows you are entitled to stay in France. In the first instance, go along to the nearest *préfecture de police* (police station), or *mairie* (town hall or municipal office) to apply. It can take several months to obtain. In the meantime you will be given a receipt (*récépissé*). You can also apply to be put on the *état civil* or population register, which comes to the same thing as applying for a *carte de séjour* and requires exactly the same documents. Prospective employers may ask you to provide a *fiche d'état civil* (extract from the population register) to show you are legally entitled to work in France, even though an EU passport is sufficient.

## Documents

A number of documents are required to apply for a *carte de séjour*: a valid passport, four passport photographs, a birth certificate, and a marriage certificate if necessary. If you are a single parent with dependent children, you will need proof that your children are permitted to leave the UK. The authorities may require you to have your birth and marriage certificates officially translated and legalised, although this seems to be happening less and less. Certainly, if you get married in France you will need a legalised translation of your birth certificate. Even original British documents are not necessarily considered legally valid, and translations have to be legalised. If you use a translator in France, they must be sworn in, or *assermenté*, all of which adds to the cost, of course. Any old translator from the yellow pages will not do. Finding a translator who is *assermenté* is difficult in the UK, so you are best advised to find a translator through your local British consulate in France. Documents can be legalised by a French vice-consul, i.e. stamped and signed, in the UK. In France, documents are legalised by a *notaire*. If you are in south-western France (e.g. Dordogne or Lot) your nearest consulate is in Bordeaux. It is advisable to have several copies made of documents and have them all legalised at the same time, in case you need them in the future. At some point you are also likely to be asked for copies of your parents' and grandparents' birth certificates: these can easily be obtained from the Family Records Centre in London (☎ 0845 603 7788; email certificate.services@ons.gov.uk; www.familyrecords.gov.uk).

## Financial resources

In the past it was always necessary to show that you had an income equal to the French minimum wage or SMIC, about £8,000 a year, to receive a *carte de séjour*. The French authorities accept that two people can live on this income. The situation now is less clear: although you can stay as long as you want in France without the *carte de séjour* you will still need to show that you have a job or an income if you decide to apply for the *carte de séjour* voluntarily. If you already have work, or have been offered a job, you can use your contract of employment; you can also ask your employer to make out a *Certificat d'Emploi* on headed paper, confirming your passport number, the date you started work, and your salary. If you want to be self-employed, you will need some proof that you are a member of a professional body and that you have registered with the local *chambre de métiers* or *chambre de commerce*. If you are living on a pension or not working, you can use bank statements, witnessed by a notary. You will also have to show that you are paying social security contributions in France and are registered for tax purposes. Applying for a *carte de séjour* necessarily implies that you are tax resident in France. It can be used as one piece of evidence to convince the British HM Revenue and Customs that you have left the UK for good.

## Proof of residence

If you have bought a property, your notary can supply a *certificat* giving proof of residence. If you rent, then rent receipts will be adequate proof. If you are staying with friends, and not paying rent, then your friend will need to supply an *attestation d'hébergement* and proof of their identity. Further proof of residence includes telephone or electricity bills (from EDF) with your name and address.

Local officials can react in very different ways to applications for a *carte de séjour*. Much depends on how much experience they have of processing applications. Problems can arise with officials who do not understand the regulations themselves very well, or who have no English. You need to be well prepared and patient if obstacles seem to be put in your way.

## Documents required for the *carte de séjour*

- Passport, with copies of the main pages, stamped as *copie certifiée conforme* by the *préfecture* or town hall.
- Four passport photographs of each member of your family.
- Birth certificate, with an official translation if requested, notarised by a French consulate or French lawyer.
- Marriage certificate/divorce papers/custody papers (officially translated and notarised only if requested).
- Certificate from the town hall stating that you are living in *concubinage notoire* if you live with a common-law partner.
- Proof of residence: *certificat* from the notary who handled your house purchase, or rent receipts, or *attestation d'hébergement* from the person you are staying with.
- Proof of entry: your travel ticket may be sufficient; or ask the immigration police when you enter the country.
- Proof of employment.
- Proof of financial resources.
- You may be asked for proof that you have no criminal record.
- Medical certificate (for non-EU citizens).

## Renewing your residence permit

The first *carte de séjour* is for a year. You need to apply for a renewal before it runs out. EU citizens will usually receive a 10-year residence permit as long as they are in regular employment in France. You will have to prove that you have paid all your taxes. The permit is then renewed again for five or 10 years at a time. The same documents as above are required, except that you will not need to produce your children's or parents' birth certificates. If you change address within France, you are required to inform the police of your new place of residence.

## Residence permits for non-EU nationals

Non-EU citizens require a Schengen visa to enter France; normally this allows you to stay for 90 days (*visa de court séjour*). Citizens from some countries – in particular, the USA, Canada, Australia and New Zealand – are automatically allowed to stay for 90 days in the Schengen area (which includes France). If you come from one of these countries and you want to stay more than 90 days, you will need to apply for a *visa de long séjour* well before you leave. The application form for the *visa de long séjour* can be found at: www.service-public.fr/formulaires/index.htm or at www.diplomatie.gouv.fr (under 'Venir en France'). The requirements are similar to those for the *carte de séjour*, but you will also need a certificate of good conduct from the state police, health insurance and proof of financial resources. Family connections within France, or a statement from a French citizen promising to support you financially, will also help. If you go to stay with a private person in France, then they will not only be asked to confirm that they are providing your accommodation (*justificatif d'hébergement*), but also that they will take financial responsibility for you for the length of your stay. Your host needs to submit the application for the *justificatif d'hébergement* to the *mairie* or the *Office des Migrations Internationales* (www.omi.social.fr); the charge is €15. You have to sign an undertaking not to work in France (unless you are applying for a work permit).

# Work Permits

EU citizens do not require work permits; they only need to follow the same regulations as French citizens as regards self-employment and business formation. They have exactly the same rights as French workers. Non-EU citizens need to apply for a work permit well before they take up employment in France. This can only be done through an employer who has offered you a post in France. You may try to enter France as a student, au pair or trainee, which will allow you to work legally. Your local French consulate will be able to advise you. If you want to start a business in France, you will need a *carte de commerçant étranger*, obtainable through a *chambre de commerce*. Note that US citizens have, since 1959, had a right to start up a business in France, or at least to transfer their existing business to France. For more information see the French government website: www.service-public.fr.

See the The Directory for a list of consulate and embassy addresses.

# My House in France
## Catherine Davis

Catherine and her husband Philip have bought a second home near Toulouse.

### Why did you choose this area of France?

We've skied at many French resorts but find they tend to die in the summer, Dordogne and Provence are lovely but expensive and too far from the mountains, and the weather in Brittany seemed similar to England. This area is just over an hour's drive away from the nearest ski resort (La Mongie) and property here costs less than a third of the equivalent rural property in the UK. Plus the architecture is beautiful and the landscape is unspoilt.

### How did you find the buying process?

We hadn't made any definite decision about buying in France but had pored over internet sites of property in the region for several months. A whirlwind trip tagged on to a business trip, led to us putting in an offer for a *maison de maitre* near Boulogne-sur-gesse. The agents put us in contact with a *notaire* nearby who drew up the *compromis*, both parties signed, and then we had to send a return confirmation that we had received a signed version, and pay a 5% deposit to the *notaire*. We had a second visit together and opened a bank account at Crédit Agricole, and arranged for insurance. We then opened an account with a currency exchange company, bought the euros to pay for the property when the mortgage came through and waited for the legal processes to be completed in France.

All in all we found the buying process very simple. I have a French friend who translated the contracts for me. Our agent and *notaire* both spoke English and replied promptly to our emails regarding bits we weren't sure about.

### Did you have to do any work on the house?

We have painted several rooms (one twice as we decided the colour was wrong), hung up lights, and put up shelves. The biggest disaster was when we removed the electric radiator from the kitchen wall and part of the wall came way with it (clearly that task was beyond our DIY skills). We also had an amazing storm accompanied by enormous hailstones which have broken a couple of windows, so we now have a new skill replacing panes of glass.

There is no shortage of recommended workmen, we have inherited the man to maintain the pool and another to maintain the garden; best of all is a friendly German neighbour who is happy to check the house and empty the post box when we are away.

## What are the main advantages of being in France as far as you are concerned?

Feeling part of a community; everyone is so friendly. Our French neighbour spoke of how the influx of foreigners had revitalised the area, and certainly we have been made to feel welcome in all the shops and by all our neighbours.

## Is life better, worse or about the same as you expected?

For us this is still a *maison secondaire*, but the intention is to retire here. Life so far has been better than expected. We just didn't think people would be so welcoming, it just wouldn't happen in an English village.

We have been here just a few weeks, so maybe are still in the honeymoon period, but given that the previous owner wept as he handed over the keys, I think we will enjoy our years here. I had worried that my student-aged children might get bored, but they have developed an addiction to croquet, boules and cycling. They seem to have forgotten they have finals/A levels looming on the horizon.

I somehow feel that we could never get bored here; the house will keep us busy indefinitely, we have visions of converting the barn into a *gîte*, and the children are working on their own designs for the loft. Then there is the garden, a whole acre of parkland with a couple of 400-year-old oaks, and numerous fruit trees and conifers. I just never thought we would live anywhere so beautiful.

# PART TWO
## Location, Location, Location

# 4 Knowing Your Patch

## Administrative Organisation

FRANCE IS DIVIDED UP INTO 100 *DÉPARTEMENTS,* or provinces, including four overseas *départements,* known as the DOM-TOM (*Départements d'Outre-Mer et Territoires d'Outre-Mer*). Each *département* has a two-figure number, used for postcodes and car licence plates. The present system of *départements* only dates back to 1789 and the French Revolution: most of them are named after rivers or mountain ranges. The system was intended to divide the country into more or less equal-sized provinces, while discouraging anti-revolutionary regional movements. As a gesture towards reviving more of a sense of regional identity, 22 *régions* with directly elected assemblies were set up from 1972.

In 2002 the right wing embarked on a process of decentralisation. All local *communes* now have to join up in *intercommunalités,* within the limits of their competencies, and these will come under 'supermayors'. The regions have been given more powers in the areas of culture, tourism and economic matters. The departmental prefects are still the intermediary between Paris and local administration, and their influence remains considerable, but their power has being reduced in favour of more local bodies. When one considers that there are already 56,000 intercommunal organisations in France, the potential for chaos is obvious, and the more republican-minded French are not that happy with the current government's experimentations with decentralisation.

The complexity of administration is not helped by the fact that there are more than 200 *pays* (smaller regions) which you will be constantly reminded of as you drive around France. The locals will tell you they come from such-and-such a *pays,* rather than from a *département.* The *pays* will often have organisations that deal with cultural or tourism issues. In the 2007 presidential election there was talk of simplifying France's local government – possibly even by merging the *département* council assemblies with the regional ones – but it remains to be seen whether anything will come of this. For most new residents the first point of contact with French administration remains the local *mairie*.

The regions are considered here from the aspect of their scenic and cultural attractions, accessibility, the value of property and the likelihood of finding employment.

# Information Facilities

Tourism is France's biggest money-earner – generating 12% of GDP – and every region has lavish brochures on offer to advertise its uniqueness. In 2006 the country welcomed 78 million foreign tourists, making it the world's most popular tourist destination. Three-quarters of these were European, but an interesting sign of likely future trends is shown by the fact that 600,000 Chinese were among those visitors. If you can, it is worth visiting the French Government Tourist Office, where there are brochures for every part of France, otherwise you can order the information by email.

## Useful contacts

Maison de la France Great Britain:

☎ 0891 244 123;    💻    info.uk@franceguide.com; www.franceguide.com or www.tourisme.fr or www.tourism-office.com or http://uk.franceguide.com.

Maison de la France USA:

☎ 514 288 1904;    💻    info.us@franceguide.com; www.francetourism.com. Also in Los Angeles and Chicago.

Maison de la France Canada:

☎ 514 288 2026;    💻    canada@franceguide.com.

FrenchEntrée regional guide:

💻    cwww.frenchentree.com/fe-regions.

Since the SNCF took it over from British Rail, Rail Europe has run from the same building as the French tourist office in London, so you can book a train ticket at the same time as looking at brochures. The main city in every region has a *Comité Régional du Tourisme* who organise information facilities. *Départements* have a *Comité Départemental du Tourisme*, which may be more informative than the regional office. Towns and cities have their own *Office du Tourisme*; in smaller places the equivalent is the local *Syndicat d'Initiative,* which may have a small welcome office, but their opening hours are generally shorter than those of the *Office du Tourisme*, and their function is more to promote business in general in their area. The *syndicats* are still not all on the internet. For more practical information about living in France, the best starting point is the French Embassy's website: www.ambafrance-uk.org. Each *département* has its own website: just search on 'Conseil Général' + the name of the *département*. The regional websites are under 'Conseil Régional'.

# Geographical Information

## Physical features

France is popularly called 'l'Hexagone' on account of its (roughly) six-sided shape. It is the largest country in the EU with a surface area of 544,500 sq km. It is also one of the most thinly populated, with a mere 109 inhabitants per square kilometre. Most of the land is habitable, being less than 200 m above sea level. The three main mountain ranges are the French Alps, including Europe's highest mountain, Mont Blanc, the Pyrenees, running along the border with Spain, and the less mountainous Massif Central, in south-central France. The English Channel – which is called *La Manche* – is just 22 miles wide at its narrowest point. France has land borders with Belgium, Luxembourg, Germany, Switzerland, Italy, Andorra and Spain. The main rivers are the Loire, the Rhône, the Seine and the Garonne. In total there are 8,500 km of navigable rivers and waterways.

## Population

The most recent census indicates that as of 1st January 2007 there are 63.4 million people living in France. This may include up to possibly 3 million illegal immigrants. The recent rise in population, however, is mostly due to a high birth rate. The rate in France is two children per woman, making it one of Europe's most fertile countries. Life expectancy has gone up too, with the average woman living until the age of 84 years and the average man until 77 years old. There is a continuing and steady movement from the countryside to the towns; around 75% of the people are urban dwellers. There is also a strong tendency for people to move towards the Atlantic coastline and the south of the country. The areas with the fastest growing population in recent years are Corse, Aquitaine, Midi-Pyrénées and Languedoc-Roussillon. Paris and surrounding areas make up Europe's largest conurbation with 11.49 million people living in l'Île-de-France. Other urban areas are:

| | | | |
|---|---|---|---|
| Lyon | 1,600,000 | Bordeaux | 890,000 |
| Marseille | 1,400,000 | Nice | 556,000 |
| Lille | 1,100,000 | Rouen | 450,000 |
| Toulouse | 920,000 | | |

In 2004 it was estimated that 4.3 million of the population were of foreign origin, including 2 million from the EU. Algerians and Moroccans make up 1.2 million.

## Other territories

Along with metropolitan France, there are a number of remnants from the French Empire, which are loosely labelled the DOM-TOM. DOM stands for *Départements d'Outre-Mer*, and includes French Guyana, Martinique, Guadeloupe, Mayotte and Réunion. The Territoires d'Outre-Mer (TOM) include French Polynesia, New Caledonia, the Antarctic territories, Wallis and Futuna Islands, and St Pierre et Miquelon off the coast of Canada. The DOM are full *départements* of France, with some degree of autonomy, while the TOM are directly administered from Paris.

The Principality of Monaco is neither a *département* of France, nor a truly independent country. The head of state is a hereditary prince, but France controls many aspects of the government. The small mountain principality of Andorra in the Pyrenees recognises the French president and a Spanish bishop as heads of state, but is more or less independent.

## Climatic zones

France has substantial variations of climate, due to its great size. The north-west, bordering the Atlantic, has a similar climate to south-west England, if somewhat warmer. The dividing line between north and south as far as climate goes is the Loire valley.

### Continental zone

The north and east of France have a continental climate, characterised by predictably warm summers and cold winters, with fairly high rainfall, similar to southern England. Auvergne and Burgundy come under this zone.

### Mediterranean zone

The south and south-east experience a Mediterranean climate, with regularly hot summers and mild winters, and unpredictable low rainfall. The south is subject to strong winds such as the mistral, and sudden storms.

### Mountainous zone

The mountain regions of the Pyrenees, Alps and Massif Central generally have heavy snowfall in winter, and cool, sunny summers with frequent rain.

# Choosing the Right Location

Location is everything, as Conrad Hilton said. Nothing could be more true. The first thing to look at is where your potential property is in relation to airports and motorways. Properties near TGV stations are worth considerably more than those which are not. There is always a rush to buy property once it becomes known that a new TGV station is going to be built somewhere. A property on a main road is generally cheap to buy and very difficult to resell.

The next point to consider is whether there are any nuclear power stations in your area. There are 20 locations in France with nuclear reactors, some of them in tourist areas. See

## Average monthly temperatures (°C) and rainfall (mm)

| | Jan | Feb | Mar | Apr | May | Jun | Jul | Aug | Sep | Oct | Nov | Dec |
|---|---|---|---|---|---|---|---|---|---|---|---|---|
| **Bordeaux** | | | | | | | | | | | | |
| Max | 9 | 11 | 14 | 16 | 19 | 23 | 26 | 26 | 23 | 18 | 13 | 10 |
| Min | 2 | 3 | 4 | 6 | 10 | 13 | 15 | 15 | 12 | 9 | 5 | 3 |
| Rainfall | 76 | 64 | 66 | 66 | 71 | 66 | 53 | 58 | 71 | 86 | 89 | 86 |
| **Cherbourg** | | | | | | | | | | | | |
| Max | 8 | 8 | 10 | 12 | 15 | 18 | 19 | 20 | 19 | 15 | 12 | 10 |
| Min | 4 | 4 | 5 | 7 | 9 | 13 | 15 | 14 | 13 | 10 | 8 | 5 |
| Rainfall | 110 | 75 | 61 | 50 | 37 | 36 | 52 | 73 | 77 | 100 | 125 | 118 |
| **Dijon** | | | | | | | | | | | | |
| Max | 5 | 6 | 12 | 16 | 20 | 23 | 26 | 25 | 22 | 16 | 9 | 6 |
| Min | −2 | −1 | 2 | 5 | 9 | 12 | 14 | 13 | 11 | 6 | 2 | 0 |
| Rainfall | 48 | 41 | 48 | 51 | 58 | 69 | 64 | 64 | 53 | 74 | 71 | 58 |
| **La Rochelle** | | | | | | | | | | | | |
| Max | 9 | 10 | 13 | 16 | 19 | 23 | 24 | 25 | 23 | 18 | 12 | 8 |
| Min | 3 | 3 | 4 | 7 | 9 | 13 | 14 | 14 | 12 | 9 | 6 | 3 |
| Rainfall | 63 | 59 | 64 | 57 | 54 | 50 | 44 | 49 | 52 | 90 | 97 | 93 |
| **Lille** | | | | | | | | | | | | |
| Max | 6 | 6 | 9 | 12 | 17 | 19 | 22 | 23 | 19 | 14 | 9 | 7 |
| Min | 1 | 1 | 3 | 4 | 8 | 11 | 13 | 13 | 11 | 7 | 4 | 2 |
| Rainfall | 48 | 41 | 43 | 43 | 51 | 56 | 61 | 58 | 56 | 64 | 61 | 58 |
| **Marseille** | | | | | | | | | | | | |
| Max | 11 | 12 | 14 | 17 | 21 | 26 | 29 | 28 | 25 | 20 | 14 | 12 |
| Min | 3 | 3 | 6 | 8 | 12 | 16 | 19 | 18 | 16 | 11 | 7 | 3 |
| Rainfall | 48 | 41 | 46 | 46 | 46 | 25 | 15 | 25 | 64 | 94 | 76 | 58 |
| **Paris** | | | | | | | | | | | | |
| Max | 6 | 7 | 11 | 14 | 18 | 21 | 24 | 24 | 21 | 15 | 9 | 7 |
| Min | 1 | 1 | 3 | 6 | 9 | 12 | 14 | 14 | 11 | 8 | 4 | 2 |
| Rainfall | 53 | 48 | 37 | 43 | 54 | 52 | 55 | 61 | 53 | 50 | 51 | 50 |
| **Tours** | | | | | | | | | | | | |
| Max | 6 | 8 | 12 | 16 | 19 | 23 | 24 | 24 | 21 | 16 | 10 | 7 |
| Min | 1 | 1 | 3 | 6 | 9 | 12 | 14 | 13 | 11 | 7 | 4 | 2 |
| Rainfall | 60 | 55 | 48 | 46 | 60 | 48 | 48 | 60 | 58 | 60 | 62 | 65 |

*'Ideally, you need to spend several months renting a property in your chosen area to see how you like it out of season'*

the website http://nucleaire.edf.fr to make sure you are not near one. Another point is to check whether there are any small airfields nearby. Noise from neighbouring farmyards can also be hard to cope with for city dwellers. Wind farms are being built in many parts of France. Although they are not bad for your health they can ruin your view and some neighbours also complain about the noise they make.

Ideally, you need to spend several months renting a property in your chosen area to see how you like it out of season. Even the Côte d'Azur has wintry weather from time to time and many Britons, for example, who have bought in places such as the Limousin have been surprised at how cold it can get. Meanwhile, French holiday homes by the coast can be awful places to live out of season. Buses may not run, and services may be reduced. Many shops and restaurants close down for the winter; there are few people about, and the place could be dead for several months.

## Potential Hazards

One should not be taken in by over-optimistic property agents who try to kid you that you will have no problems moving to France. Finding work in rural areas may be next to impossible. Naturally, if you are a writer or painter there is no problem at all, otherwise it is simply a fantasy to think that local businesses are going to employ someone who doesn't speak French in preference to a local.

### Insider Tip

The ideal business will use English as a selling point, or you could consider starting a business specifically to service other foreigners. Internet-based businesses can be run from anywhere; the French countryside is ideal if you are not tied to a location and the vast majority of areas now have high-speed internet connections. Make sure you check on this before you buy if the internet is going to be important for your work.

Another major consideration is your social life. Some are happy with the company of a small circle of other foreigners, but in most of France you will have to find friends among the locals. Is your French good enough to talk about more than the weather and the price of vegetables? Isolation and the lack of clubs and societies can spell trouble. It is essential that both partners can drive. The availability of cheap alcohol is another of the main hazards. Relationships that are under strain can fall apart if one of the partners starts drinking, as happens all too often. Business failure is often accompanied by divorce.

Everyone who has successfully settled down in France has two pieces of advice: learn French as soon as possible, preferably before you leave home, and do spend some time renting in an area before you buy.

# General Property Trends

As with any country, the property market in France is affected both by national/global factors and by local ones. By 2007 there had been an overall slowdown in house price rises compared with the steep increases seen in 2002, 2003 and 2004. Reasons for this include France's relatively weak economic performance in recent years, growing personal indebtedness among consumers and a drop (whether real or perceived) in people's spending power. Generally, buyers have become choosier and in 2007 some sellers were being forced to drop their unrealistic asking prices by as much as 15%. However, there are reasons to believe that French property prices will continue to remain buoyant in the next few years, even if a return to the extravagant increases of the recent past are unlikely. One reason is that France still has a long way to go in terms of property ownership; owner-occupier rates in France are rising but are still around 65%, which is below the EU average. In Spain, by contrast, the rate is well over 80%. President Nicolas Sarkozy has meanwhile promised to help his country become a nation of home owners in a country where renting has been commonplace. A combination of more relaxed borrowing plus a growing desire to own property suggests that the market will remain strong. Demand is also likely to increase as social factors such as divorce and separation, demographic change, an ageing population etc., mean that more people live on their own. Another important long-term trend that property buyers need to be aware of is that French people are gradually moving towards the coastal areas. This is one reason why coastal properties are considerably more expensive than those further inland. This trend shows little sign of slowing down. When looking at price trends one must also consider France's neighbours – and this doesn't just mean the British. More and more Germans are starting to buy in regions such as Lorraine, which will have an impact on prices there. In the south-east of France and along the south coast there is also a very strong Italian influence.

# Changing Climate?

Finally, there is the rather more complex and long-term subject of global warming. It is possible – and one has to stress the uncertainty here – that if global temperatures continue to rise, this could have an impact on skiing and other winter sports in the Alps and Pyrenees. This in turn could have an impact on property prices – house prices in the French Alps are among some of the highest in the country. The same climatic change could also mean that water usage and shortages become an issue in the southern half of the country and particularly along the Mediterranean strip. Against this, parts of central and northern France could become more attractive if, as some French climatic experts suggest, these areas benefit from shorter but wetter winters and longer summers. And second-home buyers, for example from Britain, may choose to buy in areas they can reach either by car or boat or train, rather than having to fly. However, given the current uncertainty over predicting future climate trends you cannot rely too much on such forecasts. The 'climate change factor' is likely to remain an uncertain one when it comes to property trends in France.

## Prices by region

| | Apartments per sq m (€) | Average price of older houses (€) |
|---|---|---|
| Alsace | 2,800 | 212,700 |
| Aquitaine | 2,500 | 204,500 |
| Auvergne | 2,200 | 122,400 |
| Brittany | 2,500 | 173,300 |
| Burgundy | 2,100 | 143,200 |
| Centre | 2,350 | 153,600 |
| Champagne Ardenne | 2,800 | 145,200 |
| Franche Comté | 2,100 | 147,800 |
| Languedoc Roussillon | 2,300 | 197,500 |
| Limousin | 1,700 | 115,400 |
| Lorraine | 1,800 | 145,100 |
| Lower Normandy | 2,300 | 147,600 |
| Midi-Pyrenees | 2,600 | 186,100 |
| Nord Pas-de-Calais | 2,300 | 152,900 |
| Pays de Loire | 2,200 | 170,500 |
| Picardie | 1,650 | 162,000 |
| Poitou-Charentes | 1,750 | 140,600 |
| Provence-Côte d'Azur | 3,000 | 379,100 |
| Rhône-Alpes | 3,500 | 240,500 |
| Upper Normandy | 2,300 | 163,500 |

Source:
Flats: *Crédit Foncier de France*, 2006, based on prices in major cities
Houses: *Perval/Notaires de France*

# 5 Where To Find Your Ideal Home

Alsace borders Germany in the north-east of France, and has its own very particular traditions, and its own Germanic language, Alsatian or Allemanic. The locals consider themselves neither French nor German, but Alsatian. After being incorporated into France in 1681 by Louis XIV it was reabsorbed into Germany after the Prussian victory of 1870, only to be returned to France in 1918. During the Second World War, 140,000 young Alsatian men were conscripted into the German army to fight on the Russian front and many never returned. The use of French was also forbidden in the region for the duration of the war. These days the Alsatian language is still widely used. Lutheranism is the established church here.

There was a vogue in the 1990s for Germans to buy properties near the border and commute to work in Germany. Many of them have now gone back to live in Germany, disappointed to find that Alsace is not as Germanic as they had hoped. The French, on the other hand, go across to Germany to shop where it is easy to see that prices are cheaper because of the common euro. The greatest appeal of Alsace lies in the Vosges mountains, good for skiing in winter and walking the rest of the year. Fishing and horse-riding are also popular. The region is 45% forest; the climate is fairly wet.

Alsace consists of two *départements,* Bas-Rhin (67) and Haut-Rhin (68), both bordering onto Germany, with the Rhine on the eastern side. The main city, Strasbourg (pop. 388,000), houses the plenary sessions of the European Parliament, as well as being home to the Council of Europe, but the MEPs only stay for 10 days at a time. Both Strasbourg and Mulhouse have very high crime rates. There are flights from Strasbourg to London. The introduction of a new

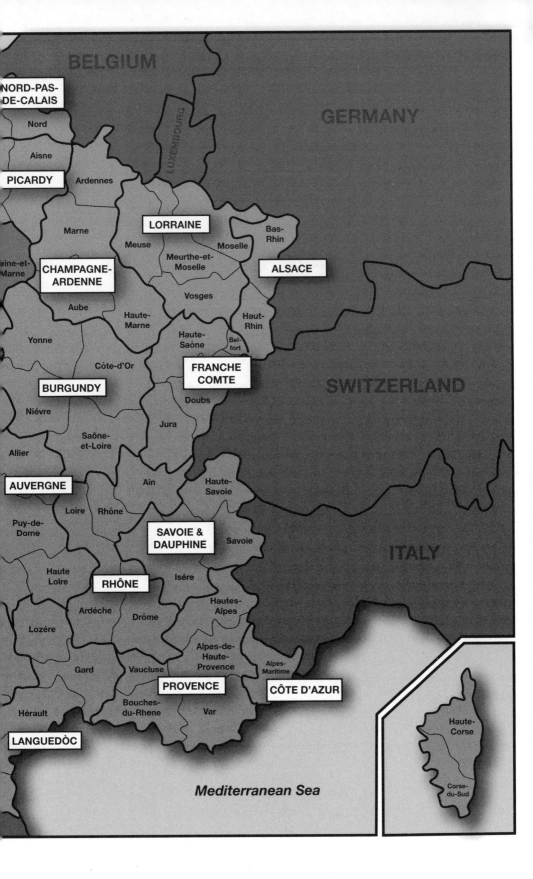

TGV high-speed train service between Paris and Strasbourg in June 2007 has also improved communications with the area.

## Cuisine

The cooking draws heavily on the fish that are caught in the local rivers. The term *à l'alsacienne* means 'with sauerkraut', or *choucroute*. Alsace has a great tradition of producing white wine (and to a lesser extent rosé), such as Gewürztraminer, but the area is equally known for its beer, of which Kronenbourg is the best known.

## Property

The classic Alsace house has half-timbering (*fachwarik*) with a hipped and sometimes mansard roof. The massive German style with all the functional spaces under the one roof is common. Houses are generally well looked-after and tidy. For protection against the weather farm walls are sometimes covered with shingles. The townhouses are similar to those over the border with Germany, typically with dormer windows, windowboxes, and decorative shutters. Generally one is limited to a choice between apartments and large houses. There is only a limited second-homes market in Alsace; houses to renovate are few and far between. Property is expensive compared with most of France, partly driven by the proximity to Germany.

## Property TRENDS

Alsace is already the fourth most expensive region in France and so it is not the best place for anyone looking for a cheap property bargain. The new TGV service to and from Paris and a recovering economy in neighbouring Germany are unlikely to change that. Indeed, they mean that property prices are likely to rise generally over the next couple of years. One interesting growth area is likely to be in investment properties, in new developments in cities such as Strasbourg. Here it is still possible to find studios or small one-bedroom flats in some areas for around €90,000. Also prices in the Haut-Rhin are lower than those in Bas-Rhin. Property around the relatively cheaper areas of Guebwiller and Altkirch could start to rise in price as people are priced out of more expensive zones. Meanwhile property in attractive towns such as Colmar, benefiting from the faster rail link, is also expected to go up in value.

## What you can get for your money

| Price range (€) | Location | Type | Description | Price (€) |
|---|---|---|---|---|
| Under 100,000 | Strasbourg (67) | Flat, 50 sq m | 2-room flat on 2nd floor with balcony and parking space | 95,000 |
| 100,000 to 200,000 | Barr (67) nr Strasbourg | House | Pretty 2-bedroom townhouse, with study, kitchen and lounge/diner | 149,000 |
| 200,000 to 300,000 | Masevaux (68) nr Thann | House, 150 sq m | 4-bedroom house with spa, terrace, study and garage | 262,000 |
| 300,000 to 500,000 | Strasbourg (67) | Flat, 115, sq m | Upmarket new development, 3 bedrooms, large living area, south-facing terrace | 390,000 |
| 500,000 and over | Colmar (68) | House, 300 sq m | Stylish detached modern home with large garden, 4 bedrooms | 690,000 |

# Aquitaine

**CRT:**

☎ 05 56 01 70 00;    🖥 tourisme@crt.cr-aquitaine.fr; www.crt.cr-aquitaine.fr; www.bordeaux-tourisme.com.

**Percentage of population:** 4.85%; percentage of GDP: 4.24%.

**Airports:** Bergerac: www.bergerac.aeroport.fr
Biarritz: www.biarritz.aeroport.fr
Bordeaux: www.bordeaux.aeroport.fr
Pau: www.pau.aeroport.fr

The Aquitaine region covers a large and diverse area of south-western France, stretching from the borders of the Massif Central down to the Spanish border and the Pyrenees. The regional capital, Bordeaux, also the prefectural town of the Gironde (www.tourisme-gironde.cg33.fr), has a long and close association with the UK and Ireland. The city (pop. 700,000) stands next to the Garonne river, where it turns into the Gironde estuary.

*'The Dordogne and Lot-et-Garonne are two départements strongly associated with second homes for Brits; the latter is rather cheaper than the first'*

The British demand for Bordeaux wines, or 'claret', led to the expansion of the port, and made this a rich city. It was substantially rebuilt in the 18th and 19th centuries with classical-style buildings and boulevards. It is the gateway to the world's most prestigious wine-producing region, but also well known for its excellent cuisine. The port is not as important as it was when France had an empire; the city is a centre for high-tech industries, aerospace, wood-based products and food processing. It has been rated second for economic dynamism and quality of life after Toulouse in a survey conducted by *Express* magazine amongst managers. Recent urban regeneration projects, such as a new tramway linking the city with the suburbs, have caused considerable disruption, but are helping the property market. The rebuilding of the waterside, Les Quais de la Garonne, to be completed in 2008, and the extension of the TGV from Tours (though perhaps not until 2016) and then on to Spain, will certainly cause property prices to rise.

Aquitaine has five *départements:* Pyrénées-Atlantiques (64), Landes (40), Gironde (33), Lot-et-Garonne (47), and Dordogne (24). Pyrénées-Atlantiques is certainly the least typical *département* in this region, as it incorporates the French Basque country bordering on Spain. The Basques in this area are not particularly militant; their main demand has been for the creation of one Basque *département*, but all they have gained is the status of a territorial collectivity. The most militant acts these days are spraying graffiti in Basque, or defacing road signs. Some such graffiti urge outsiders to keep their hands off local, i.e. Basque, property. Basque villages, with their *pelota* courts (a rougher version of squash), banana trees, and red peppers drying on the balconies, present more of an image of Spain than France. The churches are also redolent of Spanish-type Catholic fervour. By comparison with the French, the Basques are rather introverted and supposedly surly, but outsiders find them friendly enough. They appreciate it if you try to pronounce Basque words correctly: *z* is pronounced as 's' and *x* as 'sh'.

Biarritz, close to Spain, is a popular and expensive resort for surfers, once popular with British royalty. It is home to one of France's leading rugby teams who in recent years have made strong efforts to develop their 'Basque' appeal by playing some of their matches in Spanish Basque country. The prefectural town of Pyrénées-Atlantiques is Pau, another town well known for its rugby team. The main attraction is the mountainous scenery, excellent for walking and camping.

The Landes (www.tourismelandes.com) is a rather empty region of forests and sandy soil, though for some people it has an eerie beauty of its own. It can also boast the longest and straightest beach in Europe, the Côte d'Argent, stretching from the Gironde estuary down to Biarritz. The flatness of the landscape makes it ideal for cycling and camping.

The Dordogne and Lot-et-Garonne are two *départements* strongly associated with second homes for Brits; the latter is rather cheaper than the first. It is estimated that the presence of foreigners looking for second homes has pushed prices up by some 30% over what they would be otherwise. Lot-et-Garonne is an agricultural region about half the size of the Dordogne, and not that well known. Its main town is Agen. The main Bordeaux–Toulouse railway and motorway bisect the *département*. The town of Archachon in the Gironde is a typical French resort noted for its seafood restaurants and well worth a visit – though it does get very crowded in August.

# Cuisine

The Gironde around Bordeaux is home to some of France's great vintages. To the north-west, Médoc produces only red wines, the most prestigious being Château Margaux. The St Émilion/ Pomerol/Fronsac region near Libourne is famed for superior reds. The Entre-deux-Mers, actually between the rivers Garonne and Dordogne, specialises in white wines. To the south-east of Bordeaux as far as Langon, lies the Graves region, with red and white wines that formerly had a poor reputation but which have now regained some credibility. Past Langon you come to the Sauternes and Barsac region, world famous for its sweet golden dessert wines; the use of 'noble rot' or botrytis allows the grapes to shrivel before picking them, giving the wine its powerful taste. Wine is very much an industry; only the expensive *appellation controlée* wines are picked by hand these days. Part of the Armagnac (brandy) region extends into the Lot-et-Garonne – the Ténarèze around Nérac and Mézin, and into the Landes; most production is in the Gers.

The cooking of the Landes and Gironde is rather overshadowed by the wines. The main dishes are the oysters cultivated in the Arcachon basin, lampreys, and lamb cooked over vine leaves. The prefectural town of the Lot-et-Garonne, Agen (pronounced 'azheng'), is world famous for its prunes; duck cooked with prunes and similar dishes are the local speciality.

The Basque country offers Bayonne ham, *palombes* (pigeon), tuna and a strong ewe's milk cheese, *tomme* or *gasna*. Red peppers can be seen drying on many housefronts; *pipérade* is an omelette with chilli peppers, ham and tomatoes; *piquillos* are sweet red peppers stuffed with cod. The Pyrenean potato and cabbage soup – *garbure* – is an everyday item. Seafood is often on the menu, for example stewed squid, *txiperons*, and fish soup, *ttoro*.

# Property

The styles of construction are closely related to the building materials available. The western Landes and Gironde is an area with very little stone, but plentiful forests. The typical farm building is made of closely set wooden beams filled with *hourdis* – tiles set in mortar. The surface area is very substantial; all the storerooms and animals sheds are set under one low-pitched roof. In some *landaise* farmhouses the main entrance leads directly into the stables, or *court*, where you formerly dismounted from your horse. The downside of this type of design is that it is not really possible to add any extensions to the building, as they would spoil its appearance. The *landaise* is copied in modern villas; otherwise one finds the usual rather uniform ochre-washed holiday bungalows with Spanish tiles. Properties are most expensive on the coast, particularly at Arcachon, the high-class yachting resort. The upmarket wine regions are also expensive.

The Pyrénées-Atlantiques has one typical style, the Basque villa, which became popular after 1920, and copies features of the traditional local farmhouse, the *labourdine*. The *maison labourdine* is similar to a Landes farmhouse, except that it generally has two or even three

# Regional Voices – Lot-et-Garonne

**Amanda Lawrence** is a writer who has lived in the area for many years. Here she gives her impressions.

Glorious Aquitaine, fabled land of many rivers, once stretched from the Loire valley to the Pyrenees; that was many years ago when it was a rich, medieval dukedom, when Eleanor was its Duchess and her court attracted the greatest troubadours of the age. Now it has been absorbed into modern France and is a fraction of its former size. But the fairytale châteaux are still here – some of them are even for sale – it's still a beautiful, rolling landscape and after all those years when it formed part of the vast Plantagenet Empire, there's something about it that remains quintessentially English. Perhaps that explains the number of British who have elected to settle here, and are still coming in droves.

   Apart from the Dordogne, one of the most favoured departments is the Lot-et-Garonne. Watered by the two great rivers for which it's named, this is the fruit bowl of France, home of the world-famous Agen prunes and the enormous, delicious Marmande tomatoes. There are huge orchards of plum, peach and nectarine, melon fields and asparagus beds. The climate is a degree or two warmer than its neighbours inland, another good reason for the high British population. If you're looking for an area that may be a little less expensive, with fewer second homes, the further south you go the better your chances. The land around Agen, lively capital of the Lot-et-Garonne, is relatively sparsely populated whilst Agen itself offers excellent facilities. The style of the old farmhouses change as you travel south; the turrets and pigeonniers are left behind and long slanting roofs, typical of the region, appear. For those prepared to roll up their sleeves there are bargains to be found amongst these properties. This is also an excellent place to look if you fancy a smallholding. Agricultural land is cheap, the soil is rich, fertile and free of the rock-strewn ground that so delights the tourists but exasperates farmers in the neighbouring Quercy. Many rural enterprises have appeared over the last few years, farming everything from lettuces to llamas. They can sell their surplus in the local markets whilst enjoying all the benefits of a benevolent climate and contributing to the local economy at the same time. This is the kind of enterprise of which the astute and statesmanlike Eleanor would undoubtedly have approved.

For more of Amanda's views on the area and its property visit: www.amandalawrence.fr.

storeys. The base is stone, with half-timbering on the upper floors, and painted shutters. The roof is low and double-pitched. This type of house is similar to the *landaise* insofar as the front entrance goes directly into a garage or storeroom, called an *eskarratza,* and the living quarters are often all on the first floor. Animals were once housed on the ground floor. The design was adapted for the neo-Basque villa; these are all whitewashed and the timbers painted red or green, in the Basque national colours, making for a rather monotonous effect. Ornately carved galleries and shutters are added for decoration. Rather different in style are the Edwardian holiday villas in Biarritz and all along the coast.

In the Hautes-Pyrénées one finds an entirely different kind of design – the type *basse Navarre* – a massive stone-built farmhouse, with four-pitched roof, and a second farm building at right angles to it. At the lower elevations the abundance of pebbles on the river beds is put to use to make walls of geometrically arranged pebbles in mortar.

# Dordogne

The Dordogne (www.dordogne-perigord-tourisme.fr) was the first area of rural France to be invaded by British second-home owners. After the first discoveries of human bones belonging to the Cro-Magnon people in the valley of the Vézère river in 1868, British prehistory buffs started to buy properties around the small railway town of Les Eyzies, between the departmental capital Périgueux and Sarlat. Dordogne even has its own English monthly newspaper, *French News,* published from Périgueux, but covering the whole of France.

The Dordogne is known as Périgord to the French; foreigners tend to use the word Dordogne for a wider adjoining area. Certain areas of the Dordogne are being taken

> *'The Périgourdins are naturally friendly and sociable, and this has certainly been a factor in drawing foreigners here'*

over by foreigners, the heaviest concentration being around Ribérac north-west of the capital Périgueux, Sarlat to the south-east and Eymet in the south-west (the latter even boasts its own cricket team). The Ribérac area originally became popular because it was cheaper than the southern Dordogne, and now it probably has the most foreigners. In the village of Bouteilles-St-Sébastien, outside Verteillac in Périgord Vert, 60% of the houses are owned by foreigners, but 90% of these are rented out to holidaymakers and remain shuttered in winter. In the wake of this invasion, some Britons have bought bars and hotels, or started art galleries or antique shops. The large properties that outsiders want are becoming scarce and expensive; some Brits are even buying smaller houses in the towns; old barns or watchtowers are optimistically put on the market in the hope that someone will be brave enough to do them up.

The French locals view the foreign invasion with resignation. The kinds of properties that foreigners buy are generally beyond the means of the locals anyway. In one sense the outsiders keep the countryside alive, but the locals are less happy if they try to bypass the local economy entirely. The Périgourdins are naturally friendly and sociable, and this has certainly been a factor in drawing foreigners here, rather than to some other areas of central France where people are more difficult to get to know.

Périgord is remarkable in that it has evidence of continuous human occupation going back to 500,000 BC. The cave paintings of Lascaux are no longer open to visitors, but there is a respectable recreation at Lascaux II. The appeal of the Vézère valley for cavemen is easy to understand, as they could find easy shelter under the overhanging limestone cliffs called *abris*. Périgord is geologically complex, but about half of it is limestone, as is much of south-central France, easily cut through by rivers to form the typical gorges and limestone plateaux called *causses*. The region is on a slope going down from the Massif Central towards the plains of the Landes; the bottoms of the river valleys are only a few feet above sea level.

# Four colour-coded regions

Périgord is divided into four different areas: Purple, Black, White and Green. In the south is Périgord Pourpre (www.bergerac-tourisme.com) named after the grapes that are grown here, with Bergerac at its centre. Monbazillac, a little to the south, is famous for its sweet white apéritif wine. Bergerac is known for robust red wine as well as dry whites; the town has no connection with the well-known English detective series. There are direct flights to London Stansted.

East of the purple country is Périgord Noir (www.tourisme.fr/module3/sarlat/), which takes its name from the dark oak forests here. This *pays nègre* or 'black country' was a place of refuge during the wars that have often been waged around the area. The main town, Sarlat, is a tourist trap in the summer, understandably thanks to its superbly preserved Renaissance architecture. Les Eyzies, an unpretentious little town with a fine museum of prehistory, is the gateway to an area of well-preserved prehistoric caves along the Vézère river which leads up to the market town of Montignac, near Lascaux.

Périgord Blanc (www.ville-perigueux.fr) cuts a swathe across the *département*, with Périgueux at its centre, but is the least touristic area of the *département*. The departmental capital, Périgueux, is rather dull, and most tourists try to leave as fast as possible.

Finally, there is the northern area of Périgord Vert (www.perigordvert.com), where most foreigners aspire to buy property, an area of lush countryside dotted with maize fields, but not as hilly as the south. The Friday market in Ribérac is well known, and you will meet a large section of the foreign population here. There are quite a few Dutch and Germans in the area. The chocolate-box town of Brantôme, west of Ribérac, is built on an island in the Dronne river, and is always overrun by tourists in the summer. The northern part of Périgord Vert has not been so heavily taken over by foreigners yet.

Probably more than anywhere else, the Dordogne offers the possibility of making a living offering services to other foreigners. There is, in any case, precious little work outside of agriculture and tourism. The climate is warm and humid much of the year, although it can occasionally snow on the hills in winter, when temperatures can plunge well below freezing.

# Cuisine

The culinary traditions of Périgord are a main factor in drawing foreigners here. Périgord is well known for its agricultural products: nuts, apricots, strawberries, truffles, *foie gras* and even

# In the know

**Has the Dordogne become too popular with the British for its own good? Charlotte Clarke, of Sextant French Property Agents (www.sextantproperties.com) gives a French perspective:**

I believe that the Dordogne, which has proved very popular with buyers over the last two decades, will continue to be a property hotspot in the future. Why? Because of its unchanging qualities. This area has a consistently mild climate (slightly warmer in the summer), spectacular scenery and a notable ability to preserve the past. For example its incredible heritage of prehistoric archaeological and artistic work, its caves and paintings, have all been conserved. For centuries, the French have been rebuilding and reconstructing long abandoned buildings and villages, remaining faithful to original layouts and features.

Sarlat-le-Caneda, the capital of the Dordogne, is now known as one of the best preserved medieval centres in France. A beautiful town situated north of the River Dordogne, it has the highest concentration of medieval and Renaissance facades anywhere in France; narrow cobbled streets, picturesque archways, delightful squares and ochre-coloured stone houses rich in ornamental detail. There is also a twice-weekly famous market, overflowing with fresh produce, including local specialities such as *foie gras*, walnuts, black truffles, wild mushrooms and pork delicacies. And the town further upholds tradition via annual fairs and festivals: Festival des Jeux de Théâtre, for example, one of France's most important theatre festivals, takes place every July.

The Vezere Valley meanwhile, renowned for its impressive sights, has been classified as a world heritage site by UNESCO, and the whole area is also full of châteaux, gardens, forests, rivers and other medieval villages such as Domme, the bastide town of golden stone, La Roque-Gabeac, regular winner of France's prettiest village contest, Belves with its 7 towers, troglodyte houses and annual Bach Festival, and St Cyprien with its labourers' cottages.

Added to this are the facts that, though property prices may rise, house prices in the Dordogne will always be a lot cheaper than those in England. And travel links are easy, with the number of flights to Bergerac (the nearest airport) steadily increasing. Cheap airlines, for example, have increased to four flights every Saturday. There is also plenty of space in the region.

Decent weather, beautiful landscapes, an attachment to antiquity, comparatively cheap houses, easy access and space .... together this creates a region filled with winning factors. I am confident that the Dordogne, especially the area in and around the capital, remains and will continue to remain one of the places to be in France.

tobacco. The richness of the soil – the *terroir* – is reflected in the cooking. This is a land of truffles, odd fungi that only grow underground on the roots of oak trees, which have to be dug out using a sniffer sow or dog to locate them. While truffles cannot be cultivated, oak trees have been planted over the years, and they are carefully kept clear of weeds. A large truffle can fetch over £10,000. The only explanation for such prices must lie in the truffle's reputed aphrodisiac powers. The great French cookery writer, Brillat Savarin, remarked: 'Truffles make the ladies loving, and the gentlemen gallant.'

Paté is another speciality: geese are force-fed with cooked maize until their livers reach a kilo in weight. Opinions are divided on whether the geese enjoy the process. Preserved goose or duck (*confit d'oie/canard*) goes into making *cassoulet*, a dish of beans, *confit,* pork and sausage. The Périgourdins are also keen on game or *gibier:* one favourite dish consists of larks, thrushes and quails. Chestnuts are also an important ingredient in the local cooking; for poorer families they were a staple part of their diet.

| What you can get for your money | | | | |
|---|---|---|---|---|
| **Price range (€)** | **Location** | **Type** | **Description** | **Price (€)** |
| Under 100,000 | Dax (40) | Flat, 37 sq m | 3-room flat in sought-after area, newly renovated | 81,000 |
| 100,000 to 200,000 | Biarritz (64) | Flat | 3-room flat just 100m from beach | 194,000 |
| 200,000 to 300,000 | Nr Agen (47) | Stone house, 280 sq m | 17th-century house, fully and authentically restored with 5,000 sq m land | 262,000 |
| 300,000 to 500,000 | 10 km, Bergerac (24) | Perigord-style, 155 sq m | 4 bedrooms, swimming pool, easy reach of Bergerac Airport | 401,450 |
| 500,000 and over | Property 1: Bordeaux (33) | Townhouse | 8-room home in city centre, garage, garden and outbuildings | 560,000 |
| | Property 2: Nr Blis-et-Born (24) | Manor house | 5 bedrooms, tower and pigeon loft, vaulted cellar, cottage to renovate plus barn (see photo No. 1 in colour section) | 698,384 |
| | Property 3: Nr Orthez (64) | Béarnaise house | Imposing 4-bedroom home, edge of village, 1 hectare land, original features (see photo No. 14 in colour section) | 577,600 |

# Property

The types of properties foreigners look for in the Dordogne are generally traditional and may be in need of renovation, although there is less available in the latter category than there used to be. The demand is so great, however, that even new houses in the towns on estates (*lotissements*) are being bought by foreigners. The typical massive farmhouses or *périgourdines* are built from rough-hewn limestone, anchored with quoins (*chaînes d'angle*) at the corners from shaped stone, with massive oak beams running through them. Dormer windows are not that common in older property, but it is a tradition to have a couple of little V-shaped decorative openings called *outeaux* in the roof. One step up from the *périgourdine* is the *gentilhommière*, a gentleman's residence, usually with one or two separate wings, more recent and constructed from cut stone.

In the somewhat drier southern part of the Dordogne, one can also find Provençal-style *mas*, or manor houses, with flat tiled roofs and arcades. Newer holiday homes reflect the prevalent liking for the Provençal style of ochre rendering and Spanish tiles. Because of the price inflation in Dordogne, foreigners are prepared to consider doing up any building that is still standing, and the locals are quite happy to try to offload a collapsing barn (*grange*) for an apparently paltry sum on an unsuspecting foreigner. Damp and woodworm are prevalent in older properties.

As far as finding property goes, there are several foreign-run estate agents, so there is less scope for agents who might act as intermediaries between you and the *immobilier*. One could try the Wednesday or Friday edition of the regional newspaper *Sud-Ouest Périgueux*. There is no shortage of agents in the UK who can put you on to the kind of property you want.

# Property TRENDS

There's little doubt that the huge rise in property prices that took place in the middle of the first decade of this century has slowed down. As in other areas where foreign buyers have moved into the market, a combination of economic factors, over-valuation by sellers and more cautious buying have stabilised prices. Interestingly, however, and despite the past rises and foreign interest, average prices in the Dordogne remain well below those in other parts of the region. This suggests there could still be room for price rises in the future. The presence of very expensive areas such as Bordeaux and Biarritz can distort the situation in other parts of the region. For example, in the Pyrénées-Atlantiques average property prices around Biarritz are more than double those of Oloron-Sainte-Marie and even higher than around Pau. Both these areas could see increased activity in coming years. Finally, a growing trend in the region is for the building of new developments, some of them based around golf courses or other forms of leisure activity. These offer scope not just for living in but for investment too. However, a new-build one-bedroom home in the Gironde, with spa, golf course and swimming pool can cost around €300,000, so they are not necessarily cheap investments.

**Auvergne**

**CRT:**

☎ 04 73 98 65 00;  💻 www.auvergne-tourisme.info.

**Percentage of population:** 2.18%; percentage of GDP: 1.77%.

**Airports:** Clermont-Ferrand: www.clermont-fd.cci.fr/aeroport/aeroport.php
Saint-Etienne: www.saint-etienne.aeroport.fr

Auvergne includes four *départements:* Allier (03), Cantal (15), Haute Loire (43) and Puy-de-Dôme (63); the region sits on the Massif Central, a thinly populated region, much of it above 3,000 ft. The typical landscape features are the dome-shaped extinct volcanoes (*puys*) that litter the area. With its high moorlands, interspersed with oak, beech and birch, or man-made pine plantations, it has its own peculiar charm, especially with the mists settling in between the hills. Historically, the Auvergnats have been hostile towards central government; their strong sense of self-sufficiency and rebellious streak led many to convert to Protestantism during the Wars of Religion. As with the rest of central France, there is a move from the land towards the cities by young people, and there is every likelihood that the population will fall in the coming years, while the countryside becomes more and more a preserve of the elderly. On the other hand, Auvergne is traditional and more genuinely French than much of the country.

The Auvergne has a number of interesting landmarks. The most well known, the Puy-de-Dôme, is one of the highest points in the Massif Central (4791 ft/1452 m), but it has lost some of its mystique as you can drive all the way to the top. Where the Romans had a temple to Mercury, there are now radio antennae and an observatory. You can reputedly see 70 extinct volcanoes from here on a clear day. Near Puy-de-Dôme are the springs from which Volvic and other mineral waters derive: the extinct volcanoes in the area act as a perfect filter, and half of all the mineral water in France comes from the Auvergne. The western half of Auvergne is covered by the Parc des Volcans d'Auvergne, spreading all the way from Vichy in the north to Aurillac in the south.

Clermont-Ferrand, the regional capital, was originally two cities: Clermont and Montferrand, but the former won out. Michelin tyres has its headquarters here. The symbol of the city and of Michelin guides, the Michelin man, real name Bibendum, was dreamt up in 1898 by a cartoonist called O'Galop. It is home to a leading rugby side who seem to change their name constantly; currently they are known as Clermont Auvergne

In the *département* of the Haute-Loire, the main town of Puy-en-Velay (on the Loire) has a lot of charm, and an amazing church built on a rock, the Aiguilhe St Michel. The Loire actually rises in the Ardèche *département* east of Le Puy. Among the man-made attractions of the Auvergne, two stand out: one is the Viaduc de Garabit, a 125 m high railway bridge, designed by Gustave Eiffel, in the Cantal near St Flour, also a very attractive little town built on the outcrop of a volcanic plain. The other is the Forêt de Tronçais, an 11,000 hectare forest of oaks and other trees planted under Louis XIV to provide wood for the French navy. The forest lies in the north-west of the Allier, near the town of Cérilly and is open to the public.

Cantal is reputed for the cheese of the same name (www.cdt-cantal.fr). The departmental capital, Aurillac, specialises in making umbrellas. The other distinguishing feature these days are the cattle markets. North of Clermont-Ferrand is the spa town of Vichy, which has unfortunate connotations of wartime collaboration, but is actually a very pleasant spot, with abundant hotels for those who want to take the waters. Vichy is only a sub-prefectural town, the capital of the Allier *département* being Moulins further north. Allier is cereal and cattle-farming country. Before the Revolution this was the Duchy of Bourbonnais. It is particularly rich in Romanesque churches.

> '*Auvergne is traditional and more genuinely French than much of the country*'

The main attractions of the Auvergne for property buyers are cheapness and space, the main drawbacks remoteness and poor public transport – and of course very cold winters. Railway lines have been replaced by buses in many areas. There are direct flights from London to Clermont-Ferrand and St Étienne, some way to the east.

## Cuisine

Auvergne was once an important wine region, but the phylloxera epidemic of the 19th century virtually wiped the industry out. The vineyards are making a slow comeback; the Côtes d'Auvergne stretches from north of Riom to the south of Issoire. The area is famous for its cheeses, such as Bleu d'Auvergne, Salers, Saint-Nectaire and Cantal. The typical local dish is *potée auvergnate*, a hot pot of vegetables and pork. The term *à l'auvergnate* means with cabbage, bacon and sausage. *Truffade* is a hearty dish of potatoes and Cantal *tomme* cheese. The other speciality of the area is ham; *pounti* is a terrine based on ham, pork breast, prunes and beet leaves. The town of Puy has trademarked the local green lentils; this was the first French vegetable to gain an *appellation controlée* mark.

## Property

There is not much of a market in holiday homes here, but on the positive side, prices are still reasonable. The Allier has the most active second-homes market. One should bear in mind that it can be cold in winter on the higher ground, so good heating is essential. Village houses are sometimes built in terraces to save on building cost and to ward off the cold. Not surprisingly the most plentiful building material in the Auvergne is the local lava or basalt. Stone tiles with scalloped edges, or in the shape of fish scales, are used on older buildings in the mountainous parts.

The Allier, in the north of the region, has its own unusual styles of building. Large farms, known as *domaines*, are groups of houses in a U shape, which housed both the owners and their tenant-farmers. Smaller farms are called *locateries*. In the south one can find the *maison à galerie*, a house with a wooden gallery with the living quarters upstairs, as well as Spanish tiles, a sign of the nearness of the Languedoc. A *maison de montagne* or *maison auvergnate* is a cottage of rough-hewn stone with a tiled roof.

# *Property* TRENDS

The Puy-de-Dôme and Haute-Loire are two *départements* that were more or less ignored by second-home buyers until recently. The French call this *le désert* – long-term depopulation has caused havoc here. Their cheapness is one reason why more British people are looking at this area as a place to live and even for a holiday home. In the last few years there has been a growing trend for Britons to buy in this area, with low prices being the main reason. Prices in the Auvergne are the lowest in France, with property cheaper even than the Limousin next door. The main attraction is the plentiful and cheap land.

Areas that are popular with Britons now are around Ambert, such as the Livradois and Craponne-sur-Arzonne. About 50 km south of Clermont-Ferrand, check out the Brioude region; Vieille-Brioude is spectacularly located in a gorge and the modern town of Brioude has good facilities and is close to the E11 motorway to Montpellier. The altitude of your property is a major consideration; above 3,000 ft (900 m) and you are looking at an extra month of winter. Prices are rising fast, as local people realise that they can sell renovated properties to the British that no one would have looked at a few years ago. It is essential to haggle; you can reasonably try to get the price down by 15%. Expect to pay from €120,000 for a farmhouse with an acre or two of land. Of the four departments, Allier has the cheapest property of all; in 2006 the average house price was below €100,000.

## What you can get for your money

| Price range (€) | Location | Type | Description | Price (€) |
|---|---|---|---|---|
| Under 100,000 | Property 1: Vichy (03) | Flat | Renovated 2-bedroom flat, parking space | 91,200 |
| | Property 2: Issoire (63) | New development, 25.5 sq m | Studio flat (see photo No. 6 in colour section) | from 70,965 |
| 100,000 to 200,000 | Sainte-Florine (43) south of Clermont-Ferrand | New-build | 4-room house with 110 sq m living space and large garden | 192,000 |
| 200,000 to 300,000 | Billom (63) near Clermont-Ferrand | Stone farmhouse | 6-room house with outbuildings and 5,000 sq m of land | 248,000 |
| 500,000 and over | Nr Clermont Ferrand (63) | Country house | 5 large bedrooms, 105 sq m living room with beams, swimming pool, 7,000 sq m land and separate studio flat | 625,000 |

# Brittany (Bretagne)

**CRT:**

☎ 02 99 36 15 15; 💻 tourism-crtb@tourismebretagne.com; www.
tourismebretagne.com; www.tourisme-rennes.com.

**Percentage of population:** 4.85%; percentage of GDP: 3.92%.

**Airports:** Dinard: www.dinard.com/aeroport-dinard-saint-malo.php
Brest: www.airport.cci-brest.fr
Rennes: www.rennes.aeroport.fr

Brittany has for many years been one of the prime tourist destinations for the British. The area even has the same name as Britain; while Great Britain is Grande Bretagne, Brittany is Petite Bretagne. From the end of the Roman Empire in the 4th century until the 10th century, Celtic speakers emigrated here from Britain, thus keeping alive Celtic language and culture. Brittany only became a full part of France in 1532; before that it was an independent dukedom that generally stayed outside the Anglo-French wars. The Breton language has been severely repressed by the central government in Paris, and it is mixed with French. Speakers of Welsh and Cornish can understand a good deal of Breton. There is also a Breton liberation front; up until now their most violent act was to bomb a McDonald's in 1999, accidentally killing one of the workers. Not many Bretons are now interested in independence. There is some hostility towards so many outsiders buying second homes and forcing up prices, with demonstrations and burning of estate agent leaflets. Things have not yet reached the point where holiday homes are being torched. Very few Bretons would support such actions; the worst that one will see is some graffiti and perhaps a less friendly welcome in some cafés than before.

The four *départements* that make up Brittany are: Finistère (29), Côtes-d'Armor (22), Ille-et-Vilaine (35), and Morbihan (56). The Bretons divide Brittany into Haute and Basse Bretagne (Upper and Lower Brittany); the dividing line runs between St Brieuc in the north and Le Croisic on the south coast. Ille-et-Vilaine is often called 'Haute-Bretagne'. The most popular tourist spots are along the north coast of Ille-et-Vilaine and Côtes-d'Armor, which has a ferry port at Roscoff with services to Plymouth and Cork. The main town of Ille-et-Vilaine (www. bretagne35.com), and regional centre, Rennes, was made capital when Brittany became part of France. These days it is a dynamic and trendy university city. The TGV will be extended from Le Mans to Rennes by 2013, and will bring Brittany much closer to Paris.

## Insider Tip

The main advice is to learn to speak French (and Breton preferably) and show some sensitivity towards the locals. The Bretons particularly dislike foreigners who buy houses and leave them empty for most of the year. It is galling to the Bretons to see the only café in a village being taken over by English-speakers.

The old port town of St Malo, at the mouth of the Rance estuary, is a main tourist attraction, mostly for the great *citadelle* that overlooks the town. There are ferries to Jersey. Dinan (Côtes-d'Armor), 25 km to the south on the Rance estuary has an equally superb *citadelle* or castle with a medieval town centre and well-preserved ramparts all the way around. West of St Malo, the small town of Dol was once a fortress barring the way to the Dukes of Normandy; there is still a cathedral. The rocky coastline around St Malo and the Paramé is a protected national park, known as the Côte d'Émeraude (Emerald Coast).

The *département* of the Côtes-d'Armor (www.cotesdarmor.com) was until quite recently known as the Côtes-du-Nord and appears as such on pre-1990 maps. The prefectural town of St Brieuc is more industrial than touristic. Further west, the coast between Perros-Guirrec and Trébeurden — the Côte du Granit Rose (Pink Granite Coast) — is outstandingly beautiful and a national park.

To the west is the most Breton *département*, Finistère (www.finisteretourisme.com), the only area where Breton is still a living language amongst the younger generation. The southern part of Finistère — which means 'end of the world' — is called Cornouaille. The port of Brest, at the western end of Finistère, was completely obliterated in the Second World War and only has modern buildings. The properties are some of the cheapest in France, but it would not be a place for a second home. Brest does have direct flights to London Stansted. Inland Finistère has the highest rainfall in France: over 50 inches a year. The area is subject to severe storms in winter.

Along the south coast is the fourth Breton *département*, Morbihan (www.morbihan.com). The port of Lorient holds the annual Inter-Celtic Festival where the Celts congregate. The prefectural town of Vannes was once the seat of the Breton parliament. It is rated as one of the best places to live in France. To the south-west is Carnac, Europe's most important prehistoric site, with hundreds of mysterious menhirs, or standing stones, aligned according to the moon and stars.

The appeal of Brittany for many lies in its Celtic folklore and spirituality (even if this is more imaginary than actual). The landscape is both rugged and beautiful, as are the houses.

# Cuisine

For the French, Brittany symbolises *crêpes* or thin pancakes sprinkled with icing sugar. Every *crêperie* in France declares itself to be Breton. The other speciality in this line are buckwheat *galettes,* thick unleavened cakes. Buckwheat, or *sarrasin,* came back with the crusaders. The Breton rulers encouraged its use as a substitute for wheat, which was grown for export, so that the very poor would have something to eat. The locals call it *blé noir* (black wheat).

Brittany, with its long coastline, is a seafood paradise; the official authentic *plateau de fruits de mer,* is expected to have at least six kinds of shellfish, served on a bed of the local seaweed, *goémon.* Restaurants who meet these criteria have a symbol. The Pays de Léon in Finistère is the main producer of artichokes in France. Brittany as a whole produces a lot of green vegetables, cauliflowers, broccoli and peas. The image of the Breton onion seller is well fixed in our collective memory. These days the Bretons can be found at markets in Britain selling a wider range of produce.

# Property

Brittany was and is a poor region; the only good agricultural land is around Rennes. The typical building started with a double wall of schist or sandstone rocks filled in with mortar strengthened with ash, straw or animal hairs. The front of the house would face away from the prevailing winds from the west and south. Where houses face towards the west, one may see slates coming down to street level.

The basic longhouse was divided between a cattle-shed, living quarters and stables. Grain was stored above the living room, and hay above the stables. Families cooked and slept in one room until hay-lofts were converted into bedrooms. The most common roofing was at one time thatch, but this has been entirely replaced by slates because of the risk of fire.

In Ille-et-Vilaine, where there are more trees, upper storeys of houses were made of half-timbering filled with wattle and daub. The batons in between the beams are generally in a fishtail or cross pattern. Stone archways and quoins in red sandstone became popular in Brittany from the 16th century and are a recognisable feature of the architecture. Another feature is the irregular placing and size of windows, and the use of different coloured stones in elaborate patterns. The Bretons have always taken a lot of trouble to make their houses as individual and attractive as possible.

Floors were once almost universally of rammed earth (terre battue) covered with clay and earth strengthened with ash and straw. There was at one time a tradition of inviting the neighbours to come and dance on your floor to make sure that it was well trodden down. Most have now been replaced with flagstones or concrete.

## Property TRENDS

Brittany is one of the most attractive areas of France, and some 20% of properties are second homes. The main drawback is the wet climate in much of the area, especially in winter. Closer to Poitou-Charentes around Vannes the climate is drier and sunnier and has a very active second-homes market. The cheapest properties are in Finistère and Côtes-d'Armor, where house prices are on average close to 20% lower than those in Morbihan and Ille-et-Vilaine. Reckon on a minimum of €75,000 for a 2-bed house. Better transport links between Brittany and the UK and also the rest of France should help keep prices buoyant in coming years, even if the growth of recent times may not return. Low-cost flights to Dinard and also neighbouring Nantes have already helped, as will the planned improvement of the TGV line to Rennes. Meanwhile for those who prefer not to fly for environmental or security reasons, Brittany can be reached from the UK by ferry. A growing trend in the region is new developments and self-builds, with mayors encouraging building on small plots in villages, often to encourage younger people into their community. In parts of the Côtes-d'Armor for example it is possible to find plots of land of around 800 sq m to build on for about €15,000.

# Regional Voices – Brittany

**Susan and Derek Pearse** left Cornwall to move to Brittany in 2003. Their home is now in the Morbihan in a tiny village near Pontivy.

We bought three broken-down buildings, none of them inhabitable, and set about renovating them from scratch. At one time there had been tenant farmers here, but they had left 20 years ago. Our village now has three inhabited houses; in the Second World War there were 10 houses, each with a large family.

The main farmhouse is of granite, with a cowshed attached, with a grey and black striped pattern of granite and schist. The cowshed had once been a kitchen; the floor had been replaced with sloping concrete up to 2 ft thick. We knew there was a fireplace in there; it had been filled in with granite and cement that was awfully hard to dig out. We found an old granite lintel in the fireplace with the date 1864 on it. Lintels had been taken out of the cowshed in order to make smaller windows; unfortunately they had broken up this decorative lintel. The original roof of the main house was thatch, which had been replaced with corrugated fibro-cement. The cowshed has a corrugated iron roof. We plan to redo the roof with imported Spanish slates.

We gave ourselves 2 weeks to find a property, and this was the third one that we saw. We bought it through an English estate agent, who has since moved on, using the services of an English intermediary. We signed a compromis de vente on the spot, but there was a condition suspensive that we could obtain planning permission to convert the building to accommodation, so it took a long time before any money actually changed hands. With farms, there is a limit on the amount of square metres that you can convert to residential use.

The local people are amazed that we would want to take on such a huge task – we don't know ourselves how far we will go in renovating the place. It depends on funds as much as on our enthusiasm for the job. I have become good friends with the cement mixer, after a small spat, when I threw the bucket into the mixer, and the mixer threw all the cement back at me. That was no excuse to stop work, though.

In the main house there is a rotten wooden floor that we have had to dig out; in the cowshed it is concrete, and up to 2 ft thick in points. Underneath you find the typical Breton terre battue – beaten earth – which is so hard it looks like slate; this we have to remove using a pickaxe. We have also rented a pneumatic drill to break up concrete; we burnt out a couple of small drills from the local Bricorama.

The soil here is superb, and our neighbours know the best spots to grow vegetables. Over the course of time most of the stones have been removed, leaving a beautifully fine tilth. Underneath it's red clay. The buildings came with 1 acre of land, and we were able to buy another 1400 sq m; because the sellers knew we wanted it, they were able to get more for it than for ordinary agricultural land.

## What you can get for your money

| Price range (€) | Location | Type | Description | Price (€) |
|---|---|---|---|---|
| Under 100,000 | Brest (29) | Flat | 3 bedrooms, 67 sq m living space | 91,800 |
| 100,000 to 200,000 | Chantepie, (35) nr Rennes | Modern flat | 2 bedrooms and balcony in new development | 175,000 |
| 200,000 to 300,000 | Property 1: Theix (56) nr Vannes | Modern house | 4 bedrooms, garage, 530 sq m garden | 243,500 |
| | Property 2: Nr Questembert (56) | Stone house | 17th-century house, 3 bedrooms, edge of village, exposed beams (see photo No. 2 in colour section) | 279,034 |
| 300,000 to 500,000 | Saint-Cast-le-Guildo (22), west of St-Malo | Country house | A mile from beach, with 4,800 sq m garden | 424,000 |
| 500,000 and over | South Finistère (29) | Stone country house | 18th-century house with 7,500 sq m garden, tennis court, swimming pool and jacuzzi | 633,450 |

# Burgundy (Bourgogne)

**CRT:**

☎ 0380 280 280;  ▭ crtb@centrerelationsclients.com; www.burgundy-tourism.com; www.dijon-tourism.com.

**Percentage of population:** 2.7%; percentage of GDP: 2.34%.

**Airports:** Dijon: www.dijon.aeroport.fr

Burgundy is a vast area where most of the prosperity is concentrated along the Saône river in the east, with vineyards that cling to the *côtes* or slopes, whose stony soils are particularly suited to producing world-class wines. Vineyards were originally planted by monastic communities who were skilled in producing wine and brandy. Burgundy is one of the three main centres of French wine production; the other two are Bordeaux and Champagne.

There are four *départements*: Côte-d'Or (21), Saône-et-Loire (71), Nièvre (58), and Yonne (89). The regional capital, Dijon, was the seat of the Dukes of Burgundy, who were powerful enough in the 15th century to threaten the French king. The Burgundians were originally a Germanic people who migrated into the area after the fall of the Roman Empire. The last Duke, Charles the Bold, died at the siege of Nancy in 1477 fighting the Swiss. His body could only be recognised by the length of his fingernails.

The best wines are produced in the Côte d'Or region south of Dijon, that gives its name to the *département* of Côte d'Or (www.cotedor-tourisme.com). The most expensive wines come from the Côte de Nuits region, around Nuits-St-Georges and Gevrey-Chambertin. The Côte de Beaune specialises more in white wines, e.g. Meursault and Montrachet. Further down the Saône is the Challonais wine region, followed by the Mâconnais, between Mâcon and Tournus, in the *département* of Saône-et-Loire to the south; the name of Pouilly-Fuissé (named after two villages here) is well known to wine-lovers. Burgundy wine brings with it a whole tourist paraphernalia of visits to châteaux, wine-tastings and cookery courses for the enthusiasts.

> '*If, as has been rumoured Ryanair resume their service to Dijon, the region's popularity would increase even more*'

The western part of Saône-et-Loire (www.cg71.com) is one of the more desolate regions of France; the soil is generally too poor for growing crops so this has become cattle country. The name of the best beef cattle breed, Charolais, originates from the town of Charolles between Macon and Digoin. Montceau-les-Mines was the centre of a coal-mining industry that has died out; miners were brought in from Poland in the 19th century and many stayed on. Digoin, to the west, is the centre of pottery manufacture in France.

The Morvan plateau, a desolate and under-populated region, stretches over the northern half of the Saône-et-Loire and into the Nièvre next door. The emptiness and stillness appeal to those who like to leave the rat race behind. The creation of the Parc Naturel du Morvan in 1970 (www.parcdumorvan.org) has given the area a better image. The main attractions are fishing, canoeing and rafting.

The sub-prefectural town of Autun (www.autun.com), was founded by the Romans under Augustus, as Augustodunum, as a replacement for the Gaulish capital Bibracte, nearby, and was one of Roman Gaul's major cities for centuries. This is a city that seems to have been asleep since the Middle Ages; it hasn't grown much outside the medieval walls, which were built on Roman foundations, and there is a Roman amphitheatre. Autun has one of France's great Romanesque churches, the Cathédrale St Lazare, with perfectly preserved 12th-century carvings of scenes from the Bible. There is a TGV stop at Le Creusot, about 20 km away; the regular train service from Paris is scenic, but slow.

The *département* of the Nièvre (www.cg58.fr), west of Saône-et-Loire, is much the same: rather sleepy and with few inhabitants. The Nivernois is cereal and cattle-farming country. Nevers, the prefectural town, on the east bank of the Loire, is a pleasant spot, with a tradition of porcelain manufacturing, and regular jazz concerts. The Grand Prix racing track at Magny-Cours is only 10 miles to the south.

The Yonne, north of Nièvre, is also quite thinly populated. The area closer to Paris has attracted some second-home owners from the capital. The prefectural town of Auxerre has two claims to fame: some of the oldest church architecture and frescoes (9th century) in France, and also one of the country's better football teams. The town of Poligny to the north-east, was a major monastic centre started by the Cistercians in the 12th century, but not much remains of the original monastic buildings; Thomas à Becket took refuge here to escape the wrath of King Henry II. The monks here also started the tradition of planting vineyards that produce the dry white wine called Chablis, named after the town a little to the south.

## Cuisine

The Burgundy region is most of all known for its wines. Cooking in red wine has given rise to the standard dishes *bœuf bourguignon* and *coq au vin*. Anything *à la bourguignonne* is cooked in a red wine sauce with shallots, mushrooms and bacon bits added. To go with the beef, the Burgundians came up with Dijon mustard.

Snails (*escargots*) are cooked for hours in Chablis to make them edible. The Morvan plateau is known for its hams, especially flavoured with parsley. Burgundy also has its local cheeses, none of which are very well known abroad, such as St Florentin, Epoisses and Chaource.

## Property

Nièvre is an area rich in high-quality limestone as well as granite and schist in the east. Buildings are of stone with rendering; flat tiles are in use everywhere. In the wine-growing region a rather different type of building came into existence, the wine-grower's house, with storerooms on the ground floor and living quarters above, with a wooden gallery and external staircase. Half-timbering has also been quite common in the wine-growing region between Dijon and Macon, an area poor in stone materials. The Morvan is limestone in the north and granite in the south; the typical farmhouse is of uneven stone.

# Property TRENDS

Burgundy is slowly growing in popularity among British and other non-French buyers. The British are more likely to live here permanently than to have a second home. If, as has been rumoured, Ryanair resume their service to Dijon, the region's popularity would increase even more. The areas closer to Paris, Yonne and Nièvre, now have a high proportion of second homes, and there are opportunities for renovating old farmhouses. Southern Burgundy does not have rural depopulation, and cannot be characterised as poverty-stricken. There are not that many derelict properties to renovate. House prices are cheapest in Morvan. Indeed the region has a huge disparity in house prices; those in the Côte d'Or for example are nearly double those in Nièvre. Prices are determined by the closeness to Paris, and the TGV. Expect to pay from €75,000 for a 2-bed house in an isolated part of the region.

| What you can get for your money | | | | |
|---|---|---|---|---|
| Price range (€) | Location | Type | Description | Price (€) |
| Under 100,000 | Bligny-sur-Ouche (21) nr Beaune | Stone house | 3-bedroom renovated house, 450 sq m garden | 95,000 |
| 100,000 to 200,000 | Villeroy (89) | Modern house | 3-bedroom house, new development, garage, 1,000 sq m plot | 160,440 |
| 200,000 to 300,000 | Nr Chalon (71) | Wood house | 3 bedrooms, double glazing, geothermic hearing, 1,600 sq m land | 283,500 |
| 300,000 to 500,000 | Nr Luzy (58) | Modern stone house | Oak finish, 5 bedrooms, swimming pool | 399,500 |
| 500,000 and over | Nr Dijon (21) | Modern house | Heated enclosed swimming pool, 800 sq m garden | 565,000 |

# Centre (Val-De-France)

**CRT:**

☎ 02 38 24 05 05;    💻 crtcentre@visaloire.com; www.visaloire.com; www.coeur-de-france.com.

**Percentage of population:** 4.2%; percentage of GDP: 3.5%.

**Airports:** Tours: www.tours.aeroport.fr

The Centre region includes the pre-revolutionary counties of Touraine, Berry and Orléanais. To the Anglo-Saxons this is 'the Loire Valley'. The main attractions are the châteaux and churches – and of course the wine. The Loire has given its name to several *départements*, in several different regions; in the Centre you are never far from water, or marshlands. There is also the Loir river, which runs north of the Loire parallel to its bigger sister. The Centre counts six *départements*: Eure-et-Loir (28), Loir-et-Cher (41), Indre-et-Loire (37), Loiret (45), Indre (36) and Cher (18). Tourism is the main industry, along with food processing, agriculture and manufacturing.

The prefectural capital of the Eure-et-Loir, Chartres, can boast one of the world's great cathedrals, a UNESCO world heritage site, most of it dating from the 12th and 13th centuries. The Loire Valley is most of all associated with châteaux and cycling holidays. The main city of the region is Orléans, which lies on the motorway from Paris to Toulouse. The Loire starts to make its massive curve towards the south at Orléans, eventually forming the boundary between the Centre and Burgundy. The Loire Valley evokes the struggle of the French to eject the English in the 15th century, and the extravagance of enormous châteaux built for the idle rich of the *ancien régime*. The Loire Valley châteaux were developed as playgrounds for the aristocracy starting with François I (r.1515–47).

The regional capital, Orléans (pop. 245,000), is only an hour from Paris, and it is quite possible to commute to Paris for work. The city has an important place in French history; Joan of Arc, nicknamed the Maid of Orléans, lifted the siege of the city in 1429 and started the reconquest of France from the English.

The Loire represents the boundary between south and north as far as weather goes, and is often shrouded in mist; supposedly it presents a natural barrier to the clouds going further south. The Sologne area south of Blois straddles the Loir-et-Cher and Loiret, but as most of it is marshland or lakes it has little scope for house buying. It is also the stronghold of the French hunting fraternity, and houses the world's biggest hunting museum at the Château de Gien on the Loire.

*'If you want something a little unusual, you could try a troglodyte dwelling cut out of a cliff-face, used by the vineyard workers near the River Loire'*

Further downriver, the city of Tours stands at the centre of the traditional county of Touraine (www.tourism-touraine.com), as well as being the prefectural town of the Indre-et-Loire. Here the clearest French is reputedly spoken. This was also the home of the great 15th-century writer François Rabelais. The old part of Tours has numerous restaurants and is well worth a visit on a summer's evening.

Bourges, the capital of the Berry region, or Berrichonne, and prefectural town of the Cher, is another pleasant town with a cathedral that is listed as a world heritage site by UNESCO. The unfortunate *dauphin* Charles VII retreated here after Agincourt in 1415 until Joan of Arc gave him the courage to fight back.

## Cuisine

The Centre is a fertile region, and produces more cereals than anywhere else in France. Soft fruits, such as strawberries and pears are also grown. The area of the Loire has no fewer than 22 AOC wines: Vouvray covers several types of whites; Bourgueil and Chinon are mainly reds; Sancerre is more known for whites. The Berry specialities are game, river fish and crayfish, and the AOC goat's cheeses, Pyramide St Pierre and Crottin de Chavignol. Loir-et-Cher has its own AOC goat's cheeses, Selles-sur-Cher and Cendré de Vendôme.

The Orléanais is the home of the favourite French dessert, Tarte Tatin or 'upside-down tart', made with pears or quinces, discovered by two sisters called Tatin in Lamotte-Beuvron. Quince jelly – *colignac* – is a speciality of the Loiret. Pears are used a lot in cooking and for making the pear liqueur Eau-de-Vie d'Olivet.

## Property

There is an active market in second homes in the northern part of the Centre, particularly Eure-et-Loire, which is within easy reach of Paris. It only takes 45 minutes by train from

Chartres to the Gare de Montparnasse. In spite of the competition from the Parigots, prices are not unreasonable. About 17% of properties are second homes. The relative flatness of the landscape is a factor in dissuading Brits from buying here, but there are plenty of cultural festivals to make up for the indifferent scenery.

The typical older property is the *longère angevine* or stone-built longhouse, with white coping stones at the corners for decoration and solidity. There are plentiful villas, bungalows and similar modern-style brick-built houses. If you want something a little unusual, you could try a troglodyte dwelling cut out of a cliff-face, used by the vineyard workers near the River Loire. The cheapest houses start at around €100,000.

# Property TRENDS

After a surge in property prices in 2003 and 2004, the market has certainly calmed down. Partly this is because overseas buyers, including the British, have become more choosy and demanding. Travel to and from the UK is quite easy, with low-cost flights to Tours, while the TGV thunders through the heart of the region. It is possible that planned improvements in the TGV service may make the area yet more popular with many people, including Parisians looking for second homes within easy reach. The cheapest *départements* are Cher and Indre – the latter's price are on average nearly half of those in the Indre-et-Loire immediately to the west. The Indre could become a hot spot in the future but it's still possible to pick up a decent sized two- or even three-bedroom house for around €100,000.

| What you can get for your money | | | | |
|---|---|---|---|---|
| **Price range (€)** | **Location** | **Type** | **Description** | **Price (€)** |
| Under 100,000 | Choue (41) | Bungalow | 3 bedrooms, new development, 895 sq m plot | 91,137 |
| 100,000 to 200,000 | Orléans (45) | Flat, 80 sq m | 5 rooms, close to trams and shops. | 142,600 |
| 200,000 to 300,000 | Gallardon (28) | Modern house | 7 bedrooms, 2 bathrooms, 706 sq m garden | 260,500 |
| 300,000 to 500,000 | Avoine (37) | Longère | 4 bedrooms, well, 2 bathrooms, outbuildings, 3,800 sq m land | 399,000 |
| 500,000 and over | Valencay (36) | Maison bourgeoise | 5 bedrooms, 3 bathrooms, 2 hectares land, surrounded by forest | 600,000 |

## Champagne-Ardenne

**CRT:**

☎ 03 26 77 45 00;    📠    contact@tourisme-champagne-ardenne.com;
www.tourisme-champagne-ardenne.com;
www.reims-tourisme.com.

**Percentage of population:** 2.23%; percentage of GDP: 2.02%.

**Airports:** See Ile de France

The name of the region says a lot, but there is much more to the region than just bubbly. In the 17th century a monk and cellar master near Epernay, Dom Pérignon, tried adding yeast to the bottles of fermenting wine in his abbey cellars; most of the bottles exploded but those that didn't made the cork pop when drawn. Large-scale champagne production didn't really get under way until the 19th century, when glass-making techniques had advanced enough to make stronger bottles. Dom Pérignon is also credited with coming up with the idea of blending the three different wines that go into the drink.

Champagne-Ardenne is a rather flat and wooded region that is overlooked by tourists and property buyers alike. The four *départements* are: Ardennes (08), Marne (51), Aube (10), and Haute-Marne (52). The Ardennes borders on the Belgian provinces of Hainaut and Luxembourg. The dense forests of the Ardennes traditionally specialised in metalworking and slate quarrying, but these are dying industries. Agriculture doesn't thrive here either. The prefectural town of Charleville-Mézières is the world centre for marionettes, and there is a large festival every three years devoted to them. The main attraction of the area is the stillness of the forest, and the fact that properties are cheap – especially in the Haute-Marne. Access to the UK is also fairly quick. Brussels and the Channel ports are about three hours away.

The regional departmental capital, Reims (pronounced 'Rengss') has a great history; 26 of France's kings, going back as far as Clovis in 496, were crowned in the Gothic cathedral. Reims is also the capital of champagne; the tourists can go around the great *maisons* such as Heidsieck, Taittinger and Veuve-Clicquot for *dégustations*. The real centre of champagne production is the town of Epernay, 26 km to the south of Reims, where the best-known name, Moët et Chandon has its *maison*.

South of the Marne is the Aube, a region of undulating wheatfields that rises up to the Plateau de Langres on the border with Burgundy. Troyes, the traditional capital of the champagne region and prefectural city, is architecturally very rich, with half-timbered houses, Renaissance mansions and a fine Gothic cathedral. In most respects the Aube is a rather deserted region, and not much visited by tourists. One can get from Troyes to Paris in about 90 minutes.

## Cuisine

Most tourists visit Champagne-Ardenne for the fizzy drink. The Marne also produces still whites and rosés; one vintage goes under the name of Bouzy.

Champagne-Ardenne is not one of France's great gastronomic regions. There are the usual hams and patés; the most noteworthy local dishes are *boudin blanc* or white sausage from Rethel, and pig's trotters from St Ménehould. Troyes is the home of fried chitterlings or *andouillettes*. There are some fine cheeses in the Ardennes: e.g. Grand Condé, Remparts and Rocroi. In the Haute-Marne there is the creamy Chaource and the strong cheese named after the town of Langres.

## Property

The original building material of the Ardennes forest was, naturally enough, the local timber; clapboard or slate was attached to a wooden frame. More recent farmhouses are of shale with stone surrounds, and a heavy layer of rendering.

Traditional construction in the Champagne region was half-timbering, with closely positioned posts braced by long diagonal ties. Farmhouses have large square cart entrances with wooden lintels, called *porterue*. An unusual feature of Champagne farmhouses is the use of the space on the street front for storage.

The Ardennes has been more or less ignored by foreign buyers; its main selling point is the cheapness of the properties and the proximity of the Channel. Broken-down farmhouses can be picked up for next to nothing. Both Ardennes and Champagne are wet and humid areas, with a climate similar to southern England. There is never likely to be a great market for second homes here, but at least you won't be surrounded by English-speakers.

# *Property*
# TRENDS

The region lacks the climate or stunning countryside to make it a popular destination for foreign property buyers. And despite its closeness to Paris property prices have remained low in comparison with many other parts of the country. For example, in 2006 the average price for a traditional house in Aube was just €85,500 – though in Marne the average is double that. It is hard to imagine a sudden surge in prices right across the region. However the new high-speed TGV train service from Paris to Strasbourg passes through Reims and will undoubtedly increase price houses there and in the immediate area in the next couple of years. Meanwhile for the discerning visitor a smart two-bedroom flat can be picked up in the fine old town of Troyes for little more than €120,000.

## What you can get for your money

| Price range (€) | Location | Type | Description | Price (€) |
|---|---|---|---|---|
| Under 100,000 | Chalons (51) | Flat | 2 bedrooms, 52 sq m living area | 98,000 |
| 100,000 to 200,000 | Mohon (08) | Stone house | 3 bedrooms, garage, office, 400 sq m land | 135,800 |
| 200,000 to 300,000 | Nr Troyes (10) | Pavilion-style house | 3 bedrooms, garage, 690 sq m garden | 242,000 |
| 300,000 to 500,000 | Nr Bourbonne les Bains (52) | Modern house | Swimming pool, outbuildings, 2 hectares garden | 380,000 |
| 500,000 and over | La Forestiere (51) | Farm complex | Stables, 2.4 hectares land, 4 bedrooms | 566,000 |

## Corsica

**Agence du Tourisme de la Corse:**
☎ 04 95 51 00 00;  ▭ www.visit-corsica.com.

---

**Percentage of population:** 0.43%; percentage of GDP: 0.34%.

---

**Airports:** Ajaccio: www.ajaccio.aeroport.fr

The island of Corsica consists of two *départements:* Haute-Corse (2B) and Corse-du-Sud (2A), although the division is rather arbitrary. Corsica (or La Corse) has more associations with Italy than with France, but has always had a strong antipathy towards foreign rulers. In reality, Corsica has never been independent since the time of the Romans. The local language is closely related to Tuscan in Italy. The French bought the island from the Genoese in 1768. The Corsicans staged a mass revolt but were defeated in 1769. Napoleon Bonaparte, born in Ajaccio in 1769, made the island a lot more noticed. Corsica's other famous son, Christopher Columbus, born in Calvi, is claimed by the Genoese as one of theirs.

Corsica is a mere 180 km long and a maximum of 80 km wide, is sparsely populated and very mountainous, with deep gullies and tree-covered slopes. The interior is covered with *maquis* (a mix of wild flowers, herbs and dense scrub). Viewed from the sea the island looks like a mountain. The French often refer to it as the *île de beauté* or the 'island of beauty'. The 600-mile long coastline has Europe's finest beaches, which bring in the tourist hordes to the western coast in July and August. The east coast is uncomfortably hot in summer. And thanks to its mountains parts of Corsica gets snow in winter and for much of the year. In May 2007 three hikers died from the cold in the island's chilly and mountainous interior.

## Insider Tip

*The usual access to the island is by ferry from Nice, Toulon or Marseille; these services are sometimes affected by industrial action. There are direct flights during the tourist season from London to Ajaccio and Bastia, on Air France and from London to Bastia on British Airways. Otherwise one has to change at Paris or Nice. There is also an airport at Calvi.*

Corsica has little else but tourism to live from, but the profits go back to mainland France, fuelling the discontentment of the locals. The FLNC (Corsican liberation movement), has been in the habit of shooting up government buildings and dynamiting foreign-owned villas. France goes to great lengths to keep the Corsicans satisfied, by pumping in huge subsidies; the island also gets some €1 billion a year from the EU. The present trend towards decentralisation threatens to make the FLNC irrelevant; in any case, they spend as much time pursuing vendettas amongst themselves as they do fighting the French.

Corsica has exceptional natural scenery. The centre of the island is a national park, with the highest peak, Monte Cinto, reaching 8,943 ft (2,710 m). Driving between the main cities on the island is fairly easy; there is a limited railway network.

## Cuisine

The lowland areas grow all kinds of fruit: clementines, nectarines, peaches and avocados. There are the traditional chestnuts, olives and figs. The local cooking is strongly flavoured with the wild herbs that grow here in profusion. The national dish is *cabrettu a l'istrettu* (stewed kid goat). All kinds of game are found in the mountains, so you can taste wild boar, hare, partridge and wood pigeon. The local cheeses are *brocciu* – a soft cheese from ewe's milk – and a hard cheese, *fromage corse*. Sea fish and shellfish are available in abundance. The island also produces some decent wines: Santa Barba and Fiumicicoli reds and rosés around Sartène in the south, and sweet muscat apéritif white wine from Cap Corse.

## Property

Stone has always been the preferred material, as it is found everywhere on the island. The traditional Corsican village consists of tightly grouped houses without a central square which emphasises the closed nature of the society. The living room (*sala*) for entertaining guests traditionally has a rifle by the door; the bedrooms are protected by religious icons. On the coast one will find the same types of villas and apartments as one would in the rest of southern France, with the proviso that planning laws are very strictly applied, and designs have to be approved to fit in with the local style.

Estate agents on Corsica do not produce statistics on average prices of property, although individual agents can give rough figures per square metre. As of 2006, the average price of recently constructed holiday homes was estimated at a maximum €5,000 per square metre, meaning that a 2-bedroom home would come out at some €290,000 (with a sea view and in perfect condition). Older buildings are far cheaper. One can still pick up a small apartment by the sea from €125,000. Houses for renovation inland can be as little as €85,000. Building land with a sea view costs some €120–160 per square metre near towns; without a sea view the cost is €30–50 per square metre. Land that is not *constructible,* where no building permit can be obtained is worth as little as €2 per square metre.

# Property
# TRENDS

Corsica has not seen the slowdown in property prices seen on the mainland in 2006 and early 2007. 'I keep thinking it will slow down in the future but there is no sign of that at the moment,' says estate agent Stephanie De Richaud of Balagne Immobilier based in the north-west of Corsica. 'There is a lot of new building going on at the moment on the island.' This extra capacity might help bring down prices in the future but it seems unlikely. The overseas market on the island is driven mainly by fellow French people from the mainland or by Italians. The Italians are probably more popular with the locals than the mainland French. Britons, Americans and the Irish have not bought there in great numbers and this is unlikely to change in the future. The distance to travel there – plus the relatively high prices – are probably the main reasons for this. For foreigners wanting to live and work here, the prospects are not that hopeful either. About a third of the islanders work directly for the French state, but there is little or no work to be had for outsiders. You would probably have to pay protection money if you wanted to start a business. The cost of living is considerably higher than in mainland France.

## What you can get for your money

| Price range (€) | Location | Type | Description | Price (€) |
|---|---|---|---|---|
| Under 100,000 | Porto-Vecchio (2A) | Modern flat | 1 bedroom, communal swimming pool, air-conditioning | 84,000 |
| 100,000 to 200,000 | Nr Bastia (2B) | Modern flat | New development, close to sea, parking, balcony, 3 rooms | 164,000 |
| 200,000 to 300,000 | Nr Bastia (2B) | House | 3 bedrooms, terrace, garage, 1,239 sq m garden | 270,700 |
| 300,000 to 500,000 | Ajaccio (2A) | Townhouse | 3 bedrooms, garage, 96 sq m living area | 382,500 |
| 500,000 and over | Calvi (2B) | Modern house | 4 bedrooms, covered terrace, 1,500 sq m garden with olive trees | 548,550 |

# Franche-Comté

**CRT:**

☎ 03 81 25 08 08;    💻 crt@franche-comte.org; www.franche-comte.org.

**Percentage of population:** 1.86%; percentage of GDP: 1.57%.

**Airports:** Mulhouse: www.euroairport.com
             Dijon: www.dijon.aeroport.fr

The Franche-Comté has four *départements* within its boundaries: Haute-Saône (70), Territoire de Belfort (90), Doubs (25) and the Jura (39). The region was historically not part of France until Louis XIV took it over in 1678.

The city of Belfort has changed hands many times over the course of history. From the 14th century it was a stronghold of the Austrian Habsburgs; in 1648, by the Treaty of Westphalia, it became French, and was ruled by the Princes of Monaco. It gained a special prestige by its resistance to the Prussian siege of 1870, and so escaped becoming part of the German province of Alsace in 1871. It was made a separate *département* in 1922, the Territoire de Belfort. The city is 10 miles away from the Swiss border, and there is naturally a strong Swiss influence on the architecture.

Besançon (www.besancon.com), the regional capital, stands on a bend of the River Doubs; it has preserved many of its original buildings, including a spectacular citadel. The city has traditionally specialised in clock making. Besançon is also the departmental capital of the Doubs (www.doubs.org). The river of the same name rises near the Swiss border south of Besançon at Saut du Doubs, and briefly enters Switzerland before making a hairpin turn back into France, eventually flowing into the Saône 200 miles to the west. It's popular with pleasure boats and barge owners from all over the world and stretches of it are stunningly beautiful.

The Jura (www.jura-tourism.com) is in the pre-Alps, a green landscape of pastures and forests. It has something like the appearance of Switzerland; chalet-like houses with steep roofs and colourful windowboxes, interspersed with flowery meadows and pine forests.

Franche-Comté is remote from the UK; the region is also devoid of airports though there is a TGV connection between Besançon and Paris. This could be a region to live all year round, but is not an ideal choice for a holiday home. On the plus side, there are areas close to ski fields, and one can enjoy white-water rafting, fishing and walking. There is superb scenery to enjoy, and more than half of the region is covered in forests.

## Cuisine

Franche-Comté is known for its *charcuterie* – cold meats – in particular for smoked beef (*brési*), sausages and hams. The semi-hard Comté is the most popular cheese in France. The majority of the local wines are whites. Four areas of the Jura have AOC wines: Arbois, Château-Chalon, Côtes du Jura and L'Étoile; they are not well known outside France. Some are unusual, such as *vin de paille*, matured on a bed of straw, and wines flavoured with walnuts.

# Property

The timber-framed farmhouse is standard in the Belfort region and the Haute Saône. In the Jura there are stone-built vinegrower's houses with the storerooms on the ground floor. In the Vosges area of the Saône red sandstone is used, with red sandstone roof slates. The higher Doubs has inclusive farm building, with lower storeys of stone with white rendering, and planks covering gable ends for insulation. Some have a survival of the centrally-placed hearth: a pyramid-shaped hood over the whole kitchen that pierces the roof with a massive plank-lined stack. Building land is cheap. Houses start from about €75,000.

# Property TRENDS

Tourist officials are working hard to sell Franche-Comté as a holiday destination. Based on its natural beauty this is a possibility. However, thanks to its relative remoteness and its cold winters, it is hard to see this region becoming a major destination for British and other overseas buyers. At €145,000 for a standard house, average prices in the region are well below the national average of €183,600 (based on late 2006 figures). However the region could be opened up somewhat during the next decade with the opening of the new TGV link between the Rhine and the Rhone that will run from Strasbourg down to Lyon. And this could make Besançon, already basking in the reputation of being France's most environmentally friendly city, a more attractive place to buy for foreigners. Studio flats currently start at around €70,000. In the Jura, the attractive town of Dole which has a TGV stop, is another place where prices could rise.

| Price range (€) | Location | Type | Description | Price (€) |
|---|---|---|---|---|
| Under 100,000 | Nr Lure (70) | Farmhouse | Needs restoring, 2,000 sq m orchard | 91,000 |
| 100,000 to 200,000 | Nr Bourg en Bresse (39) | Village house | Restored 3-bedroom house, garage, cellar, attic | 137,000 |
| 200,000 to 300,000 | Nr Besancon (25) | Village house | 5 bedrooms, 750 sq m garden | 252,000 |
| 300,000 to 500,000 | Nr Belfort (90) | Modern house | 5 bedrooms, terrace | 409,000 |
| 500,000 and over | Nr Lons-le-Saunier (39) | Maison de maitre | 10 rooms, swimming pool, 600 sq m living area, 7,400 sq m garden | 550,000 |

**What you can get for your money**

## Languedoc-Roussillon

**CRT:**

☎ 04 67 22 81 00;    🖳 edition.crtlr@sunfrance.com; www.cr-languedo croussillon.fr/tourisme; www.sunfrance.com.

**Percentage of population:** 3.82%; percentage of GDP: 2.87%.

**Airports:** Carcassonne: www.carcassonne.aeroport.fr
Montpellier: www.montpellier.aeroport.fr
Perpignan: www.perpignan.cci.fr
Nimes: www.nimes.cci.fr

The region consists of the *départements* Lozère (48), Gard (30), Hérault (34), Aude (11) and Pyrénées-Orientales (66). Languedoc derives from *'langue d'oc'*, that is the language – Occitan – in which the word for 'yes' is *oc*, or southern France, as opposed to *'langue d'oïl'* or northern France, while Roussillon is another word for French Catalonia. Languedoc cannot really be defined as a precise geographical area; it covers anywhere where Occitan was once spoken. During the Dark Ages, the area was a refuge for the Spanish trying to reconquer Spain from the Moors. Generally, the idea of Occitan identity is still very strong here, but few people can speak the language, which was effectively obliterated by French with the introduction of universal education.

Catalonia first came into its own when the Counts of Barcelona became Kings of Aragon in 1137, and then joined up with the Counts of Toulouse to form a united front against the French. The Occitans and Catalans suffered a setback when Toulouse fell to the French in 1229; the Catalan kingdom split into two in the next century, with the Kings of Majorca ruling from Perpignan over the French area. After centuries of disputes, Louis XIV finally managed to gain control over Roussillon with the Treaty of the Pyrenees in 1659, thus making the mountain range the border with Spain.

The heart of Catalonia is the Pic du Canigou (9180 ft), where a Catalan flag perpetually flutters from a wrought-iron cross; every true Catalan is expected to climb this mountain once in their lives. On the night of June 23rd, fires known as *feux de Saint-Jean* are lit and then carried to every village and town in Catalonia. This is the occasion for traditional Catalan *ferias* or festivals.

## Pyrénées-Orientales

This *département* (www.cg66.fr), formerly known as Pyrénées d'Or, includes part of the grape-growing region of Corbières in the north, and the former Catalan county of Cerdagne in the west, around Fort-Romeu. The coast between the capital, Perpignan, and the Spanish border is known as the Côte Vermeille (Vermillion Coast). Generally, the coast has been over-developed. The picturesque town of Collioure, near Spain, gave the impetus for the colour experimentations of the painters Matisse and Derain in 1905, known as *fauvisme,* and there are Fauvist paintings everywhere. The city of Perpignan's main interest lies in the Palace of the Kings of Majorca. It is also home to one of France's leading rugby teams, a club that fiercely promotes its Catalan identity.

# Aude

The prefectural town of the Aude (www.audetourisme.com), Carcassonne, is one of France's most popular tourist destinations. The huge citadel, where knights jousted long ago, evokes the Middle Ages better than anywhere in Europe. Carcassonne lies on the Canal du Midi, a waterway running 240 km from Toulouse to the sea at Agde which was conceived by a wealthy nobleman, Pierre-Paul Riquet, who spent every last penny he had on financing it. The canal was built between 1667 and 1681, and involved constructing 99 locks and 130 bridges, as well as diverting water from the mountains. Rather incredibly, it goes uphill for half its length and then downhill again. The canal had the desired effect of revitalising the local economy but was abandoned with the advent of the steam train. It is one of France's great tourist attractions; the poplar-lined canal with its classical buildings is a wonder of elegance and ingenuity. However, recent droughts in the area have affected the water levels of the canal, amid fears about whether it can remain navigable to all the vessels wishing to use it.

On the western end of the Aude is the Lauragais, a farming region that spreads out into the Tarn, Ariège and Haute-Garonne. North of Carcassonne is the area known as La Montagne Noire (Black Mountain), whose people suffered severely during the anti-Cathar crusades of the early 13th century. The national park of the Haut Languedoc extends over the south-east of the Tarn into the Hérault and Aveyron; here you might bump into a *mouflon,* a wild mountain sheep.

# Hérault

Above the Aude is the *département* of Hérault (www.cdt-herault.fr), mostly arid vineyard and olive country at lower elevations, and deserted hills higher up. The surrounding country is known as *garrigue,* a stony landscape almost bare of trees, originally forest degraded by over-grazing and bushfires. The coastline of the Hérault, the Côte d'Améthyste, is equally arid. Saltwater lagoons separate the land from the sea, providing an ideal environment for breeding oysters and clams. The coastline is popular with sailors; much of it is unsuited for building, so over-development is more of a localised problem. The prefectural capital, Montpellier, is one of France's most dynamic cities, and has become its main centre for medical research. This is also the region's main city (it shares the title with Narbonne and Béziers) and focus of investment in new industries. The Hérault is seen by the French as the most desirable area to live in France, and it has seen spectacular property price rises, hitting 30% back in 2004.

# Gard

The neighbouring *département* of the Gard (www.cdt-gard.fr) is noted for its Roman ruins, and has only a short coastline. The Gard does, however, have a part of the Cévennes national park. The prefectural city of Nîmes is best known for its Roman amphitheatre, and the blue denim cloth named after the city. Visitors may be surprised to find out that this is also the centre of bullfighting in France. The Gard has always been popular with British property buyers, especially the pretty hilltop town of Uzès, north-east of Nîmes.

# Lozère

North of the Gard, the Lozère (www.lozerefrance.com) has some of the country's finest scenery and includes most of the Cévennes national park, an area of forests and mountains, and few people. The *département* is one of France's most thinly populated, ideal for holidays, but rather bleak when the weather closes in. The south-western quarter of the Lozère includes the Tarn Gorges – the Tarn rises at an altitude of over 5,000 ft on Mont Lozère, and the headwaters of the Lot. The area consists of high limestone plateaux, known as *causses*. Geologically, the rest of the Lozère is more granite and schist.

The Cévennes is remote; it takes about two hours to drive from Nîmes airport. The northern Lozère is about 120 miles from St Étienne, which also has flights to London Stansted. Train and bus services are limited, but if you want to get away from it all this is the place to be. The area attracted hippies in the 1960s looking to set up alternative communities and some of them still remain.

The people of the Languedoc have traditionally rebelled against central domination. They came out strongly in favour of Protestantism in the wars of religion; the Protestant guerrillas or Camisards started out from Ganges in 1702. In the Second World War, the people took a leading role in the Resistance against the Germans. In the 1970s the main focus of discontent was cheap foreign wine imports, and the necessary reorganisation of the wine industry.

This is one of France's poorest regions; much of the land is only suitable for grazing goats and growing cork-oaks. A great deal of investment has gone into new industries along the coastal strip, which has attracted job-seekers from the rest of France. The region has plenty of sunshine – up to 300 days a year – and has preserved more local traditions than most parts of France. One of these is the *transhumance*, the practice of moving flocks of sheep from the Alps across to the Languedoc every year, which has given rise to local festivals.

Languedoc-Roussillon has a distinctly extreme climate: although rainfall is adequate – around 25 inches per year – it tends to be infrequent and falls mostly in October and November. The Gard is particularly prone to flash flooding, caused by cold fronts from the Massif Central colliding with warm fronts from the south. They even talk here of 'horizontal rain', which can do serious damage to your property. In September 2002, 27 people were killed and a large area between Nîmes and Alès was cut off from civilisation after several days of torrential downpours. Flooding is a real risk in the area and should be taken into account when buying property. During the winter and spring a strong cold wind, the *tramontane*, comes down from the north-west, blowing away the clouds, but also freezing everything in its path. In summer a pleasant breeze from the south, the *garbi*, brings rain and cools the land.

# Cuisine

The Aude produces the best wines of the region. The reds that have achieved AOC status are Corbières, Minervois, Fitou and Cabardès. A *vigneron* in the town of Limoux south of Carcassonne claimed to have discovered how to produce *brut* or sparkling white wine. Crémant and Blanquette de Limoux are now AOC as well. The strong sunshine and short cold winters are ideal for the vines. Locally, sweet wines are very popular.

French Catalonia has cooking traditions similar to those over the border with Spain. The national dish is *boles de picolat,* pork and beef meatballs in olive sauce; other specialities are *cargolada* (grilled snails), *botifarre* (black pudding), and *fuets,* thin, dry sausages. Grilled peppers, aubergines and tomatoes combine with tuna and cod dishes or omelettes.

The coastal areas of the Languedoc tend to specialise in seafood, such as mussels, oysters and clams. Other typical dishes include *tapenade* (black olive paste), duck cooked in red wine, *foie gras* and *confits* from Lauragais. The Foreign Legion town of Castelnaudary calls itself the capital of *cassoulet,* the southern French dish of beans with duck and sausage.

# Property

Languedoc-Roussillon generally has few trees in low-lying areas, so few properties are built around wooden frames; termites are also a problem. Wooden rafters are used for supporting roofs, and some wood may be used for decoration on the exterior of houses. The main building material is granite, or limestone, where it is available (e.g. Corbières). Baked brick is generally only used for internal walls. Second homes make up 30% of the total housing stock in Languedoc-Roussillon.

Substantial houses are traditionally known as *mas* and some of them stand on the sites of Roman villas. The *mas* is a large farmhouse, also known as a *campanha* or *boria* in Occitan, with storehouses and cottages for the workers built on to it. These days, a new *mas* is a villa, usually with an arched terrace and swimming pool. The wealthier wine-growers also used to build castle-like structures with stone towers. The farm-workers lived in *masets,* small stone-built cottages with two storeys and a chimney, but rather small for foreign buyers. It was also traditional to build a small stone structure – a *cabana* – next to the vineyards, to live in during the warmer season, and for picnics and parties. Another type of village structure is the wine-grower's house – *maison vigneronne* – typically with a large archway for wagons to pass through. Some have *celliers* or storerooms for the wine, attached. In the silk region of the Gard, a specialised stone building – a *magnanerie* – was used for breeding silk-worms. These have very large ground-floor windows, but only small openings on the first floor. The *magnanerie* would be heated and the windows sealed with paper while the silkworms were incubating on a wooden framework, and then opened up to the elements once they had emerged.

Traditional farmers' houses are sometimes built in modern material next to fields, and could be used as a basic holiday cottage. On the whole the Languedoc uses Spanish tiles (*tuiles canal*). Additional protection from the rain is afforded by several layers of half-tiles – *génoises* – set in mortar in a cornice along the edge of the roof. Roofs can be leaky, and may need lining.

The Cévennes has its own particular style of architecture: the granite-built houses are narrow with fairly thin walls (60–70cm), and often have three or more storeys. Roofs may be quite flat, the reasoning being that a thick layer of snow on the roof would act as insulation and stop water from going through the gaps between the tiles. Due to the narrowness of the houses, exterior staircases were sometimes built on to houses when there was no space for an internal staircase.

In the upland regions of the Lozère, the main building material is the local grey schist or granite, and the style is more that of the Massif Central, with the stone slates known as *lauzes.*

# Property TRENDS

Pyrénées-Orientales is French Catalonia or Roussillon, rather than Languedoc. The typical older buildings are of Pyrenean granite. In the mountains one can find ski chalets. One can see the Catalan influence in the flat roofs and arched shutters. In the Pyrenees there are even crude stepped gables, or *pignons à redents*. The hot and dry climate and Catalan culture hold a lot of attraction for retirees. In summer you can go to take the waters at spas such as Amélie-les-Bains; in the winter there is skiing. There are direct flights from London to Perpignan and the planned high-speed rail link to Barcelona and ultimately Madrid should open up the area even more. However, in other respects this is a remote area. The current property market is fairly flat, with not that many properties on the market, so one should not expect prices to rise. Expect to pay from €60,000 for a basic village house or a slightly larger house to renovate.

The region as a whole saw a huge rise in prices from around 2002, notably in the Aude. By 2007 prices had stabilised. One reason was that many ordinary properties had been over-valued so it's worthwhile trying to knock sellers down on their asking price. In the longer term some claim that Languedoc-Roussillon will become the 'next Provence' as would-be home owners there get priced out of the market. The area is now attracting many new developments, often aimed at the investment and leaseback market. In Pyrénées-Orientales, for example, one can find new studio or small one-bedroom flats starting from around €80,000.

| What you can get for your money | | | | |
|---|---|---|---|---|
| Price range (€) | Location | Type | Description | Price (€) |
| Under 100,000 | Blavignac (48) | Land | 2,400 sq m plot, edge of village | 53,800 |
| 100,000 to 200,000 | Perpignan (66) | Modern flat | 2 bedrooms, 60 sq m area | 140,000 |
| 200,000 to 300,000 | Nr Carcassonne (11) | Modern villa | 3 bedrooms, garage, views of countryside | 250,000 |
| 300,000 to 500,000 | Between Narbonne and Beziers (34) | Village house | 4 bedrooms with space to create more, 2,000 sq m land | 370,000 |
| 500,000 and over | Nr Narbonne (11) | Country house | 5 bedrooms, 4,100 sq m plot with outline permission to build gîtes | 550,000 |

# Limousin

**CRT:**
☎ 05 55 45 18 80;   🖳 tourisme@crt-limousin.fr; www.tourismelimousin.com;
www.crt-limousin.fr.

**Airports:** Brive: www.aeroport-brive-souillac.com
Limoges: www.aeroportlimoges.com

The western escarpments of the Massif Central consist of thinly populated river valleys, with forests of beech, chestnut, and birch, with oak at lower elevations that clothe the region in superb autumn colouring. The countryside is sparsely populated and the roads are a pleasure to drive on.

The eastern Limousin is reputed as a desolate region where tough, dour farmers work hard to make a living from breeding Limousin cattle. Above 3,000 ft there is no arable farming, only pasture in between densely wooded valleys. The only other substantial industries are logging from managed pine plantations and gravel quarrying, with the attendant heavy lorries.

Tourism is a seasonal industry; the beauty of the landscape is the main attraction, although there are the usual cultural and gastronomic festivals. The Limousin is rather lacking in the literary connections the French find so fascinating. Auguste Renoir, the painter, came from Limoges. A more dubious celebrity is the current president Jacques Chirac, who is from Sarran in Corrèze. There are plenty of Romanesque churches in the area; their granite block construction has barely weathered.

The regional government has poured money into new roads; the Paris-Toulouse motorway runs past Limoges. The east–west A89 from Clermont-Ferrand meets up with the A20 at Brive. The train services are scenic but limited; a lot of routes are only served by buses. There are daily flights to London from Limoges, and also a planned service to and from Brive.

The city of Limoges, whose inhabitants are called Limougeauds, is noted as a traditional centre of porcelain production. These days it is carried on for the benefit of the tourist industry; the museums are full of porcelain. Limoges is the prefectural capital of the Haute Vienne (www.tourisme-hautevienne.com), and the regional capital of the Limousin. The limousine car takes its name from the all-enveloping shepherd's cape once worn around here, although there are not all that many sheep to herd these days. As an industrial city, Limoges has a strong socialist tradition and has become a centre for refugees from the former Eastern bloc. Whether one would want to live in Limoges is debatable; there is a verb in French – *limoger* – meaning to send someone to Limoges, i.e. give them the sack. The expression came about because Marshal Joffre sent an incompetent general to Limoges during the First World War, to be rid of him. But if you are interested in porcelain or enamel then Limoges is the place to be. Most of the Britons moving to the area prefer to live in the surrounding countryside, much of which is stunningly beautiful, even if the winters can be very cold. One of the iconic images

# Regional Voices – the Limousin

British estate agent **Andrew Merchant** works for Agence Marche Limousin (www. ieafrance.com). Here he gives his views on an area increasingly popular with overseas buyers.

The Limousin is a very rural, tranquil farming region, with many medieval market towns – one of the most picturesque being the town of La Souterraine, with its weekly markets of fresh produce and animals. Because this is such a vast open region of France you get the feeling of really living a French life – and not being overrun with expats as so many parts of Europe are. The hills are rolling with a mixture of altitudes from 400 m above sea level to its highest points of 1,400 m above sea level. Everything is so green and lush, with the wildlife second to none. The region also has over 8,000 lakes and has been named as the 'lake district' of France. These lakes offering a variety of water sports and fishing.

Over the past 10 years this region has gone from being a very poor, forgotten rural farming community of France to a thriving well-maintained and growing area. It offers a lifestyle similar to that of England 50 years ago, with zero pollution, very little crime and fantastic integration with the French.

Buying a property in the Limousin has never easier. Top French companies have gained vast experience working and employing professionals coming to France to work, and a majority of the estate agents here now not only have English-speaking staff, but also have a fully bilingual legal service, with all sale contracts drawn up in English.

of the area is that of Limousin cattle grazing peacefully in a buttercup-filled meadow on a late spring day.

The sub-prefectural town of Aubusson, in the valley of the River Creuse, along with neighbouring Felletin, had an international reputation as a centre of tapestry weaving, started around 1400 by immigrant Flemish weavers. There is still something of an industry in repairing old tapestries. The northern half of the Limousin region corresponds to the pre-Revolution county of La Marche. South of Aubusson is the evocative Plateau de Millevaches, which sounds as though it should mean '1,000 cows' but actually means '1,000 springs'. The Plateau, at a height of between 1,650 and 3,250 ft, is the source of several major rivers, including the Vézère and the Vienne. The *département* of La Creuse (www.cg23.fr) is very green, and it is known as La Verte for this reason.

The south-western corner of the Limousin tends to be lumped in with the Dordogne in the minds of Britons. Brive-la-Gaillarde (Brive the Jolly Wench) is a main railway junction on the line from Paris, but not a place one would want to buy property. A little to the north, the town of Uzerche on the upper reaches of the Vézère is a lot more attractive. Tulle, the departmental capital of the Corrèze (www.cg19.fr), deep in the valley of the river of that name, is known for its stitched lace.

## Cuisine

As a region with limited agricultural resources, the cooking here is simple and filling. The uplands are cattle-farming country. Hams are also a delicacy. The *cul noir* or black-bum pig of St Yrieix has its own festival. In the markets one can buy all kinds of cheese, from cows, ewes and goats. The forests yield wild mushrooms. Chestnuts are a local product in La Creuse. Corrèze has a *vin de pays*; there is also some cider production.

## Property

The typical granite constructions with grey slates tend to accentuate the gloom; a certain amount of red sandstone is also used here and there, and you may even see the odd half-timbered house or *colombage*. The wetness of the climate can be gauged from the steeply tiled roofs and even the occasional northern-style slate-covered wall facing to the west.

The Limousin countryside perhaps has more to offer a second home rather than somewhere to live all year round, though this has not stopped many foreigners – mainly British and Irish – moving to live in the area. Rural depopulation is a serious issue here; property prices are low – in 2006 they were the lowest in the country, lower even than the Auvergne – and they are never going to rise by very much. The trend in French property buying is that people are looking to buy in coastal areas rather than in the country's interior. Buying a home in the Limousin should not be seen as get-rich-quick property speculation. One might also add that the rural population are noted for being rather suspicious of outsiders; if you are looking for Latin jollity and a warmer climate you might be better off a bit further south. That said, many Britons living in the area report that they have been made very welcome by their neighbours. And if you like a relaxed pace of life in a rural area then this is the region for you.

# Property TRENDS

La Creuse and Haute Vienne are two *départements* that are attracting increasing interest from foreign property buyers who have been priced out of the Dordogne and Lot. South-west Haute-Vienne has been made into a regional park, the Parc Naturel Régional Périgord-Limousin. The area has strong associations with Richard the Lionheart; there is a route one can follow.

La Creuse is a fairly empty region. There is just one golf course at Gouzon. Haute Vienne has three, and Corrèze two 18-hole courses. In La Creuse there are still small farms for renovation for as little as €18,000. Even the tourist town of Aubusson has some extraordinarily cheap properties in quite good condition. Most French people would look at you blankly if you told them you were planning to live in La Creuse. In the Haute Vienne the prices are a little higher. The main consideration is whether one would want to remain here all the year round. The valleys can be gloomy in winter with lingering fogs and quite severe frosts. And some people moving to the area have been unprepared for the climate. In 2007 there was a move away from large-scale renovation projects with overseas buyers looking instead for habitable homes, from €80,000 to €150,000. Prices are not expected to rise sharply in the foreseeable future.

| What you can get for your money | | | | |
|---|---|---|---|---|
| **Price range (€)** | **Location** | **Type** | **Description** | **Price (€)** |
| Under 100,000 | Boussac (23) | Traditional house | 2 bedrooms, barn, 450 sq m garden, well | 57,650 |
| 100,000 to 200,000 | Bussiere Poitevine (87) | Renovated townhouse | 3 bedrooms, garage, close to shops | 135,000 |
| 200,000 to 300,000 | Ussac (19) nr Brive | Village house | 3 bedrooms, 2,500 sq m garden, 15 minutes from motorway | 214,700 |
| 300,000 to 500,000 | Jarnages (23) | Traditional house | 11 rooms, large barn, separate cottage, 2,400 sq m land | 369,600 |
| 500,000 and over | Nr Limoges (87) | Maison de maître | 7 room 17th-century house with barn, stables, separate apartment and *gîte*, near river Vienne | 656,000 |

# Lorraine (Lorraine-Vosges)

**CRT:**

☎ 03 83 80 01 80;　　💻 crt@crt-lorraine.fr; www.crt-lorraine.fr.

---

**Percentage of population:** 3.85%; percentage of GDP: 3.06%.

---

**Airports:** Nancy/Metz: www.metz-nancy-lorraine.aeroport.fr

Lorraine is a region with strong Germanic influences, and was more or less independent for much of its history. The name Lorraine derives from Charlemagne's son Lothar who called his kingdom Lotharingia from 855. Lorraine split into two separate entities, Metz, Toul and Verdun on the one hand, and the Duchy of Lorraine on the other. The Dukes of Lorraine maintained their independence from the French until the end of the Thirty Years' War in 1648; Lorraine was finally incorporated into France in 1766. Parts of Meurthe and Moselle were annexed by Germany in 1871 after the Franco-Prussian War, and then joined with Alsace, but were returned to France in 1918.

As a frontier region Lorraine was heavily fortified by the French from the 17th century and there are still some massive fortresses, the most remarkable being the citadel at Bitche constructed by Vauban, in the north-western corner close to Germany. The battle for Verdun in 1916 gave the French their greatest success in the First World War, inasmuch as they blocked the German advance without the help of their allies, but at the cost of 400,000 lives. The Maginot Line, a sophisticated, but ultimately useless, defensive system meant to keep out the Germans after the First World War, runs through Lorraine and is kept up in parts as a museum.

The conurbation of Nancy, with some 335,000 inhabitants, is less of an industrial city than it used to be, but has developed other industries such as banking and IT and has a major university. The designer Emile Gallé, known for his glass and ceramics, came from here, and started the Nancy School of Art Nouveau.

The other major town in the region, Metz, the departmental capital of the Moselle, has some 195,000 inhabitants. Lorraine has four *départements:* Meuse (55), Meurthe-et-Moselle (54), Moselle (57) and Vosges (88) in the south. As well as the main rivers, there is a canal connecting the Rhine to the Marne (Canal de la Marne au Rhin) and the Canal de l'Est, connecting the Meuse up to the Moselle. For 200 years the canals were major transport arteries for shipping coal, iron and steel from Lorraine to the west, but they fell into disuse with the coming of the railways, and are kept up now for holidaymakers.

The Meuse *département* (www.tourisme-meuse.com) is closely identified with Verdun and the First World War; the departmental capital is Bar-le-Duc south of Verdun. Meurthe-et-Moselle (www.cdt-meurthe-et-moselle.fr) separates the Meuse and Moselle *départements*. The little town of Pont-à-Mousson on the Moselle supplies virtually all the manhole covers in France. Metz, the capital of Moselle (www.cdt-moselle.fr) is more or less due south of Luxembourg and there are regular trains to Germany. Lorraine does not have any direct air links with the UK, however, the nearest airport with flights to London being Strasbourg in Alsace.

The southernmost *département*, Vosges (www.vosges.fr) with the attractive town of Epinal, is a land of lakes, forest and spectacular gorges, and good skiing in winter. The southern part of the Vosges is a national park, Le Parc Naturel Régional des Ballons des Vosges. There is a tradition of taking the waters here, and both Vittel and Contrex mineral waters are produced in the area.

## Cuisine

Everyone has heard of quiche lorraine, the local speciality; much of Lorraine is dairy-farming country. Because of the abundant rivers and lakes, Lorraine is also noted for its fish, such as pike, perch, trout and carp, typically cooked in white wine or cream. The area also shares the Moselle and its wines with Germany, mainly white wines such as Gris de Toul, Côtes de Meuse and Moselle, and some rosés. This is also the second beer-producing region of France. All in all, you can expect to eat and drink well here.

## Property

Lorraine is generally rich in stone. The west is limestone, and the mountains sandstone and granite. Stone and brick are the main building materials, but there are still a number of timber-framed houses with brick *hourdis* or pugging. More modern properties are brick-built with internal exposed beams and slate roofs.

Lorraine is unusual in that the traditional roofing was of Spanish tiles, with Flemish curled tiles in places. Overhanging roofs are another local feature. The typical farmhouse is the *usoir*, usually with an arched entrance for carts. Lorraine has a number of notable châteaux, if not the kinds of wrecks that Brits like to do up. As with Alsace, there is not a great market here for second homes, and the main interest comes from the Germans. The Vosges attracts the most interest for holiday homes. Houses start from about €105,000.

# *Property* TRENDS

Property prices in this region tend to be influenced slightly by trends in neighbouring Germany, so the fact that Germany's economy appears to be getting stronger may have an impact on the future. However average home prices in Lorraine are below the national average, especially in the Meuse. In 2006 the average price for a house in and around Commercy was just over €80,000, making it one of the cheapest areas in the country. It's hard to see prices rising significantly in the region in the near future except perhaps in Vosges.

## What you can get for your money

| Price range (€) | Location | Type | Description | Price (€) |
|---|---|---|---|---|
| Under 100,000 | Ubexy (88) | Farmhouse | Farmhouse and outbuildings to renovate, 2 bedrooms | 75,000 |
| 100,000 to 200,000 | Nr Commercy (55) | Modern bungalow | 3 bedrooms, garage, terrace | 139,000 |
| 200,000 to 300,000 | Metz (57) | Flat | 3 bedrooms, 2 balconies, shared garage, parking | 230,000 |
| 300,000 to 500,000 | Heillecourt (54) | Pavilion-style house | 4 bedrooms, games room, attic | 350,000 |
| 500,000 and over | Nr Vittel (88) | Country house | 3 bedrooms, library, heated swimming pool, 2,200 sq m garden | 600,000 |

## Midi-Pyrénées

**CRT:**

☎ 05 61 13 55 55;   ▭ information@crtmp.com;
www.tourisme-midi-pyrenees.com.

**Percentage of population:** 4.25%; percentage of GDP: 3.6%.

**Airports:** Rodez: www.rodez.cci.fr
Tarbes: www.tarbes-lourdes.aeroport.fr
Toulouse: www.toulouse.aeroport.fr

Midi-Pyrénées covers a diverse area of mountain, high plateaux, low-lying river valleys, and areas of rolling hills with rich, dark soil called *terreforts*. Most of it is situated within the former province Guyenne-Gascony, more or less the same as Aquitaine in its widest sense. In the 12th century the Counts of Toulouse presided over a federation of independent cities stretching as far as the Alps, with a tradition of tolerating all kinds of religious belief. All that was snuffed out by the Albigensian Crusade sent to stamp out the Cathars, a sect who considered themselves without sin: *katharoi* meant 'pure' in Greek. The land was laid waste between 1209 and 1229 by the English warlord Simon de Montfort. The final act was the fall of the castle of Montségur in 1244. The county of Toulouse became part of France, and the great Occitan troubadour tradition disappeared overnight. The region suffered again from the English occupation during the Hundred Years War (1340–1453). More *bastides* (fortified hilltop villages) were built by both sides, until the English were finally booted out.

Most of the region, especially the Ariège, has experienced severe rural depopulation. It is reckoned that half of the houses in Ariège are now second residences. The region's capital, Toulouse, is one of France's most dynamic cities in terms of economic opportunities and lifestyle, largely thanks to the effect of Aérospatiale and its European Airbus factory.

Midi-Pyrénées consists of eight *départements*: Ariège (09), Haute-Garonne (31), Hautes Pyrénées (65), Gers (32), Tarn (81), Tarn-et-Garonne (82), Aveyron (12) and Lot (46), all areas that should interest second-home buyers. Toulouse is in the Haute-Garonne (www.cdt-haute-garonne.com). The Gers (www.gers-gascogne.com) is already a well established area for second-home buyers.

The Lot (pronounced 'lott') covers a large part of the old county Quercy, a wilderness of gorges and limestone plateaux (*causses*) that has an irresistible appeal for foreign buyers (see www.quercy-tourisme.com/le-lot). Next to the Dordogne, the Lot, in its widest sense, is the place where most British buyers would like to find a house. The prefectural town, Cahors, on the Lot, is a typical sunny, sleepy southern town. North of Cahors lies the Causse de Gramat, a dry limestone plateau, and to the south the Causse de Limogne. The most attractive town in the Lot is Figeac, east of Cahors, on the pilgrimage way to Santiago de Compostela; in the past the main industry was tanning. The remarkable church on a rock pinnacle at Rocamadour is the other major attraction.

The prefectural city of the Tarn-et-Garonne, Montauban, was the first *bastide* – fortified town – built by the Counts of Toulouse against the English and French in 1144. At the eastern end of the Tarn-et-Garonne is the castle town of St-Antonin-Noble-Val on the Aveyron river, in the vicinity of the 'golden triangle' which has recently been seen by cinema audiences as the setting for the Resistance film, *Charlotte Gray*.

The Tarn is one of the most popular areas for British property hunters; suitable properties in the so-called 'golden triangle' of Gaillac, Cordes-sur-Ciel and Albi are becoming scarce and expensive. Only the out-of-the-way corners of the Tarn have cheap properties nowadays. The remoteness of the area is both an advantage and a minus: it can take a good two hours to get here from Toulouse or Bordeaux airport. Most tourists head for Albi, the prefectural town, with its remarkable red-brick cathedral that resembles an ocean liner.

The Aveyron (www.tourisme-aveyron.com), east of the Tarn, is an area of steep hills and forests in the southern Massif Central, with few inhabitants, which is much in vogue for camping and walking holidays with the French. The prefectural town of Rodez has a fine Gothic cathedral in red sandstone; it stands at the centre of a remote and wild region, little frequented by foreign visitors, where properties are still cheap and fairly plentiful.

## Cuisine

The higher elevations of the Midi-Pyrénées are the home of goats, which are kept for their milk to turn into small cheeses or *petits chèvres*. There are numerous other cheeses from cow's and ewe's milk, called *tommes des Pyrénées*. Ducks and all kinds of dishes from ducks, such as *magret, confit, foie gras* and so on are native to the region. The Ariège has its own version of the ever-popular *cassoulet*, known as *mounjetado*, cooked slowly over a wood fire at village festivals.

# Regional Voices – Quercy

**Amanda Lawrence** is a British writer who has known the area for many years and now lives near Cahors. Here she gives her impressions of the area.

The Midi-Pyrenees is the largest region in France, and possibly the most diverse, stretching from the undulating charm of the Dordogne valley in the north to the snow-capped peaks of the Pyrenees in the south. The two northernmost departments are the Lot and the Tarn and Garonne; together they form the ancient province of the Quercy. It's a lost little corner of France that time seems to have passed by, industry is almost non-existent and the main business is agriculture; vineyards and sunflower fields, walnut groves and vast orchards of peaches and plums.

The centre of this beautiful, untamed area is Cahors, capital of the Lot department and ancient capital of the Quercy. This old city sits in a loop of the river Lot, surely the most enchanting in all of France. Its serpentine course starts in the high causses, east of Cahors, lazily wends its way past soaring cliffs filled with troglodyte caves and crowned with bastide villages, then flows on through the sun-baked vineyards that produce the famous Cahors wines.

Because of its wild beauty the area has long been a favourite with world-weary Parisians, and there are numerous second homes here. In the last 10 years the British and Dutch – who would traditionally have been looking at the Dordogne – also discovered it. For that reason alone prices have risen sharply, and although the region can't be considered particularly expensive there are fewer bargains. It is still possible to find a traditional stone-built property, but before deciding on a rural location you may like to consider the villages. Village properties represent extraordinarily good value for money, they can be half the price of their country cousins, and as the turreted stone villages of this region are amongst the prettiest in France it can be a shrewd move. Many young families now prefer the village option. They are warmly welcomed at local schools and are able to enjoy the convenience of boulangeries, restaurants and cafes, a mere stroll away. Another increasingly popular option is the self-build route. Land is inexpensive and there's plenty of it. Many villages are expanding, plots on the fringes are now available with CU, and several companies have sprung up to take care of the design and build. Food for thought, especially for retiring couples: no renovation, little maintenance, and of course the views are still delightful.

For more of Amanda's views on the area and its property visit: www.amandalawrence.fr.

Pork products are essential to *cassoulet* and used down to the last detail. In the Tarn you could try pig's ears and snout cooked in wine, or perch in nettle butter.

Tarn-et-Garonne produces 80% of the fruit in the Midi-Pyrénées. Chasselas table grapes from Moissac are well known, as are the local Reine Claude plums. Tarn-et-Garonne is also the second biggest producer of garlic in France.

The mountainous areas of the Pyrenees are too cold for vineyards. The rest of the Midi-Pyrénées has a vinegrowing tradition going back over 1,000 years; there are now some 14 *appellations* ranging from the Vin d'Entraygues et du Fel in the Aveyron, to the Gaillac wines, both red and white, and sparkling, to the popular rustic reds of Cahors in the Lot.

# Property

The Midi-Pyrénées has 260,000 second homes out of 1,320,000 units. The property market around Toulouse has generally been transformed by the opening of the A20 motorway from Toulouse to Limoges and Paris, and cheap flights to the UK. The Tarn has recently become fairly expensive, and one has to look in the more out-of-the-way areas for a bargain. The Ariège was a well-kept secret until about 2000, but is now very fashionable. It combines views of the Pyrenees with charming hill-top villages. The extension of the motorway from Toulouse to Foix has stoked up property prices.

The Midi-Pyrénées is rich in various rock types and traditionally an area of stone building. There is also a lot of red-brick building between Toulouse and Albi, one of the few areas of France with no local stone for building. One of the distinctive features of the Midi-Toulousain is the use of brick door- and window-surrounds and quoins even in stone buildings. Wood was scarce and expensive in the past due to deforestation in the mountains, and was mainly used for balconies, haylofts and the internal framework of houses. One can find some half-timbering with *torchis* or cob – a mix of plaster and woodshavings called *massaca*. Farmhouses in the Haute-Garonne and Ariège are sometimes partly built into the rockface; the cellar walls are bare rock. Higher up, roofs are of slates; smaller houses of the lower country use tiles. Around river valleys one may see another type of construction, using layers of pebbles set in mortar alternating with brick or with brick quoins. The local nobility built *maisons de maître,* which they tried to turn into something like châteaux. These are on four storeys with servant quarters at the top. There is a great vogue for *pigeonniers* – purpose-built pigeon towers in stone with nests out of clay pots or wood. These served a useful purpose for manure and pigeon meat. They were also a status symbol; only those of higher social rank could have one.

# Property
# TRENDS

It's fair to say now that few parts of this large region have remained untouched by foreign property buyers. The sharp rise in the market from around 2003 has been followed by the stabilisation in prices seen in other parts of France. Prices are expected to remain relatively static in much of the region or to rise slightly over the next couple of years. The trend towards new-build developments is seen here as elsewhere, with many buyers claiming they represent better value for money than older properties. New houses priced between €180,000 and €250,000 have proved especially popular. Prices in Hautes-Pyrénées have started to catch up with more expensive parts of the region, aided by cheap flights to neighbouring Pau, but it's still possible to find interesting renovation projects from around €80,000.

South-west of Toulouse, towards the Pyrenees, is an area with relatively few estate agents that has plenty of potential for second-home hunters. The Comminges region, between Bagnères de Luchon and Toulouse, has become popular; it tended to be overlooked by foreigners, but there are plenty of properties in good condition. During the winter there is skiing in the Pyrenees. The rest of the year there is climbing, fishing, sailing and walking for the active. Hautes-Pyrénées is generally regarded as one of the up-and-coming regions for British house buyers, mainly because of the very sunny climate; with luck you can be sunbathing for 10 months of the year here. The property market is geared to outsiders; the failing economy has left the *département* virtually dependent on tourism. The dryness of the climate makes it especially attractive to retirees. Hautes-Pyrénées has very cheap property on the plains around Tarbes; closer to the ski fields expect to pay €150,000 upwards for renovated properties.

| What you can get for your money | | | | |
|---|---|---|---|---|
| Price range (€) | Location | Type | Description | Price (€) |
| Under 100,000 | Nr Belfort (09) | Village house | 5-room house to renovate, well, cellar | 99,000 |
| 100,000 to 200,000 | Armagnac (32) | Modern house | 3 bedrooms, new development, terrace, 2,500 sq m garden | 145,000 |
| 200,000 to 300,000 | Millau (12) | Chalet-style house | 3 bedrooms, swimming pool, views of Millau viaduct | 260,000 |
| 300,000 to 500,000 | Nr Graulhet (81) | Maison de maître | 6 bedrooms, swimming pool, outbuildings, 1,500 sq m garden | 392,000 |
| 500,000 and over | Nr Beaumont (82) | Modern villa | 4 bedrooms, office, annex, sauna, jacuzzi, swimming pool, 5,600 sq m garden, countryside views | 552,000 |

# Nord-Pas-De-Calais

**CRT:**

☎ 03 20 14 57 57;    🖥 contact@crt-nordpasdecalais.fr;
www.crt-nordpasdecalais.fr;
www.northernfrance-tourism.com.

**Percentage of population:** 6.65%; percentage of GDP: 5.25%.

**Airports:** Lille: www.lille.aeroport.fr
Le Touquet: www.aeroport-letouquet.com

A triangle of territory running with the Belgian border in the north and the English Channel on the west is made up of the two *départements* that give it its name: the Nord (59) and the Pas-de-Calais (62). This is one of the smaller regions, but very densely populated. The western half was once part of the county of Flanders. Louis XIV brought the area under French rule from 1668. Flemish culture mainly survives in a small area in the centre of the Nord *département* (www.cdt-nord.fr); place names and family names are Flemish, but the language has almost died out.

The regional capital, Lille, joins up with the towns Roubaix and Tourcoing to form the only real urban sprawl in France, spilling over into Belgium. The industrial heritage of this area, once the main coal-mining and textile region of France gives the Nord-Pas-de-Calais its special identity. The French will tell you that the people of the Nord-Pas-de-Calais are very *sympathique* and sociable. They are generally less excitable than the rest of the French, thanks to the calming influence of the slow and solid Flemish. The Lille conurbation counts as France's fourth largest city, with 960,000 residents. The Nord-pas-de-Calais has the highest unemployment in France, at 20%. A great deal of money has been spent on beautifying the city centres – Lille was European Capital of Culture in 2004 – but no amount of money seems to be able to deal with the endemic industrial decline here.

Pas-de-Calais (www.pas-de-calais.com) is well known to the English as the entry point to France if you come through Calais, Boulogne or Dunkerque. In most ways, it tends to be overlooked by tourists and property hunters who are looking for the sun and mountains. The Côte d'Opale has fine flat beaches, particularly suitable for families, but is fairly wild when the weather closes in from the sea. South of Le Calaisis and Le Boulonnais is the area of Canche-Authie, with the high-class resorts of Montreuil-sur-Mer and Berck-Plage. There are now cheap flights direct from Brighton and Lydd in Kent to Le Touquet, reviving a tradition that goes back to the 1950s. The golf course is still one of the best in France, and there are several others in the vicinity.

Inland is the ancient county of Artois and part of French Hainaut. In a corner of Artois one can visit Azincourt, the site of the Battle of Agincourt in 1415. The prefectural town of Arras was at the centre of First World War trench warfare; the nearby Vimy Ridge has been given to the Canadian people in perpetuity in recognition of their sacrifices. Historically, Arras produced fine wall hangings: an *arras* is another name for a wall hanging.

The Nord has one great advantage in that it is easy to reach from London: only two hours by train from Lille. Moreover one can get to Brussels in 40 minutes, and Paris in 60 minutes. TGVs from Lille go virtually everywhere in France, bypassing Paris.

## Cuisine

French Flanders is the centre of beer brewing in France; you can find many of the finest Flemish beers in the cafés of Lille and round about. The beer is certainly superior to Kronenbourg from Alsace. A few small breweries concoct lethal ales such as Trois Monts from Esquelbecq. The cuisine is also distinctly Flemish, for example, *potje vleesch* (meat in aspic), *moules frites* (mussels and chips), *carbonades flamandes* (beef cooked in stout) and *poêlée d'endives* (fried chicory). *Potje vleesch* was first invented to deal with a plague of rabbits in Dunkirk; the only thing to do with them was to preserve them in jelly, but the recipe now officially has to have four different kinds of meat. In the Flemish heartland of Steenvoorde and Hazebrouck you will be served *stryntjes* or small hard waffles with your coffee. Traditionally these were made to give out to the poor at New Year, but they are now an everyday item. The local spirit is *bistoul* or gin and the apéritif is Picon.

## Property

Styles of construction are influenced by Flemish tradition: red brick is used a lot, along with a variety of coloured brick for decorative effect, and there is the same tradition of whitewashing farmhouses. Flemish-style building with bare brick walls and flat façades is considered to be 'separatist architecture' by some municipalities. Flemish stepped gables – *pignons à gradins* – are also in evidence. Close to the Belgian border the houses are indistinguishable from those in Belgium. Pas-de-Calais shares the same styles of building with Picardie. On the downside, the Nord-Pas-de-Calais is France's most industrialised region, but there is still enough countryside left to find some attractive properties, particularly along the canals. Naturally enough, the coast is expensive.

# Property TRENDS

The improvements made to the centre of Lille have increased property prices there, and exclusive areas such as Le Touquet continue to have their own distinct property market. The coastline is still popular with Parisians, which keeps prices high. Estate agents have also noticed growing interest among British buyers who either want to take the train or drive to their second home – avoiding the plane. This suggests that at the very least prices will remain buoyant in the region. The reduction of train travel times from London from November 2007 is also expected to encourage more house buyers and owners to travel by train.

## What you can get for your money

| Price range (€) | Location | Type | Description | Price (€) |
|---|---|---|---|---|
| Under 100,000 | Lille (59) | Studio, 30 sq m | Central location | 76,000 |
| 100,000 to 200,000 | Verquin (62) | 1930s house | 3 bedrooms, 1,100 sq m plot | 145,000 |
| 200,000 to 300,000 | Property 1: Brillon (59) | Chalet-style house | 3 bedrooms, office, garage, 5 minutes to A23 | 275,000 |
| | Property 2: Nr Hesdin (62) | Cottage | 6 bedrooms, heated swimming pool, garage, workshop, 3,300 sq m plot (see photo No. 13 in colour section) | 251,214 |
| 300,000 to 500,000 | Nr Etaples (62) | Modern villa | 4 bedroms, office, cellar, 10 minutes from beach | 340,000 |
| 500,000 and over | Nr Dunkirk (59) | Le Touquet-style villa | 4 bedrooms, 2 bathrooms, laundry room, 2,300 sq m garden | 600,000 |

## Normandy

**CRT:**

☎  02 32 33 79 00;   🖳   normandy@normandy-tourisme.org;
www.normandy-tourism.org.

**Upper Normandy Percentage of population:** 2.97%; percentage of GDP: 2.83%.
**Lower Normandy Percentage of population:** 2.37%; percentage of GDP: 1.92%.

**Airports:** Caen: www.caen.aeroport.fr
Rouen: www.rouen.aeroport.fr

While Upper and Lower Normandy are officially two separate regions, they have a great deal in common, and are treated together here. There is a possibility that they could be combined into one region in the next few years.

# Upper Normandy

Upper Normandy – Haute Normandie – is a region rich in history linking it to England. Probably more than any other region in France it is connected with major writers and artists, who were inspired by its rural life whilst appreciating its being conveniently close to Paris. The best-known painter of the area, Monet, grew up in Le Havre from the age of five; his house at Giverny with its brightly coloured flowers and lily pond provided subjects for many of his best-known paintings. The shifting light on the frontage of Rouen Cathedral inspired some of his greatest work.

Upper Normandy is very much dairy country; the rolling hills are reminiscent of southern England, of which it is an extension. Although it doesn't have quite the cachet of the landing beaches in Lower Normandy that will go on attracting Americans for many years, Upper Normandy's closeness to England and the good ferry connections from Dieppe and Le Havre make it a popular location with Britons, particularly with those who want to keep working in England or who can work from home some of the time in France.

Upper Normandy comprises only two *départements:* Eure (27) and Seine-Maritime (76). Rouen, the capital of the region, was designed by the first Duke of Normandy, Rollo, a Viking who forced the French king to recognise his claim to Normandy in 911, on the site of the Roman Rotiomagus. Opinions are mixed on the attractiveness of Rouen, a city of 380,000 inhabitants. The central streets have been carefully preserved in a uniform half-timbered style that makes a very attractive whole. Anywhere outside the centre and you are in dull industrial suburbs with nothing much to see.

To see the real beauties of the Seine-Maritime (www.seine-maritime-tourisme.com) it is best to head towards Honfleur, a picturesque port whose narrow streets are thronged with tourists most of the year. The coastline was much appreciated by the Impressionists; Renoir and Cézanne came here to visit Monet who loved to paint here. Further north Le Havre is France's second largest port, with 245,000 inhabitants, and is completely new as the original town was obliterated in the Second World War. Dieppe is conveniently close to Rouen and has regular ferries to Newhaven, but is not otherwise of much interest. The whole coast between Dieppe and Le Havre is known as the Côte Albâtre or Alabaster Coast, from the whiteness of the cliffs.

Upper Normandy's most attractive towns and villages are situated in the Eure *département*, east of Rouen (www.cdt-eure.fr). The best rustic architecture is at Lyons-la-Forêt. The woods around here are very popular with walkers. A little to the south, Richard the Lionheart built the Château Gaillard high above the Seine at Les Andelys to keep an eye on the locals. Only 15 km away is Giverny, Monet's home. Évreux, the prefectural town, was heavily damaged in the war, but the outstanding cathedral of Notre Dame was saved, with its 14th-century stained glass, some of the finest in France.

# Lower Normandy

Lower Normandy – Basse Normandie – has strong ties with both Britain and North America. Once you cross the estuary of the Seine over the futuristic Pont de Normandie you are on the Côte Fleurie or Norman Riviera with the twin resorts of Trouville and Deauville. These were popularised by the playboy Emperor Napoleon III in the 1860s. Wealthy Parisians come here for the casino and the racecourses.

Further west are the Côte Nacre and the Normandy landing beaches, with their lovingly tended military cemeteries. The city of Caen, inland from the ferry port of Ouistreham (ferries to Portsmouth) was virtually obliterated in 1944. Further west, Bayeux is famed for its great

## Insider Tip

*Lower Normandy has some advantages over Upper Normandy: the climate is somewhat warmer, but it is also wetter. The annual rainfall in Cherbourg, in the Manche, is over 50 inches. For anyone who wants to start gîtes or chambres d'hôtes, prospects are good in Calvados if you are within reach of the plages du débarquement, the landing beaches, which guarantee you a steady stream of American tourists.*

tapestry showing the successful invasion of England by William the Conqueror, whose birthplace was Falaise in the Orne. Bayeux was fortunate to be the first town in France to be freed from the Germans, so it came out of the war almost unscathed.

The *département* of Calvados, of which Caen is the capital, gave its name to a potent liqueur, also known as *calvados* or *calva*. All of Normandy is dominated by apple growing and dairy farming. The Orne *département*, to the south, is the home of Camembert, a bland cheese popularised by Napoleon III. At the very far western end of the coast is the great tourist attraction Mont St Michel.

To the north-west of Bayeux lies the Cotentin peninsula, also with strong Second World War associations, which has found a place on the literary map in the series of humorous books by George East, such as *René and Me, Home and Dry in France*. Although the Cotentin is rustic and remote, it does have a ferry port at Cherbourg. P&O stopped running its Portsmouth to Cherbourg service in 2005, but Brittany Ferries still sails here from Portsmouth and Poole.

## Cuisine

Norman cooking is rich in cream and butter, as you would expect. The local drink is cider rather than wine, and the potent liqueur derived from it is Calvados. It is customary to have a pause between courses in the copious meals for a *trou normand* (literally 'Norman gap') to knock back some Calvados. Seafood is also eaten a great deal. All kinds of meat are popular, particularly ducks from Rouen, and *andouilles,* sausages made from cows' intestines. The apples and pears that are not turned into cider are put to use for apple tarts and cakes with cream.

## Property

The archetypal Norman property is the half-timbered *longère* or farmhouse. Anything advertised as a *maison normande* will have half-timbering (*colombages*), even if it is only a token decoration. Another typical feature of all Norman farmhouses are the *lucarnes* or dormer windows, which are there partly for aesthetic reasons to disguise the massive size of the roofs.

Modest Norman houses were traditionally made of wood, the *pans de bois* style. First a wooden frame (*charpente*) is constructed on a foundation of sandstone, limestone or bricks. Massive vertical beams (*poteaux*) are fixed into the foundations about 2 m apart. The *poteaux* are held apart by crossbeams known as *sablières*. Further massive beams of up to 7 m or more run from front to back. Batons are fixed into the spaces between the *poteaux* and *sablières*. The vertical batons are known as *potelets* or *colombes* and the latter has given the name *colombages* to this style of half-timbering.

The wooden framework is filled in with pugging (*hourdis*), consisting of clay mixed with straw or animal hair, soaked in water and then dried. Lumps of pugging are then attached to horizontal or oblique strips of wood (*palissons* or *éclisses*). Other types of pugging are cut-up tiles (*tuileaux*) fixed with mortar, arranged in geometric patterns. More rarely, bricks are used. The wall is then rendered with lime rendering to protect against the rain. This type of construction is vulnerable to bad weather, so roofs tend to overhang by as much as 50cm. Construction in *pans de bois* (half-timbering) continued far longer in the Calvados, or Pays d'Auge, than in Seine Maritime, or Pays de Caux, reflecting the greater poverty of the Pays d'Auge.

Seine Maritime started using brick quite early on; light and dark bricks are used to create decorative effects, similar to the style of Pas-de-Calais. The *département* of the Eure still has many half-timbered houses. One step up from a *longère* is a *gentilhommière*, similarly constructed but of greater size.

The landscape is far more rocky to the west in the Manche. The traditional stone structure is of rough-shaped rocks or *moellons* placed on top of each other on two faces of a wall, with the gaps filled in with smaller rocks mixed with earth. Here and there a throughstone (*boutisse parpaing*) is inserted to give the wall stability. Quoins of cut stone hold the walls together at the corners.

Thatch roofs are becoming less common; the wet climate makes slates a more practical roofing material, and it is more expensive to insure thatch roofs. Thatching has to be replaced regularly, making it an expensive luxury. A house with thatching is a *chaumière* – although this is often translated as 'cottage' these are usually substantial dwellings. There is also a vogue for converting buildings used for cider pressing – *pressoirs* – into houses; they have single storeys, and rather disproportionately large roofs.

A wealthy farmer or lord of the manor generally preferred to build his *ferme-manoir* in limestone or granite. The entrance for coaches would be a grand arch, convenient for the main residence or *grange*. On three sides one may find storerooms (*celliers*), a cart-shed (*charreterie*), stables (*écurie*), bakehouse (*boulangerie*), dovecote (*pigeonnier* or *colombier*), milking-house (*laiterie*) and so on. These days they may be turned into garages and *gîtes*. The wealthier the farmer, the more architectural detail he would try to apply. The very well-off would add on a tower to the *grange*.

One may still find properties to do up in the Eure, and to a lesser extent, Seine-Maritime. There is competition from the Parisians for holiday homes. Starting prices for renovation are €65,000 in Eure – though you'll more likely to find building plots at this price – and €80,000 in Seine-Maritime. In the eastern Calvados and Orne there are plenty of half-timbered Norman longhouses or *longères* for sale, as well as other farmhouses with half-timbering. The Orne, on the other hand, is somewhat upmarket. This is the centre for horse breeding in France, with the national stud near Argentan. One should be wary of buying half-timbered houses in bad condition, even if they look very cheap. Only a specialist can deal with this type of construction. If you buy a listed building the renovation costs could be prohibitive. There is also a serious subsidence risk where properties are built on clay that is subject to expansion and contraction in hot weather. The cheapest properties are in Calvados, starting from around €40,000 for renovation projects. In the Manche and the Orne there is not much under €85,000.

Because it is a holiday region, most new construction in Normandy is for second homes. Prices of property depend on two things: the distance from Paris and the distance from the sea. A sea view adds 50% or more to the price. A good railway link to Paris is also a plus point. Note that the climate here is much like southern England. Good insulation is a must, as is an adequate heating system. Half-timbered houses are generally colder than stone ones.

# *Property* TRENDS

The interest of both British and Parisian buyers in these regions should ensure that the housing market remains buoyant. Again, the proximity of the ports makes it an attractive area for those Britons who prefer not to fly.

A zone that looks likely to attract more foreign buyers in the future is the beautiful wooded area around Vire in Calvados and nearby towns such as St-Sever Calvados to the west and Vassy to the east (www.vire-tourisme.com). Here one can find a modern 3-bedroom pavilion-style home in the countryside for under €140,000. The very cheap properties of some years ago in Normandy have gone, but the region is a large one and with careful research bargains can still be found.

| What you can get for your money | | | | |
|---|---|---|---|---|
| Price range (€) | Location | Type | Description | Price (€) |
| Under 100,000 | Nr Verneuil | Barn, 60 sq m | Needs renovation, 30 sq m workshop, 1,300 sq m land | 80,000 |
| 100,000 to 200,000 | Rouen (76) | Flat | 1 bedroom, attic, close to old market | 150,000 |
| 200,000 to 300,000 | Nr Mont St-Michel (50) | Traditional house | 3 bedrooms, garage, 3,360 sq m land, views of Mont Saint-Michel | 275,000 |
| 300,000 to 500,000 | Sainte Honorine du Fay (14) nr Caen | Modern house | 9 rooms, 6,500 sq m land | 350,000 |
| 500,000 and over | Nr Argentan (61) | Mill | 6-bedroom stone mill, swimming pool, library, outbuildings, 7 hectares land | 620,100 |

# Paris and Ile-De-France

**CRT:**

☎ 08 92 68 3000; 🖥 www.paris-ile-de-france.com; www.parisinfo.com; http://english.pidf.com.

---

**Percentage of population:** 18.25%; percentage of GDP: 27.3%.

---

**Airports:** Charles de Gaule/Orly: www.aeroportsdeparis.fr

Beauvais: www.aeroportbeauvais.com

The nation's capital, with its surrounding area, forms one region known as Ile de France. The central core of Paris is home to 2.1 million people; the Paris agglomeration has a population of 11.1 million, more than half as much again as Greater London.

Until AD 987 Paris was not a particularly significant place; in pre-Roman times the Parisi tribe had a small fortified stronghold on the Ile de la Cité (where Notre-Dame cathedral now stands) known as Lutetia, which was conquered by Julius Caesar in 52 BC. Paris became the centre of an embryonic French state: when Hugues Capet made himself king of France in the 10th century, Ile-de-France was the only area that was really under his control. Most of the country was ruled by independent dukes and counts, who only paid lip-service to rule from Paris. Notre-Dame was begun in 1160 and took nearly 200 years to complete.

Apart from Notre Dame very little of medieval Paris survives. A section of the Roman bathhouse which forms part of the extraordinary Musée du Cluny is the only real reminder of the earliest phase of the capital. The 'City of Light' was substantially remodelled in the 19th century, and turned into a homogenously magnificent metropolis worthy of its status as the capital of a world empire. To see how Paris looked in the time of Louis XIV you need to go to the Marais district, with its sumptuous *hôtels particuliers* (*hôtel* also means an imposing private or public building). The Parisian taste for grandiose and daring building projects can be seen in the Eiffel Tower, the Beaubourg or Centre Pompidou, the first building to have all its pipes and escalators on the outside, and the fantastic Arche de la Défense to the west of the city, a modern echo of the Napoleonic Arc de Triomphe.

As with any huge urban conglomeration, Paris can seem overwhelming at first sight, but things are organised to make the city liveable. Paris has a well-integrated and cheap public transport system.

The downside to Paris is partly to do with its size, and partly with the mentality of the Parisiens or 'Parigots' as the rest of the French call them. Along with all of France's national institutions, Paris has also concentrated every aspect of the country's social problems in the capital. Paris also has the reputation of being the least friendly city in France. Everyone is in too much of a hurry to talk much with you. Foreigners tend to stick together, and form their own social clubs. The negative image of the French as arrogant and xenophobic comes in part from foreigners' contacts with Parisians. If a Frenchman is proud of his country, it follows that Parisians are twice as proud of their city as the heart of francophone culture. If you are looking for a peaceful life, and you relish relaxed conversations in the local café, you might think twice about living here, but if you want high excitement and a cutting-edge cultural experience, this would be the place to go for.

There is now a strong demographic tendency for the better off to leave the centre of the city for the suburbs, while the city is more and more packed with immigrants and young people. Paris is by far the most expensive place to live in France. Prices of basic commodities in shops are roughly comparable with those in London, far more expensive than the rest of France.

Most people live in apartments; there are few houses on the market within the Boulevard Périphérique which delimits the city. Property prices are 40% to 65% of those in London, but there are vast differences between the 20 *arrondissements*. The arrondissements are arranged like a snail shell, going clockwise from the centre. The 1st and 2nd are the historical centre, with world-famous landmarks. The 3rd and 4th are trendy with a lot of bars and discos. The 5th includes the Sorbonne and the Quartier Latin. The 6th or 7th are the most expensive and exclusive, with government buildings and large open spaces. The 8th includes the shopping centre of the Champs Elysées; the 9th is an area of theatres, cinemas and department stores. The 10th has the Gare du Nord and Gare de l'Est; the 11th and 12th on the eastern side are being revitalised with large building projects. The 13th, 14th, 15th, 16th and 17th are residential. The 18th was very attractive in the past but has gone downhill with the spread of the red light area around Montmartre and Pigalle. The 19th and 20th are more downmarket areas. The relative standing of the *arrondissements* can be judged from the price per square metre for apartments.

Outside Paris is a large area of suburbs as well as countryside. Central Ile de France is known as *la petite couronne,* and includes Hauts-de-Seine, Seine-Saint-Denis and Val-de-Marne. Paris is also a *département.* The rest of Ile de France is *la grande couronne,* comprising Seine-et-Marne, Yvelines, Essonne and Val-d'Oise. In recent years certain of the *banlieues* or suburbs around Paris have acquired a reputation for crime and lawlessness. The riots that spread across the country in the autumn of 2005 started in the *banlieue* of Clichy-sous-Bois. However not all *banlieues* are the same; Nicolas Sarkozy, elected as French president in 2007, was mayor of the wealthy suburb of Neuilly-sur-Seine.

# Property

Almost all residential property in central Paris dates back to the 19th century. There are plenty of modern villas and mansions outside the inner city. The Ile-de-France has its own traditional architecture, characterised by white-rendered farmhouses with elaborate entrance arches, and *lucarnes* with pulleys for bringing in sacks of grain. Flat tiles (*pannes*) and slates are both common. More recent detached properties imitate various styles of regional architecture.

As far as Paris goes, the only property you could expect to afford would be an apartment. Houses rarely come on the market, and are worth millions in the upmarket *arrondissements.* Nevertheless, apartments are not that expensive, and anyone on a good income should be able to afford one near the city centre. Out in the suburbs, prices are very reasonable by British standards. A three-bedroom house in a good area can be had for €250,000. There are very expensive suburbs: wealthy Americans live in a sort of ghetto in St Cloud. Versailles, Fontainebleau and St-Germain-en-Laye are very upmarket.

# Property
# TRENDS

Paris has its own distinct property market that seems largely unrelated to the rest of the country. Most foreign buyers looking to purchase a place in the city will be looking at it as an investment. The prospects look promising for the next few years at least. A report in 2007 put Paris at the top of the list of cities in which to invest, citing its economic sustainability. And though the French economy overall has been sluggish, Paris has started to attract some high-tech industries. Studio flats in and around Paris can start at around €85,000 though for one-bedroom flats in decent areas the prices start at around €155,000.

| What you can get for your money | | | | |
|---|---|---|---|---|
| Price range (€) | Location | Type | Description | Price (€) |
| Under 100,000 | Meaux (77) | Flat | Balcony, quiet area | 92,000 |
| 100,000 to 200,000 | Gare du Nord (75) | Period flat | 1 bedroom, built 1900, 3rd floor | 150,000 |
| 200,000 to 300,000 | Versailles (78) | Modern flat | 1-bedroom, lift, private parking, cellar | 265,000 |
| 300,000 to 500,000 | Fontenay-sous-Bois (94) | Townhouse | 3 bedrooms, parking, terrace, 167 sq m garden | 360,000 |
| 500,000 and over | Montmartre (75) | Townhouse | 3 bedrooms, cellar, open kitchen, beams | 550,000 |

## Pays De La Loire

**CRT:**
☎ 02 28 20 50 00;  💻 www.paysdelaloire.fr.

**Percentage of population:** 5.37%; percentage of GDP: 4.6%.

**Airports:** Nantes: www.nantes.aeroport.fr

The western part of the Loire Valley has been made into a region covering the old counties of Maine and Anjou. The capital, Nantes (www.nantes.fr), was the traditional seat of the Dukes of

Brittany – they are buried in the cathedral – but the city officially ceased to be part of Brittany in 1962. Duchess Anne brought Brittany under the French crown when she married King Charles VIII in 1491. In the past, Nantes prospered from the colonial trade (i.e. slavery) and ship building, activities whose place has been taken by diversified industries, especially IT. Nantes is a pleasant place to live and offers reasonable job prospects for foreign workers. It was rated third in a survey of French cities by *Express* magazine, for economic dynamism and quality of life.

The *départements* of Loire-Atlantique (www.loire-atlantique-tourisme.com) and Vendée offer flat sandy beaches and excellent sailing and golf, but parts of the coast have been spoilt by over-development. La Baule, west of St Nazaire – France's biggest ship-building port – is the most upmarket (and therefore expensive) beach resort on the Atlantic coast. The Vendée has had an uneasy relationship with Paris; in 1793 the Vendéens unwisely backed a revolt against the Revolution and were soundly defeated. To dramatise the blood that was spilt, the town of Cholet (just inside Anjou) still produces red and white striped handkerchiefs that are used all over France.

The *département* of Maine-et-Loire, corresponding to part of the old Anjou region, came under the control of the English when Henry I married his daughter to Geoffrey Count of Anjou. His son, Henry II, was thus an Angevin. The area is dotted with castles recalling Richard the Lionheart and other romantic figures. The city of Angers and the area round about are worth considering for second homes; the proximity of airports and the TGV to Paris and Lille make it a convenient place. One could say this is an up-and-coming region.

In the north of the Pays de la Loire lies the wild and thinly populated *département* of Mayenne (www.lamayenne.fr), reputed to have more châteaux per square mile than anywhere outside Paris. Rather confusingly, the departmental capital is not the town of Mayenne itself, but Laval further south, but they both lie on the River Mayenne. Agriculture is the main industry. Mayenne's remoteness makes it attractive to foreigners who want to get away from it all without being too far from the Channel ports. Straddling the southern part of Basse Normandie and the northern edge of Loire is the Maine Normand national park. The Maine is both flat and somewhat arid, and lacks the kind of scenery that attracts foreigners.

The capital of the Sarthe *département* (http://tourisme.sarthe.com), Le Mans, lying on the motorway from Paris to Rennes, is rightly famous for its 24-hour race, but it also has an amazingly intact medieval centre, and the best-preserved Roman fortress walls outside Rome itself. Le Mans is also connected by TGV to Paris.

The Vendée (www.vendee-tourisme.com) is now attracting a lot of attention from foreign property buyers. The fine sandy beaches and some up-market resorts attract Parisians in droves. There are two large islands off the coastline: the Ile d'Yeu (an hour by ferry from the mainland) and the Ile de Noirmoutier (connected by road), with strict planning laws about the size and design of buildings. The northern part of the Vendée coastline is known as Le Pays des Monts; along with the southern part, the Sables d'Olonne, this is an area thick with sandy beaches, dunes and holiday resorts, ideal for windsurfing, sailing, scuba diving, sand yachting and so on. There are four 18-hole golf courses. The southern Vendée includes part of the Marais Poitevin national park, a vast area of wetlands where the easiest way to get around is by punt. The town of Fontenay-le-Comte was rebuilt in Renaissance style by King François I. The inland part of the Vendée, the Bocage Vendéen, is also fairly touristic. The departmental capital, La Roche-sur-Yon, was built by Napoleon on a symmetrical plan to try to pacify the rebellious Vendéens and develop the local economy. It is rated as one of France's best places to live.

# Cuisine

The area around Nantes, near the mouth of the Loire, is mainly known for its light muscadet wines, which gain their particular flavour from the chalky soils. Saumur in Anjou specialises in a naturally sparkling white wine, the Saumur brut. There is also the red Saumur-Champigny. A little to the south, around the Layon and Aubance rivers, some fine sweet dessert wines such as Coteaux du Layon have a worldwide reputation. The light, fruity wines of the Vendée, which go under the name of Fiefs Vendéens, are not well known and hardly exported. Sarthe and Mayenne are more apple-growing regions.

Thanks to the long coastline, seafoods are plentiful in the western Loire, especially mussels and oysters. The local sardines, anchovies and baby eels, called elvers, are well known throughout France. The abundance of waterways in the region gives a wide range of freshwater fish, notably trout, pike, pike-perch (*sandre*) and carp. Free-range poultry from Challans in the Vendée and Loué in the Sarthe have their own *appellation*, the Label Rouge. The mild climate of the western Loire has led to the development of market gardens, growing small new season vegetables such as carrots, leeks and salads. There are all sorts of cow's milk cheeses. The rather bland Port Salut from the Mayenne is popular everywhere.

# Property

About 20% of properties are second homes in the region, mainly concentrated along the coast. Mayenne is famous for its châteaux; there is scope for finding stone farmhouses to renovate. Sarthe is an area of small stone-built farmhouses. Habitable properties start from €60,000. One may also find something situated next to a river quite cheaply. Nantes, the regional capital, is one of the trendiest places to live in France, and is experiencing something of a housing shortage as a result, while Le Mans is a lot cheaper.

The traditional style of the Vendée is the low, whitewashed *pisé* or adobe farmhouse in the marshlands, and stone inland. The low, double-pitched roofs with their curled Spanish tiles testify to the dryness of the climate. The rainfall is as little as 24 inches per year. There has been a lot of new building on the coast to cater for Parisian holidaymakers, but this seems to have reached its limit as far as available land goes. Anyone who wants to get away from the usual boxy developments by the sea can find cheaper properties inland. Angela Bird, the author of the guidebook *The Vendée* has set up a useful website for visitors and prospective buyers: see www.the-vendee.co.uk. The main attraction of Vendée is the very mild climate, with sunshine on a par with the Riviera.

# Property
# TRENDS

The cheapest property in the region is to be found in the Mayenne, where the average home is nearly half of that in the Loire-Atlantique. This area and Sarthe represent good value for money in the region and are likely to become more popular in the next few years with overseas buyers, especially those on a limited budget. The Vendée and the Loire-Atlantique remain popular places to live for the French and prices are likely to rise in the coming years. An attractive area where one can still find some renovation projects is around Saumur in Maine-et-Loire.

| What you can get for your money | | | | |
| --- | --- | --- | --- | --- |
| **Price range (€)** | **Location** | **Type** | **Description** | **Price (€)** |
| Under 100,000 | La Roche sur Yon (85) | Studio, 42 sq m | New development, 10 minutes from station | 99,000 |
| 100,000 to 200,000 | St Jean du Bois (72) | Farmhouse | 2 bedrooms, cellar, attic, wells, 3,000 sq m land | 155,000 |
| 200,000 to 300,000 | Nantes (44) | New flat, 67 sq m | 2-bedroom flat, new development, close to shops | 250,000 |
| 300,000 to 500,000 | Nr Angers (49) | Country house | 6-bedroom restored Longère, 2 offices, 2 bathrooms, studio flat, 1,400 sq m garden | 350,000 |
| 500,000 and over | Property 1: Château Gontier (53) | Country house | 6 bedrooms, 12 rooms, separate cottage, 1 hectare parkland | 625,000 |
| | Property 2: Nr Chateau-du-Loir (72) | Château | 19th-century château divided into 8 flats, would make business, quiet town location, close to le Mans (see photo No. 7 in colour section) | 813,474 |

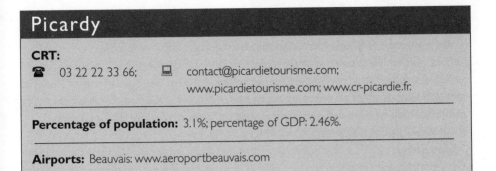

# Picardy

**CRT:**

☎ 03 22 22 33 66; 🖥 contact@picardietourisme.com;
www.picardietourisme.com; www.cr-picardie.fr.

**Percentage of population:** 3.1%; percentage of GDP: 2.46%.

**Airports:** Beauvais: www.aeroportbeauvais.com

The Picardy region has three *départements:* Somme (80), Oise (60) and Aisne (02). The name Somme naturally evokes the First World War, and the senseless waste of human life that occurred at the battles of the Somme starting from 1916, in which some 1,353,000 died in a vain attempt to win some land from the Germans and relieve the French defenders at Verdun. The area is dotted with memorials and cemeteries of the combatants, particularly around the town of Albert on the road to Cambrai. The main British, Irish and Canadian memorial is at Thiépval, along with the Ulster Monument. Around the bay of the Somme, the region has one of the best stretches of unspoilt sandy coastline in France, ideal for sand yachting. The coast drew the painters Seurat, Sisley and Dégas to try to capture its ever-changing light. The old holiday resort of Mers-les-Bains is noted for its *belle époque* (Edwardian) villas. The writer Marcel Proust enjoyed taking his holidays here.

The departmental capital, Amiens, will be familiar to anyone who travelled by train from the coast to Paris in the days before the Eurostar and cheap flights. Picardy is a land of gently rolling hills, criss-crossed by waterways and river, where the people are known for their love of flowers. Amiens has taken on the name of Venice of the North, thanks to the water gardens called Hortillonnages that can be explored in punts.

The Oise was the furthest south the Germans reached during the First World War. The prefectural town of Beauvais specialises in the manufacture of tapestry, but is otherwise fairly uninteresting. It is only a short distance from here to Paris, and a short drive to Charles de Gaulle Airport at Roissy-en-France. There are flights from Beauvais to London and Birmingham. The Oise has one of France's finest châteaux, Chantilly, whose origins go back to the 12th century; the town of the same name is known for its lace, and, of course, cream.

The Aisne was heavily fought over in the First World War; the front line stayed static here for most of the war. For anyone interested in cookery, Fresnoy-le-Grand, near St Quentin, should be a place of pilgrimage, as this is where cast-iron Le Creuset saucepans are manufactured. The Aisne has a short stretch of border with Belgium at the far north-east corner. Although Picardy was never under Flemish rule, certain traditions are similar, such as the popularity of archery, cards, skittles and other café games.

The region at one time had its own language, *picard,* one of the *langues d'oïl* (northern French dialects) that has fallen into oblivion. Its industrial and working-class traditions led Victor Hugo to use the area in some of his novels. Picardy generally prides itself on its literary traditions and holds some major literary festivals.

## Cuisine

Picardy is not one of France's outstanding gastronomic regions. Its main contribution is the fresh produce from its market gardens. Apart from the Maroilles cheese, there is smoked river eel, lamb from the salt-flats of the Somme, and waterfowl. In the south-eastern corner of the Aisne, there are champagne cellars, which are the source of 7% of France's output. There is also some cider production, and Colvert Beer, made at Péronne between Amiens and St Quentin.

## Property

The agricultural plain of Picardy has traditionally been short of stone for building; brick is the most widely used material. Earlier buildings have timber-frames and clay and lath *torchis*. The more recent style is similar to Flanders, with low, tiled roofs, and whitewashed brick. It is not always obvious what material has been used as everything tends to be covered with a thick layer of rendering. Farmhouses are narrow; the farm buildings are usually arranged in a square, sometimes without any windows on the street side.

The Somme is one of the less interesting regions for foreign property buyers. The climate is wet and the landscape flat, and heavily farmed. The after-effects of the coal-mining industry are still in evidence, with many slagheaps that are gradually being returned to nature. Away from the main roads to Paris, the Aisne and the Oise have a lot more scope; generally they are more hilly and green, with more space.

# Property TRENDS

Property in the Oise is considerably more expensive than the other *départements*; in 2006 the average price for a house was €193,500 compared with €114,900 in Aisne, and €120,600 in the Somme. Of the last two Aisne is probably the most likely to attract overseas buyers and prices are likely to remain reasonable. For just under €90,000 purchasers can find a two- or three-bedroom house in a rural or village location, ready for habitation. It is unlikely the property prices are going to increase sharply in this region.

## What you can get for your money

| Price range (€) | Location | Type | Description | Price (€) |
|---|---|---|---|---|
| Under 100,000 | Peronne (80) | Bungalow | 2 bedrooms, outbuildings, 2,000 sq m land, next to lake | 75,400 |
| 100,000 to 200,000 | Vauxaillon (02) | New-build | 1 bedroom, 2 reception rooms, 900 sq m garden | 145,979 |
| 200,000 to 300,000 | Pierrefonds (60) | Stone house | 2 bedrooms, attic, outbuilding, 900 sq m garden | 250,000 |
| 300,000 to 500,000 | Meru (60) | Chalet-style house | 7 bedrooms, garage, 912 sq m garden, country setting | 350,000 |
| 500,000 and over | Epaux-Bezu (02) | Château | 20 rooms, 1,376 sq m living area, 2.94 hectares, river | 577,500 |

## Poitou-Charentes

**CRT:**

☎ 05 49 50 10 50; 🖳 accueil-tourisme@interpc.fr; www.poitou-charentes-vacances.com.

**Percentage of population:** 2.73%; percentage of GDP: 2.11%.

**Airports:** Angouleme: www.angouleme.cci.fr/aeroport.asp
La Rochelle: www.larochelle.aeroport.fr
Poitiers: www.poitiers.cci.fr/aeroport/

As the name suggests this is really two regions in one, the coastal area of Charente-Maritime (and neighbouring Charente) and the inland Poitou. Poitiers, the capital, was the scene of a great English victory against the French in the Hundred Years' War in 1356. This was also the seat of the Dukes of Aquitaine. The virtual reality theme park, Futuroscope, about 8 km outside the city, has turned Poitiers into a popular tourist destination for families. The building of the TGV station means you can get here from London with only one change of train at Lille; it also means fast connections to Bordeaux and Toulouse as well as Paris.

The neighbouring small *département* of Deux-Sèvres (www.deux-sevres.com) is poor agricultural land with low rainfall, like the Vendée. It includes part of the national park of the Marais Poitevin, the largest expanse of wetland on the western side of France, popular for the wildlife including otters, kingfishers, herons, and other rare birds.

# Regional Voices – Deux-Sèvres

**Graeme and Graziella Swan** run gîtes in the Deux-Sèvres (www.lescygnes.net), offering the chance for holidaymakers to reduce their carbon footprint. Here they describe their experience of the area.

When we decided to move to France one of our main priorities was to live in the countryside or a small village – as after 17 years in London we were all 'cityed out'. The Deux-Sèvres is one of the most agricultural areas in the country – not unlike Norfolk – so it fitted the bill perfectly. The pace of life is a lot slower and in many ways is like stepping back 30 or 40 years. The department is one the nicest and least exploited areas in France, and is part of a weather system which makes it the second sunniest area in France, after the Med.

We actually found the area by booking a gîte for a week for a holiday before seriously house hunting much further south in the Charente Maritime, but soon we were drawn by the naïve charms of the area. We still looked south but found it overpriced and more touristy. Soon we were offered the chance to buy the house we now own and it fulfilled most of the criteria we had set ourselves. It had a main house separate from the barns which we wanted to convert into gîtes, was in very good condition, was on the edge of a pretty village – and was priced at less than a studio flat in London.

If anyone were to ask whether it has been worth it the answer is a resounding yes, but it has been difficult as well. The main pieces of advice I would give someone wanting to move here are; when house hunting don't get depressed when you can't find it immediately. The house you want is out there somewhere – it took us 3 months and hundreds of properties. Also, pay heed to people who have lived here for a while – they've probably been through the mill and come out the other side.

Charente-Maritime is a holiday region. The prefectural town, La Rochelle (www.ville-larochelle.fr), was once the main port for the trade with Canada and the West Indies; many colonists came from the Charente. Thanks to the policies of the local government, the town centre has remained largely unspoilt by uncontrolled building of holiday apartments that tends to blight much of the French coast. Holiday properties here have rocketed in price in recent years. La Rochelle is linked to France's second largest offshore island, the 20-mile long Ile de Ré, by a modern bridge; the type of building and the traffic on the island are strictly controlled; it is naturally very popular with tourists in summer. South of La Rochelle, opposite the old naval base of Rochefort, lies France's largest island after Corsica, the Ile d'Oléron, also linked to the mainland by a massive bridge.

The coast of the Charente-Maritime (www.poitou-charentes-vacances.com) benefits from one of France's sunniest climates, over 2,250 hours a year, on a par with Provence. Inland in Charente the climate is also quite sunny. The prefectural town of Angoulême was once the paper-making centre of France and Charente is also known for its indoor footwear – *une charentaise* is a carpet slipper. To the west, Cognac is the centre of the brandy industry; vast amounts are stored in *chais* – warehouses – that line the streets; they are sometimes put on the market for conversion. The grapes that go into making cognac can only be grown in the triangle between Royan, La Rochelle and Angoulême. This is one business that is rarely subject to recession and in 2007 business was booming. Charente is also home of the aperitif *pineau*.

## Property

Patterns of settlement in the past have depended on the presence or absence of water. In the marshlands of the north-west, houses were generally small and of wattle and daub, or mud, covered with bundles of rushes. The use of *pisé*, or adobe, meant that walls could not be built very high. This type of construction is more a historical relic, but the habit of using white rendering persists, and you will notice many low buildings. The rest of the region is rich in stone, and not much timber is used. In fact authorities in the Charente have been discouraging the building of modern log cabin-style homes, on the grounds that they do not blend in with the surroundings. This is generally a low-rainfall region; the water supply had to be drawn from very deep wells, so houses tended to cluster together close to the wells; village streets are narrow to try to diminish the effects of the strong winds.

Because of the shallowness of the soil, rocks were constantly dug up in the fields. Houses required only minimal foundations; the construction would be resting on rock in any case. The central swathe of the Poitou-Charentes consists of limestone and chalk, the rest of more ancient crystalline rock. In the roughest constructions the walls would be wider at the base and taper at the top. Since mortar does not adhere to limestone as well as to granite or schist, builders used cut stone quoins at the corners and inserted throughstones, and these can sometimes be seen protruding from the walls.

The Charente is already popular with foreign house buyers; the area bordering on the Dordogne is the most attractive: Aubeterre-sur-Dronne is particularly expensive. The area around Ruffec in the north is also very popular with foreign buyers, and home to an ever-increasing number of Britons and Irish. Charente-Maritime, is considerably more expensive than the rest of the region.

# Property
# TRENDS

The small *département* of Deux-Sèvres, inland from the Vendée, is likely to see more interest from British home-buyers in the next few years. The climate is dry, and there are still farmhouses for renovation available. Houses to renovate start from €45,000. This is an area of plentiful stone for building, mainly granite and gneiss. The improvements in communications make this a more easily accessible area than it was: there is a TGV as far as Poitiers, as well as flights from London. While the Vendée is becoming more and more popular with Parisians, Deux-Sèvres, which has no coast, remains cheap. There is the possibility of finding a house in the wetlands, next to water. The Charente-Maritime is likely to see prices continue to rise steadily as foreign buyers and Parisians compete with the natural tendency of the French to gravitate towards the coastline. To find cheaper property in the *département* you will need to search inland. In the Charente, the Charente-Limousine next to the Limousin still offers some cheaper property; you can still find renovation properties on a reasonable plot of land starting from just over €40,000. Plans for low-cost flights between Stansted Airport and Angoulême – scheduled for some time in 2008 – would be likely to increase property prices in the Charente.

## What you can get for your money

| Price range (€) | Location | Type | Description | Price (€) |
|---|---|---|---|---|
| Under 100,000 | Nr Chef Boutonne (79) | Village house | 7-room large house in need of total renovation. 1,762 sq m land | 59,950 |
| 100,000 to 200,000 | Nr Jarnac (16) | Modern bungalow | 3 bedrooms, garage, 1,510 sq m garden | 145,800 |
| 200,000 to 300,000 | Royan (17) | House | 3 bedrooms, veranda, garage, outbuildings, 800 sq m garden | 245,100 |
| 300,000 to 500,000 | Nr Montmorillon (86) | Longère | Restored house, 2 bedrooms, swimming pool, attic, 5,000 sq m land | 365,000 |
| 500,000 and over | Property 1: Nr Confolens (16) | Maison de maitre | 4 bedrooms, separate cottage, outbuildings, 3.5 hectares land crossed by small river | 530,000 |
| | Property 2: Nr Archiac (17) | Character house with *gîtes* | Immaculate 7-bedroom house, swimming pool with two *gîtes*, with their own swimming pool., quiet location (see photo No. 11 in colour section) | 837, 134 |

# Provence-Alpes-Côte D'Azur (PACA)

**CRT:**

☎ 04 91 13 89 00;   💻 information@crt-paca.fr; www.crt-paca.fr;
www.visitprovence.com.

**Percentage of population:** 7.51%; percentage of GDP: 6.62%.

**Airports:** Marseille: www.marseille.aeroport.fr
Nice: www.nice.aeroport.fr
Toulon: http://aeroport.var.cci.fr

The Provence-Alpes-Côte d'Azur region, or PACA as it is usually called, has everything that the second-home owner might want in terms of sunshine and natural beauty. There is a sharp contrast between the overdeveloped coastal region and inland Provence, an area of poor agricultural land and high unemployment. There has been a recent trend for high-tech companies to move to the south-east, creating a sort of Silicon Valley around Antibes, at Sophia-Antipolis. The success of Peter Mayle's books *A Year in Provence* and *Toujours Provence* in the 1980s set the trend for writing about one's experience of buying property in France, and probably led to foreign buyers being priced out of a lot of Provence. As one might expect from an advertising executive, Mayle used a lot of imagination in his writing. The French were grateful enough to give him a Légion d'Honneur. He has had to flee the Luberon to escape the tourists camping on his lawn.

The capital of the PACA region, Marseille (not Marseilles), is France's oldest city. After being founded by the Greeks in the 5th century BC the Romans took it over in 49 BC, when it was called Massilia. In the Middle Ages it was under the Counts or Kings of Provence; it finally became French in 1481. In the 19th century it took on more importance as the gateway to French North Africa. In recent years it has absorbed large numbers of immigrants. A sprawling, untidy city, it is regarded as not really part of France. It is certainly cosmopolitan, and a million miles removed from the expensive resorts of the Côte d'Azur. Counting its twin city, Aix-en-Provence, the population of 1.4 million makes it France's third city; it was once considered France's second city, but this honour now goes to Lyon. Marseille has recently undergone something of a renaissance and has started to shed its dirty, crime-ridden image. Development work in the city has started to push up prices fast, as has the high-speed rail link to Paris, which is now just three hours away. The surrounding area is one of the most industrialised in France. By some criteria, Aix-en-Provence is reckoned to be the best place to live in France.

The PACA attracts large numbers of outsiders from elsewhere in France, and from abroad. It is reckoned that the population will increase by 20% by 2020, because of high birth rates and immigration. The *départements* are: Vaucluse (84), Bouches-du-Rhône (13), Var (83), Alpes-de-Haute-Provence (04), Hautes-Alpes (05), and Alpes-Maritimes (06). The first four of these *départements* make up Provence; the region's capital was traditionally Aix-en-Provence, but this has been taken over by nearby Marseille. The Vaucluse represents one typical image of Provence: namely sunflowers and lavender fields, rich in Roman remains. The city of Orange has an amphitheatre that is still in use, and a Roman triumphal arch. Between 1559 and 1697 it was held by the Dutch Princes of Orange-Nassau.

The prefectural city of Avignon is more touristic, surrounded by its city walls, with the well-known bridge that stops halfway across the Rhône. Avignon was also the centre of Christendom for nearly a hundred years. In 1309 Pope Clement V came here at the invitation of the French King to escape unrest in Rome. The Papacy returned to Rome in 1378, but another pope was elected in Avignon, starting the Western Schism; the situation was resolved in 1403 when the last Avignon pope fled the town. The magnificent Palace of the Popes is one of France's great tourist draws. The tourists also draw crime; Avignon has the highest rate in France.

Bouches-du-Rhône (www.visitprovence.com) is named after the delta of the Rhône which spreads out into the Camargue region, wild-horse and cowboy country. The gateway to the Camargue, Arles, is a down-to-earth place that happens to have a Roman colosseum and amphitheatre in the middle of it. Being next to the Rhône it gets the full force of the *mistral*, a biting wind that blows down from the Alps for much of the year.

The Var (www.tourismevar.com), east of Marseille, can boast the celebrity playground of St Tropez, and the Roman town of Fréjus, amongst other things. Sailing and beaches are two major attractions here. This is one of the sunniest regions of the south, with over 2,500 hours of sunshine a year. This is also the stronghold of the neo-Fascist *Front National*.

# The French Riviera

Les Alpes Maritimes (www.guideriviera.com) includes the main part of the Côte d'Azur, or French Riviera, stretching from Cannes to Menton on the Italian border. The region east of the River Var belonged to the Kings of Sardinia, and was incorporated into France in 1793, but then returned to Savoie after Napoleon's defeat. It became part of France in 1860, as a gift from the Italian government to France for her support in their war against the Austrians. The French Riviera is naturally synonymous with high living; as far as property prices go, the coast is in a league of its own, on a par with Paris and the most exclusive ski resorts in the Alps. Between Nice and Menton, lies the semi-independent principality of Monaco, stuffed to the gills with millionaires.

From around 1850, the Riviera became popular with wealthy convalescents thanks to the year-round warm climate, and lack of extreme weather. As Biarritz and the Atlantic Coast declined, so the Riviera gained in status. Overall, the coastal part of the Riviera may not be that attractive to British property buyers. The area suffers from high crime levels; the rich and famous have to employ armies of security staff to feel safe here. Some high-profile murders in Monaco have scared many off. If you can do without the sight of the sea, an inland property has many advantages.

Behind the Alpes Maritimes lies the *département* of Alpes-Haute-Provence (www.alpes-haute-provence.com), traditionally the route for invaders between the sea and the mountains. The prefectural town of Digne-les-Bains lies at a comfortable 1,800 ft above sea level. In 1980 a private company reopened the Digne to Nice railway; the Train des Pignes passes through pine forests up to 3,000 ft.

The border with the next *département* – Hautes-Alpes (www.hautes-alpes.net) – once marked the frontier between Provence and Dauphiné. Following the invasion of Dauphiné in 1692, Louis XIV ordered his military architect Vauban to build massive fortresses in the Hautes

Alpes, at Briançon, Montdauphin and Fort Queyras. These no longer serve any military purpose, but are used for recreation and walking. The key to the French defensive system, Briançon, at 4,000 ft, is one of the highest cities in Europe; it is noted for its many frescoes and carved wooden doors, and some remarkable historic buildings. Hautes-Alpes is tourist country; ideal for water sports, walking, fishing, skiing, climbing and bird-watching.

# Cuisine

Provençal rosés are good to drink in hot weather; the region is equally noted for its red wines, and a few whites. Inland Vaucluse along the Rhône has several vintage wines. The town of Châteauneuf du Pape is one of the great names in wine. The Côtes-du-Rhône around Visan, Séguret, Cairanne and Sablet are home to dark and heady wines. The Luberon and Mont Ventoux also produce some fine AOC wines. If you prefer something sweeter there are the Muscat dessert wines from Beaumes de Venise and Rasteau. The everyday drink is *pastis,* an aniseed-flavoured spirit that is drunk mixed with water.

Provençal cooking is one of the healthiest in France: a lot of fresh vegetables, fish and olive oil. The best-known dish is *bouillabaisse,* a fish soup, served with a red pepper paste, *rouille.* The garlic-flavoured mayonnaise – *aioli* – is well known. On the coast *fruits de mer* – mixed seafood – is served in the better restaurants. The area around Nice has a more Italian type of cuisine, in particular ratatouille, small pizzas, ravioli, and a bitter salad called *mesclun.* The Camargue is the rice-growing region of France.

Local specialities of the Alpes de Haute Provence include *fumeton* (smoked leg of lamb), olives, truffles and herbs. There are some 200,000 sheep in the Haute Provence. The Hautes Alpes has some unusual dishes: *oreilles d'âne* (donkey's ears), which is actually wild spinach rolled in pastry and *tourton du champsaur* (potato or prune fritters). The Queyras area produces some classic cow's milk cheeses, such as Tomme d'Izoard, Bleu du Queyras and Gruyère Fontu.

# Property

Provence is an area of stone building; the only exception is in the high Alps. There are numerous limestone quarries; the yellowish tint of the limestone is one of the defining features of Provence. Before the use of cement, dry-stone construction with mortar covering was common in the countryside. In the back country one will see many *villages perchés:* villages built up or on top of a hillside in a defensive formation with a small castle. Houses are built facing south, if possible, sometimes without windows at the rear and sides, to combat the effects of the mistral. You can have sunshine almost every day of the year, but you need to be sure that the prevailing wind isn't blowing through your front window. You can use the mistral as a mitigating circumstance if you murder someone in Provence.

The *maison de maître* or wealthy farmer's house here is the *mas,* sometimes with one or more defensive towers at the corners. The asymmetrical style of architecture is actually a throwback to Roman ground plans. Houses on the plain are generally surrounded by trees; higher up they may be quite exposed to the elements. Roofing is of Spanish tiles in the countryside. An original solution to combatting the sudden storms was to fix two or more rows of half-tiles (*génoises*) into mortar along the edge of the roof. You will notice that the roofs never jut out; this is to stop a strong shadow falling over the walls, which would look unattractive.

# Regional Voices – the French Riviera

**Michael Frost** runs a luxury bed and breakfast near Miramas in the Bouches du Rhône, about 15 km from the Etang de Berre.

*I had been working in Burgundy and was looking for somewhere with more or less good weather all the year round. I deliberately looked in January to be sure. Not everyone realises that it can get quite cold in winter inland; e.g the Lubéron. It's always nice here. Where I am there are virtually no holiday homes owned by French people. It's not fashionable here. I spent 3 months looking, full-time. I had no preconceived ideas; I had just retired. I bought the place because it was in a nice location; but it is a modern building. It's halfway between Aix and Arles. I wanted to be reasonably close to an airport and the TGV so my children would come and visit. If you are up some country track then people are less keen to come and visit you. One great thing about the property is that it has air-conditioning; when I bought it I didn't care about this but now it is very convenient, particularly if you're cooking for people. I didn't plan to run a B&B; in the first place I had a lot of Bosnian refugees staying here. When they left, I realised that I liked having people around, and I didn't feel that I was ready to do nothing at all, so I started on B&B. The crucial thing is that you must like having people around you; you can't view them as intruders.*

*There was a problem with the land itself. The seller showed me the garden, which was fenced off, and I assumed that all of it belonged to him, but in fact a part of it did not belong to him. So I had to find out who actually owned it. I went to the Section des Domaines, part of the Ministry of Finance, and they went through a long process of finding out who owned that bit of land. They put up notices: 'Does this land belong to you?' and 'Has anyone paid taxes on this land recently?' As there were no claimants the land was forfeited to the state and they could then sell it to me. So I got it at 4 francs per square metre. But of course the state made money out of it for nothing. For this reason it's important to check that all the land you are shown is actually owned by the seller.*

The Riviera around Nice is expensive as it is not subject to the mistral wind that affects the Rhône delta. The architecture of Nice and the former county of Nice has more in common with Italy than France. The Alpes Maritimes hinterland has many second homes. The population in the upper valleys has fallen by more than half since 1900, leaving plenty of abandoned old houses for renovation.

# *Property* TRENDS

Though the Côte d'Azur has its problems – notably with crime – it remains very popular with wealthy foreigners, which means that prices stay high and in many cases continue to rise rapidly. The average house price in the Alpes-Maritimes in 2006 was €511,00, more than two and a half times the national average. The latest wave of wealthy foreigners are the Russians, and many predict that it will not be long before Chinese property buyers arrive in number for a slice of this distinctive part of France. Yet venture north in the same *département*, towards the Italian border and the mountains, and you will find village houses to renovate for around €100,000. Marseille has recently become a hotspot and has attracted many investment buyers and long term may still offer some of the best value for money in the region; but prices are rising fast. Inland there is a growing trend for new developments built around leisure facilities.

| What you can get for your money | | | | |
|---|---|---|---|---|
| Price range (€) | Location | Type | Description | Price (€) |
| Under 100,000 | Avignon (84) | Studio, 19 sq m | Lift, shared garden, close to station | 76,000 |
| 100,000 to 200,000 | Port d'Hyeres (83) | Flat | 1 bedroom, veranda, parking, view over marina | 180,000 |
| 200,000 to 300,000 | Grasse (06) | New bungalow | 2 bedrooms, terrace, gated estate with shared swimming pool and tennis court, lake views | 263,000 |
| 300,000 to 500,000 | Nr Banon (04) | Traditional villa | 4 bedrooms, 130 sq m living area, 1 hectare land | 353,000 |
| 500,000 and over | Property 1: Marseille (13) | Loft apartment | 2 bedrooms, in Vieux Port area, beautifully decorated, sold with furniture including €50,000 billiard table | 550,000 |
| | Property 2: Nr Fayence (83) | Modern villa | 3 bedrooms, immaculate condition, swimming pool, 40 minutes Nice airport (see photo No. 12 in colour section) | 707,274 |

## Rhône-Alpes

**CRT:**

☎ 04 26 84 74 74;    💻 crt@teleperformance.fr; www.crt-rhonealpes.fr; www.lyon.fr.

**Percentage of population:** 9.4%; percentage of GDP: 9.5%.

**Airports:** Geneva: www.gva.ch
Grenoble: www.grenoble.aeroport.fr
Lyon: www.lyon.aeroport.fr

The Rhône-Alpes region revolves around two main natural features: the River Rhône and the Alps. The capital, Lyon, is France's second largest city (pop. 1,600,000). Its main claim to fame is the high density of restaurants. Lyon suffers from its population growth, and parts of the city are not attractive, but the centre is still very impressive. Lyon does have excellent transport connections, the TGV runs through here on the way to Geneva, although very slowly beyond Lyon, and there are frequent flights to the UK from the Satolas airport to the east of the city. By 2018 Lyon will have a full TGV service to Turin via a 35-mile tunnel under the Alps.

Rhône-Alpes is a very varied region, stretching from the Massif Central in the west to the Italian border in the east, and down to Provence in the south. The Rhône is not so much an artery of commerce as a place to dump industrial effluent, and also serves to cool the nuclear reactors along its banks. Because of the concentration of chemical and other industry around the Rhône pollution is a factor here.

The region encompasses eight *départements:* Rhône (69), Loire (42), Ardèche (07), Drôme (26), Savoie (73), Haute-Savoie (74), Isère (38), and Ain (01). North of Lyon, in the Rhône, starting from Villefranche-sur-Saône, one enters Beaujolais country, named after the small town of Beaujeu. Properties in the wine region are hard to come by; the most active market is around Lyon itself. The Rhône (www.rhonetourisme.com) is the smallest *département* in France after Paris; it is basically rural, and quite hilly.

The *département* of the Loire (www.loire.fr) stands on the eastern edge of the Massif Central. The prefectural town of St Étienne has an airport with daily flights to London. The Loire does not stand out as a touristic region; it is more an extension of the wine-growing country of Beaujolais.

Ardèche (www.ardeche-guide.com) can be divided into two halves, the north and east with good transport connections to the outside world, and the rather remote western half. The northern end is a mere 50 km from St Étienne airport and Lyon. The town of Annonay was the birthplace of the Montgolfier brothers, and holds an annual hot-air balloon festival. The eastern boundary of the Ardèche is formed by the Rhône; the prefectural town of Privas is a short distance from the river. The Gorges de l'Ardèche is one of France's main scenic sites; central Ardèche has been designated a national park, the Parc Naturel Régional des Monts d'Ardèche. The TGV from Lyon to Marseille runs on the other side of the Rhône.

# Cuisine

The Valley of the Rhône is one of the premier vine-growing regions of France. North of Villefranche-sur-Saône, still in the Rhône *département*, lies the heart of the Beaujolais, centering around the village of Fleurie. South of Lyon, there is the Côte Rotie, a premier *appellation*. The quality of Ardèche wines is variable; the reds in the north-east are generally made from Syrah grapes, which require favourable conditions to ripen well.

In the Rhône, Lyon takes pride of place for its restaurants. The style of cooking favours cream and eggs in abundance, and is naturally based on all kinds of meat. Specialities are *quenelles* (meat or fish dumplings), cooked salads, and very rich cakes and desserts. Lyon is known for its pork *charcuterie,* and use of offal, such as tripe and calf's or sheep's feet.

The Ain has one particular claim to fame, the chickens from the Bresse region around Bourg-en-Bresse. The birds are especially patriotic, as they have blue legs, white feathers and red crests. The area of Bugey near the Rhône was the homeland of Brillat-Savarin, the great authority on cookery. It is noted for an onion and walnut tart, drunk with local wine, Le Manicle.

The Ardèche exports a lot of honey, especially from the southerly Vivarais region. It is also well known for its candied chestnuts. In the Drôme one can find Picodon goat cheese from the pre-Alps, alpine lamb, walnut liqueur, and raviolis from Royans.

# Property

The Rhône Valley is a vast region with a great variety in prices and types of property. In the Forez mountains of the Loire *département,* the architecture is similar to that in the Massif Central or Auvergne, using a bluish granite and slate roofs, thick walls and small windows.

The Lyonnais on the plain has, in the past, generally favoured the *pisé* method of construction: raw clay or concrete is pressed between wooden boards to make walls at least 2 ft thick. The walls are supported on stone or brick otherwise the rain would wash them away. More recent construction resembles what you would find in the Paris region.

The Ardèche tends to attract interest from foreign buyers who are looking for a permanent move to France rather than a holiday home, and there is a well-established British community. There are fewer cheap properties available now for renovation. Many properties are handled by estate agents in Montélimar, which is on the other side of the Rhône in the Drôme.

# Property
# TRENDS

The diversity of the region means that property trends tend to follow more local factors rather than a general pattern. As befits a large city Lyon has its own distinct market and prices should remain strong in the coming years. The Ardèche has become very popular with oveeseas buyers and bargains are harder to find; nonetheless you can still find habitable homes in rural areas from €90,000. The best value for money is in Loire, where the average house price was under €150,000 in 2006. However it is hard to see this area, sandwiched between the Massif and Central and the Rhône, becoming a property hotspot in the coming years.

| What you can get for your money | | | | |
|---|---|---|---|---|
| **Price range (€)** | **Location** | **Type** | **Description** | **Price (€)** |
| Under 100,000 | Nr St Bonnet le Château (42) | Village house | Stone built, 3 bedrooms, 90 sq m living area | 79,000 |
| 100,000 to 200,000 | Nr Privas (07) | House | 3 bedrooms, garage, large kitchen | 146,000 |
| 200,000 to 300,000 | Nr Lagnieu (01) | Traditional house | 3 bedrooms, mezzanine, garage, 922 sq m land | 245,000 |
| 300,000 to 500,000 | Property 1: Lyon (69) | Flat | 3-bedroom garden flat with 30 sq m garden, cellar | 350,000 |
| | Property 2: Nr Allex (26) | Stone cottage | 3 bedrooms, rural area, easy reach to motorway, swimming pool (see photo No. 8 in colour section) | 471,834 |
| 500,000 and over | Alba la Romaine (07) | Stone house | 5 bedrooms, vaulted cellars, outbuildings, 1,407 sq m garden | 550,000 |

# Savoie and Dauphiné

**CRT:**

☎ 04 76 42 41 41;    🖳 welcome@grenoble-isere.info; www.grenoble-isere.info.

---

**Population, GDP:** *See* Rhône-Alpes.

---

**Airports:** Chambéry: www.chambery.aeroport.fr
Geneva: www.gva.ch

Although officially part of the Rhône-Alpes region, Savoie and Dauphiné are quite different in character from the Rhône Valley, and so are treated separately here. Dauphiné was semi-independent until 1486, when the ruler had to sell it to the French to pay off his debts. It then became the personal property of the *dauphin* – the heir-apparent of France – and thus got its name. Dauphiné comprises the *départements* of the Drôme (26) and Isère (38). The Drôme (www.drometourisme.com) is a deserted and scenic region; south of the prefectural capital, Valence, you have a feeling of being in the Midi, the south of France. This is an area of vineyards and orchards, and olive trees. Côtes-de-Rhône wine comes from here. Straddling the Drôme and the *département* of the Isère is the dramatic Vercors plateau, a centre for the Resistance in the Second World War and the scene of a massacre by the Germans just after D-Day, that has been made a national park. The Isère stretches from the Rhône to the Alps, with the prefectural city, Grenoble in the middle. Grenoble is considered as one of the best places to live in France. A survey of managers by *Express* magazines rated it ninth in terms of economic dynamism and quality of life. The downside is pollution.

Stretching north-eastwards from Grenoble to Chambéry in Savoie lies the national park of the Chartreuse Massif, named after the Carthusians who started their order in the 12th century as a protest against the Cistercians' lax ways. Seventeen of their monasteries still exist; many were devastated in the French Revolution. Ironically, the name Chartreuse these days mainly conjures up the image of the lethal colourful liqueur made by the monks.

Savoie takes in two-thirds of the French section of the Alps – the Alpes du Nord – including Europe's highest peak, Mont Blanc (15,719 ft) on the Italian border. Savoie was first a county, then a duchy and finally a kingdom, with its capital in Turin. In the 18th century the Kingdom of Savoie was linked with Sardinia under one crown. The final union of Savoie with France only occurred in 1860 after a referendum of the inhabitants. Chambéry, the gateway to the ski fields and prefectural town, was capital of Savoie for 200 years until 1583. Chambéry is on the TGV line to Paris and Lille and is also served by direct flights from several British cities. The ski scene has expanded since the 1992 Winter Olympics were held in the depressingly modern tourist town of Albertville. Tignes, on the Italian border, at about 13,200 ft, is the only place in France that can boast all-year-round skiing, if the weather is right.

The most spectacular scenery is closer to the Italian and Swiss border in Haute Savoie; the mountainous *massifs* attract the climbers, but virtually every part of the Haute Savoie is exceptionally scenic. The departmental capital, Annecy, is an upmarket tourist destination. The star attraction, however, must be the old resort town of Mégève, stunningly located under the Alps. At the northern edge of Haute Savoie lies Lac Léman, known to the Swiss as Lake Geneva. The beauty of Savoie and the wildness of the weather in the mountain passes were an irresistible attraction to the English pre-Impressionist Joseph Turner, who came here again and again for inspiration.

# Cuisine

The Drôme, with the Rhône as its western border has some renowned wines on the *côtes* above Valence; most notably the Hermitage, and Crozes-Hermitages *appellations* (both reds and whites). There are also the appellations Côtes-du-Rhône Régionales and Villages, and the sparkling Crémant de Die. Virtually all the wines from the region are first class. Montélimar, south of Valence, is synonymous with nougat. For the French, Dauphiné evokes *gratin Dauphinois,* a simple dish of thinly sliced potatoes with a browned covering of cream cheese and butter. The Isère is known for *noix de Grenoble* – walnuts – which are used in *gateau au noix* and other desserts. The local cheese, St Marcellin, is made into *marcelline,* slices of cheese with streaky bacon.

Perhaps reflecting its harsher environment, Savoie comes out less well gastronomically, as it has only given its name to a kind of cabbage in English. Savoyard cooking favours simple heavy fare, made from potatoes, bacon and cheese, rather like the Swiss; the term *à la savoyarde* means with a gruyère sauce. Savoie produces both white and red wines, as well as mineral waters like Evian.

# Property

In Savoie one will see Swiss-style chalets, with richly carved balconies and steep roofs. At high altitudes houses were traditionally built around a massive wooden framework, with the ground level of stone. Traditionally the stables were next to the living quarters, with a hay loft on the first floor, providing natural insulation. It was also common to use pine shingles: about five or six layers are nailed to the roof – sometimes weighted down with rocks – to provide a weatherproof surface. Shingles or wooden panels may also be nailed to the walls, to increase heat rentention. At lower altitudes more German-style constructions are popular, with hipped roofs (*croupes*). Generally houses have a tidier appearance than in the more French areas. Whitewashing, decorative shutters and colourful windowboxes all give a rather alpine feel to the area.

Skiing resorts such as Chamonix and Morzine have become very popular with British buyers, who see that these are attractive places to live and also run a business all the year round. The resulting inflation in property prices is alarming to the French locals, as well as tour operators, who see their customers no longer needing to rent property in ski resorts. Some of the most expensive properties in France are large ski chalets which can provide a high rental income, which will set you back over £350,000. Much of the ski accommodation is in unattractive concrete apartment blocks; they are a good investment but the initial purchase costs are steep.

# *Property* TRENDS

Property prices already vary greatly across this area. In the Drôme, for example, the average house price in 2006 was just above the national average at €188,000. And around the remote area of Die, the average was even lower at €162,900. In remoter areas of the *département* it's still possible to find renovation projects from around €65,000. Prices are unlikely to rise rapidly either here or in the Isère. If you are on a limited budget but want to be reasonably close to both the Alps and the Mediterranean then these two departments may well worth be considering over the next couple of years. The market in Savoie and Haute Savoie is of course a distinct one and dominated by skiing and, increasingly, the Alpine summer holiday industry. Prices have risen dramatically in recent years to the point where property in exlusive resorts such as Val d'Isère and Tignes can cost more than in Paris. That sharp rise has slowed down and there has been a trend for foreign buyers in particular to look for property slightly further away from the slopes – to which they then drive when they want to go skiing. This trend is likely to continue. One note of caution. No one can be certain what long term impact, if any, global warming will have on snowfall, temperatures and of course the skiing industry. The Alps have been through poor seasons of low snowfall before and recovered. It is however a good idea for long-term investors to take into account the potential impact of climate change when buying property in an area still dominated by winter sports.

## What you can get for your money

| Price range (€) | Location | Type | Description | Price (€) |
|---|---|---|---|---|
| Under 100,000 | St Pierre d'Entremont | Barn | To renovate, 80 sq m area, village location | 75,000 |
| 100,000 to 200,000 | Châteauneuf du Rhone (26) | New-build | 4 bedrooms, garage, 920 sq m plot | 175,000 |
| 200,000 to 300,000 | Grenoble (38) | Flat | 3 bedrooms, lift, balcony, parking place, close to shops | 260,000 |
| 300,000 to 500,000 | Property 1: Nr Chambery (73) | Modern house | 3 bedrooms, terrace, large basement area, 1,500 sq m land | 362,000 |
| | Property 2: Le Nevada development, Tignes (73) | Modern flats, 55 sq m | 2-bedroom flats in modern development, parking space, ski locker, shared swimming pool and sauna (see photo No. 3 in colour section) | from 372,000 (exclusive of VAT) |
| 500,000 and over | Chamonix (74) | Modern flat | 2 bedrooms, living room with chimney, cellar, 75 sq m living space, views of Mont Blanc | 556,000 |

# My House in France
## Richard and Christina Coman

Richard and Christina Coman owned a property in the Vendée from 1982 to 2000 at St Étienne-du-Bois – a village south of Nantes – which they sold to a relative. They have now bought another property in the Deux-Sèvres.

**How did you go about buying your first property in France?**
We were over in the Vendée in August and we signed a *compromis de vente*; it took another 4 months for the final exchange of contracts. The property was a granite farmhouse with a barn, an oven house, a piggery and a hectare of land (10,000 sq m). The day we moved in I asked what we were going to do about the broken-down barn next to our house, until someone pointed out that it was my property as well. In the meantime the notary had to get the signature of everyone in the village that they had no right of way; there were terrible problems getting one 80-year-old lady to sign.

**Any problems?**
The farmer who was retiring kept the surrounding land for hay and maize. We were offered another 10 hectares adjoining at the very cheap price of £3,000, but we foolishly didn't take it. If we had taken it the farmer's two sons would have inherited the tenancy. The next year a much younger farmer who was only interested in raising beef cattle rented it. In the beginning we were on good terms and regularly bought wine from him. But then his cattle roamed over our land so we had to put up a *clôture* around our hectare at great expense. On top of that he put two huge mounds of silage covered with plastic on the land, so we got the smell; our notary told him to move it but he refused point-blank. Then he insisted on driving his tractor between our house and barn leaving huge ruts in the earth, and then drove into our boundary fence. He was generally disliked in the village and never spoke to us again.

**Did you have a swimming pool?**
There was quite an amusing situation with the swimming pool. After a lot of phoning around in London we got a plastic swimming pool with a metal frame from Harrods. It was so heavy we could barely get it over to France in my car. When we unpacked it we

was so heavy we could barely get it over to France in my car. When we unpacked it we saw the label: Made in Nantes – just up the road. The pool was fine but the next time we got one locally.

## Any other advice?

It isn't necessarily a good idea to have too much land attached to your property, otherwise you may find yourself spending your holidays cutting back grass and brambles. There is not much point bringing over British-made showers and piping: you won't be able to fix them later if they're in imperial measurements. For us, having this property was marvellous because we have nine sons and we had 18 years of free holidays. But you do need to accept that there are always going to be some difficulties when you buy a property in France: it's just part of the deal.

1. €698,384 – 5 bedroom manor house in the Dordogne with tower, vaulted cellar, barn and a cottage (to renovate)

2. €279,034 – 17th-century stone house with exposed beams situated on the edge of a village near Questembert, Brittany

3. From €372,000 – 2 bedroom 55 sq m flats in modern development in Savoie. Comes with ski locker, shared pool and sauna

4. €85,000 – Windmill for conversion in Arles, between Avignon and the coast

5. €495,000 – Town house near Perpignan, Pyrénées-Orientales

6. €70,965 – 25.5 sq m studio flat in smart new development Issoire, Auvergne

7. €813,474 – 19th-century chateau in the Loire Valley, close to Le Mans. Divided into 8 flats

8. €471,834 – 3 bedroom stone cottage with pool in a rural area of Rhone-Alpes within easy reach of the motorway

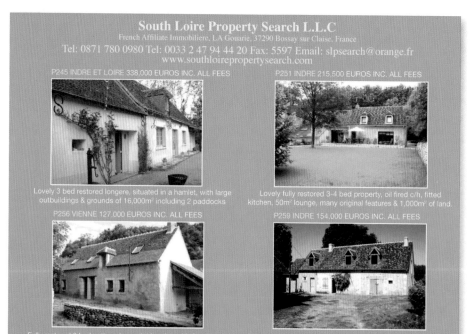

9. €397,113 – Manor house with turret, in need of renovation near to Limoges

10. €410,000 – Normandy town house with 2 bedrooms and original features

11. €837,134 – Immaculate 7 bedroom house with pool and 2 gîtes (each with their own pool) in a quiet location near Archiac, Charente-Maritime

12. €707,274 – Immaculate modern villa with 3 bedrooms and pool, 40 minutes from Nice airport

13. €251,214 – 6 bedroom cottage near Hesdin, Pas-de-Calais, with 3,300 sq m of land. Heated pool, garage and workshop

14. €577,600 – Imposing 4 bedroom Béarnaise house near Orthez, Pyrénées Atlantiques. With original features and 1 hectare of land

15. €109,000 – Converted barn in the Auvergne region with 3 bedrooms and stunning views of the Puy de Dome

# PART THREE
## Before You Buy

# 6 Financial Considerations

## Importing Currency

WHEN BUYING PROPERTY IN FRANCE, you will, under normal circumstances, have to pay in euros, the local currency. In the days of foreign exchange controls, before 1974, it was usual to take a suitcase full of pound notes over to France to pay for your property. Thanks to the Single Market, you can take as much cash as you like with you, but there is no advantage in doing so, and it is certainly risky. If you take more than €8,000 in cash with you into France you are required to declare it. Taking a large amount of cash is not only risky; you could be suspected of being a drugs dealer or terrorist by the French customs if they find out.

The French have been slow to take up the IBAN system, which is gradually becoming compulsory all over the EU.

Since the UK is not part of Euroland, anyone buying property abroad is confronted with the painful possibility that a percentage of their money is going to disappear into the pockets of a high-street bank. Fortunately, this need not be the case, since a number of specialist foreign exchange companies have now started to lessen the pain of the transaction.

A specialist company such as Currencies Direct (☎020 7813 0332; www.currenciesdirect.com), Moneycorp (☎020 7589 3000; www.moneycorp.com) or HiFX (☎01753 751 751; www.hifx.co.uk) can help in a number of ways, by offering better exchange rates than banks, without charging commission, and giving you the possibility of 'forward buying' – agreeing on the rate that you will pay at a fixed date in the future – or with a limit order – waiting until the rate you want is reached.

### Insider Tip

Currency is nowadays normally sent using electronic transfer; the SWIFT system is the best known. There are charges involved at both ends so you need to know who is paying for them, and how much the receiving bank in France is likely to charge. The receiving bank should charge very little. The use of banker's drafts is not recommended as they are far too slow, and there is the risk of losing the draft. If you are transferring to a French bank, it is useful to know the IBAN (International Banking Number).

*'since the UK is not part of Euroland, anyone buying property abroad is confronted with the painful possibility that a percentage of their money is going to disappear into the pockets of a high-street bank'*

For those who prefer to know exactly how much money they have available for their property purchase, forward buying is the best solution, since you no longer have to worry about the movement of the pound against the euro working to your detriment. Payments can be made in one lump sum or on a regular basis. It is usual when building new property to pay in instalments.

There is a further possibility, which is to use the services of a law firm in the UK to transfer the money. They can hold the money for you until the exact time that you need it; they will use the services of a currency dealer themselves.

# Offshore Accounts

While the idea of offshore banking sounds attractive, you need to be clear about what you hope to gain from it. Changes in EU law mean that lists of bank accounts held by EU citizens in other countries are exchanged with the home country authorities, under the 'exchange of information' rules. It is no longer feasible to open an account in another EU country and collect the interest without declaring it to the UK taxman. In the case of tax havens such as the Isle of Man, Jersey and Guernsey, you are given the choice between information on the interest you have been paid being sent to the UK tax authorities, or agreeing to a 15% withholding tax. If you pay tax on this income in France you will be better off going for the first option, so you are not taxed twice. Switzerland and Luxembourg are also falling into line with the EU's demands for greater openness. An offshore account in the EU can still pay more interest and may be convenient if you live abroad, but it is not a way to avoid taxes. You could try more exotic locations such as the British Virgin Islands or Belize, but eventually even these countries will not be safe hiding places.

Bank accounts in Monaco are completely transparent as far as the French taxman goes. The French authorities can look at your accounts at any time. Even if you live in Monaco you may be treated as a French resident, so you will need some expert advice if you choose to become a tax exile there.

# Banking

Sooner or later you will need to open a bank account in France. It is best to wait until you know where you are going to live before you open one. It may happen that an estate agent advises you to open an account when you are looking for property in a certain area, merely because he gets a commission from the bank for introducing new customers. Opening an account prematurely can influence your judgement if you are looking for property. Crédit Agricole Calvados has set up a service for non-residents who want to open an account without going in person called Britline.

As far as changing cash in France goes, you generally pay commission and the rate of exchange is very variable. The worst rates on offer are at railway stations. *Bureaux de change* in areas with large numbers of tourists do not necessarily offer bad rates. In Paris some of the best rates can be found around St Michel.

If you are staying in one of the major cities you may be able to open an account with a branch of a British bank. Barclays is the best represented. Lloyds has

## Insider Tip

While you are still looking for property, you can withdraw money with a cashpoint card with the Visa or Cirrus symbol, or you can use a credit card. There is a charge for using your card to withdraw money abroad, and you may not get the best possible rate of exchange. You need to know your PIN code otherwise you may not be able to use your card.

branches in Paris, Lyon, Cannes and Marseille; HSBC owns CCF. NatWest has no branches in France. British banks in France have to operate under French law; they mainly target wealthy expats with a lot of money to invest. Unless you have special requirements, you are probably better off having an account with a French bank. Prospective house buyers in France often take out mortgages with UK banks in France. Abbey National, which has its main office in Lille, is particularly active.

The best tip for exchanging money on a long-term basis is to come to an agreement with a UK resident with an account in France, whereby you pay equal sums into each other's bank accounts at the median exchange rate, thus completely avoiding the *agio*, the difference between selling and buying foreign currency.

# Money Transfers

There will be situations where you need to send money to someone in France or vice versa. A transfer of money to or from France is a *transfert* in French, rather than a *virement*, a transfer within France. Telegraphic Transfer, via Western Union or American Express is the most expensive way, but may be unavoidable if you want to send money to the USA. The most usual system between banks is SWIFT, which takes a day or two, and costs from €25 upwards. A more cost-effective method is to open a post office account in France and a Girobank account in the UK. Transfers between post offices take three to 10 days, and there is only a fixed charge to pay however much money you transfer. The least effective way of transferring money is to send a cheque drawn on a foreign bank account; it could take a month to clear and the charges will be very high. If the amount is small it would be simpler to send cash with an International Registered Letter.

There is another possibility for making payments to French companies, which is to use a postal order, or *mandat cash*, obtainable in a post office. You pay a small charge in addition to the actual amount. The *mandat* is made out to a specific beneficiary; if for some reason you don't use the *mandat* or the beneficiary doesn't cash it, you will receive a notification from the post office so you can get a refund. If you lose the receipt then you have to go back to the post office where you originally bought the *mandat,* otherwise it is refundable at any post office in France.

To transfer large sums, i.e. for your house purchase, the best method is to use a specialised company, such as Currencies Direct.

# Credit Cards

Strictly speaking, there is no such thing as a credit card in France, rather there are charge cards with a deferred debit. Every 30 days the amount you owe is automatically debited from your bank account, meaning that you may pay for something the day after you bought it. In the UK the credit is for 30–60 days, in France for 0–30 days. In France if you want to defer payment you will need to open a sub-account, which allows you to borrow money at a lower interest rate than you would pay in the UK on a credit card. There is an annual charge for credit cards in France. A Gold Card costs about €90 a year.

The national French debit card, the *Carte Bleue* (CB) can only be used in France. If you need a credit card that functions abroad, you can ask for *Carte Bleue/Visa* or *Mastercard.* Visa is the most widely accepted card in France; although there are others of course. The credit card company and the bank are separate organisations. You are expected to clear your bill at the end of each month, unless you have arranged to borrow money.

It is sensible to go on using your UK credit card. This has become more convenient as it is now possible to make your payments via the internet. HSBC Bank has the most sophisticated internet services of the main UK high-street banks.

# Bank Accounts

Opening a bank account is not difficult. You don't even need to be a resident. If you are resident in France then you simply take along your passport, *carte de séjour* (if you have one) and proof of your fiscal address in France. The basic form of bank account is the *compte de chèque* which comes with a cheque book.

When you open a bank account you will be offered a CB originally conceived as a substitute for writing cheques. The CB is a cashpoint card which can also function as either a debit card or credit card; you choose one of the two. CB also stands for *carte bancaire,* i.e. any kind of credit card. CBs work with a chip rather than magnetic strip; you key in your PIN number when making transactions in shops, so you need to remember it.

The longer you delay reporting your card lost or stolen the greater the difficulties you will have in regaining the stolen money. Bank employees are not permitted to ask your PIN code. If you lose your cheque book call 08 36 68 32 08.

# Resident and non-resident accounts

Whether you are considered resident or non-resident, from the bank's point of view, depends on where you are fiscally resident, i.e. where your centre of interests lies. If you spend more than 183 days a year in France you will normally pay your taxes there, so you are fiscally resident. As a non-resident you can only open a *compte non-résident*. Correspondence will be sent to you in your home country. It is also possible to open an account by post through a French bank branch in the UK (mainly in London). After choosing your branch in France, you need to supply a reference from your UK bank, a legalised copy of your signature, photocopies of the main pages of your passport, and a draft in euros to start you off. If the bank has doubts about your creditworthiness, they may require proof that you have never been barred from holding a bank account in France (*non-interdit bancaire*). The main advantage is that you will have everything explained to you in English at the beginning, but there is no guarantee that anyone will speak English in the

## Insider Tip

As well as the bank's own number, there is one central number for reporting lost bank cards – 08 36 69 08 80 – the Centre d'Oppositions. Your bank's website may also enable you to enter an opposition by email. In any case it is advisable to note the number of the Centre d'Oppositions for your bank; entering an opposition to stop your card being used takes priority over contacting the police. Your Carte Bleue should come with insurance against unauthorised payments.

branch you have chosen. It is far simpler to open an account in person in France after talking to the local bank staff. For Americans it may be useful to open an account through the Banque Transatlantique which has an office in Washington DC: see www.transat.tm.fr.

# Banking practices

Banking services are not as sophisticated or as liberal in France as in the UK or USA; the banks are not at all keen to lend money in a hurry. The main rule to remember is that you must never go into the red without prior arrangement, otherwise you risk becoming an *interdit bancaire*. It is also worth bearing in mind that if you go into the red any standing orders that you have will automatically be stopped, so your telephone and electricity could suddenly be cut off. You need to anticipate standing orders so they do not make you go overdrawn.

When you open your account you opt for monthly or fortnightly bank statements, or whatever arrangement suits you. There are charges for most transactions, apart from statements. You can authorise utilities companies to debit your account automatically (*prélèvement automatique*) for bill payment, but this is not obligatory. This is not the same as a standing order (*ordre permanent/ virement automatique*) although it might sound the same. If you have the internet, you can see what is going on with your account; the antiquated French version of the internet, Minitel, is still used for some online banking services.

As far as statements go, watch out for underhand attempts to get you to borrow money: sometimes you may see a message such as 'You have €15,000 to buy a car', when in fact all it means is that the bank hopes you will borrow the money to buy a car.

With your cashpoint card you can withdraw up to €300 per week from any cashpoint. You can always take out more by going in person to your bank. If you want to take out money above the limit from any cashpoint, you need to ask for a 'gold card' for which there is a charge. It is best to carry some cash in France, in case the cashpoint machine swallows your card and refuses to give it back; the simple solution is to carry two or three cards. There are card-operated filling stations and hi-tech hotels where you can only pay by card. Credit card theft and fraud are widespread in Paris and on the Côte d'Azur, where the mafia are very active.

Bank opening hours are a favourite gripe with foreigners in France; there is a law that prevents banks opening more than five days a week, so your bank may close on Mondays. Very small branches (*permanences*) in country areas may only open one morning a week. The internet is making things easier.

# Cheques

Cheques are more widely used in France than in the UK, and there are no cheque guarantee cards, but you can be asked for other identification. Cheques are written out in a similar way to those in the UK, but with the information positioned differently. Your bank will send you your first cheque book once there are funds in your account. The cheque book has to be returned to the bank if they demand it. French cheques are not negotiable to a third person. The basic form of cheque is the *cheque barré*, which only the payee (*destinataire*) can cash; the bank has to inform the tax inspectors if you want to use open cheques.

## Insider Tip

Tips for handling your french bank account.

- Practise writing cheques in French.
- Use the french crossed '7'. The french '1' looks like an English '7'.
- Carry your cheque book separately from any ID.
- Never, ever go overdrawn unless you have an agreement.
- Keep a close eye on your standing orders.
- Remember that cheques take a long time to clear in france, up to 10 days, and plan accordingly.

## Bouncing Cheques

If you write a 'wooden cheque' (*chèque de bois*) you will be given 30 days to rectify the situation. The Banque de France is informed immediately, and you are not allowed to write any further cheques until matters are resolved. You not only have to pay money into the account to cover it, but also a fine of 15% of the amount, which goes to the French treasury. There is also a form to fill in, declaring that you have dealt with the problem or 'incident'. If the money is not paid you are put on a Banque de France blacklist, and you are barred from writing cheques in France for five years. Bank cards and cheques have to be surrendered to the bank. Any attempt to write a cheque within the five years will be reported to the police.

A cheque is considered the equivalent of cash and cannot be cancelled, unless it has been lost or stolen or is deemed fraudulent by the bank. A police report has to be submitted to the bank in both cases.

# French banks

There are several types of bank in France: clearing banks such as Crédit Lyonnais; cooperative banks such as Crédit Agricole; corporate banks, e.g. BNP Paribas, and savings banks or Caisses d'Epargne. The Crédit Lyonnais went spectacularly bust recently and had to be bailed out by the French state; the clearing banks have all been privatised. The Crédit Agricole has an immense advantage in that it has the largest number of branches, 7,500 in France alone. The departmental branches of Crédit Agricole function as separate banks and issue their own shares. Other cooperative banks include the Crédit Mutuel and Banque Populaire; if you want to take out a mortgage with a cooperative bank you are usually required to buy shares in the bank, but not if you just want a cheque account. The post office, La Poste, has 17,000 branches in France and longer opening hours than banks, so it could be convenient to have a post office account, or Compte Courant Postal (CCP). The number of your post office account is a RIP rather than RIB; the number of an account with a Caisse d'Epargne is a RICE.

The French bank you choose will depend a lot on whether there is a branch near you, and whether you need specialised services. It is worth finding out if there is anyone who speaks English in your branch; where there are large concentrations of English-speakers some banks are trying to recruit English-speaking staff. In a number of areas French banks have become very aware of the presence of English-speaking customers and even in some rural branches it's possible to find staff who speak English. In 2007, for example, Crédit Agricole Charente-Périgord revealed that 10% of its customers were British.

The Calvados region of Crédit Agricole has now started a service called Britline (with offices in Caen, Normandy), which allows you to open a bank account in France by post (☎02 31 55 67 89; email britline@ca-calvados.fr; www.britline.com). Britline has stalls at French property fairs. Banque Populaire in Nice has started an English-speaking service that is very popular (see www.cotedazur.banquepopulaire.fr).

## Major French banks

Barclays Bank SA: www.barclays.fr
Banque Populaire: www.banquepopulaire.fr
BNP Paribas: www.bnpparibas.net
Britline: www.britline.com
Caixa Bank: www.caixabank.fr
Crédit Agricole: www.credit-agricole.fr; www.ca-[name of department].fr
CCF: www.ccf.com
Crédit du Nord: www.credit-du-nord.fr
Crédit Lyonnais: www.creditlyonnais.com
Lloyds Bank SA: www.lloydstsbiwm.com
Société Générale: www.socgen.com

# French Mortgages

French mortgages – *hypothèques* – work in a rather different way from those in the UK, even if they appear similar at first sight. Fixed rate mortgages are by far the most common; it is also possible to mix fixed and variable rates, or to adjust the number of years you need to pay off your mortgage. The variable rate mortgage is the most flexible. Lump sums can be paid off and the mortgage redeemed early without any financial penalties. You can also move to a fixed rate without any charge. There can be hefty financial penalties for early redemption of a fixed rate mortgage.

## Capital and interest repayment mortgage (variable rate)

This is probably the most flexible of mortgage products. You know what your repayments will be. The interest rate applicable to your loan is revised on a regular basis. Should interest rates fluctuate, your repayments stay the same – only the term of your loan is affected. A rise in the interest rate will increase the term of your mortgage. A fall in the rate of interest will reduce the duration of the loan. There is a maximum of five additional years that can be applied to your mortgage. You are able to make lump sum payments or redeem your mortgage early without incurring any financial charges or penalties and you can change to a fixed rate at any time. However, if you do convert to a fixed rate you will have to pay a charge in the event of early redemption.

## Capital and interest repayment mortgage (fixed rate)

The repayments are fixed for the whole term of the mortgage. You know exactly what you will be paying each month and how many payments you will have to make. Fixed rates are usually higher than variable rates. Financial penalties can be charged for redeeming your mortgage early, or even changing to a variable interest rate. Each bank and lender will differ and it is advisable to check their financial penalties.

## Interest only

The majority of interest only mortgages offered by French banks are quite different from what you might expect. There are two products. With both products, the term of the mortgage is divided into two phases. During the first phase you pay only the interest on the mortgage. During the second phase you pay both the capital and the interest.

Because you are repaying the capital over a shorter period, during the second phase your monthly repayments will suddenly be much higher.

With the alternative product, your deposit is used as collateral that is estimated to grow at a set rate. Again the term of the mortgage is divided into two phases.

## In the know

**Carole Bayliss runs Mortgage France (www.mortgagefrance.com) with her husband, Tony, and offers the following advice about mortgage products and their uses:**

In France, mortgages have in the main been used to purchase property or to fund improvement works. Significant changes between 2004 and 2006 saw the introduction of the EuroSwitch mortgage and Equity Release mortgages. Some of the French banks and mortgage providers have adapted to the increase in numbers of international buyers and their needs, they have enhanced their range of products, changed some of their terms and conditions, and also introduced a few new mortgage products.

A mortgage can be used to:

- purchase a property which may or may not need renovation or improvement works
- purchase a new property or one under construction
- release equity from your French property
- replace a loan in another currency that you used to purchase your French property and would now like to pay it back and take out a new loan in euros
- refinance an existing mortgage on your French property if you would like to reduce your monthly payments and/or benefit from lower interest rates
- bridge finance – only available when selling a property in France to buy another French property and only if supported by a new mortgage.

Choosing the right type of mortgage which is suitable for you and your circumstances is essential.

During the first phase you pay only the interest on the mortgage, but because your deposit is working on your behalf, you pay interest on the whole amount of the purchase price. At the end of the first phase your collateral is valued and is deducted from the amount you originally borrowed.

During the second phase you pay the capital and interest on the outstanding mortgage. Once again, you will probably find that your monthly repayments will be higher.

A pure interest only mortgage is possible. The lending criteria is strict, but to high net-worth clients it is a very useful and tax-efficient mortgage.

# Equity release

For those who bought their property in cash, or when a property has significantly increased in value, this is an opportunity to release some of the locked-in equity. It is a standard capital and interest repayment mortgage. The interest rates are higher, and there are financial penalties attached, but it is possible to release up to 70% of the equity in a property. Again the criteria is very strict and can exclude many from qualifying.

The basic type of mortgage is the *hypothèque conventionelle*, the only type available if you intend to use the loan to carry out renovation or to build a new house. There are non-refundable costs of 2%–3% payable on taking out the loan. Where you are buying existing property, whether new or old, you can apply for another type of mortgage loan, the *privilège de prêteur de deniers* (PPD), which is not subject to 0.615% registration tax and is thus less costly. Some loans are guaranteed by a mixture of PPD and *hypothèque*; the PPD cannot be used to borrow money for construction or renovation costs. The third type of loan is the *caution* or *fonds de garantie* where another person or organisation stands surety for the repayment of the loan. Banks will only grant the loan when it is backed up with a mortgage on the actual property as well.

There is also a basic difference in concept: the mortgage lender does not hold the deeds to your property as security; these remain with the *notaire*. All property and land is registered with the *cadastre* – the French land registry – and given its own unique number. This is stated in the *acte de vente,* which remains with the *notaire*, while you have a copy. Your mortgage is registered with the local *bureau des hypothèques,* and there is a fee to have the mortgage removed once you have paid it off. When you take out a loan (*prêt*) you give the lender a *hypothèque* or charge on the property, which allows them to auction it off if you default on the loan.

There are two possibilities: one is to remortgage your UK property, the other is to take out a mortgage with a French bank using a French property as security. UK-based banks will not lend money on foreign properties; French branches of UK banks, as well as one or two specialised UK lenders, will. All banks and mortgage providers, even those with a British name, are registered in France. They all operate under French banking regulations and only offer euro mortgages.

Remortgaging in the UK is easier in some ways: banks lend cash more readily than in France, but you could end up putting your UK home at risk for the sake of buying property in France. Interest rates are less stable in the UK than in France, and likely to remain higher. The French mortgage interest rate is generally about 1.4% higher than the European Interbank Rate, which was about 3.75% in 2007. The charges involved with setting up a French mortgage (*frais d'hypothèque*) are high and have to be paid up-front. French banks and mortgage providers have very strict rules about how much they will lend. Lower interest rates, however, make the French mortgage more attractive at the end of the day.

The market is highly competitive: lenders advertise all sorts of attractive rates. One trick is to forget to mention the cost of death insurance – *assurance décès*. What you need to look at is the final rate – the *taux effectif global* or TEG – including insurance and charges. Lenders are required to furnish detailed information on the monthly repayments, the rate of repayment, and total amount repaid. You should not sign a mortgage contract until the small print has been explained to you in English.

# French mortgage lenders

There are French banks and there are French mortgage providers, and they are very different. Banks, such as BNP, Crédit Agricole, etc., will usually only lend in their own particular area local to the branch and will usually insist that you visit them in person to open your bank account with them and complete and provide all the mortgage paperwork. Mortgage providers, such as BPI, will lend in any region of France regardless of which office you go to. The mortgage providers do not have any banking facilities of their own, but many have arrangements with other banks to allow them to open an account for a mortgage applicant without the need to visit a bank.

French lenders will not pre-approve mortgages. All mortgages are full status, meaning full proof of identity, income and loans, up-to-date bank statements etc. have to be provided. To underwrite a file completely for mortgage approval is as much work as underwriting a mortgage application. There is no guarantee that the client will return to the lender for their mortgage. This does not prevent you from sounding the lender out about a mortgage, but it is up to you to find out whether you are going to qualify or not.

# The *Loi Scrivener* and protection for borrowers

Borrowers are generally well protected, but in spite of the strict rules defaults among foreigners are common, mainly because the borrower has spent too much doing up a dilapidated property, or hasn't worked out a proper business plan. In the case of default, the property is compulsorily sold at auction and will fetch considerably less than if you had sold it yourself. The law generally favours owners, and it takes a long time before a forced sale can take place.

The *Loi Scrivener* – passed in 1979 and named after Madame Scrivener who promoted it – provides for transparency in the mortgage application process, and some protection for borrowers. The main provisions are as follows.

1.  The lending organisation must first state in writing: the lender's name and address, the type of loan, the property that is to be acquired, the rate of interest, total repayment and the time period of the loan, and the fact that the property purchase is dependent on obtaining the loan. There is a *délai de réflexion* (cooling-off period) of 10 days before the offer of the loan (*offre de crédit*) can be accepted and any funds transferred.
2.  The initial offer of credit (*offre préalable de crédit*) will state in writing: the identity of the lender and borrower, the type of loan, the amount of the loan, and the date from which

funds will be available, and the repayment terms. In the case of variable rate mortgages, the interest rate taken as a reference point, and the actual repayment rate, are stated. The offer also includes the insurance required by the bank, namely death/invalidity insurance; the guarantees and guarantors (if any) in case of default; and the costs of early repayment, or transfer of the loan.

3.   Once the offer has been received by registered post by the borrower and guarantors (if any), the borrower has 10 days to reflect before they can accept it. The acceptance can be sent by ordinary post. The offer of credit remains open for 30 days.

# The actual loan contract (*contrat de prêt*)

The lender cannot change the conditions of the loan offer for 30 days; during this time the borrower can look at other offers. Personal guarantors (*cautions personnes physiques*) may guarantee all or part of a loan. No money will be paid to the borrower or any third parties, until the offer has been accepted.

It will be stated in the *compromis de vente* that the purchase of the property will only take place on condition that the purchaser obtains a mortgage: the so-called *condition suspensive de prêt* (loan get-out clause), also known as the *clause suspensive de prêt*. Once the prospective buyer has obtained an offer of a mortgage, they are obliged to go through with the purchase of the property, even if they turn down the mortgage. The buyer will be in breach of contract if they have not made efforts to obtain a mortgage within a reasonable time, or if they have made misleading statements about their income or assets. The *condition suspensive* cannot be used as a way of evading one's obligations.

The offer is accepted with the proviso that if the actual mortgage contract is not concluded within four months of acceptance, then the borrower is no longer bound by the contract. If, for reasons beyond the borrower's control, the sale of the house does not go through within four months of acceptance of the mortgage, then they are freed from the mortgage contract. The borrower will, however, have to return any moneys, and pay a small compensation to the lender.

If the borrower becomes involved in litigation in connection with building work related to the house purchase, he/she may not stop repayments. This is only allowed with the authorisation of a magistrate. Once the case has been settled repayments recommence.

In the case of early repayment, the penalty cannot exceed the equivalent of 6 months' interest, and never more than 3% of the total of the principal sum remaining. The amount can also be less.

If the buyer has stated in the *compromis de vente* that they do not intend to seek a loan, and then decide to ask for one anyway, they are no longer protected in the same way by the *Loi Scrivener*.

In order to understand the likely amount of your monthly repayments, the following table gives monthly payments per £1000. Euros or dollars can be substituted for pounds.

| Monthly loan repayments | | | | | |
|---|---|---|---|---|---|
| Interest rate % p.a. | Repayment mortgage with a term of n years: amount in pounds sterling (or other currency)* | | | | |
| | 5 | 10 | 15 | 20 | 25 |
| 1 | 17.08 | 8.75 | 5.98 | 4.60 | 3.77 |
| 2 | 17.51 | 9.19 | 6.42 | 5.05 | 4.23 |
| 3 | 17.93 | 9.63 | 6.88 | 5.52 | 4.72 |
| 4 | 18.36 | 10.07 | 7.35 | 6.01 | 5.23 |
| 5 | 18.78 | 10.53 | 7.83 | 6.53 | 5.77 |
| 6 | 19.21 | 11.00 | 8.33 | 7.06 | 6.33 |
| 7 | 19.65 | 11.47 | 8.84 | 7.60 | 6.91 |
| 8 | 20.08 | 11.95 | 9.37 | 8.17 | 7.51 |
| 9 | 20.52 | 12.44 | 9.90 | 8.74 | 8.12 |
| 10 | 20.95 | 12.93 | 10.44 | 9.33 | 8.75 |
| *Interest calculated daily. | | | | | |

The above figures will vary slightly with different lenders. There is a useful French mortgage calculator on www.french-property.com.

# The amount you can borrow

French regulations mean that your monthly repayments cannot exceed 33% of your gross income less social charges (which are far higher than income tax). The 33% has to include the monthly cost of existing mortgage/rent, other loans, credit card repayments, maintenance payments and the repayments of the proposed mortgage itself. At the same time, the costs and taxes associated with the property purchase, between 10% and 15% of the purchase price will also be taken into account. Mortgage lenders' websites will give you a rough idea of how much you can afford to pay (see www.adomos.com; www.guideducredit.fr; or www.patrimoine.com). If you have a partner their income will be taken into account. Lenders are not keen these days to take projected rental income into account; this should be taken into account if you are purchasing a property through a leaseback scheme.

French lenders will lend rather less for a second-home purchase than for a principal residence. The amount may be only 50% of the purchase price. The greater the proportion that you can pay in cash (*l'apport personnel*) the more likely they are to go to the 33% ceiling on your personal income. They are not keen to lend if you are still paying off a UK mortgage, depending on how much there is to pay and your income. On the other hand, they tend to ignore National Insurance contributions (which are relatively small compared with French social charges) and take your gross monthly income as a basis for calculation.

## Mortgage calculation (*capacité d'endettement*)

Your net (joint) monthly earnings including investment income     £

    take 33% of this amount     £

    deduct rent, loan repayments, alimony payments, etc.     £

The result is the amount that you can repay per month on a French mortgage     £.

## Documents required for a French mortgage

- Copies of all the usual identification documents of all applicants: i.e. passport, birth/marriage/divorce certificates, and *carte de séjour* if you have one.
- Notarised letter from your partner agreeing to a mortgage being taken out on the property, if they are not an applicant.
- Your last three months' salary slips.
- Letter from your employer stating that you are employed.
- Tax returns/statements from previous year.
- Full accounts for three previous years, and current accounts, if you are self-employed.
- Proof of current outgoings, such as rent, loan repayments, alimony, child support payments, etc.
- Business plan, or projected rental income, if you plan to make money from your property.
- Application form and fee.
- Copy of the *compromis de vente* (preliminary contract).
- Results of a medical examination (sometimes required).

## Charges and procedures involved with French mortgages

The amount, interest rate and payment terms of the mortgage must be the same in the *acte de vente* as in the mortgage contract. Any discrepancies should be rectified. The charges are:

- the *frais de dossier* (lender's fees): approx. 1% of the loan
- fee for opening the dossier (*ouverture de dossier*): €150–€950
- fee for arranging insurance: 0.4%–0.5% of the loan
- *notaire's* emolument on a sliding scale: €889 on €100,000
- fee for registering the mortgage with the Bureau des Hypothèques: 0.615%
- further small charges and taxes.

The maximum fees come to about 5.9% for a loan of €50,000, or 3.5% on €200,000. Some of the above fees are negotiable. French mortgage lenders generally only cast a rapid eye over the property to satisfy themselves that it is not about to collapse; they are well informed about the property market and know better than foreign buyers how much money it is safe for them to lend. You need to have money available in your French bank account to pay the fees given above when the *acte de vente* is signed, otherwise the deal cannot go through. Lenders require payments to be made by direct debit from a French bank account, which you will have to open before you apply for a mortgage in any case.

If your mortgage is in sterling or another non-euro currency, a revaluation clause (*clause de réévaluation*) may be inserted in the contract. The clause can work in favour of the lender or the borrower. If the euro has fallen in value against sterling during the repayment period, you will be required to make up the difference to the original value in euros. The borrower may ask for a clause protecting them against a rise in the euro.

Only once the *acte de vente* has been signed, and the mortgage registered, will the *notaire* arrange for the release of the loan funds. A different situation exists if you are having a new house built. Funds are released in stages (stage payments), depending on how far construction has advanced. You only pay interest on the amounts released, not on the whole.

Once the mortgage has run its course, there is a further two years to wait before it is automatically erased from the mortgage register. If you sell your property before this time, you will have to pay to have the mortgage cancelled. A property cannot be sold with a mortgage charge attached to it, unless the loan is about to be paid off.

## Life insurance for mortgages

Mortgage lenders insist that you take out life/disability insurance – *assurance décès/invalidité*, even if it is not compulsory by law. The type of insurance is *assurance décès temporaire*, running for the lifetime of the mortgage contract. Strictly speaking, this should be called death insurance. The premiums are lost; there is no payout at the end. Another type of life insurance – *assurance décès vie entière* – which runs until the time you actually die, does have a payout. French life insurance – *assurance vie* – is another type of savings product, unrelated to mortgages. About 2% of applicants for death insurance are turned down because of serious health problems; another 8% are only offered limited insurance; 90% are accepted.

For older borrowers, the obligatory mortgage life insurance can become prohibitively costly. On average, a 50-year-old borrower in good health would pay insurance at an annual rate of 0.53% to borrow €100,000 over 20 years. This jumps to 1.26% for a 60-year-old borrower. Tahminae Madani from France Home Finance recommends either limiting the duration of your mortgage if you are over 50 years old or borrowing with younger family members or trusted friends to reduce the insurance burden. You are advised to consult a company such as France Home Finance to discuss the best borrowing options for your circumstances.

Insurance against unemployment – *assurance perte d'emploi* – is not compulsory, but is used quite a lot, since France has very high unemployment. You cannot be considered for unemployment insurance until you have been working for an employer for 6 to 12 months.

It is also possible to insure yourself against being forced to sell your house at a loss – *protection revente* – because of circumstances outside your control, such as divorce. The amount covered is only 10% of the purchase price or €15,000 euros at the most. House and contents insurance is compulsory for all owners and tenants.

# How the French Buy Property

The French state has various schemes in place to encourage people to save up to buy a property. The most popular is the PEL (*Prêt d'Épargne Logement*); you are required to save up to a certain limit for 4 years, after which you are guaranteed a mortgage and you receive a premium from the state, up to €1,500. The LEL (*Livret d'Épargne Logement*) is a similar scheme but you only save for 18 months.

Then there is the so-called 1% loan, subsidised by businesses with more than 10 employees. A 0% loan is available to those who renovate properties over 20 years old, where the renovation costs exceed 35% of the price, but the loan only covers 20% of the purchase price. The state underwrites loans for properties over 20 years old, with certain conditions attached, the so-called *prêts conventionnés*. State functionaries are guaranteed loans at competitive rates. Anyone who is permanently resident in France could qualify for one of these loans.

There is also the possibility of avoiding mortgage costs completely, by using a specialised cooperative organisation (*mutuelle*) to act as guarantor for the loan (for which there is a charge). Equally, if you work for the railways, post office, Air France, the Education Ministry, etc., these bodies act as guarantors for your mortgage loan.

A list of mortgage brokers and advisors who are experienced in working with French mortgages can be found in the The Directory.

The amount that can be borrowed on a property over 5 years old is normally up to 85% of the purchase price, not including the *notaire's* or estate agent's fees. New properties are treated differently, in that if they are under 5 years old, the purchase price will include VAT (TVA) of 19.6% the first time it changes hands. It is possible to borrow up to 95% of the purchase price ex-VAT. In practice 100% mortgages are available but special terms would have to be negotiated. Note that mortgages on a property cannot be transferred from owner to owner as is possible in the USA.

# Tax and Investment Advice

The law firms listed in the The Directory (p. 361–2) will give advice on how to plan ahead to benefit your heirs.

There are several UK firms that specialise in giving advice to UK citizens who are buying or already own property in France. Some hold seminars in different locations in France. These are publicised in French property magazines and the monthly *French News*.

It really is important to take specialist advice if you are planning any major financial transaction involving France, and this includes buying or selling property and living and working in France. The French system is different from others and by seeking guidance in advance you may well save yourself from making some costly errors.

## Useful websites

*www.impots.gouv.fr.* Government site, with tax simulation programme.
*www.lesechos.fr/patrimoine/index.htm.* Finance website.

# 7 Renting A Home In France

## The Rental Scene

RENTING RATHER THAN BUYING was until recently the preferred choice of many French people. With some steep rises in the price of property, and plenty of cheap loans, the idea of buying is now becoming more popular, and there are almost as many owner-occupiers as in the UK. The most significant feature of the French rental scene is that while there are more properties for rent than in the UK, the percentage of social housing is smaller.

For overseas buyers it is a good idea to consider renting in an area before you buy. That way you can get to know a location during the good and bad times, in winter and in summer and really get a feel for the place. The cost can be relatively low and by helping you know if you really want to live in the area it can be invaluable. You can also start to make contacts and friends, and find the good and less good places to buy.

Of course, foreigners looking for property to buy are not going to remain in France long enough to qualify for subsidised rentals and are forced to look on the open market. Rents vary enormously around the country. The highest prices are in Paris, Strasbourg, Lyon, western coastal resorts, and the Riviera. The lowest can be found in the economically depressed areas of the north-west, central and eastern France. The typical rental property is an unfurnished apartment, often in a *copropriété*. Large apartment blocks are often owned by banks or insurance companies. The main thing to look for is a *digicode* – a digital entry system – or *vidéophone*. The presence of a *concierge* or *gardien* is a great advantage.

The kinds of problems found in large apartment blocks in the UK also exist on certain estates in France – the HLM. Apart from these estates with social problems, privately-run apartment blocks are acceptable places to live.

For legal reasons property must be either fully furnished or not at all. A property that lacks essential equipment such as a cooker or refrigerator is not considered furnished. It is also illegal to rent out an apartment where the principal room has a surface area of less than 9 sq m. There are plenty of studios or *studettes* with 10 sq m living rooms. There should also be cooking facilities and running water. The lessor will require evidence that you can pay the rent, such as recent pay slips and bank statements. They may not agree to rent a property to you if the rent exceeds one-third of your monthly income. The lessor will have a standard rental agreement for you to sign. There is a deposit to pay – the *dépôt de garantie*.

# Rental Deposit (*dépôt de garantie*)

The deposit is often referred to by the French as *la caution*, but the official term is *dépôt de garantie*. The amount of the rental deposit can vary: when a property is rented out by the month, the maximum is 2 months' rent, when rented out by the year, the maximum is 3 months. For some dwellings, known as *logements conventionnés*, the maximum is a month's rent. Owners are required to refund the deposit within 2 months of the tenant leaving the property, minus any deductions for damage. Where the owner fails to restore the deposit in time, the tenant can obtain a summary judgment from a lower court obliging the owner to pay up, by filling in a simple form called a *déclaration au greffe*; should the sum be over €3,800 a hearing has to take place before a *juge d'instance* (civil magistrate). If the tenant is aware that they owe money to the owner, then they can have this taken into account by the court.

Unlike in some countries, the owner can invest the deposit as they please; the tenant does not receive any interest on this.

# Advertising

The basic term for rental is *location:* every local newspaper has a section. The following property websites specialise in rentals:

## Insider Tip

If you are simply looking around shops or houses, you will come across advertisements A Louer (For Rent). Some advertisements are put up by professional agents, called marchands de listes, who look for tenants on behalf of owners. They are subject to the same regulations as agents immobiliers, who also have rental property.

www.alouer.fr
www.appelimmo.fr
www.bonjour.fr
www.colocataire.fr (for those looking for a shared house or apartment)
www.entreparticuliers.fr
www.foncia.fr
www.journaldesparticuliers.fr
www.kitrouve.com
www.lacentrale.fr
www.lesiteimmobilier.com
www.locat.com
www.pap.fr
www.RentaplaceinFrance.com
www.seloger.com.

# In the Know

**Eric Smith rented several apartments in Antibes before buying his current property. He talks about some of the problems of renting:**

There were particular problems with one apartment; it was on the top of a five-storey building, and all charges were included. But the heating didn't work. When we moved out after a year we received a bill for €1,400 for the heating. We made a mistake because we had only informed the landlady and the *syndic* (manager) of the *copropriété* verbally that there was a problem. We were then taken to court for non-payment, and eventually had to pay half. This made us realise that you absolutely must send any complaints by *lettre recommandée* (registered letter), otherwise you have no recourse. Because we were on such good terms with the owner, the agent and the manager we never imagined that they would do this to us.

Practices on the south coast seem to be generally rather relaxed. We gave the estate agent a cheque as a deposit, and he simply held on to it and never cashed it, so we got the cash back when we moved out and it had no bearing on the court case about the central heating. This seems to be a standard practice down here. Also we have never actually seen an *état des lieux* (inspection report) on a rented property. We made a list ourselves of anything that looked damaged, and there were no problems when we moved out, but strictly speaking you could get into trouble without having an official report made up when you move in. Again it seems that no one bothers around here. Our contract was for a year, because it was the owner's second home.

My only suggestion is not to do everything by word of mouth, but it is difficult to go against local practices.

# Where to Stay during Short House-hunting Trips

You may not want to spend weeks or months in France looking for places to buy. Fortunately, France has plentiful and cheap hotel accommodation for short stays which puts the UK and other countries to shame. Starting at the top end, you could check out the website www. chateauhotels.com, or order their brochure. Naturally, the prices are fairly steep, but the locations are superb. The next step down is the organisation Logis de France (www.logis-de-france.fr), which covers hotel-restaurants in the two- to four-star category; many Brits swear by it.

Because of the difficulties that gîte-owners are currently experiencing in finding tenants, you can expect to find a good deal. For Paris try the very useful website www.paris-exchange.com. If you want to be guaranteed a personal and welcoming service, the best book is Alastair Sawday's *Special Places to Stay in France*.

Longer stays in France can be more difficult to arrange than holiday lets. Because the French tend to stay put for years thanks to the letting regulations, it is less common to rent a place for three or six months than it would be in the UK. One way around this is to advertise on a website such as www.french-property-news.com or www.french-news.com to see if another foreign property owner will rent you their property (usually out of season) for a lengthy period, or you could offer to be a caretaker and live rent-free. You can also look around in your favoured location for a French owner who is willing to rent out for a few months.

## Insider Tip

*If you are looking for chambres d'hôtes or gîtes, Gîtes de France dominates the market: their annual catalogue will give you places to stay anywhere in the country; see www.gitesdefrance.com. You can get in touch with owners for long-term rentals through www.cheznous.com or www.abritel.fr (in French).*

# Formalities of Renting

House hunters will be looking for short-term rented accommodation, but not at an exorbitant price. While long-term unfurnished rentals are covered by the 1989 laws, which give tenants wide-ranging rights and make eviction very difficult, furnished seasonal rentals, holiday homes and sub-lets are governed only by the *Code Civil*, the basic civil law. Such rentals are termed *location libre*. The landlord (*bailleur*) and tenant (*locataire*) can come to any agreement they wish – unless it is illegal – regarding the length of the tenancy and the conditions of payment. This can be a verbal or written agreement. The duration of the rental agreement can be fixed or indeterminate. However, French law has now changed for some furnished rentals. Previously, there was no legal requirement to use a lease for a furnished rental and it was possible to agree any duration. As from 20th January 2005, except for holiday lets, a contract of at least a year is legally required if renting furnished property to a tenant who owns no other property or has no other tenancy agreement as his main residence. However there are ways around this (see chapter 18).

Tenants are liable for some repairs – the *réparations locatives*. Anything that is not a *réparation locative* is the responsibility of the landlord. One also needs to be aware of the *charges récupérables* – the costs the landlord can require the tenant to pay. These are fixed by law. These items are listed in great detail in the relevant books, e.g. *Propriétaires et Locataires: Qui Paie Quoi?* published by PRAT, and *Letting French Property Successfully*, published by PKF Guernsey.

## L'État des lieux

Drawing up a description of 'the state of the premises' is an important step to be undertaken before actually moving into a new home. It is meant to safeguard the tenant from being accused of damage that is not of their doing, and thus unfairly being made to pay for repairs before they can recover their rental deposit (*dépôt de garantie*). It also protects the owner from having to pay for damage caused by the tenant.

Under ideal circumstances, both the lessor and lessee agree to the *état des lieux* and are both present when it is carried out. An *état des lieux* which is signed by both parties is always valid. Where one party refuses to co-operate, the other may have the *état des lieux* carried out by a *huissier* (bailiff). Where one party decides to call in a bailiff to carry out the *état*, the other party must be informed by registered letter (*recommandée avec AR*) at least 7 days in advance. The costs are then split between owner and tenant. Where the *état des lieux* is carried out by an agent of the owner, e.g. an estate agent, the tenant is not required to pay any of the owner's costs.

When the tenant leaves the premises, an *état des lieux de sortie* will be carried out to determine any damage for which the tenant could be liable. In cases where a tenant leaves suddenly and cannot be traced, the owner is required to draw up an *état des lieux de sortie* immediately, using a bailiff. Otherwise, the owner should make this description on the day the tenant leaves. Where the owner has not taken sufficient trouble to carry out the *état des lieux de sortie* as soon as possible, any claims against the former tenant or their agents are inadmissible.

Model forms for *états des lieux* can be found at town halls and in some publications, such as *Propriétaires et Locataires: Qui Paie Quoi?*. Needless to say, the same form should be used for both the first and final *état*. Taking photographs of the premises (conventional rather than digital, which could be tampered with) will make the job easier, if neither party objects.

The whole business of the *état des lieux* may seem an unnecessary bother, but it does have advantages for both parties. Without this description of the premises, it is assumed that they were in good condition when the tenant moved in. The tenant will not then easily be able to contest the owner's demand that the premises be restored to their original condition (*remise en état*). By and large, the law favours the tenant in such situations. Detailed information on the rights and responsibilities of tenants for long lets can be at www.RentaplaceinFrance.com.

# Rental contracts

Standard contracts are sold in bookshops. A letting contract is a lengthy document. It will always state the type of lease that is involved, whether short term (*saisonnière*) or the standard unfurnished lease under the 1989 law. Tenants are always entitled to request a written lease if the premises are let under the 1989 law. The owner is not permitted to insert clauses that prevent the tenant from working from home (with certain restrictions), or from keeping a pet. The tenant is free to pay the owner by the method that he chooses. He or she cannot be compelled to pay by standing order or by cheque. A model contract with translation can be found in *Letting Your French Property Successfully*, published by PKF Guernsey (www.pkfguernsey. com).

A lease is either for three years if the owner is a private individual, or six years if the owner is a company. The tenant can give notice of three months at any time, which is reduced to a month if the tenant is compelled to leave because of job relocation, a fall in income or their state of health (but only if he or she is over 60 years old). There are strict rules about rent increases which are detailed in chapter 18. The owner can give the tenant notice to quit if they or their family intend to occupy the premises or where the tenant has committed a serious breach of the contract.

Opposite is an example of a letter from a tenant giving notice (for unfurnished premises):

Monsieur (ou Madame)

J'ai l'honneur de vous donner congé pour le … de l'appartement que j'occupe et qui m'a été loué suivant bail sous seing privé en date du …, conformément aux dispositions des articles 12 et 15-1, al.2, du 6 juillet 1989. (I hereby wish to give notice from the … for the apartment that I currently occupy and which is let to me according to the rental contract dated …, in accordance with the provisions of the law of 6 July 1989, articles 12 and 15-1, para.2.)

Je me tiens à votre disposition pour établir un état des lieux si vous le souhaitez, à l'occasion de la remise des clés. (I am available to draw up an inspection report if you so wish at the time of returning the keys.)

Je me permets de vous rappeler que vous devez me restituer, conformément à l'article 22 de la loi du 6 juillet 1989, dans un délai maximal de deux mois après mon départ la somme de … euros qu je vous ai versée en dépôt de garantie et vous remercie de bien vouloir prendre vos dispositions pour le faire. (I take this opportunity to remind you that you are required to return to me the sum of … euros being the deposit I paid to you, within at the most two months, in accordance with article 22 of the law of 6 July, and would be grateful if you would take the necessary steps to do so.)

Veuillez agréer, Monsieur (ou Madame), l'assurance de mes salutations distinguées. (Yours sincerely,)

*(Adapted from 300 Modèles De Lettres Et De Contrats, published by PRAT.)*

# 8 What Type Of Property To Buy

## The Right Property for You

BUYING YOUR FRENCH PROPERTY should be the experience of a lifetime, if it is approached in the right way. It would be disingenuous to say that no one has ever regretted buying property in France. The main causes of disappointment are buying in the wrong location, and not setting a realistic limit on your budget. This applies not just to the purchase price but to the cost of any renovation works.

By going through a list of simple questions it is easy enough to see whether a property is the right one for you.

- What is my budget?
- Do I need to rent it out to make it affordable?
- Will I be able to rent it out if I need to?
- How much work does it need doing, and what will it cost?
- How easy is the property to get to?
- Are there any airports nearby?
- Do I want to live there all the year round?
- Is the climate bearable in the winter?
- How close is it to tourist attractions?
- Will I or my partner be able to pursue our hobbies there?
- Will we or our family still want to use it in 20 years' time?
- Does it have a high-speed internet connection and do mobile phones work there?

As a general rule, it is wise to decide on your budget and stick to it, no matter how tempted you might be to spend an extra €20,000 or whatever. If the property needs renovating, ask for some quotations beforehand. You should have outline planning permission – a *certificat d'urbanisme* – before buying, if you are planning a change of use or large-scale renovations. Your *notaire* will advise you on whether you need this.

It is risky to buy a property if you can only finance it by renting it out or running gîtes. More and more foreigners are buying in France with the same idea, while the tourist market is actually contracting. It is far more realistic to have a profession that you can carry on in France which leaves you financially secure, rather than struggling.

> 'unless you know exactly what you are doing, buying in the hope of selling at a profit is a risky proposition'

Unless you know exactly what you are doing, buying in the hope of selling at a profit is a risky proposition. Historically, the French stock market has always been a better investment than property. The rapid price rises of recent years may not continue. When it comes to making money on capital appreciation you are also better off in the traditional high-growth areas such as Paris, the Alps and the Riviera. No matter how much you may love your isolated rural cottage in remote central France, you cannot expect it to rocket in value.

# Old versus New

It is an oddity of the French property scene that the French consistently prefer new-build, or completely renovated property, leaving the decrepit character farmhouses to the foreigners. Perhaps until 30 years ago the average Frenchman didn't mind living in a damp, crumbling farmhouse, with broken chairs and tables, and water coming through the roof. French women have, however, voted with their feet, and moved to the comfort of the towns or to new homes on village plots, forcing the male of the species to follow suit.

The French have seen what the British and other foreigners can do with old properties, but not that many are interested in imitating them. On the whole, foreign buyers and the French are looking for quite different types of property. The incomers look for a beautiful location and authenticity, while what the French really want is elegance and convenience. The most telling statistic is the fact that the average new property is worth 40% more than an old one. It is therefore important to understand that it may be very difficult to recoup the investment that you make in renovating an old property in a remote area, unless you are lucky enough to find another foreigner who happens to like it. Those French who do buy character properties tend to be outsiders themselves – perhaps Parisians – looking for their own slice of authentic life in the countryside.

Even though you may know what you are looking for, it is useful to consider a checklist of the pros and cons of old versus new.

**Advantages of the old**
- The property has an authentic feel and rustic charm.
- There will probably be more land attached to it.
- The garden will be well established.
- You know from the outset what you are buying.

- The view will probably be better than with new property.
- There will be more craftsmanship in the construction.
- You are more likely to be able to rent it out to holidaymakers.

### Advantages of the new

- There will be a garage or parking spaces already built.
- The kitchen will be more modern.
- The wiring and plumbing won't need replacing.
- The building is guaranteed for 10 years from construction.
- You can design the property yourself.
- The heating will be more efficient.
- There should be insulation.
- On some developments, there are shared sports facilities.

Traditionally the great majority of foreigners have preferred to buy an old property, even if it had some defects, and needed more maintenance than the new. However in recent years this trend has begun to change. It's become more and more common now for overseas buyers to purchase properties in new developments. For investors and those people who want to use the place as a holiday home for a few weeks, a new property has the advantage of being cheaper to maintain, being more secure in their absence and

*'it has become more and more common now for overseas buyers to purchase properties in new developments'*

probably having good facilities nearby. For retired people new homes can be simply easier to live in. Not everyone wants to spend their days on DIY projects and tending large gardens. The average first-time buyer in France will buy an apartment in a *copropriété*. The crucial point for foreign buyers is: Do I want to rent it out? If you plan to make a living from bed and breakfast the property will have to be substantial, and even more so for *gîtes*. If you only intend to live there for part of the year, and rent it out the rest of the time, there is more leeway. Holidaymakers will be quite satisfied with an apartment or a standard French holiday bungalow, as long as it is near the sea or the ski fields.

# Buying Uncompleted Property

It is common in France to buy property on the basis of plans – *achat sur plan* – or which has not yet been completed – *vente en l'état futur d'achèvement* (VEFA). A developer – *promoteur constructeur* – buys a piece of land, arranges for planning permission, and then looks for potential buyers before the property is built, or when it is partially built. The VEFA is defined in the Code Civil as:

*a contract by which a seller immediately transfers his rights to a piece of land, as well as the ownership of any existing construction. The building that is to be done becomes the property of the buyer as the work is completed. The buyer is required to pay the cost as the work progresses. The seller is in charge of the building until the handover [to the buyer].*

The dwelling can be an apartment, or an individual house, as in the case of a *lotissement* or estate.

The first step in the process is to sign a preliminary contract, or *contrat de réservation,* with a developer. The contract must contain certain information, as well as any get-out clauses in the sale, including:

- the habitable surface area
- the number of main rooms
- a list of any attached rooms, or spaces
- the location of the building in the estate
- the technical quality of the construction, with a list of the materials to be used
- the provisional price of the building, and any conditions that allow for the price to change
- the date by which the final contract can be signed
- where relevant, any loans that the developer intends to obtain for the buyer
- the conditions for paying the deposit.

The buyer has the right to ask for changes to the contract. Once the contract has been received by registered post, there is a seven day cooling-off period during which the buyer can change their mind.

The deposit – *dépôt de garantie* – depends on the length of time before the completion of the signing of the final deed of sale: 5% if within a year, under 2% if between one and two years, and no deposit if beyond two years. The deposit will be returned if:

- the sale does not go through
- the sale price exceeds the provisional price by 5%
- the buyer fails to obtain a mortgage
- equipment that has been promised is not installed
- the property falls 10% in value.

The developer is legally required to present a guarantee that the project will be finished, or a guarantee of full reimbursement if it is not completed. In most cases the developer will have their own guarantor, a bank or cooperative society, as a backer.

## Final Signing of Contract

The second, final, contract is signed once the building programme has been decided on, and construction can commence. A draft of the *contrat définitif de vente* is sent to the buyer at least a month before the signing date. The final contract must contain certain information, including:

- the description of the building or the part of the building to be sold
- the price, the method of payment, and any possible revisions in the payment
- the completion date
- details of the developer's financial guarantees.

There are two categories of faults that can appear in new constructions: the *défaut de conformité* and the *vice de construction*. The first is where an incorrect piece of equipment has been installed, e.g. a shower instead of a bath. Payment for the item can

*'a new building comes with a guarantee that the construction is satisfactory.'*

be withheld until the fault has been rectified. *Vice de construction* covers bad workmanship or mistakes in installing equipment. The guarantee covers any faults that the buyer may find, and ensures that all faults are corrected This *garantie de parfait achevement* is for 10 years.

## Payment

There are legal limits on the amount payable at any one stage of the building process. These are:

- 35% when the foundations are completed
- 70% when the roof has been built and the terraces are no longer exposed to water
- 95% when the building has been completed
- the final 5% is payable at the handing-over stage, unless there is a dispute.

In practice, however, there are more stage payments that this; for example, you might pay 20% on completion of the ground floor.

When the property is ready to be handed over, there has to be a formal *réception des travaux* between you (or your representative) – the *maître d'ouvrage* – and the developer – the *maître d'œuvre*. The *réception des travaux* (acceptance of the work), can take place with or without reservations. The final 5% of the payment is known as the *retenue de garantie* and this can be withheld until any defects have been put right, or to cover your own expenses in putting them right if the builder fails to do the work. If the 5% is withheld, it should be deposited in an escrow account held by a *notaire*.

At the *réception des travaux* you will sign a document – a *procès-verbal* – accepting the handover. You can only refuse to take over the building if there are serious defects or equipment is missing. Before the deed of sale is signed

### Insider Tip

Before the handing-over the buyer should inspect the building, with the help of an expert if necessary, to determine if there are any faults that need correcting. You – or your representative – will need to have plans and lists of all the equipment that is supposed to be installed. Electrics and heating should be tested.

the *notaire* has to ensure that all the mandatory insurance policies are in place. For example, the developer must have a policy to cover their *responsabilité décennale* – the compulsory 10 year guarantee against major construction faults. There is also a 2 year guarantee – *garantie biennale* – against faults in the equipment, such as the fitted kitchen, heating and double glazing.

The developer also has to present the electricity safety board's certificate of approval, the *attestation de consuel*. In order to guarantee the quality of the construction and equipment, it is possible to engage an organisation such as Qualitel, based in Paris, who will oversee the whole process of design and construction. See the website: www.qualitel.org. Another agency, Promotelec, is involved in promoting efficient energy: see www.promotelec.fr. You can also check whether your developer is a member of the Fédération Nationale des Promoteurs Constructeurs: 106 rue de l'Université, 75007 Paris; www.fnpc.fr.

# Penalties

There are, naturally, penalties where either the buyer or the seller fails to meet their obligations. If the buyer fails to make stage payments on time, the developer can add on 1% for each month in arrears. There will be a clause in the contract imposing a penalty of up to 10% of the purchase price if the buyer does not meet their payment schedule, and other clauses which allow the developer to find another buyer if necessary.

From the side of the developer, the contract should give the period of time within which the stages of construction are to be completed, in the case of an individual house. Penalties are payable by the developer once the date has been exceeded by 30 days, unless this is due to forces outside his control. The penalty is set at a maximum of 0.033% of the total price per day of delay. The buyer is in a stronger position if they can set an actual deadline, rather than a period of time in which the work has to be done. If there are no such penalty clauses on the developer in the original contract then you should try to get them included.

# Taxation

There are both advantages and disadvantages to buying a new property, as far as taxes go. The downside is that 19.6% TVA is payable, although this can be avoided in some circumstances. The costs associated with the purchase, to be paid to the *notaire*, are reduced to about 2%–3% of the price, before TVA. In addition there is the *taxe de publicité foncière* – at 0.75% of the price before TVA.

TVA is also payable if you buy a property within five years of its completion. TVA can be avoided if:

- you buy property under a leaseback scheme
- you run a hotel or similar *TVA*-registered business from the property
- you let the property to someone running a hotel
- you sell the property at a loss within five years of purchase
- you are a *marchand de biens* – dealer in property.

TVA is only payable the first time the property changes hands within the first five years after construction, unless this was through a *marchand de biens*. There are strict rules about the avoidance of TVA; professional advice is essential if you are looking for ways of avoiding TVA.

# Leaseback

Leaseback, or *le leaseback*, is a scheme that is somewhat like 'buy-to-let', but within a formal structure that guarantees your investment is safe. It was originally promoted by the French government as a way of encouraging private investors to fund new tourist accommodation. The idea is quite ingenious: you agree to buy a new or completely rebuilt property in a tourist complex, and then lease it back to the developer for a period of between 9 and 20 years. The developer's management company runs it for you, and guarantees a rental income which goes towards paying off any mortgage that you have taken out to buy the property. You can also agree to have the use of the property during the off-season for a number of weeks each year, though your rental returns are usually lower for such deals. At the end of the fixed leaseback period, you are the owner of the property; hopefully you will be sitting on a substantial profit.

*'there are real bargains to be found if you are prepared to take a risk'*

You benefit right at the start because the French government repays the 19.6% VAT that is normally charged on new buildings, thus reducing the purchase price. This is on the assumption that the management company provides specified hotel-type services for the period of the leaseback. If the company goes out of business, then you may have to repay the VAT. If you resell the property the VAT need not be repaid provided that the property continues to be used for leaseback by the new owner. You should take legal advice before entering into a leaseback purchase; there are potential pitfalls you may not be told about. You are not allowed to switch from one management company to another; you should find out what the management company charges for its services. There may be conditions attached to reselling the property after the leaseback period is finished. As with any property, you also need to consider factors that could affect the resale value, such as flooding, large new developments nearby, and so on.

Leaseback schemes will usually only be found in tourist areas on the coast, in Paris, and in the Alps. Because the term 'leaseback' is now such a buzz-word, it is sometimes used for ordinary buy-to-let, and there have been cases of mis-selling. Make sure that there is a guaranteed annual return on the property to pay off your mortgage, and that the developer takes on the task of finding holiday tenants. The box opposite lists some companies that deal in leaseback properties. Others can be found through the organisation FOPDAC; see www.fopdac.com.

# Buying at Auction

The idea of buying at auction may not occur to many foreigners, but there are real bargains to be found if you are prepared to take a risk, and the process itself holds some excitement.

*In the know*

**Nick Leach, business development manager of leaseback specialists Pierre et Vacances (www.pierre-vacances. co.uk), advises on property investment in France:**

Buying a property in France has historically been a lifestyle investment for Francophiles who love the food, wine, weather and way of life that France has to offer – the ideal destination for a second home. The reasons for buying in France have changed in recent years as pure property investors also see it as a country to make a solid rental return and excellent capital growth which has continued on average at double digit rates for more than 7 years. Areas of particular interest for pure investors are Paris, the Alps and the Cote d'Azur – because the buying possibilities are limited by supply and building constraints and yet there is long-term appeal.

The option for acquiring a property under a leaseback continues to grow as a hassle-free way of investing in French property where owners lease the *residence de tourisme* property back to a management company who manage, maintain and lease the property to their tourist clients in return for a guaranteed net yield and no running costs with the rebate on the VAT as an added incentive.

## Leaseback companies

**Azur Property Investments:** www.azurpropertyinvestments.com.

**French Buy To Let.com:** ☎01803 290004; www.frenchbtl.com; Côte d'Azur.

**Pierre et Vacances:** www.pierreetvacances-immobilier.com; large French holiday company which pioneered leaseback; properties available to rent or own around France including ski resorts.

**MGM French Properties:** ☎020 7494 0706; www.mgmfrenchproperties.com; specialise in the French Alps and the Côte d'Azur.

**Selectis Estate Agency:** ☎04 94 565 565 www.selectis.fr; based in France.

**Villas Abroad (Properties) Ltd:** ☎020 8941 4499; email villasabroad@fopdac.com; www.villasabroadproperties.co.uk; Côte d'Azur.

**VEF:** ☎020 7515 8660; www.vefuk.com.

Fewer than 1% of property transactions in France take place through auctions; in an average year only 500 properties are sold in Paris by this method, and perhaps only 250 in the rest of the country. Auctions (*ventes aux enchères*) can be divided into three types: *vente judiciaires*, *vente de notaires*, and *vente des domaines*.

## Ventes judiciaires

This type of sale occurs when the owner of a property has gone bankrupt or defaulted on their mortgage payments. It is a forced sale by the creditors, i.e. mortgage lender. These sales take place less and less and are really a last resort for creditors. They are advertised in the local press, in *Le Journal des Enchères* (every 2 months), *Les Affiches Parisiennes*, and in the *Programme des Ventes* given out by the clerk of the lower court (*greffier du tribunal*). To bid at the sale, you hire a lawyer (*avocat*) registered at the court where the sale is going to take place. You give him/her a *mandat* (authorisation) to bid up to a certain limit, and a certified cheque for 20% of the sum you are prepared to go up to. Your lawyer will not exceed the amount you have stated unless you are standing next to him at the sale and give your permission for him to bid higher.

### Insider Tip

*If your bid is successful, you have 30 days to pay in full in the case where a property has been seized by the creditor (saisie immobilière) and three months in the case of bankruptcy proceedings (mise en liquidation). Properties with sitting tenants or squatters are best avoided, otherwise you will be involved in a long legal fight to evict them.*

## Ventes de notaires

In this case properties and goods are voluntarily submitted for auction by their owners at a *séance d'adjudication* or auction. Sales are publicised in a national bulletin (*Les Ventes aux Enchères des Notaires*). Information about these auctions can be found on the website: www.min-immo.com/Encheres. Again, you cannot bid directly yourself, rather you are represented by your *notaire*. Owners use this type of auction in the hope of gaining a higher price than through the usual channels. If you are looking for prestigious older properties you may get a good deal here.

In order to take part you will have to deposit a certified cheque for 20% of the estimated price to the *notaire* carrying out the sale. You have 45 days after the sale to pay the remainder. There are hefty costs involved, between 10% and 20% of the sale price.

## Ventes des domaines

The state sometimes sells properties at auction: these are announced in the *Bulletin Officiel d'Annonces des Domaines*. You are required to deposit a certified cheque for 5% of the estimated price in order to bid.

## *Vente à la chandelle*

The 'auction by candle' is a relic going back to the 15th century. The idea is that three tapers are placed on a board: the first two are lit simultaneously, and burn down within tens of seconds, while bids are made. The third taper is then lit, and if no higher bid is made then the property is sold. Nowadays, the tapers are being replaced with electric lights. This is not the end of the matter: if a bid of 10% more than the successful bid is made then the property has to be auctioned all over again, but this rarely happens. The latter condition does not apply to the *ventes des domaines*.

## Points to watch for

It goes without saying that you should view the property in question, and try to get an estimate of the likely costs of renovation. You are required to take the property as seen; there is no comeback in case of structural faults, and there is no *condition suspensive* (get-out clause) making the sale dependent on getting a mortgage. If you fail to pay for the property in full, it will be auctioned again without a reserve price (*folle enchère*) and you will be liable to pay the difference between what you bid and the price that is finally realised. On the day of the sale be there right from the beginning. Try to attend other auctions before you bid yourself.

## Finding out about auctions

The trickiest part of French auctions is finding out when and where they are happening if you are not in France. *Notaires'* offices and estate agents are kept informed of auctions, and can help you to find one in a suitable area. Anyone who is interested in auctions should look at the magazine *Journal des Enchères* which covers every kind of auction, including furniture, antiques, etc. The following are useful websites: www.licitor.com; www.ventes-judiciaires.com; www.encheres-paris.com; www.min-immo.com/Encheres; and www.ilf.fr (for the PACA region).

# Other Ways of Buying

## Rent-to-buy/*location accession*

It is possible to enter into an agreement with an owner whereby you rent the property for a number of years before buying it. The seller incorporates a clause in the contract promising to sell you the property. The clause is only activated when the prospective buyer pays a 5% deposit into a blocked account. From then on, the tenant/buyer makes further payments towards the eventual purchase price, on top of their rent. After an agreed time – usually two or three years – the buyer then has the option of paying the remainder of the purchase price. If the potential buyer changes their mind there is a small penalty to be paid to the seller.

If the seller breaks the contract there is a heavier penalty of up to 3% of the value of the property.

## Reversion property/*rente viagère*

This is a system that is rather alien to the British, although it does have something in common with an annuity taken out on the value of your house. The idea of the *rente viagère* (literally meaning 'income for life') is that you come to an agreement with the owner of a property that you will pay them a certain monthly sum and in exchange the property will revert to you on the owner's death. The buyer also pays out an initial sum known as a *bouquet* equivalent to 20%–30% of the total price. The person who pays out the money is the *débirentier* and the one who receives money is the *crédirentier*. There are two types of *viager*: one where the *crédirentier* continues to live in the house, and the other where they live elsewhere.

Properties are sometimes sold with the elderly person included, so to speak. You may see advertisements giving the cost of the property, the age and sex of the occupant, and how much you have to go on paying them. If you want to sell your property *en viager*, you can try looking at the website: www.viager.fr.

The popularity of this kind of scheme has been on the decline as people live longer and longer, since you are gambling that someone is going to die quite soon. On average, you will pay less for a property this way than by purchasing outright.

The classic example of where the *rente viagère* turned out badly for a buyer is the case of Jeanne Calment who died in 1997 at the age of 122. A notary, André-François Raffray, aged 47, made a deal with Calment, who was then 90, that he would pay her £300 a month for the rest of her life on condition that he inherited her house in Arles, Provence (where Van Gogh once lived). Thirty years later, Raffray died, having paid out £120,000 or twice the value of the property, and his heirs were obliged to shell out for another 2 years. Calment joked to Raffray on her 120th birthday: 'We all make bad deals in life.'

Anyone thinking of entering into this arrangement would be well advised to look at the projected lifespans of the French, which as in other Western nations is rising. The current figures are that on average women live to 84 years old in France and men to the age of 77 years.

## Timeshare/co-ownership

Timeshare has as bad a reputation in France as anywhere else. The EU issues brochures warning about the dire consequences of signing a timeshare agreement and leaves them in French railway stations. Unfortunately, the paranoia about timeshare is entirely justified. The French legal system leaves less scope for timeshare crooks than other countries, however, and there is far less timeshare property available than in Spain or Portugal. Many French people have bought timeshare themselves in other countries and lived to regret it.

The idea behind timeshare seems sensible enough at first sight. Instead of renting a room in an expensive hotel on the French Riviera, or a chalet in the Alps, you buy a share in a timeshare company that gives you the right to use a property for a certain number of weeks for the rest of your life, and to pass it on to your heirs. A timeshare can cost from £2,000 to £10,000 or more. The catch is that you never actually own any part of the property: you just have a right to use it for a fixed period each year. The French often call timeshare *multipropriété* which is entirely misleading: you never own the property. It should really be called *multilocation* (i.e. multiple rental) or *multi-jouissance* or *jouissance en temps partagé*. Under the French system, you are buying shares in a timeshare company, which you can then sell on if you want or leave to your heirs. If the timeshare company goes out of business you will lose the right to use the property, and you may even be held liable for some of the company's debts. You are allowed to rent out the property for the weeks that you have bought, which could make you a profit. The contract does not have to be signed in the presence of a notary; usually it is done *sous seing privé,* or 'under hand' in British parlance.

The first disadvantage of timeshare is that other people will be using the property for most of the year, so it will never feel that it is yours. If you decide that you don't like the property it is difficult to sell your share without making a substantial loss. In addition there are still costs involved with timeshare: you can expect to pay between £200 and £500 a year in management fees. It's worth noting that some people confuse leaseback with timeshare, when in fact they are completely different. Unlike in timeshare, with leaseback you are, and will always remain unless you sell it, the owner of the freehold of the property.

## How timeshare is sold

Unlike in Spain, timeshare touts do not go looking for potential victims. The most usual way is to advertise timeshare in a property magazine or on the internet. Under French law you cannot sign a timeshare contract on the spot; it has to be sent to you and returned by recorded delivery. It is a wise precaution to ask for the contract to be sent to your address in the UK so that you have sufficient time to look at the details. This may be enough to put off dishonest sellers. Under French law the timeshare contract must include a 10 day cooling-off period after you have sent off the signed contract, during which you can change your mind. The seller is not allowed to ask for or receive any money until the end of the 10 day cooling-off period. The contract should give the identity and address of the sellers, and all the costs involved, the location and description of the property, and the weeks you can use it.

Because of the low resale value, a timeshare can be bought for less than half the original asking price, so there is little purpose in buying a new one. They are sometimes advertised in *Dalton's Weekly* and *Exchange & Mart*. The website www.redweek.com usually has some advertisements for timeshare, including reviews of the properties on offer. You can look at the Timeshare Consumers' Association (TCA) website (www.tcaforum.com) to see if there have been any complaints about the timeshare company. Dealers who resell timeshares should be members of the OTE – Organisation for Timeshare in Europe (see www.ote-info.com). French timeshare companies have their own federation – Syndicat des Professionnels en Temps Partagé, 3 square Malherbe, 75016 Paris – who can advise you on timeshare purchase.

Offers of shares in so-called *multipropriétés* can be found in some small ad magazines. These are timeshares rather than genuine offers of part ownership. The weekly *De Particulier à Particulier* and its website – www.pap.fr – always has some offers. *Le Journal des Particuliers* (www.journaldesparticuliers.fr) has many of the same offers. Weeks at peak times of the year are hard to find. The fact that the week on offer falls during a school holiday is a key selling point.

# French-style co-ownership: *multipropriété*

Instead of getting involved with timeshare, it is more sensible to buy a property jointly with some other like-minded people, and agree on who will use it at what time of the year. This is not a cheap option, but you will at least be a part-owner of the property. The important thing is to draw up the deed of sale correctly, and this can only be done with a lawyer who is familiar with French property law. The law companies mentioned in chapter 15 can advise. The most suitable form is a *Société Civile Immobilière,* as long as it is constituted correctly. The SCI allows one to get around French inheritance laws, which would automatically favour children over spouses. It is particularly useful where several unrelated people own shares in a property, and wish to be free to pass their share on to others. The SCI is a company but is not subject to corporation tax. It is treated as 'fiscally transparent'; the directors are taxed as individuals. If you hold property through a company you could also be liable to UK tax on directors' benefits in kind, and the tax bill would have to be shared out between the owners. Owners pay for the running costs of the property in proportion to the number of weeks they use the place.

Selling your French property to a group of owners while keeping a part for yourself, is an ideal way to retain the use of your property for some weeks of the year, while at the same time regaining the money you invested in it. There is also an agency in the UK – OwnerGroups Company – that specialises in finding, and handling the purchase of property for the purpose of co-ownership. Their fee is 6.5% of the value of the property. In 2007 they had a share in a four-bedroom chalet in the French Alps on offer for £50,000, with £70 a month running costs. They can be contacted on 01628 486350; www.ownergroups.com.

Another approach is to find a group of like-minded people and set up a partnership in the UK with its own rules and regulations specifically to buy a property in France for the members to use. Such a partnership needs to have rules about voting out partners if it becomes necessary.

Another approach is roperty investment clubs; these often specialise in upmarket properties in upmarket resorts. One such club that covers Europe, including France, is www.thehideawaysclub.com.

# *Copropriété*

This is also a type of co-ownership, normally applicable to apartments, although it can be used for any kind of building split into several units. As there is no such thing as leasehold in France, *copropriétés,* in which a group of owners run a building themselves, are extremely common and many foreigners find themselves involved with one. It should be said that, while there is no leasehold, the land on which a building stands could be owned by someone else. A property company can buy parts of a *copropriété,* and has the right to be represented at meetings.

Any building or buildings divided between several owners with private and common areas automatically comes under the 1965 law on *copropriétés.* The group of owners, or *copropriétaires,* automatically constitutes a *syndicat de copropriété.* The owners are legally obliged to appoint a *syndic* or manager responsible for the day-to-day running of the building; they are also required to elect a *conseil syndical* (council of the syndicate) for a three-year term, and to hold annual general meetings.

There is a basic text that defines the conditions under which a *copropriété* functions, known as the *règlement de copropriété*. This includes:

- a list of the common and private areas
- the uses to which the property may be put: e.g. whether you can run a business from it
- the administration of the common areas
- the division of the charges.

A general assembly of the *copropriétaires* can be called at any time by the *conseil syndical*, or by the *copropriétaires* holding at least 25% of the votes. There has to be at least one assembly per year. If you rent out your part of the *copropriété* the tenant can also take part in an assembly, but they cannot vote on the same motions as you. The *syndic* will notify you at least 15 days before the meeting that it is happening. Any of the *copropriétaires* can ask for an amendment to the order of the meeting. You can appoint a representative to attend the meeting in your place.

Motions concerning the day-to-day running of the *copropriété* are passed by simple majority. Matters affecting the basic running of the *copropriété* must be approved by two-thirds majority. Some other matters, such as changing the division of the charges, can only be approved by unanimous vote. All the *copropriétaires* should receive a notification within 2 months of the decisions taken at the meeting. Strictly speaking, only those who opposed a decision, or were absent from the meeting, have to be informed, but it is normal to inform all the *copropriétaires*. Decisions can be challenged in a court of law, unless you have already voted in favour of them.

The general assembly is required to elect a board of management – *conseil syndical* – whose term of office runs for 3 years. *Copropriétaires*, their partners, and their representatives are all allowed to sit on the board. The board chooses a president who stays in contact with the manager of the property.

## The *syndic*

The *syndic* – the manager of the property – deals with the day-to-day running of the property. A part of their job is to keep a logbook of all the maintenance of the building, and to give advice to the owners. They are expected to present a provisional budget for the year at the AGM, and to keep accounts of the running of the property. The *syndic* maintains a bank account in the name of the syndicate. As a rule, the *syndic* does not need to go to the *conseil syndical* to carry out urgent repairs. There is generally an agreed figure which the *syndic* may spend for necessary repairs without calling a general meeting.

The *syndic* can be appointed by the general assembly of the *copropriété*, by the board of management, or they may be named in the constitution of the *copropriété*. Since their task requires specialised knowledge in accounting and law, the *syndic* usually holds a professional qualification, the *carte professionnelle de gestion immobilière*. It is virtually a requirement to have a professional *syndic* if there are more than five or so *copropriétaires*. Although any of the *copropriétaires* or their partners can act as the *syndic* they will not be able to obtain the professional indemnity insurance that is available to a professionally qualified person.

The *copropriétaires* are entitled to look at the accounts of the *copropriété* in between notification of a general meeting and the meeting itself. The accounts of the *copropriété* are separate from the *syndic*'s own personal accounts. If the *syndic* is suspected of taking bribes from suppliers you would need a court order to look at his accounts. The *copropriétaires* have a right to instruct the *syndic* to use, or not to use the services of a particular company.

## Alterations to the property

There are strict rules about what you can change in your part of the *copropriété*, since any changes to the property affect all the owners. You need the permission of the *syndic* for any redecoration, new shutters, plastering and so on. Anything that alters the external appearance of the *copropriété* is of concern to all the members.

Needless to say, any work that is to be done to the common areas is the responsibility of the *syndic*.

## Charges

You will receive a regular bill for insurance, cleaning, maintenance and so on in the communal area. The cost of heating the common areas is also shared. There may also be a charge for the television aerial. The *syndic*'s remuneration is paid by all the owners.

The percentage of the charges that you are due to pay depends on the value of your part of the *copropriété*. You will have to pay for your share of a service, even if you do not make use of it, unless there is some good reason. For example, if you live on the ground floor, you do not pay for the lift. The list of charges and their distribution is included in the regulations of the *copropriété*. There is a time limit if you want to object to the amount you have to pay: either 5 years from the publication of the regulations, or within 2 years if you buy a share in a *copropriété*, but only if this is the first time it has been sold. The percentages of charges and the way these are calculated have to be included in the regulations of the *copropriété*.

If you are thinking of buying into a *copropriété* be sure to look at the minutes of the last 3 years of AGMs at the very least.

# Other types of common ownership

When a piece of land is divided up into parcels and an estate – *lotissement* – is constructed, the owners of the dwellings can set up an *association syndicale libre* to manage the shared spaces and equipment. The creation of an ASL is not obligatory. A *copropriété* can only be set up where the land has not been divided up.

An *indivision,* where more than one person owns a share in a property – usually through inheritance – does not come under the *copropriété* regime. For legal purposes it is considered an indivisible entity. A property company – *société civile immobilière* – is not a *copropriété* either, but it can own parts of a *copropriété* and send representatives to general meetings.

# Farms and vineyards

The French government is keen to encourage foreigners to take over farms since so many French farmers are giving up and moving to the cities. Local governments in central France are particularly interested in attracting new farmers. The land and buildings are far cheaper than in the UK, but newcomers may not get a very friendly welcome from the long-established locals. There are grants available for setting up farms. The first port of call is the departmental

*'the French government is keen to encourage foreigners to take over farms'*

ADASEA or *Agence Départementale pour l'Aménagement des Structures des Exploitations Agricoles*. See the websites www.cte.fnsea.fr/adasea/adasea.htm and www.safer.fr. Also see www.eurofarms.com, www.terresdeurope.net and www.europeruris.com.

It is also possible to buy a vineyard: it takes a brave person to try to beat the French at their own game, but it has been done. You should watch out for potentially useless vineyards. One Englishman was on the point of buying one in Provence when a local informed him that all the vines would have to be replanted and he wouldn't harvest a single grape for seven years.

# 9 Building Your Own Home

IN RECENT YEARS MORE AND MORE PEOPLE FROM OVERSEAS ARE CHOOSING TO BUILD THEIR OWN HOME in france. As with anywhere this can be a rewarding process, as you can, within reason and subject to budget and planning rules, choose your location and the layout and style of your home.

However, it does require a considerable amount of organisation and work compared with buying an existing building, and is not something to take on lightly. A few brave souls choose to design and do the building work themselves but most people prefer to use architects and artisans to carry out the work according to their requirements. You will need to be aware that different areas of France have different styles of building and you'll need to satisfy local planners that your plan fits in with these. Once again, the key to a smooth and trouble free self-build is research. First of all you will need to find the right plot.

## Buying Land for Building

It is not unusual for the French to buy a piece of land with the intention of building a property on it themselves and building land is generally cheap in the countryside.

A lot of land cannot be built on, especially on the coast. Agricultural land is also protected. Many *communes* have a PLU – *Plan Local d'Urbanisme* – which states which pieces of land may be built on; the PLU is still popularly referred by its old name: POS or *Plan d'Occupation des Sols*. Linked to this is the COS – *Coéfficient d'Occupation des Sols* – a figure giving the maximum amount of square metres of surface area that can built on each square metre of land. The implication is that if you want to build a property with more than a certain number of storeys then you will have to pay a further charge, if permission is granted at all. If the *commune* has no PLU, then the use of the land is decided by central government. Planning permission – the *certificat d'urbanisme* – will only be granted where there are adequate access roads, drains, water and electricity supplies, and so on.

A usual way to buy land for building is to buy a plot in a *lotissement* or new estate; otherwise you may find a single plot or *parcelle* by looking in the usual property magazines. If you are thinking of buying land for building, it is vital to be aware of any plans on the part of the local authorities to construct new roads, industrial parks, etc. Look in the local *Plan Cadastral* or Land

Registry, to see what the precise measurements of your piece of land should be, and whether there are new developments planned near to your property. If the boundaries are not clearly defined then you will need the services of a *géomètre-expert* – see the local yellow pages – to carry out the *bornage,* that is put in markers to show the boundaries. Only a *géomètre-expert* is allowed to change boundaries.

When buying land make sure that you choose a site that you really like rather than simply going for one that you can afford. Try to imagine yourself living on the site. What will the views be like? Will there be trees one day that will block your views, or other new buildings or roads or businesses? Find out from locals whether, for example, the site you have chosen is in a frost pocket or exposed to winds or has good or poor drainage. And will you will able to be connected to the local sewage system or will you have to have a *fosse septique?*

## Companies that sell land:

www.allobat.fr
http://frenchland.com
www.terrain.fr
www.terrain-a-batir.com
www.terrains.com
www.villesetvillages.fr
www.frenchentree.com

# Pre-emptive Rights/*droit de préemption*

In many areas, state organisations or the local council can have pre-emptive rights on land purchase. Even after you buy a piece of land, the state can make a compulsory purchase order; you will receive a 10% compensation. It is also conceivable that a private person has a pre-emptive right, or some other right, such as the use of the land for a fixed period, or rights of passage. In order to avoid pointlessly acquiring land, it is essential to conduct a search of all the possible *servitudes* or 'easements' attaching to a piece of land.

In agricultural areas, the main organisation to watch for is the SAFER – *Société d'Aménagement Foncier et d'Établissement Rural* – which exists to ensure that agricultural land, forests and fields are put to appropriate use, and in particular to try to bring small parcels of land under one ownership. The *notaire* handling the sale is legally obliged to inform SAFER of the impending transfer. Where it appears that there is going to be a change in the use of land, the SAFER can intervene and negotiate with the seller to find a more suitable use, or they can buy the land themselves and sell it on. Where the land is being sold to family members, or co-heirs, the SAFER will not intervene.

If SAFER does not reply to the *notaire* within two months, then the sale can go ahead. In some rare cases, SAFER may fail to notify the *notaire* and carry out a compulsory purchase even after the *acte de vente* has been signed. It is therefore essential to ensure that your *notaire* has gone through the necessary steps to obtain SAFER's agreement to the sale.

# Building your own Property

There are a number of ways you can go about building your own property. You can either hire an architect to design the building, or design it yourself, if it is fairly small, or go to a builder and ask them to supply you with a ready-made plan. If you choose to take a ready-made plan, then the contract you sign is a *contrat de construction d'une maison individuelle avec fourniture de plan*. The terms of the contract are strictly regulated by law. The builder must have financial guarantees and insurance. Payments are made according to a well-defined schedule:

| | |
|---|---|
| 15% | on starting the work |
| 25% | on completion of foundations |
| 40% | on completion of walls |
| 60% | when the roof is put on *(mise hors d'eau)* |
| 75% | on completion of walls *(mise hors d'air)* |
| 95% | when the heating, plumbing and carpentry are completed |
| 100% | at the hand-over. |

Not many foreigners go for this type of arrangement, since they would rather have a design of their own.

The more usual procedure is to hire an architect to draw the plans. This contract is not regulated in law. Evidently, it should include details of estimates of the cost, and stage payments. The actual building work is usually handled by a *maître d'œuvre*, who oversees the whole process, and engages various specialist tradesmen. A *maître d'œuvre* is not usually as highly qualified as an architect, but will have more time to spend on-site. Note that the person who engages a *maître d'œuvre* is called the *maître d'ouvrage*. The contract you sign with him is the *contrat de maîtrise d'œuvre* which is again not regulated by law. The *maître d'œuvre* will normally hire tradesmen that he has worked with in the past, or he may give the job to a local co-operative.

One final possibility is to act as your own *maître d'œuvre* and to conclude contracts – *contrats d'entreprise* – with the various builders and tradesmen that you need. Such contracts are regulated. They are more used for commercial property, and it is unlikely that a foreigner would want to go about building in this way.

# The Cost

You do not pay any *notaire's* fees when you build a house, simply the conveyancing fees. These amount to 1%–2% of the cost of the plot of land you are building on. However, there are other cost factors to bear in mind. The key point is to set a realistic budget you can afford in advance and try to stick to it as far as possible. It is also a good idea, however, to set aside a contingency fee for any unforeseen costs or overspend. This should ideally be a minimum of about 10% of the overall project budget.

As for the cost of building land itself, this will again vary enormously from area to area. In 2007 a 2,500 sq m plot of land with outline permission and with country views in the north Dordogne near the border with the Charente was on the market for €39,000. A 1,500 sq m plot on the edge of the minute a quarter of an hour from Limoges was being marketed for €24,750. Meanwhile a 2800 sq m plot of land at Sainte Maxime in the Var in the south of France was on sale for €700,000.

# Planning Permisison for New-Build and Renovation

The rules concerning planning permission both for new-build and renovation work in France were changed in October 2007 as part of a much-needed clarification and simplification of the rules. In place of the many different regimes that existed before there are now just three categories of planning authorisations:

1. *permis de construire* (planning permission)
2. *permis d'aménagement* (permission to develop or fit out an existing site, for example create a golf course, developing a housing estate or creating a leisure park)
3. *permis de démolis* (permission to demolish a structure).

There is a distinction between a *permis de construire* (PC) which is planning permission and a *certificat d'urbanisme*, which will be dealt with later.

In most cases overseas buyers looking to build a house or improve a home will be concerned with a PC, though anyone looking to develop leisure facilities, for example, may need a *permis d'aménagement*.

The basic rule of thumb now is that a PC will be required for all new building work. The law now lists those new works that do not require a PC, and which either need no form of approval or simply a preliminary declaration or *déclaration préalable*, also known as a *déclaration de travaux exemptés de permis* or *déclaration de travaux*. If the type of work you are carrying out is not included on these lists of exceptions then you will need a PC.

New work not needing any formal permission include wind turbines whose height is under 12 m, certain light constructions on a camping site or leisure park under 35 sq m in surface area and swimming pools of 10 sq m or less.

New work that requires simply a *déclaration préalable/déclaration de travaux* includes swimming pools of 100 sq m or less that are either uncovered or whose cover/roof is less than 1.8m high.

# In the know

**Michael Holmes is Editor-in-Chief of *Homebuilding and Renovating* magazine (www.homebuilding.co.uk). Here he gives some advice on building your home in France:**

■ Research the area/plot that interests you thoroughly, ideally in different seasons.

■ Find a builder and an architect you can trust, either locally or from the UK. Check that they are fully qualified and ideally registered members of their respective trade associations.

■ Set up a specific but realistic timeframe and try to stick to it.

■ Narrow down your chosen sites to a shortlist. You will need to go to France to arrange viewings of your shortlisted plots.

■ Write a list of all questions you need to ask during your viewings (noise, utilities included, cost of adding water, drains, electricity …): has it got *viabilité* or *non viabilité* – linked to mains already or not – and check proximity and access to services you need (school, shops etc.).

■ Ask for a get-out clause to be added to the preliminary contract, or *compromis de vente*, covering things such as rights of way, planning permission or a mortgage application being approved.

■ Check the site against a *plan cadastral*, the official record of site boundaries, which your surveyor can check for you or you can get it from your local town hall. By consulting the *plan local d'urbanisme* (PLU) and the related *coefficient d'occupation des sols* (COS) you will know more about the grounds and area you are about to purchase.

■ Contact the DDE, *Direction Departementale de l'Equipement* about road buildings, planned motorways or other projects that might spoil your purchase. Contact the SNCF to enquire about any new train or TGV routes.

■ Speak to local residents about local problems, noise, pollution …

■ Do not sign anything that you don't understand or are unsure of.

## Insider Tip

*(i)*

A key rule to remember is that if your restorations or new building work cover more than 170 sq m – this is the total floor area, whether one or more storeys – you have to have architect's plans drawn up. This area is 800 sq m for agricultural structures. Another important rule is that you cannot build anything within 3 m (10 ft) of a neighbouring property, or half the height of a neighbouring wall if it exceeds 6 m. These distances can vary slightly from area to area so you'll need to check with the mairie.

For existing buildings there is the reverse assumption that work does not need a PC or a *déclaration de travaux* unless it is specified in the law. The most important works on existing buildings that *will* require a PC are structures that add more than 20 sq m surface area to the building, or creating or enlarging new windows or doors (though not double glazing.)

Any work involving a change of use or which increases the number of rooms in the house (e.g. making a workshop or converting a loft into a bedroom), affecting the taxable value of the property, will require a PC. Knocking out walls always requires one; putting in new internal walls does not.

Other work exempt from a PC include terraces and walls under 2 m, or any structure with a surface area (*surface hors œuvre brute* or SHOB) of less than 20 sq m added on to an existing construction. A completely new construction with a surface area of more than 2 sq m and taller than 12 m. requires a *déclaration de travaux*; as do walls between 2 m and 12 m tall. Your *déclaration de travaux* must be displayed on the wall of the *mairie* within eight days of receipt. The administration has a month (sometimes two months) to respond; once this time has passed it is assumed that your *déclaration de travaux* has been accepted.

It is not necessary to enter the application for the PC yourself; your architect or *maître d'œuvre* or your representative (*mandataire*) can do this for you, but you are ultimately responsible if the right PC has not been acquired first. The forms you need are held by the *mairie*; they are exactly the same throughout France.

Calculating the surface area of the works is a complicated process. A distinction is made between the *surface hors œuvre brute*, or SHOB (the total surface area including cellars and roof spaces and the thickness of the walls, but not including inaccessible flat roofs or terraces at ground level), and *surface hors œuvre nette*, or SHON, the surface area used for deciding whether you need a PC or not, which allows you to subtract some surfaces according to complicated formulae. If you are unsure about the surface area concerned you can consult an *architecte conseiller* working for the municipality or other state body, free of charge.

The request for a PC is sent to the *mairie* by registered letter (*recommandée avec demande d'avis de réception* or *accusé de réception*), or it can be delivered by hand; you will be given a receipt (*décharge*).

The authorities no longer have to send you a *lettre de notification* with the number of your PC registration, and the length of time it will take them to deal with your PC.

The time limit for processing the request now starts from when the *mairie* receives the complete file. Previously, it started when the person who had made an application received notification from the town hall that their request had been received.

The *mairie* has two months for private houses (*maison individuelles*) and three months for other buildings (e.g. barn, block of flats) in order to process the application and either grant or refuse planning permission.

If however, the *mairie* requires further information, he/she must ask you for this additional information

> *'Planning permission rules are complex, and it is advisable always to ask the mairie before carrying out any building work, however minor'*

within a month of receiving the file: the town hall has a month to check whether or not the file is complete.

If the authorities fail to give a decision within the specified time then it is assumed that the PC has been granted automatically, a PC *tacite*. The *mairie* will handle the application in urban areas, or pass it on to the relevant intercommunal authority. A printed version of your application will be posted on the wall in the *mairie* with your name and address, so that anyone can raise objections if they wish. A PC is valid for two years.

If the *mairie* turns you down, you have two months to apply again. If you are refused again, you can go to a *tribunal administratif* to contest the decision or to claim damages or, in some cases, before going to the *tribunal administratif*, you can write to the *prefect* to ask him or her to intervene. You can ask for an *attestation* that no negative decision has been given if you want to be on the safe side.

Planning permission rules are complex, and it is advisable always to ask the *mairie* before carrying out any building work, however minor. It is important to understand that a *permis de construire* never allows you to demolish an existing building. For this you need a *permis de démolir*.

It is easy enough to go to the local office or *sub-division de la direction d'équipement* (there are several in every *département*) to get an opinion about what type of PC you need. The opinion of a local builder is not always reliable: the owner of the building is liable, not the builder. The authorities are tougher about PCs in some *communes* than in others; on the whole they are being applied more and more strictly everywhere in France as time goes by.

Several bodies are involved in granting the PC. Apart from the *mairie*, the *conseil municipal* and the *Direction Départementale de l'Équipement* have to give their approval. If you are carrying out work in an area subject to flooding, for example the Loire Valley or near the Rhine though there are many such areas in France, a state-appointed engineer has to assess the application. If the local *commune has* been declared a flood zone, the document indicating this, called the *plan de prévention de risques*, may say that a soil survey has to be carried out (*étude du sol*). This *étude* will be one of the documents filed with the planning permission. If you are building within 100 m of a cemetery the *mairie* has to be consulted.

The *Direction Départementale des Affaires Sanitaires et Sociales* and the *Sous-Commission Départementale d'Accessibilité des Personnes Handicapées* also have to give their approval if you are building or converting property for holiday complexes. The number of bodies that have to give their approval depends on the nature of the work.

Special rules apply if you are carrying out work on, or next to, or within view of, a listed building or site. The authorities have 4 months after acknowledging receipt of your application to consider the case. You should never assume that you have tacit approval where listed buildings are concerned, even if you hear nothing from the authorities. If the application is passed to the national ministry of public works they are not necessarily required to give you any response. If you are working within 500 m of a listed site, you may be told to use only certain kinds of building material, which can make the work far more expensive.

## Documentation for PCs

The documents and plans that are required are listed on the PC application form. Again the rules on these changed in 2007 and the law now indicates which documents must be filed with the application. The authorities can only ask for those documents and none other. These will include:

- a plan of the piece of land
- a site plan with the proposed work, between 1/100 and 1/500 with the orientation, and the property
- the *volet paysager*, two photographs of the property, from close up and distance
- plans of different floors of the property
- decisions regarding rights and obligations (*servitudes*)
- documents concerning grants
- a document outlining the use to which the new buildings will be put.

This is by no means the full list.

As in the UK and elsewhere, it is tempting to begin your building work before obtaining a PC, on the understanding that a PC is generally granted for the type of work you are undertaking. But as an outsider it pays to be doubly careful about following the rules, even if you risk making life more difficult for yourself. If you do go ahead and build before permission you risk having to see the structure demolished if the PC is turned down. All PCs are granted *sous réserve du droit des tiers* – with the reservation that third parties' rights are not affected. Having a CU or PC does not mean that your neighbours cannot raise objections if you are building something that overlooks their property, or if you infringe on some 'easement' or *servitude* that affects their property. These are matters of private civil law where the *mairie* has no say. The *mairie* will not necessarily be aware of all the easements affecting your property, unless they are mentioned in the land registry, i.e. the *conservation des hypothèques*.

When the work starts you enter a *déclaration d'ouverture de chantier* (declaration the work has begun). The authorities have the right to inspect the building site to ensure that you are respecting the terms of the PC. The PC has to be displayed on a *panonceau* or panel at the entrance to the building site for the duration of the work; third parties have two months in which they can enter objections if you have failed to take their interests into account when you applied for the PC. After building work is completed you have 30 days to enter a declaration that you have done the work according to the terms of the PC (*déclaration d'achèvement des travaux*). The authorities can inspect the work; they will then send a *certificat de conformité* within three months. No *certificat* needs to be issued if the work has not created any new surface outside the *surface hors œuvre brute* or SHOB.

Constructions requiring a PC may be liable to local taxes, the *taxe locale d'équipement* and the *taxe d'urbanisme*. The amount will be entered on the PC; if no amount is given you are not required to pay.

## Certificat d'urbanisme

Prior to applying for a PC, you may want to obtain outline planning permission, or a *certificat d'urbanisme* (CU). Anyone can apply for a CU, even before they have bought a property or piece of land. The application for the CU – *demande de certificat d'urbanisme* – requires plans and maps of the property, in four copies, and a description and drawings or photographs of the work you propose to do. You can expect a decision within two months. It is compulsory for the seller to obtain a CU where land is being sold to build on, except where this comes under the law governing housing estates or *lotissements*. This includes selling a part of the land that your property is sitting on. In other respects the CU is an opinion on whether a piece of land can be built on or not in relation to the town planning laws. Or it can be an opinion on an actual building project. Most *communes* have a *plan local d'urbanisme* (PLU), or a *plan d'occupation des sols* (POS), which states how many buildings with how much floor area can be put up on a certain piece of land. Each area of the *commune* has a coefficient – the *coefficient d'occupation du sol* (COS), a number used to calculate the maximum SHON or floor area (defined above) that can be constructed. If the COS is 0.40, then it allows you to build 200 sq m of SHON on a 500 sq m piece of land. In some cases you will be allowed to build more, but you will then have to pay financial penalties.

A CU will only be granted for land that is *viabilisé* – namely, where there are adequate roads and utilities, a pre-condition for it becoming *constructible*. Agricultural land is generally not *constructible* and is never likely to be. Not surprisingly, land that is *non constructible* is worth very little, but there are plenty of owners who will hang on to their *non-constructible* land in tourist areas, in the hope that some day in the future it will become *constructible*. The CU is delivered within two months of the application, if it is not turned down. You then have a year during which you are more or less guaranteed a PC, although it can still be denied if you do something illegal. Foreign buyers need to be especially careful that where land or property is sold with a CU included, that the CU is going to be valid for long enough for you to obtain the PC, because CUs will only run for a year. Buyers are sometimes told that a CU has been obtained, when it has in fact already lapsed. The PC can still however be refused, even if you have a CU. This is not so much because you've done something illegal, but because the CU itself is illegal – for example certain administrative prerogatives were not taken into account on the CU, or for example if the area is in a risk area (e.g. flood zone) and the mayor has omitted to indicate this on the CU.

## Insider Tip

You can still be taken to court after construction work has been completed if the alteration to the property has a real effect on your neighbours' rights to the peaceful enjoyment of their property. The best advice is to talk to your neighbours at the planning stage and try to get their agreement before you start any actual work.

## In the Know

**Lawyer Julia Jones discusses the changes in French planning laws:**

The changes in French town planning law implemented in October 2007 aim to facilitate the procedure for obtaining planning permission, which has been considered in the past too lengthy and too arbitrary. The new legislation clearly defines in what cases planning permission is required and the documents that should be filed with the application. Fortunately, the new legislation also stipulates the time given to the local authority in order to process the request. If the local authority has not provided a response in the time limit given, then, in principal, planning permission is deemed to have been granted.

Obtaining planning permission is still a complicated matter, which generally requires the assistance of an architect. It is, however, of crucial importance that planning permission is obtained when required. Failure to obtain planning permission has two important consequences. Firstly, the local authorities can require you to regularise the situation at a later date, or even to demolish the 'offending' building. Secondly, if the property is to be sold within 10 years following the completion of the works, the notary has an obligation to check that all the appropriate authorisations have been obtained. If they have not, the vendors will be advised by the notary to regularise the situation – which takes time, and is not always possible, thus making the property impossible to sell.

Julia Jones, a French-qualified avocat, works for Bright Jones, and is based in Toulouse. Telephone 05 61 57 90 86; email brightjones@wanadoo.fr.

There is another type of document that one can apply for, the *note de renseignement d'urbanisme* – also an opinion on whether something is *constructible* or not. The *note de renseignement* has no legal force, but it is popular with *notaires* because it makes them money, as does the CU. All one can say is that it gives buyers more security. Even then this may not be enough. If you are planning to construct something close to a listed building, then a departmental official, the *Architecte des Bâtiments de France* has to be involved. He may add more conditions to the permit, such as the type of building materials you can use, which will make the job far more expensive.

A recent property will have a CU: you couldn't build it without one. Older properties will not have a CU necessarily, unless someone applied for one, but there should have been a PC. There is the outside risk that a property was built without planning permission in the past. Once it has been standing for 30 years the authorities cannot make you demolish it.

# Hiring Professionals for Building Work

Most Britons will tell you that, while French builders are good at their job, they are also in great demand and booked up for months in advance. There is naturally a great temptation to bring over your own builders who are ready and willing to get on with the job. Not using the local tradesmen, however, may create resentment and put you on bad terms with the village. You also need to consider that British builders may be quite unqualified to make repairs

*'while French builders are good at their job, they are also in great demand and booked up for months in advance'*

to traditional French buildings, and will probably only have rudimentary French. Another factor to consider is that local builders will be usually know the type of building you want work done on or the local rules for new homes.

There are great risks involved in employing someone just because they speak English; many Brits have been the victims of incompetent or dishonest builders brought over from the UK, whose work carried no guarantees. Work done by builders registered in France has to be insured for 10 years – the *garantie décennale*. Registered French builders have gone through a long apprenticeship. Beware of using unregistered British builders, unless you know them well, because of the insurance implications. You are 100% liable if the builder is injured, and you will not have the usual guarantee against bad workmanship. In addition you will not qualify for grants towards doing the work, and the cost will not be taken into account in reducing your capital gains tax liability. If you have obtained a loan to do renovation work on your house from a French mortgage lender, it is a condition that you use registered French tradesmen. Another risk of working with unregistered people is that you could be considered as illegally employing someone in France, which is another offence.

All tradesmen in France should be registered with the local *chambre des métiers* and have an official business number: the SIRET. This is shown on advertisements. One will find numerous British and other English-speaking tradesmen advertising in French property magazines, such as *French Property News, France* and *Living France*; many of them have a SIRET number, the others in the process of applying for one: SIRET *en cours*. Even if someone you are employing does have a SIRET number you should find out what it covers. For example if someone has a SIRET number as a gardener but is employed by you to fix your roof, you could be in the same situation as if you were using someone who is not registered at all.

The normal procedure is to ask for an estimate – a *devis* – from several tradesmen; the *devis* is then binding. It is essential to obtain references from builders, and ask to see photographs of their previous work if possible. TVA is levied at only 5.5% on building materials and work done to restore or maintain properties more than two years old. If you use an unregistered tradesman you will pay the full rate of 19.6% on building materials. It is illegal to pay for any services in cash above €2,000.

If you are having a substantial job done, involving several tradesmen, you may wish to appoint a *maître d'œuvre* to supervise the whole operation. You will need to draw up a written contract with the *maître d'œuvre*.

Before building work begins, you can draw up an *état des lieux*, a description of the property, in the presence of the builder so that you have some evidence if they damage trees or verges. They may not, of course, agree to this. Every foreign property owner who has had work done by French tradesmen will tell you that they need to be supervised. They are generally very honest, but they may have assistants who are not.

## In the know

**David Darling 40, and his wife Shirley, from the Scottish Borders, are having a house built at Roumazieres-Loubert in the Charente. They talk of their experience so far:**

We are currently speaking to several builders to discuss styles and prices to build a house for us. We have a basic remit of a three-bedroom bungalow with garage and part covered terrace at the rear. The floor space we have asked for is around 100 Sq m on our plot of land that is 905 sq m. The house itself will run north/south with the front facing the east and rear garden to the west.

Although the plot has outline planning permission (it was sold as such), we still have to get detailed permission once we agree on a design. We also know that there are restrictions. The building has to be a bungalow, can be one of only two permitted colours and needs to blend in with other new-builds in the area.

We won't be doing the building work ourselves. Once we have spoken to the builders and confirm the design, then it's up to them, including getting final planning permission – though we shall be supervising.

In our experience, buying land was made extremely easy as the seller and the notary had a fixed price for the land and services. The notary even provided us with a translator to assist during the signing of the deeds. It would have been a far more difficult process for us to sign without one. We would suggest having a translator throughout any legal meetings and signings.

# 10 Finding Properties For Sale

## Estate Agents

THE ESTATE AGENCY PROFESSION IS NOT AS HIGHLY DEVELOPED IN FRANCE as it is in Britain, because the profession is still quite new. Until recently property sales were handled by *notaires*. On the positive side, many French estate agents are more relaxed and less cut-throat than those in Britain, but they can also seem amateurish by UK and US standards. In certain areas – especially the Côte d'Azur but also now in much of south-west France – there are professional estate agents who specialise in dealing with foreigners. You will often find either native English-speakers or French staff fluent in English working for quite small agencies in areas that are popular with overseas buyers.

The number of estate agents or *agents immobilier* in operation has grown rapidly in recent years. Most UK-based agents do not deal directly with properties themselves, but rather put you in touch with *immobiliers* in the area you are interested in, and generally organise your house-hunt for you. The advantage is that you do not have to deal directly with French *immobiliers*, and so your language abilities are not going to be so severely tested if they happen not to speak much English. There are more and more British estate agents setting up in France, so whether you feel you need another intermediary is up to you.

The English-speaking agent receives a commission from the *immobilier* which can be as much as 50% of

### Insider Tip

The need for agents arises because many British and other foreign buyers do not have the time to search for properties during their holidays. Ideally, one would spend several months living in an area and looking for property, but this is not always possible.

the total commission where there is a long-established partnership. Where agents are less well established, their commission from the *immobilier* will be less and they will charge the customer 1%–1.5% as an additional commission. It is important to be clear at the start how much commission you are paying any intermediaries. There will be a signing-on fee, which is refunded in the event that you buy the property. There are also a few conmen who pose as

## Insider Tip

*It is vitally important to find out at the start who is going to pay the immobilier's commission. It is more usual now for the seller to pay. The asking price that is advertised must, by law, include the agent's commission if the buyer is to pay it.*

agents and try to trick customers into paying deposits in advance of viewing a property, or even try to charge you simply for meeting them. You should walk away from any so-called agent who makes unusual demands before you have actually seen any property.

Apart from agents, there are property consultants who do research for potential buyers, and offer every kind of hand-holding service, which can include arranging flights and stays in France and advice on dealing with the buying process. A consultant will be paid by the customer directly for their services. French *immobiliers'* commissions vary from region to region, and are on a graduated scale depending on the value of the property. The minimum is around €2,000. With very cheap properties the commission can be up to 20%; above about €250,000 the commission will not exceed 3%. A very cheap property naturally attracts a very high percentage in commission. Upmarket properties in Paris or in tourist areas also attract high commissions; the normal range is 5% to 10%.

Some agents may try to quote you prices *net vendeur*, i.e. the price the seller will receive, so you need to be on your guard. Another dubious practice is quoting prices with all costs included, which allows the agency to slip in a few more thousand pounds unnoticed. You should always have a precise breakdown of all the components of the price.

Unlike in Britain, a French-based estate agent must have professional qualifications and have a licence from the *chambre de commerce*. Anyone who acts as an *immobilier* without a *carte professionnelle* is liable to a heavy fine and a jail sentence, and this has happened to some foreigners who, perhaps in ignorance of the law, have worked with *notaires* selling properties in France. They may have done a good job for their customers, but they still broke the law. The *carte professionnelle* has to be renewed every year. For an inside view of the estate agency business it is worth reading Alan Biggins' *Selling French Dreams* and *A Normandy Tapestry* (www.normandy-tapestry.com). Biggins worked in a grey area of the law for a while before he had to concede that the regulations made it too difficult for him to be an estate agent in France.

Estate agents are required to display the following notices in their office:

- number of their carte professionnelle
- amount of their financial guarantee
- name and address of their guarantee fund
- name of their bank and the number of the account into which funds have to be paid
- amount and percentages of commission.

Estate agents are legally required to have a minimum guarantee fund or bond of €110,000 if they maintain a blocked account for payments, as well as professional indemnity insurance. Estate agents who pass on the payments to a *notaire* with a guarantee fund only need to post a guarantee of €30,000, but they will not be permitted to join one of the main national organisations of estates agents. Members of the national organisation of estate agents FNAIM are required to have a slightly higher guarantee fund of €120,000. Members of FNAIM have indemnity insurance up to €2,500,000. The guarantee fund (*garantie financière*) ensures that you don't lose your deposit if the seller does a runner.

Estate agents have negotiators working in their offices, but each main office must have a holder of a *carte professionnelle*. Some branch offices have an *agent de commerce* or a *fondé de pouvoir*, someone who is mandated by an *immobilier* to negotiate contracts on their behalf.

The *immobilier* has a time-limited *mandat* or *mandate* from the seller to negotiate on their behalf. It is common practice for a seller to give several agents a so-called *mandat simple* to sell property on their behalf. Where the agent has the exclusive right to sell the property you will see *en exclusivité* on the advertisement; the agent has a *mandat exclusif* which may give him or her the right to carry out the sale themselves, or to allow the seller to deal directly with the client. As a general rule of thumb, if a property is advertised with several agents for a long time, you can assume that it is difficult to sell, and you can offer a lot less than the asking price. You may see the same property photographed from different angles.

Only half of properties in France are sold through *immobiliers*. The rest are sold privately, through *notaries* or at auctions. Going round villages asking if there are any properties coming on the market, or if anyone has died recently, can pay dividends. Even paying a local to act as a spy for you could save you a great deal of money.

A list of estate agents can be found in the The Directory.

## Property viewing

The role of the *immobilier* is to show people round the property. They stand to make a considerable sum of money if the property is sold through them. They will, not, however, put *A Vendre* (For Sale) on the property, for fear that potential buyers will trace the owner and deal directly with them. The For Sale sign will only be put up by private sellers, or if the owner is not easily traceable. For this reason you are accompanied on your house-viewing visits by an agent or the *immobilier* him- or herself. They do not give out precise addresses of properties, but rather put 15 km from such-and-such a village. Since several properties in a village can have the same name, you will have a hard time finding the one you are looking for.

If you are taken around by an agent, you will be asked to sign a *bon de visite* at the start to prove that the agent has taken you to see the property, and that he or she is entitled to the commission if it is sold.

### Insider Tip

You may begin the process by looking on the internet at some adverts, or in some French property magazines, and contacting an immobilier who will, if you are lucky, send you some details of the properties they have available. French immobiliers do not go for the same hard-sell techniques as their UK counterparts, and their publicity materials are not always of the same quality as in the UK.

☑ *Been there, done it...*

**Sarah Woodbridge moved with her husband, an engineer, and three children from Dorset, UK, to Antibes in the Alpes Maritimes. It took them five attempts to buy a property.**

We sold our house in the UK and had a lump sum, and we estimated that we could look for houses with an asking price of €350,000 on the basis of our salaries. We first tried to buy an old restaurant in the Fayence area (inland Var) from a private seller, as we were considering starting a business there. We put in an offer of €330,000 that was accepted, but the owner then asked us to wait for six months until January, for tax reasons. We replied by asking for a reduction in the price as we would have to rent for that period, but that was not accepted. The second property was a run-down house on top of a hill, being sold by the grandson of a couple who had died. Our offer of €295,000 was accepted, but then the owner asked us to pay €45,000 under the table in return for reducing the price (this was to avoid inheritance tax), something we refused to do.

The third property was very nice in Fayence, in a valley. We bargained the price down from €365,000 to €358,000, but it was still rather expensive for us. Also we had not taken into account the *notaire's* fees, which would add to the price.

The fourth property belonged to a person who had died. We put in an offer (for the asking price) of €309,000, but when the estate agent telephoned the vendor to confirm, he said he would have to withdraw as the family had refused to go along with the sale. We were sitting there ready to sign but they would not discuss it any further. By that time we felt rather depressed and fed up with the whole thing.

In the case of the fifth house, we were not that keen on it to start with. It had been on the market for a long time, and needed a bit of work on it. The asking price was €330,000, and we first offered €285,000, which they would not accept. Then they came back and suggested that we sign an *offre d'achat* or binding offer to buy, at €292,000. Both the seller and the estate agent had taken a cut in what they asked for. In the end the estate agent received €15,000 and the owner only €277,000. We then went on to sign an undated *compromis de vente*. It could not be dated until the report on asbestos, the *diagnostic amiante*, had been done. At the same time we made out a cheque for €5,000 to the estate agent which he said he would not cash, but in fact he did three weeks later. Finally we had our property.

## Marchands de biens

As well as the *agents immobilier* there are also the *marchands de biens* (dealers in property), the main difference being that a *marchand de biens* buys and sells properties in their own name to make a profit, while an *immobilier* is legally not allowed to buy or sell in their own name. Anyone who makes a living from regularly buying and selling property or land has to register with the chamber of commerce; they are taxed according to a special regime, not on the basis of capital gains; and they pay VAT on the profit they make on selling a property. They are only subject to very low registration charges on the purchase of property as long as they resell the property within four years. It is common practice for a *marchand de biens* to make a downpayment on a property while looking around for a potential buyer, but they do have to own the property for three months before they resell it. They take the risk of having to pay hefty tax penalties if they don't find someone to buy the property within four years, or if, in the case of land, they do not start constructing a property.

# Advertisements

The first place one might consider looking would be British newspapers: the *Daily Telegraph* has regular advertisements for French property. *The Times* also carries some advertisements; these are generally in a high price bracket; some are from private advertisers. There are generally fewer advertisements for property in French newspapers than in the UK; the national newspapers advertise very little. *Le Figaro* has a section for Paris. French magazines with an international readership, such as *L'Express* and *Nouvel Observateur* have advertisements for expensive properties, mainly in the south of France, on their inside back pages in some issues.

## Insider Tip

The main thing to watch out for is that you are actually shown the properties you are interested in. It happens all too often that foreigners go out to France to look at a cottage and then find that they are being shown châteaux and barns, and everything but what they wanted, because that is all the agent has on their books. The other pitfall is to make sure that the property you specifically want to see has not already been sold to someone else. An attractive-looking property on the internet may not be available any more by the time you get to France. Agencies in the UK may be slow to find out whether a property has been sold.

The main French property magazines distributed in the UK carry some advertisements for individual properties, and a lot of ads for agents: these are *France, Living France* and *French Property News*. The websites are a good source for advertisements. British agents' websites are a fertile source of properties; they will also send you lists. French *immobiliers* are not that keen to send lists of properties to anyone based outside France; they prefer to deal with people who are on the spot. If you are travelling around France, it is easy to pick up lists of property that are left outside the *immobiliers* all year round.

There is a wealth of French websites with property advertisements, and there are numerous French magazines with advertisements sorted by *département*. The main national magazine for second homes is *Résidences Sécondaires* which also has interesting articles about the property market. The main publisher for holiday properties and rentals is Indicateur Bertrand, and they have specialised magazines for Paris, Rhône-Alpes and the south. For more downmarket properties, it is best to try to get hold of local estate agents' lists. The cheapest properties are often in the hands of *notaires,* who advertise on the internet. There are separate magazines for new property developments, mainly apartments, such as *Immobilier Neuf.*

# The internet

Thousands of properties are advertised on the internet in French and English. Estate agents' websites are one starting point. *Notaires'* websites (see The Directory) often have a section on property and carry some very general information about legal issues. General websites on property carry a wealth of useful information (in French), and offer the possibility of advertising your own requests. Newspapers have *immobilier* sections on their websites (see The Directory); reading the local news can help you to know more about an area. Property magazines have their own specialised websites. There are also government websites with information on regulations and changes in the law.

# Property fairs

There are also now a number of property fairs and shows in the UK and Ireland where you can meet estate agents selling property and see property for sale. These are advertised in French property-related newspapers, magazines and websites. The French Property Exhibition and A Place in the Sun Live are among two of the better known shows.

# Interpreting property advertisements

Property advertisements in French are not always that informative and can be hard to interpret. Estate agents do not give the kinds of detailed measurements of rooms that you would expect from a UK estate agent. By law, the advertised price must include the estate agent's commission. Some agents still advertise *net vendeur* (i.e. the price the seller gets), which will be indicated by the abbreviation HNC or n.c.

The price given in an advertisement is only the starting point for your negotiations. It is usual to offer 10%–15% less than the price stated. French sellers are aware that foreigners pay over the odds for property, but if you are in an area where the other potential buyers are also foreign then your room for haggling will be much more limited. There is more scope for bargaining in central and eastern France, much less in the south and west.

Some aspects of property terms are baffling: the terms T1, F1, Formule 1, and Type 1 all mean exactly the same thing: one room plus a kitchen and bathroom (which may be very small). The word English people take to mean a room – *une chambre* – actually means a bedroom; a room

> '*the price given in an advertisement is only the starting point for your negotiations*'

is *une pièce*. Some words can give rise to odd misunderstandings. If the advertisement says there is a *verger* included, you shouldn't imagine that you are taking over a vicarage; it means an orchard. Advertisements also use the English word *standing* meaning quality, rather than parking.

The term *haut standing* implies a high-quality development, while *moyen standing* might be a warning that this is not such a good area. There is no such thing as *bas standing*. Some adverts have *hors lotissement,* 'non-estate' in English estate-agent parlance; the implications of being on an estate are not necessarily as dire as they would be in England. Houses on *lotissements* are modern and uniform in style, but not necessarily in a bad area. Properties can be said to be in a *quartier difficile* or *quartier à problèmes* – an area with social problems. The absolute pits is a *quartier sinistré* – a seriously rundown area.

The term *maison de bourg* is used for a town-centre house; the original meaning was a house within a fortified hilltop village. Nowadays, *bourg* implies that there are some shops in the vicinity; *bourgade* means much the same. The term *bungalow* is not the same as in English as it implies a wooden garden house which is unsuitable for year-round occupation. A *plain-pied* is on one storey; it does not necessarily mean the same as a British-style bungalow. A *pavillon* originally meant a hunting lodge, but now refers to a two- or three-bed holiday villa or simply an up-market detached house in the suburbs. There are virtually no semi-detached houses in France (which says a lot about how the French view neighbours).

It is normal, but not obligatory, to give the habitable surface area of the property in the advertisement. Advertisements for apartments should always give the surface area; there is a law that requires the surface area of an apartment in a *copropriété* to be given in the contract, the *Loi Carrez*. Advertisements for newly built houses will always give the habitable surface area. The glossary on should guide you through the idiosyncrasies of property ads.

# My House in France
## Richard Burton

Richard was at one time Professor of French at the University of Sussex. He is now living about 100 miles south-east of Paris.

### What made you decide to move to your area?
The main reason is that it hasn't been taken over by other Britons. Also it's one-and-a-half hours from Paris. For this reason quite a few Parisians have second homes here. Generally, the countryside is quite nondescript and it's fairly cold in winter, but it suits me fine.

### How was the buying process for you?
Everything went very smoothly. Fortunately, I had the assistance of two French friends, but I could understand the documents myself in any case. I admit that the buying process could be a lot more complicated if you don't speak fluent French, but on the other hand, I haven't come across any Brits who have had serious problems with buying a property. After signing the *compromis de vente* it took just 11 weeks before I took possession of the house.

### How are the neighbours?
I was careful to look out for any possible problems with neighbours, such as loud dogs and other noise nuisances, but I hadn't reckoned on two parrots living next door. I asked the owners to get rid of them, and they agreed; they were fed up with them too. Generally, the French practise a 'live and let live' ethos. The French are noisy people, and they don't respond sympathetically to complaints about barking dogs and the like. On the whole, I didn't check nearly enough on the neighbours and the locality; it is not as quiet as I expected. I didn't realise that there is a private airfield 20 miles from here – they are common in France – so that came as a nasty surprise. At least look on a map to see if there is one in the vicinity.

### How about the heating and utilities?
I'm waiting to see what it's like in winter. I have lots of wood. I'm only going to heat half of the house with central heating. This is *gaz de ville* which is a great advantage. In addition I plan to use paraffin heaters, which are a lot better than in England and don't smell. Heating is crucial in a cold area; at least check that your central heating is working and get in plenty of fuel.

As for electricity, there are never enough power points, and a lot of French wiring is dangerous, so check up on everything, especially the earthing (*raccordement à la terre*). A lot of these old systems would never pass a safety test, so you must have it all checked by a professional. Finally, contrary to what some might say, British electrical equipment works fine here, apart from TVs. If you want to watch UK videos, bring a UK video and TV which will work OK, but you won't be able to watch French TV.

**What is your opinion of French tradesmen?**
Generally, extraordinarily slow and unreliable. You have to put continuous pressure on them to do something. I would advise getting estimates (*devis*) from three or four people, because some of them won't deliver. I was frequently let down because I didn't get enough estimates. The *professionnels,* especially builders, here have a huge backlog of work, so think six months ahead. You must follow them up at weekly intervals. And use local tradesmen.

**What advice would you give to prospective British buyers?**
Firstly, take your time. The more time you can spend looking around the better. If you go to an *agent immobilier* make sure that they have their professional certificate displayed on the wall, or ask them to show it. I would also advise on learning French as soon as possible, otherwise your social life is going to be limited to other foreigners. Certain areas of Normandy and the Dordogne are now so over-populated with Britons that you can walk into a bar and not find a single French person. This is not really a problem as far as the French are concerned, but it rather defeats the object of going to live abroad.

# PART FOUR
## The Purchasing Process

Buying a property in France needs a sense of wild adventure and daring-do if you are the type that thinks surveys are a waste of money. Even after 40 years in my profession as a building surveyor I am amazed at the condition of some French properties I come across. I have surveyed a host of rural, ex-farm properties and this could account for the catalogue of test-book defects I see on a regular basis. I have said to many a young trainee-surveyor that France is the place to learn about house surveys.

When I do a house survey in the UK I am rarely on the point of trying to suppress a smile. However in France I know that I am probably going to have a problem keeping a straight face, especially if the house is advertised as "renovated". I was in one the other day in Northern France that had been "renovated" solely by the application of several sheets of plasterboard to some internal walls. I say this because I could see no other evidence of any renovation whatsoever even though I looked really, really hard. The outside walls which are fairly important in that they hold up the main structure, support the roof, keep out the weather, etc. were on the verge of collapse. The bricks were held together by the adhesive properties of the ambient air that passed through the joints where traditionally mortar is found. The brick joints would have breached the Trades Description Act in the UK as they did not actually join the bricks. Only gravity (and the adhesive air) was holding them all in place.

I have to mention the staircase because it was as if Tommy Cooper had built it as one of his props. I could write several hundred words on this alone but suffice to say it used less wood than a laminate floorboard and there was no access for anyone over the height of 5 feet. The accepted joinery principles of each riser being the same height and each tread being the same depth were obviously rejected out-of-hand at the design stage. It is worth noting that French Building Regulations are entirely optional and avoiding them is the second favourite pastime after tax avoidance. The stair warranted a health warning although it was probably safer than the house walls.

This French house was not an exception so my advice is beware and expect the unexpected in France. If you are inexperienced in house buying or building construction have a survey done. Expect to have a very interesting report for your money particularly if the place is old and "renovated".

Martin Quirke FRICS MCIAT

**Advertorial**

# 11 Peace Of Mind

## Inspections and Surveys

HAVING A PROPERTY SURVEYED BEFORE YOU BUY IT is more or less a matter of course in the UK, but not so in France. Fewer than 3% of buyers have a survey done, against 95% in the UK.

The reasons for the lack of interest in surveys are cultural. In the countryside people assume that if a house looks solid it is not likely to fall down within their lifetime. French property sellers may not accept a clause such as 'subject to survey' in the preliminary contract. Any general survey should be done before signing the preliminary contract. If you want to secure the property by signing a preliminary contract, but you have a concern about a specific aspect of the property, then it may be possible to insert a clause requiring further checks to be done.

There is also the fact that there is no such profession as 'chartered surveyor' in France. There is the *géomètre-expert,* whose job is to calculate the surface area of buildings and land, and then there are architects who do some surveying as well. Specialised firms of surveyors are hard to find, and their services are expensive since they have to keep a whole group of different professionals working together under one roof. Information can be found on www.geometre-expert. fr, or contact: Ordre des Géomètres-Experts, 40 ave Hoche, 75008 Paris; ☎01 53 83 88 00; email ordre@ geometre-expert.fr.

### Insider Tip

Surveys for termites and lead paint are not required in every case. The inspection is done at the expense of the seller of the property, who has to present the expert's report when the pre-sale agreement is signed. The expert who carries out the work is not allowed to have any links with firms who carry out treatment for termites, asbestos or lead paint.

## Compulsory surveys

In some respects, there is protection for buyers from *'vices cachés'* – latent faults – in that an inspection has to be done everywhere in France for the presence of asbestos. Surveys for termites and lead paint may also be required. There is a national organisation of experts in these three areas, grouped under www.expertimmobilier.com, or one can look under *expert* in the yellow pages. Note that the term *expertise immobilière* refers to valuations; people who carry them out are often *notaires*, not surveyors. Technical surveys come under *expertises techniques*. Some *notaires* have surveyors working for them.

## Termites

The original law intended to protect house buyers from insect infestations dates from 1999; it was originally intended to cover not only termites but also other kinds of insect infestations, such as death watch beetle (*grosse vrillette*) and woodworm (*petite vrillette*), as well as dry rot, wet rot and other fungi. The subsequent decree passed in 2000 only mentions termites. Other wood-eating insects are not covered; nor are dry rot and wet rot. Inspections only have to be done where a prefectural decree has been issued requiring one; much of the south-western quarter of France comes under this category. The expert will draw up an *état parasitaire*. If the expert notices other signs of wood-eating insects apart from termites, he will mention them, but the search is basically only for termites. The report is valid for three months and must be presented at the signing of the *acte de vente*.

The worst infestations of termites are in the Landes, followed by Gironde, Charente Maritime and Lot-et-Garonne, where over half the *communes* are affected. The Dordogne is also quite badly affected, as are parts of the Loire Valley. For maps of infested areas and those where there is a prefectural decree in force requiring a report, look at the CBTA website: www. termites.com. The only way to be entirely certain whether there is a termite infestation in your *commune* is to ask the *préfecture* or *mairie*. If treatment has to be carried out for termites, etc., check that the company is a member of the CBTA in France, or the BWPDA in the UK. The cost of the work is tax-deductible.

## Asbestos/*amiante*

The requirement to carry out inspections for the presence of asbestos has been extended to all properties for sale that were built before 1997. The *compromis de vente* cannot be finalised without the survey report, which is carried out at the expense of the seller. Out of the three types of asbestos, blue and brown asbestos are known to be dangerous; white asbestos is apparently harmless. Asbestos can be found mixed with cement, plaster and paint, and has been used for pipes, wall panels, floor tiles, corrugated sheeting and slates. It has also been used a lot in industrial and commercial buildings. In itself, asbestos does not present a risk unless it starts to flake and release dust. The technical expert who prepares the report will tell you what action needs to be taken. You should not try to remove or cut through asbestos-containing materials yourself.

## Lead/*plomb*

Paint containing lead was widely used until recently. It presents a danger to human health where it flakes off or turns to dust. This can cause the syndrome known as *saturnisme* in French, retardation of the brain functions, hence one will see notices about *la lutte contre le saturnisme*, 'the struggle against saturnism'. The main victims are immigrants living in damp old houses in big cities. One way of dealing with lead paint is to cover it up with wallpaper or panelling; the other, far more expensive, is to have it removed entirely.

Once you sign the contract accepting the property in the condition in which it is sold, there is no way to obtain compensation if you find lead paint later on, unless you can prove that the seller deliberately misled you.

## Radon gas

This is a colourless, odourless, gas, released by the breakdown of uranium. About 9% of all lung cancers are caused by radon gas. Unhealthy concentrations can be found in houses built on granite, such as one might find in some parts of Brittany. There is as yet no law requiring a seller to have the air tested for radon.

## Energy efficiency

Yet another test on property has arrived in France, as it will in due course in other parts of Europe. This is the test of a home's energy efficiency. In French this is known as a *diagnostic de performance énergétique* (DPE). This test has to be carried out by a qualified person, and it measures how efficient the heating is, the quality of the insulation and so on. The expert grades the house and lists any major faults and how to put them right. However, though it is attached to the sale contract, the energy certificate has no legal effect – the seller is not obliged by law to carry out the work and nor is the buyer. The cost of the test can vary from €250 up to €700 or more. Since July 2007 it has applied to new homes as well as older properties. The scheme is part of the EU's efforts to combat global warming and save energy. To find someone to carry out the survey if you are selling you can simply type *diagnostic de performance énergétique* plus the name of your department into a search engine and this should give you the names and details of experts in your area. You can also use www.dimexbat.com to help you find one.

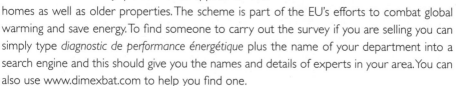

### Insider Tip

The seller of a property is required to call in an expert to prepare a report – a *diagnostic plomb* – in areas where there is a prefectural decree in force. This only concerns properties built before 1948. The report is valid for a year and is to be presented before signing the pre-sale agreement. Where there is no prefectural decree in force requiring an inspection, you need to be on your guard that there is no lead paint in the basement of the property you want to buy, or elsewhere.

# Boundaries

When buying a property, you need to know where the boundaries lie, otherwise you may find that you have less land than you expected. It is quite common for there to be no precise boundaries between properties. It is a *géomètre-expert*'s job is to establish *bornes* or boundary markers. It is important to study the *plan cadastrale* for the area surrounding the property to ascertain which numbered parcels are included in the sale. See www.geometre-expert.fr.

# Droughts and subsidence

The risks of damage due to drought are becoming more serious in many parts of France. With global warming one can expect more abnormally hot summers such as in 2003 when temperatures reached 46 °C.

Houses built on clay (*argile*) are particularly at risk. While clay is impermeable, the surface can absorb water, which makes the clay expand. In a temperate climate, clay is normally close to its saturation limit and cannot expand much, but it is also furthest removed from its dry state. With successive droughts, the clay shrinks causing shifts in the foundations of properties. The worst problems are in the Paris area, Normandy, Haute-Garonne, Gers and Tarn-et-Garonne. Where there is a lot of granite, such as Lozère, Haute-Vienne and Brittany, there is no problem. The *Bureau de Recherches Géologiques et Minières* produces reports on changes in clay, under the heading *L'aléa rétraits-gonflements de l'argile*; see www.brgm.fr/retraitGonfl. htm. Another problem is that a lot of the older built stone houses are constructed without adequate foundations with the bottom layer of stones being simply laid on to excavated earth

The cure is to fill cracks with mastic, and if necessary drive small piles into the foundations. For new-build, driving the foundations into a substrate that is not affected by the weather is one expensive solution. Small streams or gutters that channel water towards the house need to be diverted. Certain trees suck up water and thus dry out the clay: the worst offenders are poplars, cedars, willows and oak. The *vigne vierge* or Virginia creeper is a very thirsty plant. Trees can destabilise foundations by drawing water from one part of the foundations to another. If necessary, put a screen into the foundations to stop roots from growing. Avoid planting trees too close to your house in any case. You can also build an impervious pavement all the way around your house to limit evaporation directly next to the outer walls. Finally, ensure that the foundations are on an equal level at the base.

## UK surveyors

Since there is a gap in the market not filled by French surveyors, a number of British chartered surveyors have started business in France, mainly in the south-west where there is a lot of old property to be bought for renovation. Some are based in the UK and France, and will travel out to France for you. There are also British architects who carry out surveys, prepare applications for building permits, etc. French surveyors should belong to the *Ordre des Architectes*. Names and coordinates are given in property magazines and English-language newspapers.

A list of qualified surveyors can be found in The Directory.

## Checking with the planners

As well as knowing that your own house and boundaries are in good shape, you need to know about the area too. Are there any plans for the future near your house that might affect your enjoyment of it – and its value? Your first point of contact on this should be the mayor's office who should be able to tell you about about any plans for new roads or rubbish tips or other major developments in the area – for example new nuclear

> *'Are there any plans for the future near your house that might affect your enjoyment of it – and its value?'*

power stations. The local *Direction Departementale de l'Equipement* (DDE) – which is organised by *département* – should also be able to tell you about any plans for large scale roads or motorways. If you ask the mayor's office nicely they may agree to contact the DDE on your behalf if they are unsure of any plans outside their immediate area of influence. The mayor's office should also know about any plans for new railway lines in the area – the TGV (*train à grande vitesse*) high-speed network of lines (LGV or *ligne à grande vitesse* ) are being extended throughout France. If not, you can contact the railway company SNCF (www.sncf.com). It's also a good idea if you can to chat to neighbours about any problems with pollution, noise, smell and so on.

# Checklist for the Buyer

Before you commit to buying your new home in France it's a good idea to step back and take a good hard look at what you are planning to do. In particular you should examine the place you are looking to buy – and work out if it really is such a great idea after all. The following are some of the questions you should ask yourself.

- Do you like the property?
- Can you afford the house?
- How easy is it get to?
- Will it be too isolated for you in winter?
- Are there good schools and shops nearby?
- Are there good medical facilities nearby?
- What is the area like – are other houses in good condition?
- Is this house in good repair? If not, do you have a good idea of how much it will cost to repair/renovate?
- Is the garden big enough/too big?
- Will the garden be easy to maintain?
- Where can you park your car/cars?
- Is there good access to the property?
- Is the house secure?
- Is it private – are you overlooked by neighbours?
- Will neighbours/schools/workshops/roads/farms cause a lot of noise during the day or night?
- Is the house on the mains sewer system? If not, can it be put onto it?

- Are there enough power points in the house? If not, how much will it cost to put in new ones?
- Is the area subject to flooding?
- How much will it cost to heat and light a year?
- If you have children, are there potentially hazardous features such as ponds?
- Is there high-speed internet access available? If not, are there any plans to install it in the community?
- Does your mobile phone work there?

# In the know

**Brian Hersee is an experienced chartered surveyor and engineer now living and working in the Charente. Here he offers his advice about buying a property in France:**

France is a vast country with a wide variety of people, property, lifestyles, cultures, surroundings, amenities etc., and it is so important at the outset that you are clear as to what your desires are– working or retirement, city life or rural retreat, medium-sized house with average garden or small château with acres of land. So many Brits start looking with no fixed idea of what they are after and end up with something completely inappropriate. I once surveyed a house for a couple who were taking early retirement and it was a 12-bedroomed house with 10 acres of land. They didn't want to use it for any business proposition but bought it because they could say 'look how much house and land I can get for my money'. I visited them about 4 months after they moved in and both looked considerably older; the man had spent nearly all his time cutting the grass on the 10 acres.

Having found the house my second piece of advice would be to have a structural survey carried out. You are buying in a foreign country with different building techniques and specific regulations regarding electricity, drainage, ventilation, swimming pools etc., and in my view it is imperative that you have as much information as possible before committing to buy.

My third piece of advice, especially if there will be any renovation or improvement work involved is to engage the services of a project manager at the outset – preferably *before* purchase. They can advise on planning matters, i.e. what can and can't be done – and more importantly advise on the likely costs of the work. So many times people discover all too late that although properties are cheaper to buy than in the UK, renovation and improvement costs can sometimes be considerably higher. Add to this the scarcity of availability of registered experienced artisans and all too often the dream quickly turns to nightmare. Very recently I advised a couple who had already bought a house that the minimum renovation cost for the project was €130,000. Unfortunately their maximum budget was €50,000 . I am currently awaiting their response.

To contact Brian: email cassiehersee@wanadoo.fr or telephone 05 45 64 94 56.

# Simone Paissoni

## IN FRANCE         FOR FRANCE

Tri lingual English Solictor based in Nice since 1995 provides advice and assistance on all aspects of property purchase and ownership in France, with emphasis on inheritance and taxation.

**Tel: +334 93 62 94 95 Fax: +334 93 62 95 96**
**Email: spaissoni@wanadoo.fr**
**22, ave Notre Dame, Nice 06000. France**

# 12 Conveyancing

ONCE YOU ARE SURE YOU HAVE FOUND THE RIGHT PLACE it is time for you to make an offer and, once it is accepted, for the French legal system to play its part. Overseas property buyers are understandably anxious about the prospect of making such a major purchase in a foreign legal system. After all, it can be nerve-wracking enough at home. However the good news is that the French system is relatively straightforward, if very different perhaps from the one you're used to.

As long as you understand clearly the different steps that are involved and what your rights and responsibilities are at each of them, you should not encounter too many nasty shocks. Many buyers find themselves pleasantly surprised by the purchasing process, and it's not unusual, for example, to hear British buyers compare it favourably with their own. First of all it's important to understand the role of the key legal figure in property transactions in France – the *notaire*.

## The *Notaire*

*Monsieur le Notaire* is a stock figure in French folklore; there are still very few *Madame le Notaires*. The institution of *notaire* dates back to a time when few people could read or write and the state needed someone to certify documents as genuine. There are a few notaries public in the UK; but on the whole this is a purely Continental institution. These days the *notaire* is a public official, appointed by the state, whose main function, as far as property transfers are concerned, is to ensure that everything is done correctly, and that all taxes have been paid. *Notaires* do not have a good reputation in France; as a foreigner you are not in a strong position to obtain redress if they make a mistake.

It is normal for the *notaire* appointed by the seller to handle the transaction. They may have handled the sale of the property in the past. The buyer is entitled to appoint their own *notaire* without paying any additional costs, in theory; the two *notaires* share the fees between

## Insider Tip

It is always wisest to have your own notaire if you are the buyer. Although a notaire may know a great deal about the property being sold, they are not likely to tell you anything more than they have to. The most important thing to understand is that the notaire does not look out for your interests. One of the biggest mistakes that Britons make in France is to imagine that a notaire is the equivalent of a solicitor.

them. There is a chance that some extra items will be added to the bill to see that both *notaires* get a fair share of the fees. If you want impartial legal advice it is best to approach a bilingual lawyer or *avocat*, most likely one based in the UK though there are some in France too. Few *notaires* speak good English, and they will be doubly cautious about giving advice in a foreign language.

The *notaire's* main concern is to ensure that he or she does not make an error and leave themselves open to being sued. *Notaires* undergo seven years of training and are experts in property law, but they do sometimes make mistakes. The chances of a foreigner successfully suing a French *notaire* are slim. Since they also act as tax collectors, you should be on your guard about what you tell them. A *notaire* has professional liability insurance. In addition, his (or her) activities are supervised by the departmental *chambre des notaires*.

## Functions of a *notaire*

You may be told: 'We don't use *notaires* for property transactions in France.' There is some truth in this. A property transaction can be carried out through private treaty – *sous seing privé* – but such an agreement is only binding on the parties who have entered into it: it is legally inferior to an *acte authentique* signed by a *notaire*. If you want a deed of sale that is binding on third parties, then the intervention of a *notaire* is legally necessary at the signing of the *acte de vente*. The *notaire* will deposit a copy of the *acte* with the deed and mortgage registry (*bureau des hypothèques*) and that is it. As a foreigner buying property in France, it would be foolish not to use a *notaire*, otherwise you leave yourself at risk of all sorts of unpleasant surprises later on after you have taken possession of your property.

Amongst other things the *notaire* will:

- conduct a search in the land registry to see whether any third parties have any claim on the property, or the right to use the land for any purpose
- transfer your money via an escrow or blocked account to the seller, while ensuring that all fees and taxes have been paid in full
- ensure that any pre-emptive rights on the property are 'purged'
- witness the *acte de vente* or other agreement to sell the property to you.

# The Offer and Pre-contracts

First of all, however, and before the *notaire* gets involved you need to make on offer on the property. You can make a formal written offer, an *offre d'achat*, or *promesse d'achat* – promise to buy – which the seller can consider. It only becomes legally binding on the seller if he or she accepts it. You are not allowed to make any deposits accompanying an *offre d'achat*. On the whole, it is simpler to make a verbal offer, and then ask for a preliminary contract to be drawn up.

If your offer is accepted, a preliminary contract – an *avant-contrat* – will be drawn up. Although there is no legal obligation to use a preliminary contract, it is universally used. There are two main types of contract in use in France: the *compromis de vente* which is binding on both parties, and, less commonly, the *promesse de vente* (promise to sell), which is binding on the seller. The latter is commonly used north of the River Loire, including Paris. It is normal to pay 5% to 10% of the sale price as a deposit.

# Before signing the pre-sale contract

Because of the binding nature of pre-contracts, it is vital to go through the following points before you sign anything.

- Are you sure that you can use the property for your intended purpose?
- Have you obtained preliminary planning permission for any work you want to do?
- Does the sale include all the outbuildings and attached land, without reservation?
- Are the boundaries of the property clearly marked out?
- Are there any rights of way over the land?
- Do any third parties have any rights relating to the property?
- Will you share property rights over boundary walls with neighbours?
- If the property is recent, have you seen the handing-over report: the *procès verbal réception des travaux*?
- Has planning permission been obtained in the past for any work?
- Has the contract been checked by a qualified person?

You have the right to obtain an extract from the land registry (*extrait de matrice cadastrale*) from the *mairie* to verify the above points. The numbers on the *plan cadastrale* should correspond with those mentioned in the *compromis de vente*.

# *Promesse de vente*

With the 'promise to sell' the seller commits himself to selling within at least a month, or more usually within two to three months. In return the potential buyer will pay an *indemnité d'immobilisation*, a sum that compensates the seller for temporarily taking his property off the market. The usual amount is 10% of the sale price. The *promesse de vente* can be signed in front of a *notaire*, or can be signed privately. The seller pays a charge of €300–€400 to the *notaire*. If the *promesse*

*'the seller commits himself to selling within at least a month'*

is signed privately, it is to be signed in triplicate, and one copy is deposited with the *recette des impôts*. It is in the buyer's interests to sign the *promesse* in front of a *notaire*. The *notaire* will not witness a contract unless they have drawn it up themselves, or they are satisfied that it is free from flaws.

It is strongly recommended that the *indemnité d'immobilisation* be paid into a blocked account held by a *notaire*, and not directly to the seller. If you exercise your option to purchase – *lever l'option* – the *indemnité* will be deducted from the sale price. If the deal falls through the *indemnité* will be returned to you if one of the get-out clauses can be invoked within the allotted time; otherwise you will lose it outright.

## Pacte de préférence

This is a variation on a *promesse de vente*, whereby the seller promises to sell the property to the potential buyer if they choose to exercise their option on it. Essentially, it is a right of first refusal. This type of contract is becoming less popular, as it is difficult to enforce penalties in a court of law if it is broken by the seller. It is still used a lot for rental properties.

## Compromis de vente

The more common type of pre-contract, or *avant-contrat*, also goes under the name of *promesse synallagmatique*, since it binds both seller and buyer. It is usual to pay 5% to 10% of the sale price as a deposit or *depot de garantie;* this is not the same as the *indemnité d'immobilisation* mentioned above. The deposit should be paid into a blocked account – *compte séquestre* – held by a *notaire* or by the estate agent.

The nature of the deposit is vitally important. If it is an *arrhes*, then the buyer can withdraw from the agreement but will forfeit the deposit. If the seller decides not to sell, then they are required to pay the buyer twice the amount of the *arrhes* as compensation. A variation on this type of deposit is a *dédit,* a specified sum that is forfeited if the buyer pulls out of the deal.

The other type of deposit, the *acompte* – which can be translated as 'down-payment' or 'instalment' – has more serious implications. In this case the sale is legally enforceable on both buyer and seller. There is no way to prevent the sale from going ahead.

The *compromis de vente* can be signed in front of a *notaire*, for which there is a charge. It can also be done privately – *sous seing privé* – in duplicate, and no copy has to be registered. In the former case, you have a week's cooling-off period after receiving the draft *compromis de vente* by registered post, or 7 days from the handing over of the contract by the *notaire* against acknowledgment. During this time you can decide not to go ahead with the deal. With the private contract, you have a week after receiving a recorded letter from the *notaire* or agent during which you can withdraw without penalties.

All payments should be made by bank transfer through the estate agent or *notaire's* blocked account. The days when the English paid with suitcases full of cash are long gone. On top of this, cash sales of properties will not be registered, as a measure against money laundering.

# The contents of the *compromis de vente*

It is vitally important to understand that signing the *compromis de vente* virtually makes you the owner of the property you are promising to buy. If you sign a *promesse de vente* the seller remains the owner of the property. Getting out of a *compromis de vente* will be expensive and difficult, so you must be entirely satisfied that the contract is worded the way that you want. You may be asked to sign a standard printed contract by the estate agent, which will not contain the get-out clauses that you need.

> *'it is vitally important to understand that signing the compromis de vente virtually makes you the owner of the property you are promising to buy'*

While there are no standardised requirements as to the content, the contract should at least contain the following:

- the *état civil* (entry in the population register) of the buyer(s) if they are already living in France
- details of passports, birth certificates, marriage certificates, divorce certificates
- official declaration as to the marriage regime, or civil partnership contract
- a description of the property, including outbuildings
- the address
- the surface area of the land
- the habitable surface area of the property (compulsory in the case of *copropriétés*)
- proof that the seller is the rightful owner of the property, i.e. an authentic copy of the previous *acte de vente*
- the agreed selling price of the property
- name of the *notaire* handling the sale
- who is to pay the notary's fees and other costs
- who is to pay the estate agent's commission
- the property's unique number in the *plan cadastral* (land registry)
- any equipment or fixtures included in the sale: e.g. fitted kitchens, burglar alarms
- results of reports on termites, lead, asbestos and energy efficiency
- details of guarantees with newer properties
- date by which the *acte de vente* is to be signed
- receipt for any deposit
- date on which you will have the use of the property
- penalties if one of the parties withdraws from the deal
- get-out clauses: *conditions suspensives*
- who will be responsible for dealing with *vices cachés* or 'hidden defects'.

The usual clauses in the *acte* make it quite explicit that the vendor is guaranteeing nothing and the buyer accepts this. There are two basic exceptions – one where the vendor is a

## Insider Tip

It is necessary to determine who will pay the costs of repairs if hidden defects are later discovered. Any clause that frees the seller from having to make good hidden defects can be challenged if they have not followed the proper procedures in relation to termites, asbestos and lead. If the property is less than 10 years old, it will be covered by a garantie décennale – a 10 year insurance policy against major construction defects.

property professional (i.e. buys and sells for his living), and the other where the vendor deliberately hides a defect. Property professionals are required to be entirely open and cannot be protected by the usual clauses. Deliberate hiding of a defect is more difficult to prove, but in effect if a vendor hides a defect in such a way that a reasonably attentive buyer could not be expected to see it then the vendor can be pursued through the courts. As the French do not understand the concept of a 'structural survey', verification is often difficult, but if in doubt a buyer should get local builders to inspect the property and quote for necessary work or find a suitable surveyor (see chapter 11).

## Get-out clauses

The negotiation of *conditions suspensives* (the precise translation is 'conditions precedent') is an area where expert legal help can be very useful. The most usual one is that the signature of the final deed is dependent on obtaining mortgage finance. This get-out clause should not be treated lightly. If you do not make reasonable efforts to obtain mortgage finance, and you are shown to be acting in bad faith, then you could lose your deposit. If you require a loan to complete the purchase, you can benefit from the provisions of the *Loi Scrivener* as regards get-out clauses (see chapter 6).

Other clauses can be inserted, for example you can make the purchase dependent on being able to sell your existing property. For example, you can put in the following get-out clauses.

- The owner has to carry out necessary repairs.
- There are no works planned by the local government that would interfere with your use of the property.
- Building permits can be obtained.
- A report on the presence of termites has to be produced.
- No one is going to exercise pre-emptive rights on the property.
- The property will have no sitting tenants.
- There are no legal constraints on the owner selling the property.
- The dimensions of the property correspond to what is in the contract.

Another possible clause is the *condition résolutoire:* a rescission clause that nullifies the contract automatically if its conditions are met.

As stated earlier, it is easy enough to find out if the local municipality is planning to construct a main road or do some other works near your property in the near future, by asking the mayor's office or the local *Division Départementale de l'Équipement,* the town-planning office.

# Rights and obligations/*servitudes*

In between the signing of the *compromis de vente* and the *acte de vente*, the *notaire* has some time in which to make enquiries about the status of the property. Between one and three months can elapse between the preliminary and final contract signings; two months is a normal interval. During this time he will be able to obtain clearance from any bodies – such as SAFER, the guardians of agricultural land use – that might have pre-emptive rights over the property: that they do not intend to exercise them. He should establish that there are no mortgages still applying to the property. The seller should have made the necessary arrangements for the purging of the mortgage from the mortgage register. In the case of property that has been completed recently the seller will have to supply a *certificat de conformité* from the *mairie* certifying that all the necessary building permits were obtained when the property was constructed, and no regulations regarding urban planning have been broken. There are cases where older properties have been constructed without planning permission, so it pays to be on your guard.

The matter of *servitudes*, that is rights and obligations, is particularly important. The most common type of *servitude* is where a farmer has the right to use part of your land, or allow animals to roam on it, or to draw water from your well. Your neighbour may have obtained the right to make windows in a wall overlooking your property, a *servitude de vue*. The biggest headache can be rights of passage – *droits de passage* – which allow hunters to walk over your grounds on their way to a designated hunting area. One Brit in Provence was shocked to see a carload of men with shotguns drawing up to his house soon after he moved in, and found himself in a long legal battle to get them to take another route. No one had warned him about the existing right of way for hunters. If you see notices saying *chasse gardée* or *chasse privée* you know that there will be hunters in the vicinity. It is quite possible that your *notaire* will ask everyone in a village to sign a document agreeing that they have no right of way over your land.

Any *servitudes* that the previous owner of a property has entered into will have been drawn up in an *acte authentique*, signed by a *notaire*, and registered with the land registry. *Servitudes* can be registered for a limited number of years, or for as long as the property exists. They come with a property, and are not attached to the owner. They can work in your favour if they give you the right to use someone else's land. The seller of the property should inform you of *servitudes*; the *notaire* will find the details in previous title deeds and the land registry.

If you are worried about *servitudes* and other claims by third parties, it is possible to take out an insurance policy guaranteeing good title to the property for a small sum.

# The *acte final*

After a period stated in the preliminary contract the parties will proceed to signing the final deed of sale, known as the *acte authentique de vente*. Only *actes* witnessed by a *notaire* are considered *actes authentiques*, and are legally binding on third parties. The *acte de vente* is signed by the buyer, the seller and one *notaire*. If there are two *notaires* involved, one acting for the buyer and one for the seller, only one of them will witness the *acte de vente*. Which one depends on local custom. The *acte final* is always signed on French soil.

You will be sent a *projet de l'acte* – a draft of the *acte de vente* – in advance; typically a week in advance for existing properties though earlier than this for off-plan purchases. This will contain much the same information as the original *compromis de vente*. You will be asked to produce originals of your birth/marriage/divorce certificates, and they may have to be translated and notarised; ask well in advance. At this point you should have made arrangements for payment of all the sums involved in the purchase, including the taxes and notary's fees. The *notaire* will in any case require advance payments to cover his expenses. If a mortgage is involved, the *notaire* will draw down the money from your bank account.

## Power of attorney

A date will be fixed for the signing. Very often there are last-minute hitches and the date may be put off. For this reason it is highly desirable to arrange to give a trusted person a power of attorney – a *mandat* – to act on your behalf if you are unable to attend the actual signing. In practice it is often given to the *notaire's* clerk.

For practical reasons, the power of attorney is best made up in the French form. It should be witnessed by a notary, by a solicitor or at a French consulate. If it is witnessed by a British notary public or solicitor, it will have to be legalised by the Foreign and Commonwealth Office (www. fco.gov.uk) to make it valid in France, unless it is an existing house with no finance i.e. mortgage involved. The document should state what powers you are giving to your representative. The power of attorney allows your representative to do virtually anything you wish, and should only be given to a reliable person; preferably a close relative.

## The actual signing

Assuming that all the loose ends are tied up, you will be invited to the signing of the *acte de vente*. This will be an interesting experience, or perhaps nerve-wracking if there are last-minute hitches. Apart from yourself, the seller and the *notaire*, and their clerk, there may be other interested parties present. By this point, all the necessary funds should have been transferred to your *notaire's* blocked bank account. There are various taxes and fees to be paid at the last minute, and you should be prepared for this. You should also have paid the first insurance premium on the property, before signing the *acte de vente*. Subsequent payment dates are based on the date of the signing.

Certain items will often be mentioned in or attached to the *acte de vente* that will not have appeared in the *compromis de vente*, such as:

- details of mortgage loans
- a full description of the property, with details of previous sales
- details of the insurance policy on the property
- the amount of capital gains tax payable by the seller; or exemption
- reports on the presence of termites/lead/asbestos (required in some areas)
- the existence of any public easements.

# In the Know

**Philip Seabrook, of A Home in France (www.ahomeinfrance.com), gives the following advice regarding translation of legal documents:**

Some agents offer a translation of the French text in the *compromis de vente* – but beware. The translation has no legal value – the definitive text is the French – and sometimes the English actually contradicts this! There is no obligation on an estate agent or *notaire* to provide a translation of the *compromis*, and a simple translation can make you think that you know what you are signing for when in fact you do not. Usually only the simplest standard *compromis* have translations, preprinted, and these by definition are not tailored to the particular purchaser nor to a specific property.

The French conveyancing system is very different to that in the UK and purchasers should get bilingual advice from someone who can explain the process, confirm what is and is not included in the sale, and ensure that you understand what you are buying. Even if your conversational French is good you are unlikely to understand the content of several pages of legal French.

Remember that once you sign the *compromis* you are committed to the purchase, so get advice before you do so – it is much more difficult afterwards.

For the *acte authentique* (deed of sale) most *notaires* will insist that a qualified translator attends the signature if the purchaser (or vendor) does not speak good French – enough to understand what he is signing – and the cost is charged to the person needing the translation. It is very rare for a translation of the *acte* to be supplied and having this done professionally is expensive. *Notaires* who speak some English will often refuse to do so during a signature for fear of unintentionally misleading an English buyer – even if they may talk in English afterwards. A good adviser will prepare you for the signature so that you understand the process and do not have last-minute surprises.

You will be asked to confirm that all the information you have given is truthful: the *affirmation de sincerité*.

# Costs Associated with Property Purchase

The high level of costs involved with property purchase is one of the main reasons that property prices have in the past not risen very fast in France. The fees and taxes that have to be paid to the *notaire* and to the state are inaccurately referred to as *frais de notaire*, when only a part of them go to the *notaire*. The *notaire*'s own emoluments are based on a sliding scale between 5% and 0.825% + TVA at 19.6%, depending on the value of the property. Some properties, so-called Group 2 and Group 3, attract smaller *notaire* fees, but most fall into Group 1. The *notaire*'s fees are fixed by the state, and are not negotiable. It is normal practice for the *notaire* to ask in advance for more than the final bill, to cover for all eventualities, so you will probably receive a small repayment.

The *frais de recouvrement* are the expenses involved in collecting the *taxe départementale*. TVA (VAT) is levied at 19.6% on new properties. The same rate is applied to extensions, garages and outbuildings added on by the seller in the last five years, which could come to a substantial amount.

There are some other fees to be paid:

- the salary of the keeper of the land registry: 0.1% of the sale price
- costs of registering a mortgage, at about 2% (see chapter 6)
- costs of paper, official forms, stamps, extracts from the land register, etc. paid by the *notaire*.

## Notary's fees

| | |
|---|---|
| up to €3,049 | 5% |
| €3,049–6,098 | 3.3% |
| €6,098–16,769 | 1.65% |
| €16,769 and above | 0.825% |

It follows from the above that the *notaire*'s fees will come to about 1% of the sale price, except for very cheap properties, where they will be slightly higher.

In addition there are the *droits de mutation* – transfer taxes – adding up to 4.89% on old property, made up of:

| | |
|---|---|
| *taxe départementale* | 3.6% |
| *frais de recouvrement* | 0.09% (2.5% of the above) |
| *taxe communale* | 1.2% |
| | **4.89%** |

# In the know

**French lawyer Marie Slavov offers some guidance on the buying process in France:**

For those used to the purchasing process in the UK you should to be aware that in France you'll find the legal process and the tax position quite different. Buying a property in France is a process, which can usually be divided into four stages.

1. The search and the offer. When visiting properties it is essential to ask the agent or the seller about several issues, such as any works carried out, the drainage system, the list of fixtures and fittings that will remain in the property and a detailed map showing where the boundaries lie. I would also recommend that you make enquiries through the local *mairie* in relation to new developments or roads in the surrounding area and any planning regulations applicable to the property and its environment. The offer can be made verbally or in writing. Under the Property Act 2001 you will still have a cooling-off period.

2. The signing of the contract. The *compromis de vente* is the most frequently used in France for buying existing properties. This document needs to be checked carefully. The contract is a reciprocal binding contract, subject to various get-out clauses (*conditions suspensives*). These are safety-net clauses as you are signing without knowing everything about what you are buying. They usually cover planning and covenants issues relating to the property; outstanding mortgages; and rights of way or any encumbrances on the property. A finance clause may also be included and the parties are free to agree and add other conditions with their solicitor's help.

3. The structure to be put in place. Buyers should investigate the options available under both English and French law with their legal representatives, in order to choose between the various options and statutes available (purchasing in their names *en indivision*, *en tontine*, with a marriage contract, a life interest in possession or through a company or a trust). The question of wills should be looked at. I recommend covering all these issues prior to signing the initial contract – enabling you to understand what can be done in France and also the impact of the French legal and tax system.

(Continued)

> 4.    Completion. Completion takes place at the French *notaire's* office. If the parties do not want to attend, they can sign a power of attorney in the UK in front of a French Consul or a solicitor/notary public.
>
> You need to understand that the role the *notaire* plays during the transaction is different from that of the solicitor. He should be impartial. You should not anticipate or assume that he will provide services or advise you as he may not be able or allowed to do so.
>
> Marie Slavov is a qualified *avocat* in the French Assets and Tax team at Blake Lapthorn Tarlo Lyons: www.bllaw.co.uk; email frenchteam@bllaw.co.uk.

Finally, there is the commission payable to the estate agent or *immobilier,* which can range from 3% to 10% or even more with very cheap properties.

Before signing the *acte de vente,* it is advisable for you or your representative to check again on what is included in the sale price. The contract will state whether you will have vacant possession – *possession libre* – or if there are any tenants present. In the UK it is assumed that once the final contract is signed the property is available to move into, but this does not always happen in France. If the sellers wish to remain for a few weeks, you can expect them to pay you something as compensation. The date by which the property is ready to move into should be stated in the *acte de vente.*

# After the Sale

Once the *acte de vente* has been signed, the *notaire* has to pay all the taxes and commissions (unless you are paying the *immobilier* directly) out of the sums that you have passed over to him. The title is registered with the *bureau des hypothèques* – the register of deeds and mortgages, as well as the mortgage, if any. Eventually you will receive a certificate informing you that the title has been registered. The whole process will take some months. The original title deed remains with the *notaire.* He is authorised to make authentic copies if necessary.

# Under-declaring the Sale Price

It was once common practice to under-declare the sale price so as to save on taxes and fees, while paying a part 'under the table', or *sous la table.* There is no advantage in the long run to the buyer, since they will be penalised with higher capital gains tax in the future when they resell. The penalties for under-declaring are serious. The one way around this is for the seller to leave some furniture or other moveable goods in the property, which can be given a slightly inflated value, thus reducing the taxes payable.

# Special Procedures for *Copropriétés*

Apart from reports on asbestos/termites/lead, there is also a requirement for the *copropriété* to draw up a report on the solidity of the structure, and many other aspects – the *diagnostic technique* – at the time of setting-up the *copropriété* where the property is more than 15 years old. This is a measure to prevent unsound blocks of flats being turned into *copropriétés* without proper repairs. You should also ask to see the *carnet d'entretien*, or log-book of the building, to see what kind of repairs have been carried out in recent years.

The manager of the *copropriété* will most likely be present at the signing of the *acte de vente*. This should contain details of what percentage of the communal areas belong to you – your *quote part* – and what percentage of the communal charges you will be required to pay.

# *Notaires* as Estate Agents

It might come as a surprise to foreigners that *notaires* also act as estate agents, especially in western France and in country areas. Many French wouldn't dream of using an *agent immobilier* to find property. *Notaires* keep lists of properties; they often have the best deals around. They make very good estate agents: they have the best database on property prices, they are keen to make a quick sale to get their clients out of difficulty, and they are more likely to give an honest description of the property, compared with an *immobilier*, who will try to embellish on its merits. The *notaire* will require a commission on the sale, but not as much as an *immobilier*; the commission is on a sliding scale of 5% on the first €50,000 and then 2.5% above, plus TVA. One can reckon on paying 3% of the sale price.

Some properties held by *notaires* have 'problems' associated with them. This mainly happens when inheritors find themselves in a situation known as *indivision* after someone has died, when two or more people have rights to the proceeds of a sale, and neither can sell without the other's agreement. It is worth asking early on whether this is the case with the property you are trying to buy, as it can sometimes lead to long delays or even the sale falling through. One British couple in Poitou-Charentes had to wait 11 months from the time they put in an offer to the time they became owners, because there was a dispute over whether to sell among the inheritors of the property. There are also properties which have *servitudes* or obligations attached to them, for example someone has the right to live in the property for the rest of their life, or someone has a right to use the land or rights of way.

# Law Firms Dealing with French Property

Ideally, one will want to use the services of a UK law firm, with lawyers qualified in both UK and French law. Some firms have French lawyers working for them in the UK, or have offices in France. Such lawyers can advise you on whose name to put the property in, and what measures to take to minimise inheritance taxes. The *acte de vente* still has to be signed in front of a French notary and registered in France.

A list of law firms dealing with French property can be found in The Directory.

# My House in France
## James Ferguson

James, 49 years old, is married with two children, and owns a semi-detached Cévenol-style house in a village in the Gard (Provence).

### How did you come to buy this property?

My father owned it, and I inherited it along with my brother. My father bought it back in 1971 from another Englishman. When he died we declared the value to the UK taxman and paid inheritance tax on it at UK rates. As my father had always been domiciled in the UK and never lived in France, the French tax authorities did not have to be involved, but we did get a notary to draw up a declaration that the property was legally ours. It was a lot simpler to deal with the UK tax authorities, rather than having to go through the French legal system, and there was in any case no obligation to pay French inheritance tax.

### How do you find the locals?

We go down there during the summer with our children, and occasionally at other times. We have many friends in the area, but they tend to be other incomers, especially French-speaking Swiss and Belgians. Many of the older people in the village know me and address me as *tu* but I have to address them as *vous* back. There are others of my age that I can *tutoie*. As we don't live full time in the village it is natural that we don't get to hear all the local gossip. The local society is fairly closed.

The fact that our house adjoins the post office has been helpful in preventing burglaries. On the other hand the neighbours won't allow the water from our roof to run onto their property. On one occasion a tennis ball got lodged in a down pipe and caused a catastrophic leak; water cascaded into the house and the whole place had to be redecorated and replastered. The insurance didn't pay the full cost of the work as the original plastering wasn't in such good condition.

> *'local craftsmen are unfailingly late, but their work is always good'*

### Have you tried to renovate the house?

This is a traditional house in the village square, made of local rough-hewn stone and mortar; we had the original thick layer of roughcast rendering or *crépi* removed which greatly improved the appearance of the property. Originally it was three small shops side by side, but with the decline in the rural population all the shops have closed down, so there is now only one entrance where once there were three. My parents had the roof redone in 1972, and we plan to do the same soon. The roof beams and laths are very primitive; they tend to rot here because of the rain that is driven horizontally by the wind through the tiles. The roof is of Provençal curled tiles and you can see daylight in between the gaps, so we will have a membrane put in to make it waterproof. Local houses tend to be several storeys high with small rooms, which helps to keep warm; we have knocked one wall through and put in a joist to make a larger living room.

### How are the local craftsmen?

They are unfailingly late, but their work is always good. Our neighbour had the misfortune of hiring a plumber who was an alcoholic to put in a new toilet. He forgot to make sure the outlet was sloping so they ended up having to put their toilet onto a tall platform; the effect is amusing to say the least.

### What do you use for heating?

We have a combination of paraffin, calorgas and wood-burning stoves. The cast-iron free-standing stove generates a lot of heat. We have thought of getting a *citerne* to have a gas supply, but we decided against it. There is no *gaz de ville* here.

# PART FIVE
## What Happens Next

# 13 Making The Move

## Import Procedures

### EU citizens

AS FAR AS CITIZENS FROM OTHER EU COUNTRIES ARE CONCERNED, there are few restrictions on the importation of household goods and tools required for your work. Thanks to the provisions of the Single Market, which have been in force since 1993, moving from the UK to France should not be a lot different from moving from Scotland to England. If you are an EU citizen entering France with your household effects you should have a notarised certificate of ownership of your French property or your rental contract with you. The French authorities can also ask for an official statement that you have left your town or village in your country of origin (you would have to ask your local town council for one). There are restrictions on the importation of firearms, alcohol, tobacco and medicines. The British HM Revenue and Customs has a Helpline on 0845 010 9000 to advise you, or look at the website: www.hmrc.gov.uk.

Many would like to save money by transporting their furniture and other goods with a trailer to their new home in France. One should sound a note of caution here. French customs at ferry ports have the right to inspect your goods and may ask questions about where you got them from. It is best to be as polite and cooperative as possible. If the *douane* want to be awkward they can ask you for proof that the goods are really yours, and this does happen to a small number of foreigners every year. Producing receipts for your household goods is likely to be difficult. If you are moving very valuable goods you need to have some explanation as to why, and receipts. You should on no account carry large sums of cash with you: there are regulations in force requiring you to account for movements of money over €8,000 (to prevent money laundering).

Another difficulty can arise if the French customs think that you are carrying a large amount of one particular item, which might lead them to believe that you are actually going to France to sell the goods you have with you.

## Non-EU citizens

Assuming that you have registered with your *commune* and are planning to move your residence to France, you are entitled to import household goods, your car and tools needed for your work without paying import duty, as long as you can show that you have owned these items for over 6 months or if there is some wear and tear on them. Importation must take place within 12 months of your registration as resident in France. Subsequently you are not allowed to sell or otherwise dispose of your goods for a period of 12 months, unless you have the permission of French Customs. Contact your local French embassy for details.

### Insider Tip

You need to register your car with the local authorities. The local préfecture will send you a leaflet explaining how to obtain your French registration document, the carte grise. Generally you will need to make modifications to the headlights and the exhaust for your car to pass the required norms. France is the only country in Europe that insists on yellow halogen headlights.

## Importing a car

Under EU regulations, you can bring in one car for your personal use, as long as you can show that you are going to be permanently resident in France. There are few conditions attached to importing a car: you need to have the original registration papers, invoice and proof that you have paid VAT in your home country.

Once you are resident in France you will need to change your number plates. Ask at the nearest *préfecture de police*. For further information see *Live and Work in France* (Vacation Work; www.vacationwork.co.uk).

There are very good reasons for buying a left-hand drive vehicle once you are in France:

- the roads here are dangerous enough without having the added handicap of having the steering wheel on the wrong side
- having a foreign-registered car in front of your house attracts the attention of burglars
- you run a higher risk of car-jacking if your car looks foreign
- spare parts for British-made cars can be very expensive or impossible to obtain
- most cars are cheaper in France than in the UK.

Nonetheless many Britons do keep their right-hand drive cars with them in France. An alternative to buying a new car in France is to buy one in another EU country where prices are low, and then pay the VAT in France. There are dealers in Belgium who specialise in this kind of arrangement and who will do all the paperwork. One could also try Luxembourg or Portugal. New-car dealers are under pressure from manufacturers not to sell to foreign buyers, thus, while Denmark has the cheapest ex-VAT cars in Europe, the dealers will put a lot of obstacles in your way if you try to buy your car there. You may not get the model you want, but you may have to wait a long time. You can buy through a *mandataire* or person appointed to act on your behalf.

Once your car has been delivered in France you have 15 days to pay the VAT to the *recette des impôts du département d'immatriculation* and you will then have a provisional *immatriculation*. The downside of getting a new car abroad are potential problems with the warranty in France. A Peugeot in Belgium is considerably cheaper than in France; legally, French garages are required to carry out service checks on French models. A better plan could be to buy a second-hand upmarket car in Belgium, where they are very cheap, to import into France.

## Insurance

With French car insurance it is the car rather than the driver which is insured, so you can give anyone permission to drive your car. Well-known insurers include AXA, AGF, CNP, Generali France, Matmut and Groupama. You may get a good deal if you are moving from the UK if you can convince your French insurer to take over your no-claims bonus from the UK. A letter from your British insurer confirming your no-claims status can be enough to convince the French firm. In France it takes up to 13 years before you get the maximum no-claims reduction of 50%, and any claims you make are heavily penalised with higher premiums. Much depends on your degree of responsibility if you have an accident. If you were breaking the law when the accident happened you may lose the no-claims bonus entirely. If you have records from the UK showing you have made no claims in the last 13 years then you should certainly bring these with you to show the French car insurer.

# Removals

The first principle is to consider what the bare minimum is that you will actually need, and then try to cut it down. Using a removal firm will cost you a minimum of £600 for the areas of France close to England, and much more if you are further away from the ferry ports. Electrical equipment should function satisfactorily in France with adapters, bearing in mind the generally dubious nature of older French wiring. Household appliances are generally more expensive in France than in the UK (and far more than in the USA), but it may be simpler to buy some new items in France than to ship over old equipment which you may not be able to have repaired if it goes wrong. It's not a good idea trying to run energy-sapping appliances such as irons or kettles using an adapter, and it is best to buy these items in France.

With furniture, and larger items, it is worth considering whether the contents of your English semi are going to fit into a cottage in the Dordogne, or whether British-style armchairs would look good in Provence. If you plan to rent out your property in France, then it is far better to furnish it locally.

Individuals normally have to pay the removal company up front for the removal so if you are worried about the removal company going bust or what will happen if your most precious items are damaged or lost, the British Association of Movers (BAR) has set up International Movers Mutual Insurance so that clients of any of the companies belonging to BAR will be compensated for loss or damage, or in the case of bankruptcy the removal will be taken over by another member company.

Companies with offices in France as well as in the UK are generally the safest bet, although they will be more expensive. The BAR can provide a list of international removers in your area and other information in return for an SAE (BAR, Tangent House, 62 Exchange Road, Watford, Herts WD18 0TG; ☎01923 699480; email info@bar.co.uk; www.bar.co.uk). Removals can be done door-to-door or your possessions can be put into a warehouse in France. Charges start at around £700 for 3 cubic metres, but the exact price depends very much on the total distance involved at both ends, and whether you are flexible about the delivery time.

# Exporting Pets to France

Many expats would like to have their four-legged friends – *animaux de compagnie* – with them abroad, and in some ways this has become a routine procedure. France declared itself rabies-free in 2002, but there was a case of rabies in the Aquitaine area in August 2004 – following the illegal importation of a puppy from Morocco – since then dogs and cats in the *départements* of the Gironde, Dordogne and Lot-et-Garonne have to be vaccinated against rabies and also microchipped or tattooed. All cats and dogs entering France must in any case first be microchipped and then vaccinated against rabies. The vaccination should be given at least 21 days and not more than 12 months before leaving the UK; your vet will give you an EU pet booklet, which you must have with you when you enter France. The French authorities do not require cats and dogs to be treated for ticks and tapeworm before they enter the country. If you are planning to bring the pet back to the UK then a blood test is also necessary, in order to obtain a Pet Passport, which can only be issued by a licensed veterinary inspector. It is essential to obtain your Pet Passport as early as possible before you travel, because of the time involved before you can return your pet to the UK.

If you want to bring in pets other than cats and dogs, there are other rules. There are no particular formalities for importing rabbits, guinea pigs and hamsters. If you want to bring in a parrot or similar you will have to swear that you are not going to resell it in France, and agree to a veterinary inspection. The local French consulate will advise you on other types of animals. The UK Department of Food, Environment and Rural Affairs (DEFRA) can provide forms for France. If you are thinking of exporting animals other than cats and dogs the PETS Helpline will give you the number of the section you need to call.

## Non-EU pets

The situation for dogs coming from outside the EU changed in late 2002. From then on a blood sample taken from your pet has to be sent in advance to a laboratory in Nancy for testing. The animal also has to fulfil the conditions given above for UK animals. It should be stressed that regulations change, and the best people to ask for up-do-date information are specialised pet-carriers (see The Directory) or your nearest French embassy. The French government does not publicise its rules on the internet.

## Pets returning to the UK

The British authorities require an animal to be microchipped first before being vaccinated, and the French authorities have changed their legislation to fit in with this. In the past the order in France was the other way around.

When in France, you must have your pet vaccinated against rabies annually, otherwise the British authorities will consider it as having originated from France, and you will need to apply for a new PETS Certificate in France. Call the PETS Helpline on 0870 241 1710 or look at the website, www.defra.gov.uk for further information.

If you are coming from France, take your pet to a government-authorised vet for the necessary certificates. The animal has to be treated against ticks and tapeworm between 24 and 48 hours before leaving France.

Pets originating from France require a globally standardised tattoo (*tatouage*) or microchip (*micropuce*), as well as vaccinations, if you intend to take them abroad. The British authorities will only accept an animal that has been microchipped before it is vaccinated. If you buy a dog or cat in France, there is no legal requirement to have a tattoo or microchip implanted unless you are taking it abroad, except in the three *départements*

### Insider Tip

You can bring your pet back into the UK as long as you follow the rules laid down by the UK Department of Food, Environment and Rural Affairs (DEFRA) in the Pets Travel Scheme (PETS). Six months have to elapse after a successful blood test following vaccination against rabies before you can get a re-entry certificate from your vet, so you need to plan ahead. When in France, the cat or dog can first be microchipped and then vaccinated and blood tested. An animal that has been microchipped does not need to be tattooed as well.

affected by the rabies scare in 2004. There is, however, an odd tradition in France that pedigree dogs are given a name beginning with the same letter depending on the year; if your dog was born in 2004 then the name had to begin with V. A similar tradition applies to horses.

## Pet travel insurance

There are a number of companies offering this service. See the websites:

www.mrigroup.com
www.petplan.co.uk
www.pinnacle.co.uk
www.rapidinsure.co.uk.

# 14 Living In France

## Culture Shock

FRANCE IS A COUNTRY WITH A STRONG TENDENCY TOWARDS UNIFORMITY, so it is not exactly difficult to make generalisations about it. The social mores are very similar everywhere, but there is no doubt that people are generally friendlier and less formal in the south than in the north and centre.

Taken as a whole, French social customs are old-fashioned by Anglo-Saxon standards, and there is a whole system of etiquette and formal behaviour that you will need to learn about if you want to mix with any of the social classes and not constantly offend people. It is well worth investing in a manual of French etiquette, the best being *French or Foe?* and *Savoir Flair* by the American Polly Platt (www.pollyplatt.com). Unless you learn about the customs of the French, your stay could be unnecessarily difficult.

## Making Friends

The first thing to remember is that the French draw a very clear distinction between people they know and strangers. Walk into a bar in rural France, and people often look at you as though you have just landed from Mars. No one will say a word to you, thus confirming your worst prejudices about the locals. Until you have made some kind of personal contact, such as found something that you have in common, not much conversation will take place. It is quite possible to start chatting with people on trains and buses, but there has to be some good reason. People are generally suspicious of strangers, and would rather not get involved with them too quickly.

Smiling at everybody regardless is a big mistake. Smiling is reserved for appropriate occasions, otherwise it is seen as insincere. There is also no need to make much effort to make people like you. You will be judged on what you are, rather than what you want people to think you are.

*'smiling is reserved for appropriate occasions, otherwise it is seen as insincere'*

Talking loudly in public places should be avoided. You will notice that the French generally keep their voices down in public places. Groups of British visitors are easy to spot in restaurants: they make a lot of noise and laugh too much.

Being accepted into French social circles is difficult, admittedly, and if you are it is an honour. The French generally have networks of friends dating back to their early schooldays, so it is hard for a foreigner to get a look-in. By all accounts, Paris is the most difficult place of all to make friends; it can be a very lonely place for outsiders. The French from the provinces also dislike *les parigots* or Parisians. Foreigners will tend to stick together; if your workplace is informal you may become friendly with your colleagues outside working hours. Joining a sports club or ramblers' group is a good way to meet people, but in general the French are not great ones for organised social activities. However, in many villages you will find communal meals organised by local associations and going to these is an excellent way of meeting people and making new friends.

> '*being accepted into French social circles is difficult, admittedly, and if you are it is an honour'*

France is an intensely competitive society; from the time children go to school they are conditioned to compete and they are criticised mercilessly by their teachers and parents if they fail to do their best. Every foreigner in France soon notices that, while the French are always making fun of foreigners, they become very upset if anyone criticises them or their country. There is always a light-hearted banter going on between the French – everyone appreciates witty repartee – but when foreigners try the same thing, it sounds as though they are making personal criticisms, and the well-known French touchiness manifests itself. The French are undoubtedly volatile and often appear inconsistent to northern Europeans and Americans. The French want excitement and drama in their day-to-day life. There is, too, a basic contradiction here; while the French are generally excessively serious, they are also masters of frivolity and fun.

## Insider Tip

Conversation is an art form here. There are things that you must not talk about with people you don't know well, in particular French politics, or anything concerning one's private life. The fact that there are virtually no taboos about what close friends can talk about should not mislead foreigners into thinking that they can reveal everything to casual acquaintances.

Brits and Americans may feel their self-esteem rapidly sinking in the face of so many one-sided jokes at their expense, so it is vital not to take things personally. The French respect people who are self-confident and proud of their country; they dislike the kind of self-disparagement practised by the British because it reminds them of their own insecurities.

A key issue in whether you can get on in French society is the degree to which you master the French language. The importance of mastering the language cannot be over-emphasised; it is the key to being able to fit in here. If you can read French literature in the original you will never be at a loss for a topic of conversation, and you will gain a great deal of respect. Being up on French *chansons* will win you a lot of brownie points. The French have boundless respect for education and learning: your status in life is determined by how much you have of it. Everybody, regardless of their social class, is interested in ideas and politics. Everyone is ready to have a serious discussion about philosophy. The French much prefer the theoretical over the practical. This is perhaps because they are really a nation of aristocrats, who would rather not sully their hands with menial work. Nobility of purpose is tremendously important; if you have some great cultural or philosophical obsession then you will get on well here. On the other hand, they dislike pomposity. It is a major social gaffe to monopolise the conversation or talk too much about oneself. In a typical conversation, people interrupt each other or talk at the same time; the main thing is to be entertaining.

## Meeting and Greeting

You will also need to understand the etiquette of kissing. It is customary to give women two pecks – *deux bises* – on the cheek on leaving a party, or once one is on friendly terms. For a man to give a woman three pecks – *trois bises* – implies something more than just being casual friends; to do so may give offence. For family and close friends it is expected, but you should take your lead from other people. One kiss on the cheek is also over-familiar. Rather confusingly, some women give four pecks to their good friends. In the south of France, three pecks is more acceptable between casual friends. When work colleagues meet for the first time in the morning, it is normal to kiss twice; foreigners should follow the lead of the locals.

Knowing how to greet people is a must. At the very least you should shake people's hands when you meet them. It is very important to use people's titles; Monsieur, Madame (or Mademoiselle for girls under 16 years old), but not with their surname. If they have a professional title, then you should use it: Monsieur/Madame le Professeur/le Docteur and so on. In the workplace you will not be on first-name terms with superiors unless you are working for a foreign-based company. The boss will always remain Monsieur le Directeur.

## The French and Authority

One of the typical features of the French is their ambivalent attitude towards authority. While the British make jokes about sex, the French make jokes about authority. In the 18th century, authority rested with an aristocratic class who had absolute power. These days it is civil servants who exercise absolute power. Once you are admitted to a post of civil servant, you are virtually irremovable, and you can make life and death decisions about citizens' lives. About 25% of the French work for the state and are therefore *fonctionnaires* or civil servants. There are plenty of reasons to try to become a *fonctionnaire* – it means that you are set up for life. France is one of the world's most bureaucratic countries: you can hardly do anything in this country without filling a form in. But at the same time, if you happen to know the right people, almost anything becomes possible. Everything depends on personal relationships: state functionaries can make a telephone call and fix things for you should they so wish. It is very much at their whim, just as it was under Louis XIV. France rates as one of Europe's more corrupt countries: on a par with Portugal but not as bad as Greece and Italy.

## Insider Tip

Hand-shaking is another big ritual which you need to get right. The first time you meet in the morning in your office you should shake hands with male colleagues (if you are male), and when you leave in the evening. The person who is socially superior or doing you a favour takes the initiative in shaking hands; you should not extend your hand to your boss before he or she does so. There is no need to shake hands with tradesmen or cleaners, but you should shake hands with notaries, architects and other professional people. If you enter a room, shake hands with everyone starting from the left and going around clockwise.

The all-pervasive interference of the state in every aspect of life was, in the first place, intended to counter the anarchic tendencies of the French, but it has also led to a backlash, a desire to defy authority and completely ignore all rules. The worst manifestation of this anarchic mentality is the way the French drive without any consideration for other motorists, and so turn the streets into a war zone. You are almost twice as likely to be killed in a car accident here as in the UK. There are the daily irritations of drivers not signalling left or right, or driving much too close to you. In recent years there has been a campaign to cut down on road deaths, which is having some success, but it must be doubtful whether the French will ever learn to emulate northern European driving behaviour.

It would be a mistake to think that everyone just does as they please here. If you are going to break the rules, then you have to know how to do it, otherwise you will simply get into trouble. Because this is essentially a socialistic society, there are a lot of rules which exist to protect weaker members of society. Other regulations, however, appear to be completely irrational or arbitrary, and designed to make life difficult, such as the rule that you have to submit certified copies of your degrees and qualifications every time you apply for a job, or the fact that anyone who graduates from secondary school can go to university.

If you come to live in France from another country, then it is just as well to understand how things are done here, and not to get too upset when it doesn't match your expectations. After all, you came here to experience a different culture …

## Quality of Life

By any objective standards, France should be a paradise to live in. The citizens are well looked after; according to UNESCO, France has the second highest quality of life after Canada (a country with a strong French influence). For many years France had a permanent trade surplus – it is self-sufficient in food – and a style of life that led the German poet Schiller to coin the term 'to live like God in France'. Pleasure definitely comes before work here. The government started to institute a compulsory 35 hour working week back in 1997, much to the irritation of big business. The French do not actually work 35 hours a week, they simply get more holidays a year in lieu. There are still many who work far more hours. The underside of the French dream is all too evident if you walk around the big cities. With permanent high unemployment, there is a huge underclass of dispossessed poor who will never live the life that they would want.

Young people face great obstacles in finding a job; many are going over to the UK to find some work and learn English.

The fact that many French are chronically dissatisfied with their lifestyle is amazing to foreigners who would love to have a second home here. The roots of the malaise seem to lie in the excessive conformism of French society. If you don't earn a good salary and have a respectable job, if you can't afford to spend the whole of August in your holiday home, then you have failed to live up to the French model. In a sense there are two countries here: the idealised France and the reality. What appears at first sight to be a society devoted to hedonism and working as little as possible, turns out to be intensely competitive and snobbish about material possessions. One consequence can be seen in the fact that the French use twice as many antidepressants and tranquillisers as the British; the French are the second biggest consumers of pharmaceuticals in the world after Japan, another high-pressure society. It is estimated that one-third of French teenage girls are on medication for psychological problems.

While 75% of the French live in towns and cities, their roots are very much in rural France. Most of the towns are small by British or American standards; there are three huge cities: Paris, Lyon and Marseille, while the rest of the country appears quite empty. You can drive for half an hour without seeing a soul or a single house. The depopulation of the countryside started in the First World War, and is something of immense concern because it threatens to undermine the basis of what it is to be French. It does seem that the tide has turned, because so many city-dwellers are moving further and further out of town, thanks to the excellent train services. Those who can work from home out in the sticks are also boosting the deserted villages, and one should not underestimate the effect of so many foreigners buying houses in the countryside. However there is still a shift in population away from the centre of the country as increasingly the French are moving to live on or near the coast.

The key to French identity lies in the short distance that separates the people from their peasant origins. Their basic values have not changed that much. Everyone has relatives in the countryside. In some respects this is still a peasant culture, with an overlay of sophistication.

# History

## Origins

Where have the French come from? In spite of the current widespread concern about immigration, the French are a very mixed bunch, arguably more so than the British. The earliest historical peoples that one can say much about are that diverse collection of peoples known as the Celts, who came from much further east starting from around 1000 BC. While they were related to the Celts in Britain and Ireland, their language was far closer to Latin than that spoken by their offshore cousins. For this reason they quickly gave up Gaulish and started speaking Latin when the Romans arrived; there are still some Gaulish words in modern French. The ancient Greeks also colonised the Mediterranean coast starting from 800 BC; some place names, such as Nice and Antibes are originally Greek. The next invaders were the Romans, who established the province of Gallia Narbonensis from 121 BC. In the following century, in 52 BC, Julius Caesar, by remarkable feats of arms, conquered the rest of Gaul.

For some 500 years, Gaul was an integral part of the Roman Empire. After the collapse of the Western Empire, the first stable dynasty to appear were the Merovingians, from AD 451, German-speaking Franks who had come to the aid of the Romans in repelling Attila the Hun. The Frankish language was never written down, but modern French is full of Frankish words, and the Franks, of course, gave the country a new name. Three hundred years later, in 751, the Carolingian dynasty took over, and one of their rulers, Charlemagne, set up a new Roman Empire in the West. His empire, much larger than modern France, was divided up between his three sons on his death in 843, leading to a slow but inevitable disintegration.

# The English connection

The Carolingian state was weakened by internal strife and could not withstand the assault of the Vikings, who occupied Rouen in 912. A new strongman emerged, in the shape of Hugues Capet in 987. He started the Capetian dynasty of kings, based around Paris and the Ile de France. The Vikings were pacified by ceding them the province of Normandy, and it was from here that William the Conqueror launched his successful invasion of England in 1066. At the same time the English Norman kings still held on to their French possessions. The situation was aggravated when the charismatic Eleanor of Aquitaine (1122–1204) decided to divorce the dull French King Louis VI and marry the more exciting English King Henry II, bringing all of her substantial French territories with her. Eleanor was a romantic figure, one of the few significant women in French history, and the mother of Richard the Lionheart and King John of England. After her death, the French King Philip Augustus soundly defeated the English at Bouvines in 1214 and turfed them out of most of France. His is a name one should try to remember if you want to impress the French with your knowledge of history.

The Capetian dynasty gave way to the House of Valois from 1326, but this was disputed by the English Plantagenet kings, thus starting the so-called Hundred Years War. After the great victories at Crécy (1346) and Poitiers (1356), the situation looked good for the English, and all of south-western France was under their control. An even greater victory in 1415 at Agincourt led to King Henry V being recognised as the heir to the French throne, but he died before he could become king of both England and France. When French fortunes were at a low ebb, Joan of Arc appeared – inspired by visions of the Virgin Mary – and led the fightback, which saw the English losing almost all their French possessions by 1436. Although the French were rid of the English, the French kings only controlled half of what is modern-day France. The powerful Duchy of Burgundy only became part of France in 1477, and Brittany in 1491. Through constant warfare and expansion, most of the modern French heartlands were brought under control by 1610, but the country was still smaller than it is today on the northern and eastern sides.

France steered its own erratic course through the Wars of Religion between Protestants and Catholics. After the infamous St Bartholomew's Day Massacre of 1572, when thousands of Protestants were slaughtered, a Protestant king – Henri IV – came to the throne in 1589 and the Edict of Nantes was issued, giving the Protestants the right to control certain towns. Louis XIV, however, decided that he wanted to win favour with Rome, and revoked the Edict in 1685, with the result that the Protestants had to go abroad or reconvert to Catholicism. A great warmonger, Louis XIV, decided to expand in all directions, and acquired Flemish and German-speaking areas in the north and east. But he also succeeded in uniting the rest of Europe against him, and had to retreat in the face of superior British-led forces. It is interesting to note that in 1700 the population of France was 27 million, against 9 million for England and Wales, and 2 million in Holland. France was in one sense very powerful, but at the same time economically and politically backward. By the mid-18th century England was 30 years ahead of France technologically, and had a far more liberal political system, which was greatly admired by French intellectuals like Voltaire.

# Revolution

The stubborn insistence of the French ruling classes in holding on to their medieval privileges meant that when the Revolution came, it outdid all the other revolutions in terms of violence. Since France had supported the USA in its revolution, the people saw that it was possible to overthrow the established order. The first period of idealism after the storming of the Bastille in 1789, gave way to the Terror, when thousands were guillotined, sometimes for quite trivial reasons. Out of the anarchy emerged a new strong man, in the form of the Corsican Napoleon Bonaparte. Napoleon brought stability, but also pursued a policy of imperial expansion, which gave France a short-lived period of glory the French are still proud of, though Napoleon himself is a controversial figure nowadays. While Napoleon restored some aspects of the *ancien régime* in the new empire, such as reviving the orders of nobility, he followed anti-clerical policies, and the Catholic Church was severely weakened. Napoleon's final defeat in 1815 brought in a new period of monarchical rule, under Louis XVIII, a brother of Louis XVI. Louis still believed in the divine right of kings, and would not act as a constitutional monarch. The fear that the old order had come back led to more unrest and a more liberal constitution from 1830, under King Louis-Philippe.

France lagged behind the rest of northern Europe as far as industrial development was concerned. Political unrest was ongoing. The extreme inequality of French society led to the insurrection of 1848; the king was exiled to England and a Second Republic declared. It was only a few months before Napoleon's nephew, Louis-Napoleon, won the first election for president. With the myth of his uncle behind him, he mounted a coup d'état in 1851 and declared himself emperor Napoleon III. The new emperor had the same desire for glory as his uncle, and large swathes of North Africa came under French rule during his tenure. Generally, he provided stable government, and gradual reform, helped by favourable economic conditions. His disastrous decision to declare war on Prussia in 1870, however, and subsequent capture, made the Third Republic inevitable. The monarchy was finally dead and buried at the third attempt.

# Fin de siècle and beyond

The end of the 19th century saw the prestige of French culture reach its absolute zenith, with exceptional achievements in all the arts. There was also a sea of change in relations between France and Great Britain, when they formed a close alliance – the Entente Cordiale – in 1904. It was also in the early 20th century that France formally became a secular country, completing a journey that had begun with the Revolution. The secular nature of the state forms an important part of French 'republican' identity and is jealously guarded by just about all political parties, left and right. The First World War, coming soon after, changed France forever. The mass slaughter of young men on the Western Front led to the depopulation of the countryside, a phenomenon that is still very evident today. The period between 1918 and 1940 was one of constant political and economic crisis, with the extreme left and right often fighting it out on the streets. In May 1940 France was invaded again, and half the country occupied, while the other half remained under the control of a puppet regime, with the First World War hero, Marshal Pétain, as leader. The regime was known as Vichy France. Not everyone was wholeheartedly on the side of the British; the sinking of the French fleet off the coast of North Africa in July 1940 by the British still rankles with some. The maverick Charles de Gaulle carried on the fight for a free France from London, and was rewarded by being allowed to enter Paris at the head of French forces in August 1944, thus salving wounded French pride.

# De Gaulle and after

France rebuilt quickly after the Second World War, but was still plagued by political instability. The Fourth Republic, declared in 1945, was eventually destroyed by the problem of decolonisation. The humiliating defeat in Vietnam in 1954 was followed by the start of the Algerian War of Independence. Algeria had the same status as mainland France, and a large European population. When the French government appeared to be ready to consider independence for Algeria in 1958, the European settlers and French army in Algeria declared their willingness to fight against their own country; with the prospect of a military coup in Paris, the state turned to General de Gaulle to save the situation. De Gaulle assumed the powers of a dictator for six months and duly extricated the country from its Algerian nightmare. A Fifth Republic was declared, with a constitution that gave the president, who was now to be elected every seven years, far more power than before.

Algeria finally got its independence in 1962, and France had to deal with a large influx of *pieds noirs,* European settlers, as well as pro-French Muslim troops, the *harkis.* The legacy of Algerian independence still makes itself felt in modern French politics. Politics was now dominated by the right wing, one factor that triggered off serious disturbances in May 1968, protests that could have led to the overthrow of the Republic. De Gaulle survived, but was replaced by Georges Pompidou in 1969, who died in 1974 before he could complete his term in office. The next president, Valéry Giscard d'Estaing, was another conservative, ruling in tandem with a conservative administration. Against all expectations, the veteran socialist politician François Mitterrand won the presidency in 1981, and was re-elected in 1988. Mitterrand was able to rule in concert with a left-wing government from 1982. This was the year when the regions – first set up in 1972 – were given elected assemblies. In the face of severe economic difficulties, the Socialists found themselves obliged to follow more market-oriented policies. In 1986, the right won elections, and the president had to work with a government led by the Gaullist Jacques Chirac as prime minister, the first instance of what the French call 'cohabitation'. From 1988 the left were back in power, but they suffered a crushing defeat in the 1993 elections.

The centre-right Jacques Chirac won the presidency in 1995 after the death of Mitterrand. He immediately infuriated the rest of the world by conducting nuclear tests in the Pacific, probably to boost morale at home. In spite of allegations of corruption Chirac won re-election in 2002. This was inevitable once the Socialist Party candidate, Lionel Jospin, was beaten in the first round of the voting by Chirac and the anti-immigrant National Front leader Jean-Marie Le Pen. To its disgust, the French left had to vote for Chirac to ensure that the far right Le Pen did not become president. Chirac was an excellent orator while at the same time projecting a genial, relaxed image. In 2002 the right again formed the government under the little-known figure of Prime Minister Jean-Pierre Raffarin. The main features of his term of office were the attempts to water down the 35 hour week and to make cuts in the welfare system. Since 2002 the president remains in office for just five years, making it possible for parliamentary elections to coincide with presidential ones, thus perhaps avoiding the inconvenience of cohabitation. A new conservative united front was set up in 2003, the UMP (*Union pour un Mouvement Populaire*), which backed Chirac. The new star of the party became Nicolas Sarkozy, who fell out badly with Chirac when the former supported another candidate in the 1995 election.

## 'Non' to Europe

There was a political earthquake on 29th May 2005, when the French loudly said 'Non' to the planned new European Union Constitution, which their octogenarian former president, Valéry Giscard d'Estaing, had toiled over for most of his retirement. The vote against the EU Constitution was a protest against the governing party, attempts to undermine the social security system, and the threat of Anglo-Saxon economic liberalism that voters believed to be enshrined in this document. For right wingers the referendum was a chance to object to the possible admission of Turkey to the EU, and to enlargement in general. The 'Non' vote made it necessary for the existing government to step down. Jean-Pierre Raffarin was replaced by the aristocratic Dominique de Villepin as prime minister – a man who had never been elected to any political post – with the controversial figure of Nicolas Sarkozy being made Interior Minister. The reshuffle in the government changed little; the same programme of centre-right reforms continued as before until the 2007 elections. But, as ever, the most controversial policies – such as a new temporary work contract aimed at reducing youth employment – were shelved in the face of widespread protests on the streets. Soon all political attention was on who would win the 2007 poll, one seen as critical for the country's future.

## President Sarkozy

On 6th May 2007 Nicolas Sarkozy, the son of a Hungarian immigrant, finally fulfilled the ambition he had nurtured since he was a youth to become president of France when he beat the Socialist Party candidate Ségolène Royal in the second round of voting. The turnout was an astounding 85%, showing that the French people realised the importance of this election. During the campaign, Sarkozy was demonised by the left as a divisive, even dangerous figure, while the economy and unemployment were key issues. Afterwards the new president immediately injected an energy into the Elysée Palace that had been largely lacking under his predecessor Chirac. There was a real sense that French politics had moved on a generation. Sarkozy, whose first declaration was to say he would govern for all French people, not just those who supported him, sprang a number of surprises in choosing his new government, opting for a number of figures from the centre and even left of French politics. The most notable of these was his choice of the popular socialist politician Bernard Kouchner, one of the founders of the charity *Médécins sans Frontières,* as foreign minister. There was less surprise over his choice of prime minister – his close ally and campaign manager François Fillon, a former social affairs minister. Sarkozy promised during his campaign to modify the rules surrounding the 35 hour week, ensure that public transport maintained a minimum service during strikes, and reform the rules governing access to local schools. It remains to be seen whether Sarkozy will be able to carry out these and other controversial reforms. In the past French presidents and prime ministers have tended to back down in the face of the street protests to which the disgruntled French readily resort. Sarkozy, however, has promised he will hold onto his election pledges. The reaction of civil servants, teachers and public transport workers to the planned reforms will be critical; it should be an interesting 5 years. One of Sarkozy's earliest proposals was to allow homebuyers to offset their income tax against their mortgage interest payments. For those who don't pay income tax they get a credit instead. Some observers believe this could trigger a housing boom.

> 'Sarkozy has promised he will hold to his election pledges'

## The centre ground

One of the most interesting outcomes of the presidential elections was the relatively poor showing of the extreme left and right. In the first round of voting the *Front National's* share of the vote fell significantly to just over 10% (from 16.9% in 2002). The smaller candidates on the far-left also saw their share of the votes fall, as left-leaning voters opted for Royal. The French Communist Party (FCP) candidate Marie-George Buffet, meanwhile, received only 1.9% of the vote. In 1981 the FCP candidate Georges Marchais had managed 15.3%. The surprise package in the first round, however, was François Bayrou, leader of the centrist *Union pour la Démocratie Française* (UDF) Party. He polled 18.6% and at one time the opinion polls even suggested he might be a threat to Ségolène Royal. After the election Bayrou, who made it clear he did not vote for Sarkozy in the second round of voting, created a new party called *Mouvement Démocrate.* Meanwhile the Socialist Party went through its habitual agonising after defeat. As ever the question was: should it move to the centre and become a social democratic party, as has happened elsewhere in Western Europe? Or should it look towards the traditional old French left? It is just possible that a major realignment on the left and in the centre of French politics could occur in the coming years. Key figures in this respect are likely to be Ségolène Royal and the Socialist Major of Paris Bernard Delanoë.

## Permanent crisis?

In the new millennium, France is still struggling to deal with fundamental economic problems. Although it has a constant trade surplus, this is founded on its self-sufficiency in agricultural products. France lives off its capital, rather than making a living from buying and selling. Unemployment has not budged below 8% since the 1970s. The fact that unemployment has stayed around or above 10% since 2004 is seen as a kind of warning that France is in serious difficulties, but the rigidity of the labour laws and the lack of a market-driven economy are intractable obstacles to an improvement in the employment situation. However in late 2006 and 2007 unemployment was falling.

Power at the top is split between the president and the prime minister, who is appointed by the president and has far less say than the British prime minister. Recent French governments have been unable to reform the economy or social security system, because all attempts at change are blocked by the 25% or so of the population who work for the state. Special-interest groups frequently extract concessions from the government or prevent change by resorting to – sometimes violent

*'the vote in 2007 did look like a vote for change, a plea by the French people for the energetic Sarkozy to bring an end to the 'crisis''*

– protests. New legislation is passed without repealing previous laws, so that the tax and social security system is now so complicated that a layperson cannot understand it.

The French feel that they are trapped in a permanent crisis, but few are willing to embrace the liberal economic model that has transformed the British economy. Even President Sarkozy, who has been caricatured as an arch-liberal in some quarters, has made it clear that he wants to maintain the French tradition of protecting its industries from outside competition. And though the president has talked about the reform of labour markets it remains to be seen how far they go and how effective they are in the face of opposition. For a country that is notorious for its overly centralised administrative system, it is indeed surprising to see how weak its central government actually is. Napoleon understood how individualistic and self-interested the French are. As General de Gaulle once famously said: 'How do you govern a country with 363 kinds of cheese?' The answer could be that things will go on as they always have done. Life is still very good in France for many people, so for them a static situation is fine. Against that, the vote in 2007 did look like a vote for change, a plea by the French people for the energetic Sarkozy to bring an end to the 'crisis'. In the coming few years we will find out which of these contradictory trends will triumph.

# Political Structure

The first French republic was founded in 1792 after the Revolution. After the empire and several monarchs, the republican system has remained in place since 1870. In common with the USA, France has a written constitution and an executive president who is not only the head of state but also the head of the government. The president has the right to dissolve the lower house of parliament, the *Assemblée Nationale,* but not the *Sénat* or *Haute Assemblée.* If the president dies in office, or has to resign, then the Speaker of the Senate takes over temporarily as president. The upper house reviews legislation but cannot prevent its passage. One half of the 346 seats are up for re-election every 3 years, the electors being 150,000 *grands électeurs,* made up of *députés,* regional and department councillors and local council representatives.

The *Assemblée* serves for a term of 5 years, which from now on coincides with the presidential elections. The 577 members or *députés* are chosen by a double-ballot system in their constituency or *circonscription*; there is a run-off between the two candidates who receive the largest number of votes in the first round. The same system applies to presidential elections. Depending on which political grouping has the most seats, a government of 42 ministers is formed; ministers give up their seats in the *Assemblée* to a pre-selected deputy, or *adjoint.* The prime minister may not necessarily come from the same political party as the president, in which case the president tends to exercise more power. Legislation is drafted by the president's office, and then debated in parliament.

Women are very under-represented in French politics; there has only been one woman prime minister – Édith Cresson – between 1991 and 1992, and she was deemed a failure. Women did not even receive the vote in France until 1945. The original Napoleonic constitution classed them with children and lunatics. However, the emergence of Ségolène Royal as a major political force may bring about more rapid change. And as he had promised, President Sarkozy's first government in May 2007 had an equal share of male and female ministers.

# Administration

## *Régions*

The introduction of a new layer of government between Paris and the *départements* was initiated in 1972. From 1982 each *région* was given an elected assembly and an executive. This is not really devolution as we would see it in the UK. The *régions* have powers in the area of culture, education and business. The main purpose was to reduce the power of the *départements,* and to restore some feeling of regional identity, which had been deliberately negated by the organisation into *départments* after 1789.

## *Départements*

France is logically, and conveniently, divided into 100 *départements,* four of which are overseas. The rest make up what is called *La Métropole,* or *La France Métropolitaine.* Each *département* has a two digit number which is, again very logically, used for postcodes and licence plates. Napoleon placed a prefect or *préfet* in charge of each *département* in a deliberate imitation of the Roman Empire, an un-elected official directly appointed by the president. Since 1982, the prefect has been replaced as the chief executive of the *département* by the President of the General Council. The general council or *conseil général* is the elected council that runs the *département* and is responsible for such matters as maintaining schools and roads and promoting economic development. The councillors or *conseillers généraux* are elected for six years, with elections taking place every three years for half of them. However, the prefect still remains an important figure, reporting directly to the Interior Ministry, in charge of the local police and firefighters and responsible for such issues as road safety, and the provision of driving licenses and identity cards. They are the French state's local representative.

## *Arrondissements* and *cantons*

The *départements* are divided up into *arrondissements* and these are again divided up into *cantons*. These units have some significance in organising voting and public services, but no directly elected representatives.

## *Communes*

The level of government that everyone comes into contact with is the *commune*, of which there were 36,782 at the last count, most of them with fewer than 1,000 inhabitants, with 214 of them overseas. The voters elect a municipal council for 6 years, while the chief executive officer is the *maire* or mayor, who is not only an official of the municipality, but also a government agent, and a member of the *police judiciaire*. The *maire* is obliged to keep the civil register (*état civil*), and often performs marriages. He or she also draws up the electoral roll and publicises laws. The French government's policy is to encourage, or force, *communes* to work together in groups or *collectivités*, within the limits of their official competencies, in order to run the country in a more rational and democratic manner. There are now some 55,000 *collectivités* and 550,000 local and national politicians, who hold more than one office at different levels of government. At the *commune* level the *maire* is an all-powerful figure, someone that newcomers should try to cultivate at all costs, because he or she has a lot of say in who receives planning permission for buildings and can be very helpful – or obstructive – if you want to start a business.

## *Pays*

Since 1995, following the *Loi Pasqua*, different regions or *communes* can band together to form a *pays* (literally 'country'), to promote their economic interests and strengthen cultural ties. They are a throwback to the pre-Revolutionary *ancien régime*. By 1996 there were already 200 *pays* in France. The more republican French are concerned about the weakening of the *départements*, and fear a return to the pre-1789 organisation of the country. Critics note that they provide yet another tier of administration, making local government even more complex.

# Political Parties

No one political party can form a government on its own in France; the only possibility is 'cohabitation' or coalition. The main parties on the left are the *Parti Socialiste* (PS), and the very much diminished *Parti Communiste Français* (CPF). On the right there were at one time the *Rassemblement pour la République* (RPR), a Gaullist party organised by Jacques Chirac, and the *non-Gaullist Union pour la Démocratie Française* (UDF), originally started by former President Valéry Giscard d'Estaing. In theory they united into one party in 2002, the *Union pour un Mouvement Populaire,* though in practice a smaller UDF party continued, led by François Bayrou. On the fringes are the *Front National* (FN), an extreme right-wing party under Jean-Marie Le Pen (who tortured prisoners in Algeria), and *Les Verts* (the Greens). Le Pen's henchman, Bruno Mégret, started a new ultra-right party in 1998, the *Mouvement National Républicain,* which has some influence at local level. The *Front National* and *Mouvement National Républicain* are strongest around Marseille, their main programme being to make life difficult for immigrants and Muslims in particular. The French still have a nostalgic if rapidly dwindling fascination with the far-left, represented by such parties as the *Ligue communiste révolutionnaire* (LCR) or Revolutionary Communist League and the *Trotskyite Lutte Ouvrière* (LO) or Workers' Struggle. Perhaps more significantly politically is the growing anti-liberalisation or *altermondialiste* movement, represented by radical farmer José Bové in the 2007 presidential election. Capitalism, economic liberalism and globalisation are frequently targets of attack by politicians. In 2007 UDF leader François Bayrou formed a new centrist party called *Mouvement Démocrate,* building on his presidential campaign slogan of being neither right nor left.

# The French Language

The French are exceedingly proud and possessive about their language, which is the primary vehicle for spreading French culture around the world. The 20th century saw French lose its predominant position as the international language of diplomacy. The younger generation of French have given up some of their feelings of snobbery about their language; they are happy to use British and American expressions, which are creeping into the media more and more, while the *Académie Française* regularly issues edicts banning these linguistic intruders. Prospective Anglo-Saxon residents should not imagine, however, that this is a language about to throw in the towel in the face of English-language imperialism.

Many British visitors are irritated or puzzled to find that when they address the locals in their own language they will often reply in English, flatly refusing to carry on a conversation in French with you. They are just trying to be helpful: they reason that the conversation will be clearer if they speak in English, because clarity in expressing oneself is of primary importance here. By the same logic, those who are more modest will refuse to speak English at all.

On the whole, the average Brit or American tends to overestimate their own French-speaking abilities. The fact that English is full of French loanwords which came in from 1066 onwards, leads them to believe that they can instantly understand French without studying it. Most of the commonly used French words used in English don't actually mean the same in French as they do in English and there are whole dictionaries devoted to explaining these 'false friends'. The same holds true for French. One is reminded of a current tourist brochure that describes south-west France as 'a land of evasions'.

Needless to say, if you speak French well, and can talk knowledgeably about French literature, you will earn respect as someone who is '*cultivé*'. It cannot be emphasised too much how important learning French is: people who have given up and gone back to the UK often cite not speaking the language as one of the main reasons for their disenchantment.

## Where to learn French

Learning a foreign language should be fun. If it isn't, then you might as well not bother. Unfortunately, the trend in British schools for many years has been to teach French without teaching grammar – a prerequisite for learning any language. Brits and Americans also need to pay attention to their pronunciation. It is important to realise that French has no diphthongs (pairs of vowels, of which there are many in English); it also makes little distinction between long and short vowels. Taking care to pronounce French vowels correctly makes all the difference between mangling the language and sounding reasonably authentic.

The French state expends vast sums on trying to promote French abroad; if you are lucky, there may be an *Alliance Française* near you offering evening classes (they also exist in the USA). Your local college of further education, or community education centre will certainly offer courses in French; the price can be as low as £130 per year. It is a good idea to aim for an examination, such as an A-Level, so that you have some objective measure of your actual competence. If you are in France, it is worth asking at the local *mairie* to see if there are any low-priced courses available. The arrival of so many British and other English-speaking people in parts of France has led to an increase in the number of state-subsidised language courses around the country. They are an excellent way of both learning the language and making new friends.

*'The arrival of so many English-speaking people has led to an increase in the number of state-subsidised language courses around the country. They are an excellent way of both learning the language and making new friends'*

These days there are also numerous courses available on cassette, video, CD-ROM and the internet, which can be useful in supporting one's learning programme, even if they can't take the place of a native speaker. In particular, there are now some very good internet lessons available where you and the teacher speak using internet telephony software such as Skype. This means that not only do you get to speak to a native French speaker, you can also use an instant messaging service to combine oral and written work.

Courses that make absurd claims, such as 'You'll be speaking fluently in 10 days,' may not be bad courses, but you do need to know how to make the best possible use of them. If you do have to pay for language tuition, try to tape the lesson on a mini-disc or cassette so that you can go over it later. Again, you can also find French people who are willing to talk to you via the internet in return for helping them with their English.

With written French, one is confronted with an absurdly complicated system of accents, which was originally devised by the *Académie Française* in the 18th century to prevent people

## How Skype works

Using Skype or indeed other so-called internet telephony software is straightforward. You'll need a computer, a high-speed internet connection and either a set of headphones with a microphone or a special internet telephony phone. Visit www.skype.com, download its latest software, and follow the instructions to install it on your computer. You'll need to set up a Skype profile including a user name. Once the system is up and running you can call via your computer – for free and for as long as you like – anyone else who has a Skype account. For them to contact you you'll need to give them your Skype user name. You can also use Skype and other similar systems to call conventional telephones. This costs money, but works out less than using standard landline telephones. You can find out more about this on the Skype website.

## Insider Tip

*If you have some notion of language-learning methods, the cheapest and most effective way of learning is to advertise for a language exchange partner: you offer English in exchange for French. Simply listening to a French person speaking, and getting them to explain what you don't understand, can work wonders. In some places in France there are discussion groups where French- and English-speakers get together to speak first in one and then the other language.*

from changing the pronunciation of words. The great Enlightenment writers, such as Voltaire, got by perfectly well with one accent, but they are now here to stay. Unlike in Italian or Spanish, the accents may not be ignored; they serve a useful purpose in telling you how the word should be pronounced, and distinguishing one word from another.

A good dictionary is a must: Collins Robert and Harrap's are the two heavyweights. Both are available on CD-ROM. It is best to buy a new dictionary, because the language is changing so fast. You can more or less dispense with printed dictionaries if you have the internet: the website www.yourdictionary.com has several excellent online dictionaries which cover all sorts of specialised topics. The best one is the Canadian www. granddictionnaire.com.

## Language manners

As has already been said, the French take their language very seriously. They will quickly put you in your place if you try to make out that your French is better than it really is. In order not to sound uncouth, there are certain ground rules to observe. In the first place, you should address anyone you don't know as *Monsieur* or *Madame*, even if you are talking to the local drunk in the park. *Mademoiselle* is quite OK for someone under 16 years old, but otherwise stick to *Madame*.

You also need to understand when to use the formal (and plural) form of 'you', *vous*, and when to use the informal form *tu*. On initial acquaintance, you should always start with *vous* rather than *tu* (meaning 'you') unless everyone around is using *tu*. Immigrants may address

# In the know

**Céline Anthonioz runs Learn French at Home (www.learnfrenchathome.com), a distance learning company with a growing number of British clients. She explains the advantages of long-distance learning:**

Statistics show that 70% of Britons who relocate to France return to England within three years. One of the main reasons for going back is the difficulty they encounter in adapting to life in France and the frustration that comes from not being able to speak or understand the language plays a pivotal role.

Going to France with the idea that you will be able to understand French because many words are similar in English is a false concept. Language acquisition experts feel that it takes many hundreds of hours of exposure to the language to become fluent. Not only will you be faced with learning to recognise and reproduce the sounds of the language that are very different from those in English, but you will have to understand the mechanics of French grammar.

Thanks to today's technology, it is possible for anyone to start learning French even before moving to France. Long-distance learning has become very popular and effective in recent years and has been proven to be a very comfortable, less stressful way of learning. As long as you own a computer with a broadband connection, you can easily take lessons via an online communication tool called such as Skype. This system usually offers a better sound quality than the telephone and displays a chat feature which the teacher can use as a blackboard to type vocabulary and sentences for the student. Some great benefits have been found in learning the language at a distance.

- **Scheduling flexibility and time saving**: there is no need to drive to a language school and you can choose the best time for you to take the lesson.
- **Cost savings on one-to-one lessons**: studying a language on a one-to-one basis with a teacher is much more effective, but usually expensive. However, long-distance schools have fewer overhead expenses and the resulting fees are more attractive.
- **The lessons can follow you wherever you go**: you can continue to take your lessons even if you travel a lot.
- **Native French teachers located in a French-speaking country**: having a teacher located in the country will give you the opportunity to ask for information relating to life in France.

You can find these long-distance teaching programmes by typing key words such as 'learn french via skype' in the major search engines. Learning the language before you move to France will greatly increase your chances of succeeding in your new life.

everyone as *tu* (the verb is *tutoyer*), but it is best not to copy them. With people of your own age and social grouping, the transition to *tu* should happen quite quickly. If everyone around you is addressing each other as *tu* it will seem odd if you don't do the same. With people of the opposite sex you should be more careful, in case you appear over-familiar. If you look very young, older people may address you as *tu* and you will reply using *vous*.

The use of the more respectful *vous* – the verb is *vouvoyer* – is also rather loaded. With strangers you must use *vous*. If you continue to use *vous* with social acquaintances then you are keeping your distance. If you address your wife and children as *vous*, then people may think you have had a serious domestic rift, or perhaps you are just a mad foreigner. Once you start using *tu* you cannot go back to *vous*, although it is quite possible that in the course of an evening people will address you as *tu* and then go back to *vous* the following day.

## French letters

Although the expression raises a smile – the French have got their revenge by calling a condom a *capote anglaise* – writing letters in French is no laughing matter. A foreigner who wants to write a formal letter in French is best advised to use a model letter such as can be found in *330 Modèles de Lettres et de Contrats* (published by Prat, 2002). It pays to be careful when writing formal letters; the most crucial part is to get the salutation and the close right. You should never begin a letter *Cher Monsieur* or *Chère Madame*, unless you are on friendly terms with the addressee. The salutation with officials and business people is *Monsieur* or *Madame*. If they have a title, it is best to use it. One of the oddities of titles is that some of them remain masculine even when used for women: thus *Madame le Professeur, Madame le Notaire, Madame le Docteur.* On the other hand, you can say *la secrétaire* as well as *le secrétaire*. Some titles have feminine forms: *Madame la Directrice.*

It is also crucial to get the ending right. There are literally dozens of permutations of endings which can run to a whole tortuous sentence. The safest one is: *Recevez, Monsieur (or Madame), l'assurance de mes salutations distinguées.* Some people avoid using formulas which substitute '*sentiments*' for '*salutations*' with people of the opposite sex. A more informal ending is *Cordialement,* but you shouldn't use this the first time you write to someone.

# Communications

## Fixed-line telephones

The landline scene in France is in something of a state of flux. In most places France Telecom is the only company that can install your first telephone line and all calls go through them, but in some cities it is now possible to have a telephone line installed by Cegetel or Free Telecom, such as in Paris, Lyon and Bordeaux, and to pay your line rental to these companies. Gradually the landline scene is being changed by the use of VoIP, or calling via the internet. Once the preserve of computer wizards it is becoming more and more widely used. Skype is the best known of the many VoIP options and has a good instant message or chat facility that can be used while you are talking. You will need to download the software from www.skype.com. There are however many other providers and as ever it is worth shopping around. The Livebox offered by Orange (formerly Wanadoo) provides telephony, TV, and internet connection all in one. Packages start from around €30 a month though you will only be able to receive television via the internet if your broadband connection is fast enough. Another well-known provider is Alice, formerly Tiscali. Some people who live in rural areas may not be able to get this service even if they have broadband.

France Telecom has been gradually privatised and has the distinction of being one of the world's most heavily indebted companies. The website www.francetelecom.fr has a lot of information (if you can find it), including some in English. You can sign up to a sophisticated system for tracking your bill and paying it online. You can circumvent France Telecom entirely by going through another fixed-line provider, such as Primus (www.primustel.fr), and enjoy on-line usage tracking and other additional benefits. Primus does not charge for the connection, making it very economical. Many fixed-line providers offer highly misleading contracts, which appear to offer very cheap prices, but after six months you suddenly find that your charges have doubled. It is best to read the small print very carefully before you sign up to any of these seemingly attractive deals. A comparison of their prices can be found on the website www.comparatel. com. One option is to keep France Telecom as your line provider but to choose another company such as Tele2 (www.tele2.fr) for your calls. You will still pay rental to France Telecom but will be able to take advantage of the other company's usually much cheaper call rate. France Telecom's tariffs are high and you woud be well advised to look for alternatives when it comes to call charges. The advantage of still renting your line from France Telecom is that if your line is out of order – a not infrequent occurrence in rural France – they do have a team of engineers able to fix it, usually relatively quickly. Alice have been offering some very attractive deals that reduce the cost of overseas calls dramatically as part of a combined internet and telephone package.

The first step to take if you want a line installed, or restored, is to go to a Boutique France Telecom, or to telephone a France Telecom shop – the numbers can be found under

> *'Many fixed-line providers offer highly misleading contracts, which appear to offer very cheap prices, but after six months you suddenly find that your charges have doubled'*

*Régions* on www.francetelecom.fr. Or you can call 10 14 free of charge. There is an English-language helpline on 0800 364 775. In order to be connected you will need the following documents:

- a copy of your identity card or passport
- your surname, given name, date and place of birth printed on paper
- the precise address where you want the line installed and the date you want it by
- a telephone number where France Telecom can contact you
- details of the previous subscriber.

France Telecom promises to have your line working within 48 hours. If there is no existing connection, then you will have to have the necessary work done first. The France Telecom shop will direct you to a contractor.

British handsets need an adapter to work in France; the British variety have three wires, while the French ones have only two. The keys on French telephones are much the same as on British ones. The only point to note is that the hash symbol is called *dièse* – the same as a 'sharp' in music – needed for cheap-rate telephone cards. Both business and private telephone numbers are on the internet. The yellow pages are on www.pagesjaunes.fr and private subscribers on www.annu.fr. There is also the French system called Minitel, which is now rapidly going out of date and is expensive but can be used free in post offices. There is always Directory Enquiries: dial 12.

France Telecom and the other companies have a multitude of special rates and tariffs. Calls are half-price after 7pm until 9am, and also from 7pm on Friday until 8am on Monday and on public holidays. If you are not going through one of the fixed-line companies such as Onetel, then you maye be best off using a call-back service for international calls. These include Eurotel. Sat (www.eurotelsat.com) and Phonexpat (www.phonexpat.com). The main concern with telephone discount international-call providers is that while their call rates may be rock bottom, you often still pay a connection charge which means that you start paying from the moment the telephone starts ringing, and you also pay if the line is engaged or if there is no response. One of the few companies that does not make a connection charge is www.teleconnectfrance.com.

# Telephone boxes

Telephone boxes mostly work with cards; those that work with coins are inside cafés or other private buildings, so it is essential always to have a card with you if you do not carry a mobile phone. The France Telecom card is not good value for money; the post office sells a better card – Kertel (www.kertel.com) – particularly for phoning abroad. Many cards claim that you can use them in other countries, which is not true. The numbers usually turn out to be fictitious. You can also use French telephone boxes with a UK card such as BT Globalcard, which is expensive but useful in an emergency.

# Mobile phones

The topic of *le mobile* or *le portable* is as complex as anywhere else. There is the same abundance of tariffs and options. France has still not fully deregulated its mobile phone market, which is still largely limited to SFR, Orange and Bouygues, or rather these three companies have not allowed other operators to enter the market. However newer companies such as Tele2 (www.tele2.fr) and Debitel (www.debitel.fr) are now providing some much-needed competition and are worth having a look at. To find some trees in the wood, try to look at the information on www.comparatel.com, which has a great deal of useful information comparing mobile phone companies as well as internet providers. It is quite possible to carry on using your UK or US mobile phone in France, but you will be in for a shock when you get the bill. Mobile phone companies have seen an opportunity to make a killing by charging outrageous amounts for calling with your own mobile. The best policy is to change the SIM card in your mobile to a French pay-as-you-go SIM, so you can carry on using the same handset and keep your list of numbers etc. You can then top up your mobile as and when you need. A great advantage of this system is that it also protects you if your mobile is stolen in France, because once the pre-paid amount

*'Unless you are officially resident in France, French mobile phone companies will only let you use a mobile phone with a pre-paid card, on production of your passport'*

has been used up the thief can no longer make free calls with it. You can now top up your pay as you go mobile phones online via your service provider.

Unless you are officially resident in France, French mobile phone companies will only let you use a mobile phone with a pre-paid card, on production of your passport. The well-known deals are Orange La Mobicarte, SFR La Carte, and Bouygues Carte Nomad. To buy a mobile phone you need a proof of identity and a proof of address. You also have to produce a RIB – a bank account number – which is in any case unavoidable if you pay by direct debit. You will also be asked to produce a cheque written out to you that has gone through your account, or a French credit card. If you only make short visits to France, you could use a multi-country operator that offers short-term contracts. One such is Transatel which offers a two-month contract under the name LeFrenchMobile (www.lefrenchmobile.com). These are 50% cheaper than pre-paid for national calls and 75% cheaper for international calls. Additionally you get a local French number and you can keep your number for €5. You can order by filling in the form on their website or you can call +33 170 75 24 00. Another provider of discount mobile services is www.teleconnectfrance.com (+33 130 07 23 50; email info@teleconnectfrance. com). The company provides SIM cards that enable British clients arriving in France with UK mobiles to make cheap calls while in France. You can also purchase foreign pay-as-you-go SIM cards from a website such as www.0044.co.uk.

As France is relatively thinly populated in comparison to the UK, mobile phone coverage is not guaranteed, and there are areas in the countryside where you will not have any reception. Out of the three main mobile phone companies, Orange and SFR are supposed to have better coverage than Bouygues Telecom in country areas. They generally claim to cover 98% of the population and 87% of the land area. There are apparently far-fetched plans to have aeroplanes flying overhead 24 hours a day to ensure that everyone has 3G mobile phone coverage. For the three main companies see: www.orange.fr, www.sfr.fr and www.bouyguestelecom.fr.

## Internet and email

It would be fair to say that France has taken a long time to catch up with the UK and the USA as regards internet use and availability. This is to some extent because of the pioneering system known as Minitel started in 1985, which provides a service similar to the internet. Minitel is a keyboard and screen that sits alongside your telephone; although it is expensive it is still used by some people and organisations. You can access Minitel from the UK, by logging on to www. minitel.fr. There are few cybercafés outside big towns in France. Some are located in the back of cafés or clothes shops. It is advisable to create an email account with the French post office – see www.laposte.net – which is best done at home, as you cannot do it in a post office. The internet terminals in post offices take pre-paid cards, but don't raise your hopes: most have been trashed.

If you absolutely have to have internet access everywhere, then the solution is to sign up for a GPRS or 3G contract in the UK or the USA. Roaming with a wireless connection is extremely expensive – around £6 per megabyte used abroad. It is also possible to buy pre-paid cards in expensive hotels or to look for 'hotspots' (if your laptop is suitably equipped) where you can surf the internet fairly cheaply without a telephone line. The site www.mappy.fr shows Orange hotspots for wireless surfing.

The French are still trying to decide on a word for 'email'. The *Académie Française* favours *courriel*, an abbreviation of *courrier électronique*, but few people have taken this up. Most people prefer the ugly-sounding *mél*; a lot of companies use the word 'email', and though it is not likely to become the standard written form of the word, you can safely use it in everyday speech.

Once you have settled in to your new home in France, you can look at the different internet service providers' offerings, which are more limited than what you would find in the UK. However, though France may have been slow to develop the internet, it is now widely used and available and there are more and more offers on the market. If you are a light user, you may do well with www.Club-internet.fr. Orange (formerly Wanado and owned by France Telecom) can also be recommended. There are dozens of other ISPs, such as Club-internet, Alice (formerly Tiscali), Free and Freesurf who offer monthly packages. If you are connected to cable, you can get good deals with Noos. Cable offers the fastest broadband capability. Otherwise you can use ADSL. This is the high-speed internet connection that works via a telephone line but which allows you to use your telephone while surfing the internet. The limitation is that it downloads files much faster than it uploads (sends) them. You can find out very easily if your area qualifies for ADSL, by looking on www.comparatel.com and entering your address under the relevant box. The site will also tell you the best deals available for your town or even village. The vast majority of France is now covered by ADSL, though in many of the more rural areas speed will be limited to 1 or 2 megabytes per second (MB/s). For those few isolated spots not covered a variety of solutions are being tried, such as ADSL via wireless and satellite, though these vary in cost and availability. As in the UK, USA and elsewhere it is now common to have a wireless network at home to manage your ADSL connection. If you already have a wireless router or modem and are moving to France you can use them. You do not have to use the ISP's router/ modem, which usually comes at an extra cost.

Another interesting possibility is to circumvent France Telecom and use an inactive telephone line to obtain a triple service, telephone, internet and television, from www.free.fr with their Freebox (similar to the Livebox from Wanadoo). It is also a good idea to get a back-up dial-up connection in case you have problems with your ADSL connection at a crucial time. You can get a simply pay-as-you-go dial-up connection from companies such as www.Free.fr.

## Internet glossary

| | |
|---|---|
| *l'adresse électronique* | email address |
| *l'alinéa* | paragraph |
| *l'annexe* | attachment |
| *l'arobase* | @ (at) symbol (not *arabesque*) |
| *le clavier* | keyboard |
| *cursif/cursive* | italic |
| *l'écran* | screen |
| *gras/grasse* | bold (type) |
| *le haut débit* | broadband |
| *kilo-octet/Ko* | kilobyte |
| *mega-octet/Mo* | megabyte |
| *la mémoire vive* | RAM memory |
| *le mot de passe* | password |
| *le moteur de recherche* | search engine |
| *le navigateur* | browser |
| *l'octet* | byte |
| *la police* | font |
| *la pouce* | inch (screen size) |
| *le répertoire* | directory |
| *le retrait* | indent |
| *le site web/internet* | website |
| *télécharger* | to download |
| *valider* | to hit enter key |

# Computers

There is no reason why your UK or US computer (the latter with an adapter) should not work in France; the only downside is that your keyboard will be different from the French one, and it will be somewhat less convenient for typing French. The French keyboard, called AZERTY, has the peripheral characters in different places from the English QWERTY; the main irritation is that the numbers have to be accessed with the shift key, while their place has been taken by accented French characters. The spacing on the screen will also appear different from in the UK. There is a simple remedy for this, which is to go to System Tools and change the keyboard language from French to English. The downside is that the letters on the screen will not correspond to the keys you are using. It is simpler to plug a UK or US keyboard into a computer bought in France; the computer should be turned off when you change the keyboard, unless you use a USB port. You will also need a different cable for your modem.

# Media

## Newspapers

The newspaper scene in France bears no comparison to that in the UK. The national newspapers have a small circulation; regional newspapers are often more popular. At the weekend you will often have to make do with one paper for Saturday and Sunday, or Sunday and Monday. The only Sunday newspaper comparable to those in the UK is *Le Figaro*, though this is still a Saturday/Sunday edition. The highbrow *Le Monde* is pretty dry, and does not even have photographs in the news section, mainly consisting of long and well-written essays on current topics of interest. It is however an excellent way of keeping in touch with the main concerns of the French Establishment and its website (www.lemonde.fr) is well worth consulting. *Libération* is a more colourful left-wing offering, and then there is *L'Humanité* founded by Jean-Paul Sartre. The daily *Le Figaro* represents conservative opinion. The business daily *Les Échos* is considered right wing. Regional newspapers concentrate on local news and sport though they give a useful digest of national and international news too; they are also useful for property advertisements. The French produce good magazines: apart from the original celebrity glossy *Paris-Match* there are excellent general interest magazines such as *Express, Nouvel Observateur* and *Le Point*. The big development in recent years has been the emergence of rather more brash celebrity magazines such as *Closer*, the French version of the British weekly magazine. French intellectuals and commentators love to sneer at such low-brow offerings, regarding them as vulgar Anglo-Saxon inventions. However the French public is buying them in ever-greater numbers.

There are a number of useful English magazines for expats in France, perhaps the sharpest being the monthly *The Connexion*. *French News* also has a useful analyses of French news from an expat perspective.

## English magazines in France

*Anglo Riviera Times:* Quarterly guide; www.riviera-media.com.

*Connection Côte-d'Azur:* Bimonthly.

*The Connexion:* Monthly, useful reading for expat residents; www.connexionfrance.com.

*French Times:* Quarterly published from Dordogne; www.french-times.com.

*FUSAC:* Leading free weekly in Paris; stands for France-USA Contacts; www.fusac.fr.

*The Irish Eyes:* Free monthly in Paris; www.irisheyes.fr.

*New Riviera-Côte d'Azur:* Glossy magazine published every 3 months.

*French News:* Monthly, useful reading for expat residents; www.french-news.com.

*Paris Voice:* Free monthly; www.parisvoice.com.

*Riviera Reporter:* Monthly; www.riviera-reporter.com.

*Riviera Times:* Monthly; www.mediterra.com.

# Television

If you come from the UK, you will quickly be struck by the poor quality of French television. Many of the offerings are American series dubbed into French spoken at breakneck speed, so you will never catch a word. There are interesting political discussions, where everyone talks at once, but nothing like the kind of aggressive interviewing one sees in the UK. Interviewers treat politicians with kid gloves.

The main terrestrial channel is the formerly state-owned TF1. FR2 and FR3 are still owned by the state. The fourth channel is Canal Plus, a private subscription channel. Channel 5 shows La Cinq – a state-run cultural channel – in the daytime, and the Franco-German Arte after 7pm. The latter is by far the most highbrow terrestrial channel, broadcasting high-quality films and documentaries in the evening, with no news bulletins. Channel 6 – M6 – is a light entertainment channel that broadcasts a great number of American shows.

As in the UK, to watch television in your French home you need to have a TV licence or *redevance audiovisuelle*. The charge is €116 (in 2007) regardless of whether you own a colour or black and white set. If you are liable to pay *taxe d'habitation* (that is you are occupying habitable premises on 1st January of the tax year) then you will be charged. If you do not own a television you will have to opt out by ticking the relevant box in your tax declaration. Those over 65 years old and invalids (assuming they do not live with someone who is subject to *taxe d'habitation*) are exempt. It is possible to pay by three-monthly instalments, using direct debit.

## Access to British television

If you want to have access to the BBC and other English-language stations, then you could have cable, but satellite is a far more satisfactory option. The cable channel Noos (www.noos.fr) offers a variety of 'bouquets' of channels, which include BBC, CNN etc. There is no need for a dish with cable TV, but if you live too far out in the countryside you will not be able to connect to cable in any case. You can find out by entering your address in the box '*êtes-vous raccordable?*' (can you be connected?) on www.noos.fr. TPS (www.tps.fr) and CanalSat (www.canalsat.fr) are satellite subscription stations also offering English-language channels; the hire of the decoder and dish are included in a monthly charge of around €20–€30 depending on the option you choose. The two stations have now merged. There is also the possibility of receiving satellite TV through your telephone connection, via ADSL, in some of the larger French cities and wherever high-speed internet access is available. The advantage of cable is that you can have a superfast broadband internet connection included.

The satellite TV situation changed in 2004, insofar as the Astra 2D satellite, which broadcasts British stations, shifted its 'footprint' to the north somewhat. Whilst you will still have reception with a 60 cm dish

*'Another great advantage of having satellite TV is that it enables you to pick up British radio stations, without the bother of accessing them over the internet'*

(*parabole*) in the north-western quadrant of France, along the Côte d'Azur, you will need a 130 cm dish to be sure of receiving UK television. A map of the required dish sizes can be seen at www.satalogue.com. The dish is installed on the exterior of your residence. If you live in a *co-propriété* you will need the permission of the other residents.

To obtain the maximum number of English-language channels you need to obtain a Freesat card from Sky in the UK. The first step is to obtain an information pack from Sky on 08702 404 040; ask for it to be sent a UK address. The Freesat card is valid for a minumum of two years and costs £20. Sky will only send it to a UK address and you will also need to give a UK telephone number. You should never tell Sky that you are abroad. The company www.insatinternational.com (020 8886 7155) can obtain a Sky digibox and Freesat card for you, from around £150, or you could ask a friend.

Once you have your card you will need a decoder or digibox (assuming you haven't got both at the same time from someone like Insat International), which costs from £150 upwards. If you are technically minded you could buy the decoder for far less on eBay. The rest of the equipment will cost around £70, and there is still the cost of €200–€300 for someone to do the actual installation. Where there are large communities of Britons, you may be able to obtain assistance more cheaply. There are numerous British-owned companies who will provide the complete package; they advertise in French property magazines. At all events, it is advisable to download the free guide to satellite TV installation from www.satcure.com.

The third option is to take out a Sky subscription and then take the equipment with you to France. Some people find that they can continue to pick up satellite TV after their Sky subscription has expired, but the best advice is to keep your involvement with Sky to a minimum. Sky will in any case only supply you with a receiver if they install it themselves and it is a condition that you remain connected to a UK landline for a year or so, for purposes of online shopping. Be careful; if Sky find out then both the viewing card and the digibox risk being blacklisted and according to industry experts the company is clamping down on unauthorised use of their system.

Another great advantage of having satellite TV is that it enables you to pick up British radio stations, without the bother of accessing them over the internet. With hundreds of TV and radio stations to choose from you will also need a guide to this plethora of celestial entertainment, so it is advisable to subscribe to www.digiguide.com for £8.99 for two years, so you know just what sort of dross you can expect to be watching. The whole exercise of installing satellite TV will cost up to £500, assuming you are not qualified to do the work yourself.

# Education

France has the reputation of having one of the world's best education systems: it is certainly one of the most effective for stuffing facts into pupil's heads, but not that good for encouraging independent thinking or personal development. The main emphasis is on intellectual achievement, in particular in French grammar, science and mathematics. The downside is the harshness of the school regime. It is at school that the French learn how to compete; the general absence of sports (apart from gymnastics) is another difference from the British system. It is often said that it is best not to put English-speaking children over the age of seven into the French school system: the language deficit, combined with the rigorous nature of French education, could make their lives unbearable. This is unrealistic, however, for young families moving into more rural areas of France. The other alternative is to put them into a school where part of the French national curriculum is taught in English, so that they can then take a French International Baccalaureate. A few schools even mix French and British curriculums. But again, these are unlikely to be found in less populated areas. There are international schools, but these are expensive and are only in the big cities. In fact, recent experience shows that many British children have adapted well to French schooling and they usually pick up the language very quickly – far more quickly than their parents. This allows them to make French friends and to be able to make the most of their education. Many British adults find that their children soon become their unofficial translators or interpreters.

Education is compulsory between ages six and 16 years old. Until recently there was a virtually uniform system over the whole country; most schools are state schools (*les écoles publiques*). There are also private schools (*les écoles privées*), which are partly subsidised by the state or by the church, mostly religious-based. If you want to send your child to a private school, the state or municipality may offer financial assistance, depending on your means. You should in the first instance go to the *service des écoles* at your local *mairie,* who will give you a list of the schools in your area.

# Structure of education

French children go into nursery schools as early as possible. Since 1989 every child from the age of three has been entitled to a place in a nursery school (*école maternelle*). There is also the infants' school (*jardin d'enfants*) for 2–3-year-olds (which is not free).

From 6 years old all children go into the primary system – *école primaire* or *élémentaire* – which comprises grades 11 to 7. From 11 to 15 years old children go into the *collège d'enseignement secondaire* (CES), the same as a British comprehensive. Depending on their aptitudes, students go on to a *lycée* or a specialised *lycée technique,* where they prepare for one of a number of possible leaving qualifications. The more academic stream will take the General or Technical Baccalaureate, which qualifies them automatically to go on to university.

For more information on the education system, ask the French embassy to send you their leaflet 'Primary and Secondary Education in France' (see www.ambafrance.org.uk and www.ambafrance.org.us) or look at the government website: www.education.gouv.fr. Most of the English-medium schools in France belong to the ELSA (English Language Schools Association France) organisation and are listed on their website (www.elsa-france.org). The website www.FrenchEntrée.com also has detailed information on the education system.

The French higher education system is very different from that in the UK or USA. Universities are the second tier in the system; everyone aspires to go the *grandes écoles,* elite institutions that train the brightest and best to become civil servants, high government officials and the country's political masters. There are specialised colleges for engineers, scientists, businessmen and administrators; graduating from one of them guarantees high social status and a job for life. In the case of the universities, there is a chaotic struggle at the beginning of the academic year to get onto courses, and many change subjects or drop out. Because of the lack of grants, most students continue to live at home while they go to university. On average they stay with their parents until they are 22 years old. The state of their universities is a major concern to the French authorities.

## International schools

For those who can afford them, an international school, or a school offering the same curriculum as in your home country, may be the best or even the only solution. Most of these schools offer the International Baccalaureate which is accepted for university entrance in many countries. Some offer a mixture of instruction in English and French. Some have nursery sections. Tuition fees go up to £18,000 a year or more; French private schools are much cheaper. There are liaison organisations in the UK and USA who can advise you on where to find an international school in your area. A short list of international schools can be found in The Directory.

# Health

It has been acknowledged by the World Health Organization that France has the best, or at least the most cost-effective, healthcare system in the world. This has come about as the result of the French government spending liberally to bring an unsatisfactory system up to scratch. In spite of this, there are still shortages of doctors and everyone fears that the situation is going to deteriorate in the future. In particular there is a growing shortage of doctors and dentists in rural areas. France spends 10.1% of its GDP on health, as opposed to 9.4% in the UK, and 15.2% in the USA. French employees pay a specific 8% of their wages for healthcare insurance, but healthcare is still not free. You pay as you go and reclaim most of the cost afterwards. You will be treated in case of emergencies without undergoing a 'wallet biopsy'; the bills come later.

## British non-residents

If you are just going on holiday to France, or planning to stay for less than three months, be sure to obtain a European Health Insurance Card or EHIC. This gives some identification numbers but it is not a smart card. This entitles you to what is called 'necessary' healthcare during your stay in France. Application forms are available from post offices in the UK or you can visit www.dh.gov.uk/travellers or www.ehic.org.uk.

Not having the EHIC can be financially disastrous if you fall ill in France. If you do need treatment, show the EHIC to the doctor or clinic, who must be *conventionné*, i.e. part of the French state system. You will then be able to reclaim up to 90% of the costs of treatment. The EHIC is not a blank cheque to use the French healthcare system. It runs out after three months, by which time you should be paying into the French social security system. It is advisable to take out health insurance in any case for trips abroad: a stay in a French hospital can cost up to £2,000 a day in the case of major surgery.

If you forget to apply for the EHIC before you leave, the Department of Work and Pensions will send it to you (Department for Work and Pensions, The Pension Service, International Pension Centre, Medical Benefits Section, Tyneview Park, Whitley Road, Newcastle-upon-Tyne NE98 1BA; psymbol 0191 218 7547 or +44 191 218 7547). If you are intending to remain abroad for more than three months then you must register with French social security.

Once you are a permanent resident in France, you are no longer entitled to use the National Health Service free of charge in the UK, but in practice, the French authorities allow Britons to go on relying on the NHS and the EHIC for about 18 months after their arrival; this is one case where theory and practice do not match. Pensioners can continue to use the NHS in the UK longer than those who are working in France; contact the Medical Benefits Section for further details (www.dh.gov.uk). If you work in France, but pay National Insurance contributions in the UK, it is also possible to go on using the NHS; ask for form E106 or E128. If you are retiring to France and are entitled to UK state benefits (pension, invalidity, bereavement, etc.), ask for form E121 so you can receive the same benefits as French residents. You must register your E121 with French social security. Finally, there is the E106 which also applies to those who retire early from the UK to France. As long as you have paid Class 1 or 2 National Insurance contributions up until the time you leave (or at least up until some months before you leave), then you will be able to benefit from the same entitlements as a French resident for an extended period (the length of time is not entirely clear). If there is too long a gap between the time you stopped paying National Insurance contributions and your application for the E106 then it will be turned down. This type of E106 is obtainable from the Medical Benefits Section. The E106 that applies to those working for UK employers is obtained from the Contributions Agency (☎0845 915 4811). The form is exactly the same, but the details are different.

# The French healthcare system

Paying into the social security system in France entitles you and your dependants to medical treatment, and other expenses, free of charge up to a statutory limit for each type of treatment. The contributions are collected by a departmental organisation called CPAM, which then distributes the money to different *caisses*, or sickness funds, depending on your profession. Once you pay in you will receive the all-important *Carte Vitale*, a green smart card that stores all your administrative details on a microchip. The *Carte* does not hold any medical details, nor is it a payment card. You can read the information on it by inserting it into a *borne vitale* at any surgery or hospital. The reform of the healthcare system has also seen the introduction of a *Carte Vitale 2*, which will record more details about your course of treatment, which doctors you have seen, and so on, than the older *Carte Vitale*. An important – and discouraging – new rule enforced from September 2007 is that only those British residents with an E121 (see above) or who are 'economically active' (i.e. working and paying social charges) are eligible to join the French state health insurance system and thus get a *Carte Vitale*. This means people who retire early to France, who do not work and who are not eligible for an E121 will have to take out private health insurance to cover the costs of *all* their treatment. See websites such as www.FrenchEntree.com for more details on this major development.

Social security generally pays 70%–90% of the cost of treatment, and 35%–70% of the cost of medicines. Alternative medicines may not be refunded at all. The full cost will be paid for serious illnesses or in specific hospital practices. Hospitals and general practices can charge as much as they want for their services, but in every area groups of doctors agree to charge fees within the limits set by social security. Doctors who follow these agreements are known as *conventionné*. Rates for treatment are publicised on Minitel.

# Reform of the health insurance system

From 1st July 2005, there began a major reform of the healthcare system, which continued through 2006. The intention is to save the state €1 billion per year by limiting patients' choice of doctor and keeping a closer eye on their course of treatment. From then on patients are required to register with a *médecin traitant* or 'main doctor', who does not necessarily have to be a *généraliste* or general practitioner. If you require specialist treatment, then your *médecin traitant* will pass you on to a *médecin correspondent*. If you choose to go directly to a specialist or a doctor who is not your *médecin traitant* then you will pay higher charges, or rather you will be reimbursed less of the costs. To put it in concrete terms: the basic tariff for a consultation with a specialist in the *Secteur* 1, or *Tarif Sécu* is €27 of which 70% is refunded. If you went directly to the specialist then you are charged a basic €32 but the *Sécu* refunds 70% of the old tariff of €25, which means you receive €16.50. From 1st January 2006 this dropped to only 60% of €25, if you do not go along with the *médecin traitant* system. Doctors who do not charge the approved *Sécu* rates are classified under *Secteur 2*. Their basic rate is €23 and 70% is refunded by the state. For a more complex diagnosis they will charge €40; the refund is still 70%. Still further reforms are planned in late 2007 and early 2008.

There are numerous exceptions to this system; in particular paediatrics, ophthalmology, gynaecology and psychiatry are not yet subject to the *médecin traitant* procedure. Dental services are not affected by the reform. By the launch date of 1st July 2005, some 40% of patients had already signed up with a *médecin traitant*.

# Private health insurance

To cover the shortfall in the cost of treatment, it is strongly advisable to have additional private health insurance. Most French have additional insurance, but many foreign residents do not. Different professions have special plans – known as *complémentaires* or *mutuelles* – or your employer may pay for this. Well-known British-based health insurers include BUPA and Expacare. You need to verify that the insurer has an existing link with French social security and that they offer adequate cover. Once you are resident in France you have to have a social security number; private health cover taken out in another country does not exempt you from paying social security contributions. The Brittany-based insurer, Agence Eaton, has bilingual staff and deals with all kinds of insurance. A well-known French provider of this 'top up' medical health insurance is the large insurer Groupama.

Costly dental treatment is mainly paid by the patient; a good *complémentaire* will refund more than the state scheme. The situation is similar with opticians. Opticians will always accept payment by a *complémentaire*.

## Insider Tip

When choosing additional health insurance, it is important to check whether the insurer already has a direct link with the social security office in France, which will speed up reimbursement of your costs.

## Health insurers

**Agence Eaton:** Arradon ☎02 97 40 80 20; www.french-insurance.com.
**British United Provident Association (BUPA):** Brighton ☎01273 208181;
www.bupa-intl.com.
**Expacare Insurance Services:** Berkshire ☎01344 381650; email info@expacare.net;
www.expacare.net.
**Goodhealth Worldwide (Europe):** ☎0870 442 7376; www.goodhealth.co.uk.
**Groupama:** www.groupama.fr.

If you pass retirement age in France, you will only pay a small contribution from your pension for sickness cover, but you will still have to pay the difference between the cost of treatment and the amount refunded, unless you have a chronic illness.

# Doctors and dentists

Once you know you are going to remain in France, do find a local doctor and dentist. Although it is not essential to be registered with a doctor first, it is easier if you know in advance who to go to. Ask them if they are *conventionné* and what their charges are. Doctors are highly educated and most will be able to speak some English; other expat can tell you who is the most appropriate. The local *commissariat de police* can tell you where to find a doctor out of office hours.

Up until 2002, after your course of treatment was finished the doctor gave you a receipt – *feuille de soins* – which you then sent to the local *Caisse Primaire d'Assurance Maladie* to get your refund. The pharmacist would attach a price tag (*vignette*) to your prescription (*ordonnance*) for you to send to your health insurer. A new electronic system is now in operation which speeds up the process of reimbursing your payments. The paperwork follows later. Your details are registered on your electronic smart card – the *Carte Vitale* – which is read when you enter a hospital or surgery; your refund should be automatically credited to your bank account within five working days. In some areas the electronic system is not yet in use.

# Chemists

Pharmacists (*pharmaciens*) are highly trained and can give basic healthcare advice. The French consume excessive amounts of pills and remedies and there is much wringing of hands about this, but somehow it is always other people who are using too many pills. Just look in any French medicine cupboard. The main problem lies in the fact that the amount of pills prescribed is often more than what is required for the course of treatment.

As a basic principle, medicines for life-threatening conditions are free, even where the condition is chronic, which is good news for the retired. For run-of-the-mill problems the refund rate may be as low as 35%; some items will not be refunded at all. There are schemes in operation allowing you to obtain prescription medicines out of hours. There will be a hole in the wall where you can insert your Carte Vitale.

# Shopping

If you come from northern Europe or North America one of the first things you will notice in France is the way shopkeepers deal with customers. The customer is not king here; you may feel that the shopkeeper is doing you a favour by letting you into their private domain. The rudest shop assistants are, not surprisingly, in Paris. Being asked to open up your bag for inspection at the checkout in supermarkets can also be very disconcerting for foreigners. Opening hours are another bugbear. Smaller shops can only open on five days a week, so many opt to close on Monday and stay open on Saturday, which gives rural towns a strangely dead atmosphere on a Monday. This also includes estate agents.

The best advice when shopping is to appeal to the shop assistant's more helpful side: simply saying 'Pourriez vous m'aider, madame/monsieur' will work wonders, rather than 'Avez-vous un…'. The French love to help anyone in trouble, especially if you address them respectfully. It is not necessary to thank shop assistants too effusively. It is normal to wish them a 'nice day' (bonne journée).

The retail scene in France is very different from the UK. While there are supermarkets (supermarchés) – smaller than in the UK – and hypermarkets (hypermarchés), there are few shopping malls. Most French would like to keep a personal relationship with their local shopkeepers, with the idea that they will get a better, or at least friendlier, service.

## Relative prices

Comparisons of retail prices in different countries are notoriously unreliable: the data that exists are between London and Paris, neither of which is at all typical. Most Britons find that the cost of living in France is lower than in the UK, outside of the very expensive areas of Paris and the Côte d'Azur. Groceries in London and Paris cost about the same, with notable exceptions such as alcohol and French specialities like olive oil. Petrol is more or less the same price in both countries.

Among the goods that are particularly expensive in France are books and newspapers. Foreign imported goods have always been more expensive than French ones, although the difference is tending to diminish. Electrical goods are often considerably more expensive than in the USA or the UK and it is worthwhile searching among specialist French online sites which can save you money once you know what you are looking for. Mistergooddeal (www.mistergooddeal.com) is one place to start, another is the price comparative site www.acheter-moins-cher.com. Delivery is often free for larger items. For books but also for some electrical items, mobile phones and DVDs the French-language Amazon site is useful. It can be found at: www.amazon.fr.

The French equivalent of VAT – the Taxe sur la Valeur Ajoutée (TVA) is charged on most goods and services at 19.6%, while some items – including food, travel, hotels, books, non-reimbursable medicines and utilities – are only subject to 5.5%. There is a 2.1% super-reduced rate on magazines, reimbursable medicines and TV licences.

# ✓ Been there, done it...

**Pipemaker Trever Talbert from North Carolina has some wry observations on the differences between shopping in the USA and France (adapted from his website www.talbertpipes.com).**

The difference in shopping hours isn't that noticeable at first, but over time it has become a nuisance on several occasions where we've wanted to shop at odd hours. In France, most businesses close for two hours for lunch ... yes, I said close, and even the big stores like SuperU tend to close up at 7.30 pm. This means no shopping for groceries at midnight, which we did fairly often in the USA to avoid the crowds. No businesses in the USA do this. Here, the priority is on the convenience to the employees. Rather than stress half the staff while the other half is at lunch, the whole shop will simply close down.

Ignore everything you may have read about the French being rude – the people who work the counters and aisles of our local big grocers and shopping centres are some of the nicest, most polite people a person could want to deal with. On top of this, they stay where they are to a degree that is jaw-droppingly amazing to my American brain. We have now lived here for over 3 years and the same check-out cashiers are still working at the SuperU – we know them by sight and some by name now. In the USA, the entire staff of the local K-Mart would often change between weekly visits. Here, it's like stepping back to the 1970s – there are small family-owned businesses everywhere and they seem to be holding on, despite the appearance of the same big uber-stores we know from the USA. Herbignac has a little family grocer, butcher, video store, etc. – all places that have almost disappeared from the American landscape in the past 10 years.

Of all the odd things we've encountered, I think nothing else sums up the entirely different ways of thinking as much as shopping carts. In the USA, all grocery store shopping carts are the same. They all have one wheel which is permanently twisted sideways and will not turn, yet the shopping carts will soldier on in straight lines, dragging the complaining screeching wheel along with them and leaving a little black skidmark throughout the store. In France, this is completely reversed. All the wheels work, but none of them will ever point in the same direction. Trying to push one in a straight line requires lots of muscle and the sort of skill it would take to herd a bunch of eels across an open parking lot. Unlike the US carts however, they change direction in the blink of an eye ... you were aiming for the door but suddenly you are going sideways.

Generally, this area has become more and more like the USA. We have ADSL, we can buy fresh milk that isn't heat pasteurised, and there is even peanut butter, but it's pretty pallid compared to a big tub of Jiffy Extra Crunchy.

# Electrical goods and furniture

If you are moving over to France you will have to consider whether to bring electrical equipment with you or not. The general opinion is that French electrical goods are not that cheap and are of lower quality than British ones. Old plugs can literally disintegrate so you need to be very careful if you are using old equipment. The drawback with British electrical equipment is that it will be difficult to repair or find spare parts for, so it seems best to go with the French goods even if they do not last as long. Most foreign electrical goods will work satisfactorily in France with suitable adapters; the only exception are goods with an internal timer, which it would be best to buy in France. If you want to watch British videos in France, you will need to bring a British video and TV with you. There is no problem about watching French videos on British equipment. DVDs do not have any compatibility problems, unless they are from the USA. Generally, you have the option of selecting the zone you want to watch your DVD with, and then you have to stick with it.

Furniture is best bought in France; there are amazing bargains to be found if you are willing to travel around and look in at the *brocanteurs* (second-hand merchants) and *dépôt ventes*; there is always IKEA, of course. Even brand-new furniture is cheaper than in England, so there may not be much point in bringing it over from home. In any case, English furniture may look out of place in your French retreat.

# Clothes

Buying clothes in France can be awkward if you are not used to Continental European sizes. This is not the whole story; women's clothes tend to have shorter arms and legs than the supposed UK or US equivalent, since French women are generally shorter than their UK and US cousins. It is usually necessary to buy XL size T-shirts, if you want them to fit. The sizes of men's trousers do not match those in the UK or USA. For example, a 34 inch waist in the UK becomes a size 44 in France. Shirts are even more tricky: a 39 inch chest is a size 50 in France. The labels S, M and L do not correspond to UK sizes either. It is essential to try on shirts and trousers before you buy. These days many clothes have labels giving sizes for the UK and European countries, but there is no guarantee that what you are buying will fit.

# Bargain hunting

If you are looking for a bargain, the best place is a factory shop (*magasin d'usine*), where you can buy well-known brands at a large discount. For some reason the notion of flogging things cheaply is strongly associated with the north-west of France. The traders of Lille invented the idea of the *braderie* (meaning a market with rock-bottom prices). *The Factory Shop Guide to Northern France*, by Gillian Cutress and Rolf Stricker, is a useful guide, but has long been out of print. The French equivalent, *Guide des Magasins d'Usine,* by Marie-Paule Dousset, is a good alternative. You can also try to get a copy of Suzy Gershman's *Born to Shop France* and *Born to Shop Paris*, available from Amazon. In Paris, Anne and Alain Riou's *Paris Pas Cher* (published annually) has become a sort of shopper's bible, and includes 500 restaurants and every other conceivable type of retailing, graded with Eiffel Tower symbols. There is Sandy Price's *Exploring the Flea Markets of France,* which is rather out of date, but still useful. This gives dates and times of the markets throughout France as well as useful hints about buying from them. Les Puces de St Ouen is known for its second-hand clothes. The market at the Porte de Clignancourt really put the flea into markets. More to gawp at than to buy. See www.parispuces.com.

# Food and Drink

Eating and drinking mean a great deal more than just keeping body and soul together: the French have taken the arts of wining and dining to heights that can only amaze lesser mortals, to the extent that they have become a religious activity. The whole thing certainly goes too far, perhaps, but there is an undeniable sense of shock when one returns to the UK, a country where in general people only eat to live.

Traditionally, one expected a quality of food that was mostly unobtainable in the UK. The French have become complacent about their restaurants, it must be said, and the UK is catching up with France. French cuisine relies far too heavily on duck. Contrary to what one might think, it is quite possible to get a bad meal in France; chain restaurants, or those where there are excessive numbers of tourists are generally best avoided. France will always have the edge because the quality of produce in shops is often much better than in the UK. This does not always apply, however, to items such as fresh vegetables which can be very disappointing in French supermarkets. The average French household spends less on going out to eat than does a British family, but a great deal more on buying food to prepare at home. In contrast with the UK, there are still plenty of small supermarkets (*supermarchés*) and greengrocers (*primeurs*). There is also the trend towards hypermarkets (*hypermarchés*) selling every possible kind of product under one roof. Local supermarkets are generally smaller than in the UK; in small towns there is usually only a general grocer's or *superette* in the town centre. Most people prefer to go to local markets for fresh produce and meat.

> *'the French have taken the arts of wining and dining to heights that can only amaze lesser mortals'*

One of the positive sides of small country supermarkets is that the produce is often locally sourced. The downside is that fruit is sold ready to eat, and may not keep for very long. It is certainly best to buy fruit and vegetables in your local market if you can. The meat in France is sold without the fat and gristle that comes with British meat. French meat appears expensive by weight, but the quality is often far better. In general the quality of meat, fruit, vegetables and bread will nearly always be of better quality in your local shop than in larger outlets. Bread is, of course, another national obsession and local bakers take great pride in their produce. There is more to French bread than simple baguettes, and many bakers are now using traditional and organic ingredients to produce some wonderful flavours and textures.

Perhaps through poverty, the French have been inventive about finding things to eat. Everyone knows about snails and frog's legs. Spare a thought for the frogs: their legs are chopped off while they are still alive. Items like pig's trotters and tripe are still very much on the menu. It's just as well to know what you are eating. All kinds of small birds are blasted out of the sky on their migratory routes for the sake of their meat, especially larks or *alouettes*. Larks that have been captured and fattened up are *mauviettes*. Even blackbirds are not safe here. For one of his last meals, the late President Mitterrand is said to have dined on *ortolans,* a protected species of bunting, the last word in extravagance and decadence.

## The etiquette of eating out

The etiquette of eating in a high-class restaurant in France is not that different from what you would expect anywhere else. It is considered good manners to eat off the back of the fork, and to keep your hands on the table when you are not eating. You should make sure that your fellow diners' glasses are kept topped up. If you are eating out with French friends, they will know which wines go with different courses, otherwise the wine-waiter – *le sommelier* – can advise you. It is best to be clear about who is going to pick up the tab beforehand. Unless you are in informal company, one person should pay for everyone. Going Swiss – *faire suisse* – as they say, is OK if it is decided in advance. The French like everything to be clear.

*'in February 2007 smoking was banned in all public buildings in France'*

Discussing business matters during a meal is acceptable, as long as it is done after the cheese course. Before this time you should stick to other topics. By the time the fruit course comes round, everyone should be in a good mood, and you may be able to clinch a good deal. It is rather *mauvais ton* to drink too much alcohol at lunchtime – one glass of wine is sufficient – all the more so if you are trying to negotiate business matters. The evening is the time to indulge if you need to. This rule however does not always apply in rural bars and restaurants where drinking a carafe of wine is not really considered 'drinking'.

There are certain odd rituals in French cafés and *chambres d'hôte* that are worth noting. You may be expected to hold on to the same knife and fork for your hors d'œuvre or entrée as for the main course; in other words: *gardez vos couverts.* If you have bread with your meal, or for breakfast, you are not given a plate to put it on. Leaving crumbs and a few stains on the table is a sign that you had a good meal; the tablecloth is washed daily anyway.

If you order meat in a restaurant it is vital to ask for it to be well cooked: *bien cuit*. Even then it will be undercooked by British standards. The French like their meat bloody – *saignant* – and need to be persuaded that you can cook meat all the way through. There are no such problems with fish.

In cafés and bars, you are not expected to pay for your drinks or food until you are ready to leave. The bar staff will give you a ticket for each item, or you ask for the bill (*l'addition* – colloquially *la note*, a term also used for an hotel bill) at the end. They may ignore you if you ask how much you owe after your first drink. It is all right to ask for free tap water, but be careful about asking for a 'soda': you are likely to get Coca-Cola. If you want fizzy water, ask for *une eau gazeuse.* For flat mineral water, ask for *eau non-gazeuse* or *eau plate*. In rural restaurants and bars the lunchtime trade is usually very brisk; they offer great value set menus and are often frequented by local working people. By contrast, such places may be very quiet in the evening, especially outside the tourist season.

Traditionally, smokers have generally been considerate towards non-smokers in bars. However in February 2007 smoking was banned in all public buildings in France. Hotels, bars and restaurants were given an extra year to prepare themselves for this major change. The French love affair with the cigarette may not yet quite be over but it is, as in other countries, now taking to the street.

Finally, if you have to, ask for *les toilettes* and not *la toilette*, which means a washstand.

## Party animals

Whenever French people get together, it's party time. Any social meeting is a big occasion here. The emphasis is on sharing and not standing on ceremony. The French generally prefer to buy some expensive ingredients to cook at home, rather than going out to an expensive restaurant. Buying food and drink to prepare at home is often the biggest item in the family budget.

When you are invited for a meal at someone's home, which will hopefully happen sooner rather than later, you are not necessarily expected to take a gift. In informal situations you can bring something though it is not usual to take wine. Do not worry too much however because as a foreigner you will not be expected to know the rules and whatever you take will be gratefully and genuinely acknowledged. Banquets and wedding feasts can go on for hours and involve 10 courses and the same is true for many meals organised by local associations and clubs; outsiders may be shocked at such unashamed gluttony. It is considered bad form to leave a party before the end; even if it is five o'clock in the morning and you are collapsing, it is best to try to keep going as long as possible. A telephone call to thank your host or a thank you note for a good time will be appreciated.

# Sport and leisure

As in other parts of Europe, football is one of the main national sports. The French have reason to be proud of their national side which won the World Cup in 1998 and then the European Championship in 2000. To most people's surprise – including their own – they also made it to the World Cup final in 2006. The undisputed soccer idol was Zinedine Zidane, whose popularity only seemed to increase after he was sent off for head butting an opponent in their defeat by Italy in the match. After Zidane's retirement following that tournament, the remaining star name in French football was striker Thierry Henry. Most villages, even quite small ones, tend to run a football team and often a *commune's* sports club is at the heart of local community events. If you like sport, joining the local sports association is a good way to meet people. Walking or hiking is another popular pastime and there are many local groups – *groupes de randonneurs* – that take adavantage of the many pathways in the countryside. Another major sport is rugby union, which is especially popular in the south-west of France. A number of new British residents have joined local rugby clubs, which is another excellent way of getting to know a local community. Basketball, tennis and swimming are also popular sports, as is handball, a game less familiar to Britons and Americans. Though the country has plenty of space for golf courses, this is a sport that has not yet taken off as it has in Britain, Spain and Portugal. However its popularity is growing, as shown by the number of new upmarket housing developments associated with courses. A list of French courses can be found on www.golfeurope.com. Another national obsession is of course cycling, its importance shown by the media attention given to the annual Tour de France. Drugs scandals may have tarnished the top end of the sport, but cycling remains hugely popular with many French people and it is common to see cyclists on country roads, especially at weekends. Another very popular sport is *boules* or *petanque*, which is played even through winter by some hardy souls. This game can be taken very seriously but there are some informal competitions that give the outsider a chance to play. If you take part in one of these you are likely to be soundly defeated, but it is an excellent way of meeting people and most fellow competitors will thank you for making the effort.

Other leisure activities you could consider are listed below.

- *Bird-watching*. France is a great country for watching birds, even if a considerable number are shot during the hunting season (September to March) while others are kept in cages. The main organisation concerned with the protection of birds and with ornithology is the *Ligue pour la Protection des Oiseaux* (www.lop.fr).
- *Bridge*. If belotte is not your card game, then maybe bridge is. *Le bridge* is played across the country – there are about 1,300 clubs in France. If neighbours or the mayor's office don't know where the local club is then visit the French Bridge Federation website at: www.ffbridge.asso.fr.
- *DIY*. The French are becoming just as addicted to DIY as other nations. Stores such as Castorama, Bricomarché, Brico Depot, Leroy-Merlin and Mr Bricolage are cropping up all over the place. You'll often find many Britons visiting them too.
- *Fishing*. Fishing – *la pêche* – is an extremely popular pastime in France. As in other countries you'll need a permit, a *carte de pêche*. You can obtain these from the local fishing association or from specialist fishing shops – you can find these in many small towns. Ask the mayor's office to find out more about fishing in your area or visit the *Fédération Nationale de la Pêche en France et de la protection du milieu aquatique* at: www.unpf.fr.
- *Second-hand sales*. There are always plenty of second-hand sales – *brocantes* – or car boot sales – *vide-greniers* – for you to visit. They vary enormously in the quality and price of the goods on display but you can find some real bargains. They are also fun days out too.

# Crime

Taken as a whole there is less crime in France than in the UK, but what exists is heavily concentrated in certain areas such as Paris, other major cities and the Riviera. There is a widespread feeling that *'l'insécurité'* is rising, based on the idea that crime is increasing along with immigration and asylum seekers. The result was to make the neo-fascist *Front National* France's second party ahead of the socialists at the presidential elections in 2002. Recent right-wing governments have tried to be tough on crime, mainly by passing illiberal legislation. The

# In the Know

**Rachel Loos is editor of the 'Living in France' section of www.FrenchEntree. com. She suggests some ways to create a social life in France:**

*La belle vie* in France is far more enjoyable if you get out and about and spend time with other like-minded people. This is particularly true during the winter months when cold days make you less likely to spend time pottering around the garden or basking in the sun by the pool.

The good news is that creating a social life in France is pretty easy. The first thing to do is make sure you get out to local events – not only will you be seen to be supporting your local community (very important), you also get a chance to meet people, both French and English.

As well as local fetes and fairs, there are also likely to be *belotte* (a popular card game) tournaments, *boules* games and *loto* to name a few French events. The British seem to be rather partial to curry-aoke nights – Indian food plus singing! – and if you start learning French locally, you are bound to find out what's going on, and meet people who are in the same situation as you. Also check out the local papers – both French and English editions – as they will have lots of information on what is going on in your local area.

I would definitely recommend going out of your way to make French friends as this gives you the inside track on what makes the French tick, as well as making you feel like you are integrating into France. Most often, the best way to start is by asking your neighbours over for a drink. If you can buy products locally, then this will bring you into contact with others. Again, joining local French clubs will also help. In villages, the year is often marked by a series of grand *repas* – make sure you get along to these too. Even if you don't speak much French, after an *aperitif* or two you will be definitely be able to communicate!

Also, embrace all the things you love about French life, and what makes living in France different to living in Britain. As well as the supermarket, shop in your local shops as the quality of food is high, you get to practice a bit of French and again you start to build up relationships with others. Spend time at your local market and when you can, go out for lunch (the main meal of the day). Get in the car or hop on the train and start visiting the country that is your new home.

And now that you've fulfilled the dream of moving to France, why not do all those things you were always going to do but never had the time for. There are even courses that allow you to combine a passion for food, painting or other interests with learning French. *Parfait!*

interior minister, Nicolas Sarkozy took advantage of this shift to the right to gain support for his successful campaign to become the next President of France in 2007.

Crime rates vary considerably around France. There are villages where there is hardly any crime at all, while there are other places where it is dangerous to go out at night. Paris has the worst rate, with 147 crimes per 1,000 inhabitants in 2001, but this is heavily concentrated in the depressed areas such as St-Denis. Nice and the Côte d'Azur are not that far behind; muggings and car-jacking are serious problems. A disturbing new trend in the Côte d'Azur is the use of gas to render victims unconscious so that their mobile home or villa can be stripped bare. Avignon is one of the most crime-ridden cities in France. Strasbourg, Mulhouse, Lyon, Bordeaux, Marseille and La Rochelle also have very high crime rates. The presence of large numbers of tourists generates a lot of crime in the summer (part of which is committed by tourists themselves). The Riviera has a heavy concentration of private security staff to protect the rich, but this does not help the average person on the street. Crime rates are published by the magazine *Le Point* in its annual survey of French towns: see www.lepoint.fr. For a small payment you can access data on major French towns.

In the autumn of 2005 a series of serious disturbances broke out first in certain disadvantaged (*defavorisé*) areas in Paris and then spread to many other urban centres; rioting that shook France and its rulers. The immediate cause was the death of two youths who were electrocuted in an electricity sub-station in the Parisian suburb of Clichy-sous-Bois, apparently trying to escape from the police. Among the many wider causes is an almost complete breakdown of trust between the police and youths in certain areas, notably those with large immigrant populations. Little appears to have been done to tackle this problem since and some observers fear more such outbreaks of violence in the future.

For more information on anti-crime measures, caretakers and insurance see chapter 16.

# Public Holidays and Local Festivals

France does not have an inordinate number of public holidays; they all commemorate something, rather than being just bank holidays.

## Public holidays

| | |
|---|---|
| 1st January | New Year's Day |
| Easter Monday (*Pâques*) | Easter Monday |
| 1st May | Labour Day (*Fête du Travail*) |
| 8th May | Victory in Europe Day |
| May | Ascension Day |
| May/June | Whitsun (*Pentecôte*) |
| 14th July | Bastille Day |
| 15th August | Assumption |
| 1st November | All Saints Day |
| 11th November | Remembrance Day |
| 25th December | Christmas Day |

# Festivals

France has an extraordinary number of festivals each year. Many of them are put on to promote tourism in remote areas. The French love any excuse for a party and they know how to put on a good show. Festivals are important for anyone who is thinking of running *gîtes* or *chambres d'hôte* as a way of pulling in the punters. There are thousands of concerts, plays, happenings and festivals advertised on the internet on sites such as: www.culture.fr, www.francefestivals.com, www.festivalsaoste.com, www.viafrance.com – and on tourist office websites. The following is only a small selection of what is available. The telephone numbers are sometimes only in use during the month before the festival.

## Festivals in France

| Month | Festival | Telephone | Website |
|---|---|---|---|
| January | Ice Sculpture Competition, Valloire, Savoie. | 04 79 59 03 96 | www.valloire.net |
| | Foire Grasse, Limoges, Haute Vienne. *Foie gras*, truffles, goose, duck products. Also February. | 03 55 34 46 87 | www.tourismelimoges.com |
| | Journée de la Truffe-Truffles Day, Uzès, Gard. | 04 66 22 68 88 | www.ville-uzes.fr |
| February | International Festival of Short Films in Clermont-Ferrand. | 04 93 12 34 50 | www.clermont-filmfest.com |
| | Carnaval, Nice. | 04 93 92 82 82 | www.nicecarnaval.com |
| | Fête du Citron-Lemon Festival, Menton, Alpes-Maritimes. | 04 92 41 76 76 | www.feteducitron.com |
| March | International Carnival, Mulhouse, Alsace. | 03 89 35 48 48 | www.ot.ville-mulhouse.fr |
| | Grenoble Jazz Festival. | 04 76 51 00 04 | www.jazzgrenoble.com |
| April | Laughing Spring Festival of Humour, Toulouse. | 05 62 21 23 24 | www.mairie-toulouse.fr |
| | Musicora Classical Music Festival, Paris. | 01 49 53 27 00 | www.lesalondelamusique.com |

*(Continued)*

## Festivals in France

| Month | Festival | Telephone | Website |
|-------|----------|-----------|---------|
| May | Cannes Film Festival. | 01 53 59 61 00 | www.festival-cannes.fr |
| | St Émilion Open Door Days, Gironde. | 05 57 55 50 55 | www.saint-emilion-tourisme.com |
| | Chocolate Days, Bayonne, Pyrénées Atlantiques. | 05 59 46 01 46 | www.bayonne-tourisme.com |
| | Wine And Food Festival, Plombières, Vosges. | 03 29 66 01 30 | www.plombieres-les-bains.com |
| June | Summer in Bourges Music Festival, Bourges, Cher. | 02 48 24 93 32 | www.ville-bourges.fr |
| | International Garden Festival, Chaumont-sur-Loire, Loir-et-Cher. | 02 54 20 99 22 | www.chaumont-jardins.com |
| | Jazz en Franche-Comté. | 03 81 83 39 09 | www.besancon.com |
| | Bordeaux Fête Le Vin, Wine Festival. | | www.bordeaux-fete-le-vin.com |
| | Fête de la Tarasque, Tarascon, Provence. Folklore, concerts, bullfighting. | 04 90 91 03 52 | www.visitprovence.com |
| | Vinexpo, Bordeaux. Wine and spirits exhibition. | 05 56 56 00 22 | www.vinexpo.fr |
| July | Festival de Cornouaille-Celtic Festival, Quimper, Brittany. | 02 98 55 53 53 | www.festival-cornouaille.com |
| | La Félibrée-Occitan Festival, Dordogne. | 05 53 07 12 12 | www.felibree.fr.st |
| | Fête de l'Agneau-Lamb Festival, Sisteron, Alpes-de-Haute-Provence. | 04 92 61 36 50 | www.provenceweb.fr |
| | Festival International de Folklore, Gap, Alpes-de-Haute-Provence. | 04 92 52 33 73 | http://paysgavot.free.fr |

*(Continued)*

## Festivals in France

| Month | Festival | Telephone | Website |
|---|---|---|---|
| | Fête des Géants-Festival of Giants, Douai, Nord. | 03 20 14 57 57 | www.crt-nordpasdecalais.fr |
| | Les Tombées de la Nuit, Rennes, Brittany. Theatre, music, dance. | 02 99 67 11 11 | www.ville-rennes.fr/tdn |
| | Festival Européen du Pain-European Bread Festival, Brantôme, Périgord. | 05 53 05 80 52 | www.ville-brantome.com |
| | Bataille de Castillon, Périgord. Spectacular re-enactment of 1453 battle. Also August. | 05 57 40 14 53 | www.batailledecastillon.com |
| | Festival d'Avignon, Provence. Also August. | 04 90 14 14 14 | www.festival-avignon.com |
| August | Inter-Celtic Festival, Lorient, Brittany. | 02 97 21 24 29 | www.festival-interceltique.com |
| | Mimos International Mime Festival, Périgueux, Dordogne. | 05 53 53 18 71 | www.ville-perigueux.fr |
| | Tournois de Joutes-Water Jousting, Sète, Hérault. | 04 67 74 71 71 | www.ville-sete.fr |
| | Fête de la Lavande-Lavender Festival, Digne, Hautes Alpes. | 04 92 36 62 62 | www.ot-dignelesbains.fr |
| | Feria-Catalan Fiesta, Collioure, Pyrénées Orientales. | 04 68 82 15 47 | www.collioure.com |
| | Jazz à Montauban, Tarn-et-Garonne. | 05 63 20 46 72 | www.jazzmontauban.com |
| September | Fêtes Médiévales, Arles-sur-Tech, Pyrénées-Orientales. | 04 68 39 12 22 | www.ville-arles-sur-tech.fr |
| | International Music Festival, Besançon, France-Comté. | 03 81 25 05 80 | www.besancon.com |

(Continued)

## Festivals in France

| Month | Festival | Telephone | Website |
|---|---|---|---|
| | European Sand-Yachting Championships, La Barre-de-Monts, Vendée. | 02 51 68 51 83 | www.ville-labarredemonts.fr |
| | World Puppet Festival, Charleville-Mézières, Ardennes. | 03 24 59 94 94 | www.marionnettes.com |
| October | Octobre en Normandie. Throughout major cities of Normandy. Starts September. | 02 32 10 87 07 | www.octobre-en-normandie.com |
| | Fête des Vendanges-Grape Picking Festival, St Émilion, Gironde. | 05 57 55 28 28 | www.saint-emilion-tourisme.com |
| November | Jazz dans les Feuilles, Côtes d'Armor, Brittany. | 02 96 78 89 24 | www.jazzdanslesfeuilles.com |
| | Journées Mycologiques-Mushroom Festival, Entrevaux, Alpes-Maritimes. | 04 93 05 46 73 | www.entrevaux.info |
| | Fête de l'Olivier, Manosque, Haute Provence. | 04 92 78 68 80 | www.provenceweb.fr |
| | Salon International du Livre Gourmand, Périgueux, Dordogne. Cookery book fair. | 05 53 53 10 63 | www.ville-perigueux.fr |
| December | Fête aux Santons, Marseille, and Provence. Nativity crib figures. | 04 91 13 89 00 | www.marseille-tourisme.com |

# 15 Financial Implications

## French Tax

FRENCH TAXATION IS AN EXTREMELY COMPLEX SUBJECT, and not something that one can easily summarise in a few pages. For this reason, if your tax affairs are at all complex, you are urged to seek professional advice before you go to France; a list of tax lawyers based in the UK who specialise in French taxation is given in *The Directory*. You may also require professional advice in France; a French accountant or lawyer may save you a lot of money, as they will know all the ins and outs of the system, which is far from transparent.

If you become French tax resident, that is, you spend more than 183 days a year in France, then you are taxed on your worldwide income in France, and you have to fill in a French tax return. If you only own a second home in France, you will still have real estate taxes to pay, and tax on rental income.

The methods by which French income tax is calculated give one the feeling that the French are a race of super-mathematicians. The whole thing has become increasingly complex because of all the exemptions that have been negotiated by different special-interest groups. Fortunately, you are only required to state your income; you do not have to work out your tax yourself.

While French income tax may appear exorbitantly high; this is not really the case, because of all the exemptions that are applied. Most taxes in France are raised through social security contributions – *charges sociales* – and VAT, which are more difficult to avoid. Direct taxes account for less than a quarter of all tax revenues raised. In fact, only about half of French people who work pay income tax. In contrast their compulsory social charges – they go towards pension, social security and health – are considerable.

## Moving to France

### Procedure for UK residents

The situation is reasonably straightforward if you are moving permanently abroad. You should inform the UK Inspector of Taxes at the office you usually deal with of your departure and they will send you a P85 form to complete. The UK tax office will usually require certain proof that you are leaving the UK, and hence their jurisdiction, for good. Evidence of having sold a house in the UK and having rented or bought one in France is usually sufficient. You can continue to own property in the UK without being considered resident, but you will have to pay UK taxes on any income from the property.

If you are leaving a UK company to take up employment with a French one then the P45 form given by your UK employer and evidence of employment in France should be sufficient to prove that you are moving abroad. You may be eligible for a tax refund in respect of the period up to your departure, in which case it will be necessary to complete an income tax return for income and gains from the previous 5th April to your departure date. It may be advisable to seek professional advice when completing the P85; this form is used to determine your residence status and hence your UK tax liability. You should not fill it in if you are only going abroad for a short period of time. Once HM Revenue and Customs are satisfied that you are no longer resident or domiciled in the UK, they will make a note in your file not to expect any more UK income tax to be paid. However you can still pay UK income tax in some cases.

If you are resident in France and have, for example, property in the UK that you rent out then you need to declare that income in the UK as well as in France. You can indicate on the French form that this income is taxed in the UK. UK government pensions are also taxed in the UK.

## Insider Tip

*Before leaving the UK, it is important to plan your tax affairs and consider the most advantageous way to use the fact that you are moving to another country. It is even possible not to be resident in any one country for a whole year, although you can actually be considered French tax resident without spending 183 days in France, for example if your permanent home is there. Do not automatically assume that just because you are not in France for 183 days a year that you will not be regarded by the French authorities as tax resident there.*

If you are moving abroad temporarily then other conditions apply. You are not liable for UK taxes if you work for a foreign employer on a full-time contract and remain abroad for a whole tax year (6th April to 5th April), as long as you spend less than 183 days in a year, or 91 days a year averaged out over a four-year period, in the UK. If you spend one part of a year working abroad and the rest in the UK you may still be considered non-resident for the part spent abroad, the so-called split tax year concession; this only applies to someone going abroad for a lengthy period of time. If you have bought a principal residence abroad and have evidence to show that you intend to remain abroad for at least three years you will be treated as non-resident as long as you fulfil the requirements on numbers of days spent in the UK.

France has a double taxation agreement with the UK, which makes it possible to offset tax paid in one country against tax paid in the other. While the rules are complex, essentially, as long as you work for a French employer and are paid in France, you should not have to pay UK taxes, as long as you meet the residency conditions outlined above. For further information see the HM Revenue and Customs publication IR20 'Residents and

Non-Residents: Liability to tax in the United Kingdom' which can be found on the website www.hmrc.gov.uk. Booklets IR138, IR139 and IR140 are also worth reading; these can be downloaded from the above website, or obtained from your local tax office or from the Centre for Non-Residents (CNR): St John's

*'the methods by which French income tax is calculated give one the feeling that the French are a race of super-mathematicians'*

House, Merton Rd, Bootle, Merseyside L69 9BB; ☎0845 070 0040 (UK calls); + 44 (0)151 210 2222 (from outside the UK); www.hmrc.gov.uk/cnr.

## Procedure for US citizens

The US Internal Revenue Service (IRS) expects US citizens and resident aliens living abroad to file tax returns every year. Such persons will continue to be liable for US taxes on worldwide income until they have become permanent residents of another country and severed their ties with the USA.

Fortunately, the USA has a double taxation agreement with France so you should not have to pay taxes twice on the same income. In order to benefit from the double taxation agreement you need to fulfil one of two residence tests: either you have been a bona fide resident of another country for an entire tax year, which is the same as the calendar year in the case of the USA, or you have been physically present in another country for 330 days during a period of 12 months which can begin at any time of the year. Once you qualify under the bona fide residence or physical presence tests then any further time you spend working abroad can also be used to diminish your tax liability.

As regards foreign income, the main deduction for US citizens is the Foreign Earned Income Exclusion, by which you do not pay US taxes on the first $80,000 of money earned abroad (as of 2004) or $160,000 between two people. Investment income, capital gains, etc. are unearned income. If you earn in excess of the limit, taxes paid on income in France can still be used to reduce your liability for US taxes, either in the form of an exclusion or a credit, depending on which is more advantageous. The same will apply to French taxes paid on US income.

The rules for US taxpayers abroad are explained very clearly in the IRS booklet 'Tax Guide for US Citizens and Resident Aliens Abroad' known as Publication 54, which can be downloaded from the internet on www.irs.gov. You can also ask for advice from the IRS office in Paris, at the American Consulate, 2 rue St Florentin, which is open from 9am to midday for personal callers. The office is generally very busy and may not be able to deal with your enquiry. You can try phoning on 01 43 12 25 55, or you can write to: IRS, c/o American Ambassy, 2 ave Gabriel, 75382 Paris, Cedex 8.

The US tax return has to be sent to the IRS, Philadelphia, PA 19255-0207; ☎215 516 2000. The IRS office in Paris will not accept tax returns or fill them in for you.

# Aspects of tax residence

It is important to understand that the French authorities make no distinction between residence, ordinary residence and domicile in the way the British tax authorities do. In the British sense, the country where you have your longest lasting ties is your domicile; this is a concept not defined in UK tax law, but rather based on precedent. In France, *domicile* simply means 'residence', and is based on facts, such as the number of days you spend in a place, or where you have the main centre of your economic interests or principal home, for example.

The French tax authorities define tax residence (*domicile fiscal*) somewhat differently from the British. If your household – *foyer fiscal* – is in France, e.g. your family live there, then you are tax resident there, even if you work in another country. The other test of tax residence is where you have your principal residence. If you spend more than 183 days a year in France then you are tax resident. You may even be tax resident in France if you spend less than 183 days a year there, if you have spent more time in France than in any other country. Whether you have a *carte de séjour* or not does not enter into the assessment.

> 'one may well ask how the French authorities can know where you have spent most time: it is remarkably easy for them to find out'

If the main centre of your economic interests is in France, or your main employment is there, then you are certainly tax resident there.

One may well ask how the French authorities can know where you have spent most time: it is remarkably easy for them to find out, since there are no rules preventing different agencies from sharing information about your movements, as there would be in the UK. Credit card statements, medical records, passenger manifests and bank records can all show where you have been. There is every likelihood that neighbours, or anyone you have fallen out with in your village, will share information about you with the authorities, because of the culture of informing on your neighbours.

Situations may arise where one married partner is tax resident in the UK and the other in France. Partners are considered separately as far as tax residence goes, even though the location of your household is the main criterion for establishing tax residence. In this case you may have a choice between being taxed together in the usual way, or being treated separately, so that the resident spouse will declare their income to the local *centre des impôts* and the other to the *Centre des Impôts des Non-*

## Insider Tip

Although it might be tempting to try to avoid being tax-resident anywhere for a while, the consequences could be appalling for your heirs if you were suddenly to drop dead. The UK authorities will not accept that you have left their jurisdiction unless you can produce your French tax number.

*Résidents* in Paris. This is a possibility, since under French law, those married in the UK and USA are assumed to come under the regime of separation of estates – *régime de séparation des biens*. In such cases you need to seek expert advice.

As a basic principle, tax is levied on a household as a whole – the *foyer fiscal* – rather than on separate persons. It is not usual for a husband and wife to pay tax separately, unless they are in the throes of divorce and have separate households, If you have entered into a PACS – a civil partnership contract – you no longer have to wait for three years before you can be assessed as one household. If you are simply living together *en concubinage* you are treated as two separate households. Each of the *concubins* can have their own dependants, who will be taken into account when their tax is calculated.

# Trusts and French taxation

French tax residents pay tax on their worldwide income, including gains or income from trusts. They also have to pay taxes on any income from offshore companies, trusts, accounts, shares and so on.

The French for a trust is *trust*; the term *fiducie* is used as well. As far as your French tax return goes, trusts come under *structures soumises hors de France à un régime fiscal privilégié*, a catchall term for assets held in countries with favourable tax regimes *(Code Général d'Impôts, article 123)*. The tax authorities state that if you have more than a 10% interest in a foreign structure the gains or income have to be declared. The term 'favourable tax regime' applies if the tax withheld at source is at least a third less than the tax in France.

Assets held in a revocable trust must be declared for purposes of French wealth tax (ISF). If you make a loan to a trust this counts as part of your wealth. In general, irrevocable trusts do not need to be declared. If you are the beneficiary of a trust, any income or gains, or a life interest, have to be declared in your income tax return.

The French authorities take a dim view if a trust is used to deprive French nationals of their part of an inheritance. A French national who is a 'reserved heir' – i.e. entitled to a certain percentage of your estate – has the full weight of the law behind them in claiming their part of the inheritance.

Trusts are complex issues and you really need to take professional advice in this area.

## Trusts

The subject of trusts is a complex one. If you have substantial assets, then a trust of one kind or another (and there are many kinds) may be an effective way of reducing or avoiding French taxes, but this can only be done with expert advice. The concept of a 'trust' only exists in countries with common-law legal systems, e.g. the UK, USA, Canada and other former British colonies. French law is vague on this topic, so it is hard to predict how your trust will be treated by the French tax authorities. There are also moves by the government in the UK to make trusts less effective as a way of evading taxes.

The concept of a trust is simple enough: you give away or lend your money to a trust, and it is then treated by the taxman as though it were not your money. The trustees appointed to run the trust invest the money as they see fit. Income generated by the trust is taxed under a special regime in the UK, depending on the type of trust.

The two basic categories of trust are as follows.

- *Interest-in-possession trust:* this gives a person or people the right to income from the trust or the equivalent of income (e.g. the right to live in a rent-free property). The trustees have to hand over the income to the beneficiaries stated in the trust.
- *Discretionary trust:* the trustees decide which beneficiaries should receive income or capital from the trust. Where no money is paid out until the end of the trust, this is known as an *accumulation trust.* If money is paid out for the education, maintenance or benefit of beneficiaries until they get an *interest-in-possession,* then the trust is an *accumulation-and-maintenance* trust.

The French tax authorities make another distinction between *revocable* and *irrevocable* trusts. In the first case, the settlor, the one who sets up the trust, is also the beneficiary, and can revoke the trust. In the second case the settlor has entirely divested themselves of the assets in the trust, although they may still be one of the beneficiaries. The treatment of income and capital paid by the trust, and succession tax, depend in the first place on whether you have been tax resident in France for six of the last 10 years or not. As a rule, life assurance products such as endowment policies are fiscally more favourable than other kinds of trusts, and easier to set up. In any event, it is far better to set up the trust before you become tax resident in France.

# French Income Tax

## How income tax is paid

The French tax system works on the basis that you pay tax in instalments on your income for the previous year, calculated on the basis of your income in the year before that. There is, therefore, a delay before a foreign resident starting work in France for the first time pays any tax. No tax is paid in advance (except for taxes withheld at source on savings, etc.). If you work for an employer, tax can be deducted at source through the year. You can either pay 10 monthly instalments from January calculated

*'if your lifestyle is inconsistent with your declared income you may be investigated by the tax inspectors'*

on the basis of your previous tax return – the last two months are used to adjust the total tax paid – in which case you are *mensualisé;* or you pay in three instalments in February, May and September – the *tiers provisionnels.* Strictly speaking the first two payments are due on 31st January and 30th April, but no penalty actually becomes payable until 15th February and 31st May. Normally you will receive your final assessment during August/September. The final instalment is due on the last day of the following month. This is again extended to the 15th of the month after. Only after the 15th of the second month after you receive your final assessment will you have to pay the 10% penalty. Since September 2003 you are required to pay within 45 days of any tax demand, whatever the time of year.

All French residents must be registered with the local *inspecteur des impôts.* You are liable for tax on your worldwide income from the day you arrive in France. It is up to you to request a tax return (*déclaration fiscale*) if you do not receive one automatically. The final date for submitting your annual tax return was 31st May (in 2007). If you are non-resident, and live in Europe, you had until 30th June. The final dates for filing tax returns are subject to change from year to year. If you file your tax return even a single day late, you automatically receive a 10% penalty. The authorities take a very hard line with tax evasion, which is common with non-salaried workers. A growing number of people file their tax return online, which attracts a small financial bonus. The deadline for completion is also later if you file online.

| Types of income that are subject to income tax | |
|---|---|
| Wages, salaries, remunerations, pensions, life annuities | *Traitements, salaries, remunerations assimilées, pensions, rentes viagères* |
| Investment income | *Revenus de capitaux mobiliers* |
| Capital gains (short term) | *Plus values à court terme* |
| Industrial and commercial profits | *Bénéfices industriels et commerciaux (BIC)* |
| Non-commercial profits | *Bénéfices non-commerciaux (BNC)* |
| Property income | *Revenus fonciers* |
| Agricultural profits | *Bénéfices agricoles* |
| Certain directors' remunerations | *Rémunerations des dirigeants de sociétés* |

## Tax returns

There are several different types of tax returns – *déclarations fiscales* – for different types of income. The basic form is No. 2042, the *déclaration des revenus.* If you are self-employed, have capital gains to declare, or rent out property, you also have to fill in No. 2042C, the *déclaration complément*. If you are taxed as a *micro-entreprise* you also fill in No. 2042P.

There are several more forms that one may be required to fill in:

- blue form No. 2044 for *revenus fonciers* – property income
- pink form No. 2047 for foreign income
- green form No. 2049 for capital gains
- form No. 2065 for corporation tax
- form No. 2074 for capital gains on investments.

Benefits in kind are taxed at the same rate as wages, salaries, pensions and life annuities, according to their market value. Employees can claim tax deductions for some expenses, including travel to and from work.

Commercial profits – BIC – covers income from running a business, small-scale manufacturing and trading, as well as letting out shops or furnished properties. It is particularly relevant to those who run *chambres d'hôtes* and *gîtes*.

Non-commercial profits – BNC – concerns income from liberal professions, i.e. doctors, architects, lawyers, and so on.

Property income concerns the letting of houses, offices, factories, etc., agricultural land, lakes, forests, as well as hunting rights.

# Calculation of income tax – *impôt sur le revenu*

Income tax is levied on a whole range of sources of income. Bank interest and income from some savings accounts and life insurance are taxed at source, though there is an option to have them taxed at your marginal rate if this is lower.

If your lifestyle is inconsistent with your declared income you may be investigated by the tax inspectors, on the basis of *signes extérieurs de richesse*. If you possess a yacht, an expensive car, and so on, then these will be valued and taken into account. New assets can be assessed as income and taxed accordingly.

## Exemptions

Certain kinds of income are exempt from income tax, notably:

- rental income, if you rent out rooms in your own home, on a long-term basis, as long as the rent is considered 'reasonable'
- up to €760 rental income generated from short-term letting of *chambres d'hôtes*, if you are not considered a professional *loueur en meublés*
- income from certain savings plans, and investments in industry, under certain conditions: e.g PEP, PEA, and *Livret de Developpement Durable (LDD)* (replaced CODEVI)
- social security benefits, some maternity benefits, disability benefits, incapacity benefits
- redundancy payments.

Although you may not pay income tax on the above, some of these items, namely investment plans, are still subject to social security taxes totalling 11%.

## Deductions

Before any tax is calculated you are entitled to certain deductions, notably:

■  maintenance payments to parents and children, including adult children, if they can be shown to be in need
■  child support and alimony payments to divorced partners
■  voluntary payments to children up to a reasonable limit
■  voluntary payments to persons over 75 years old living in your home
■  some investments in French film production or video making
■  losses in certain business investment schemes, qualifying for tax breaks.

If your income falls under wages, salaries, pensions, etc., there are further items to deduct from your gross income before tax is calculated:

■  professional expenses – including travel to and from work, meals, hotels, etc.
■  the interest on loans contracted in order to invest in a new company can be deducted from the salary paid by the company
■  private pension contributions up to €45,891 (in 2005); compulsory pension contributions are deducted from gross salary before tax is calculated
■  abatement for disabled persons or those aged over 65 years old of €2,172 if total gross taxable income is below €13,370 ; €1086 if income is between €13,370 and €21,570.

# Pensions

French pensions are subject to a different set of tax rules from those applying to salaries. The effect of these rules is that pensioners pay less tax than workers; 60% of retirees pay no income tax at all. If you have a *rente viagère* or life annuity, tax is paid on a sliding scale, on between 70% and 30% of the pension, depending on your age. Private pensions, foreign pensions, etc., attract an additional abatement of 10% up to a maximum of €3,446 before the above deductions are applied.

If tax is or will be deducted at source in the UK from your pension, you need to contact HM Revenue and Customs' Centre for Non-Residents and ask for form FD5. Once the French tax office has stamped it and you have returned it, the Centre will instruct your pension provider not to deduct tax at source. You will then pay French tax on your pension. Contact the Centre for Non-Residents, St John's House, Merton Rd, Bootle, Merseyside L69 9BB; ☎00 44 151 472 6196 (from France); www.hmrc.gov.uk/cnr.

# Methods of income tax calculation

The basis of the calculation is the total income of the household added together. In order to compensate taxpayers with dependants or low earners in their household, the French use a 'family quotient' system – *quotient familial* – calculating tax according to *parts* assigned to members of the family. The total income is divided by the number of parts, which has the effect of calculating the tax as if each member of the family earned the same amount. Once the tax has been worked out on a sliding scale, it is multiplied by the number of parts to arrive at the final figure.

As a single person, you have one part. If you are married then you have two; if one partner is disabled the couple receives 2.5 parts; if both are disabled three parts. There are numerous different categories of parts. Dependants (*personnes à charge*) are (to put it simply) children under 21 years old, students under 25 years old, children doing their military service, and disabled children whatever their age. They are only accepted as dependants if they are based at home and still require some support from you. In the first three cases they may be 'reattached' to the household, even though they are living and working away from home, and you will receive an additional 0.5 parts for each of them. Since 2003, divorced or separated parents can receive 0.25% of the parts if they share custody.

The French tax office allows foreign residents to benefit from the family quotient system, on the assumption of reciprocity on the part of the British HM Revenue and Customs and other tax authorities, even though French residents in the UK do not actually benefit from the same system.

As a rule, the first two children each count as half a part for tax purposes. The third child and each subsequent child count as one part. Each child counts as another 0.5 parts if they are disabled. There is a limit to the amount that you can save per extra part with this system. The maximum tax advantage you can gain for *each* of the first two children is €2,121 and for each subsequent child €4,242 . Single parents and those with disabled dependants are treated more generously.

## Tax calculation by *tranches*

The French tax system resembles other systems in that tax is calculated progressively on the amount per part. The amount per slice or *tranche* has to be multiplied by the parts to arrive at a final figure before tax credits and rebates are applied. The following figures apply to income earned in 2006.

| Income tax bands (*barème*) | |
| --- | --- |
| Up to €5,614 | 0% |
| €5,614 to €11,198 | 5.5% |
| €11,198 to €24,872 | 14% |
| €24,872 to €66,679 | 30% |
| €66,679 and above | 40% |

## Tax credits

There are various tax credits and reductions, too numerous to go into in great detail. Note that these are all subject to conditions and limits. All are subject to having the correct paperwork. The more usual ones include:

- 50% of the cost of domestic help, child minding, gardeners, cleaners, etc., up to a total maximum credit for all employees of 50% of €15,000

- child-minding expenses outside the home (25%, limited to €2,300 euros)
- charitable donations; but no more than 10% of your taxable income (charities are not all treated the same by the authorities; you should check first to see what kind of tax rebate is on offer)
- renovations, extensions, and repairs to tourist accommodation in certain designated rural areas
- investment in heavy equipment for the home, e.g. central heating, solar panels, etc.
- environmentally friendly vehicles
- one-off compensation payments to divorced partners
- life assurance premiums on policies taken out before 1996
- investments in small-and medium-sized businesses
- support paid to adult children
- home improvements that promote energy savings or use renewable energy.

## The *décote*

If your tax liability is below €828 you are eligible for a rebate – *décote* – of the difference between €414 and half the tax liability. Thus if your tax liability is €600, you will have a rebate of €114 and your liability is reduced to €486. If your liability is under €61 you pay no income tax at all.

## Complete exemption from income tax

Certain persons are completely exempt from paying income tax. If your income after deduction of 10% professional costs is below €7,640 you pay no tax. This increases to €8,340 for those over 65 years old.

# Social Security Taxes and Contributions

The basic tax is the CSG (*Contribution Sociale Généralisée*) which is applied at a rate of 7.5% after a deduction of 3% for professional costs (i.e. 7.5% of 97% of gross income). All earned and unearned income is subject to this tax, which is in many cases a withholding tax, except for sickness, unemployment and some other benefits. A contribution to repaying the social security system debt, the CRDS or *Contribution pour le Remboursement de la Dette Sociale,* is levied at 0.5% on similar terms to the CSG.

Investment income is subject to an additional 'social contribution', the *Prélèvement Sociale* at 2%, to which is added to an additional contribution of 0.3%, making 2.3%. Certain tax-free savings accounts, such as the *Livret A, Livret Bleu,* existing *CODEVI and LDD* are not subject to the above social security contributions.

There are further social security contributions covering pensions and unemployment benefit, totalling some 9.3% of income, and then compulsory basic medical cover at 6.8% deducted before any tax calculation is made.

Retirement or disability pensions are liable for CSG at 6.6% and CRDS at 0.5% on 95% of the gross amount. Foreign pensions are not usually liable for these charges if the person is eligible for cover under forms E106 or E121.

# Local/Real Estate Taxes

Most local taxes are real estate taxes. There are some minor taxes that are not dealt with here in detail, namely, regional development tax, the tax to finance local chambers of commerce, and the refuse collection tax. The main real estate taxes come under three headings: *taxe d'habitation*, *taxes foncières* and *taxe professionnelle*. These are local taxes raised for the benefit of local *communes, départements* and *régions*. The rates of tax are set by the local administrative collectivities, up to specific limits set by the national government. The rate for your area can be found in the annual publication *Impôts Locaux*, published at the start of November. See www. guideducontribuable.com.

## *Taxe d'habitation*

The *taxe d'habitation* is payable by anyone who has premises at his or her exclusive disposal subject to the tax. This includes both principal residences as well as any secondary homes that are available for your use. Whether you rent or own the property, if you occupy the property on 1st January you are liable for the entire year's tax. It follows that if you move house during the year, the person whose dwelling you are taking over pays the tax for the year.

Any type of premises that are furnished so as to be habitable, as well as garages, parking spaces, gardens, staff accommodation and other outhouses within 1 km of the main building are assessed for the *taxe d'habitation.*

Some buildings are exempt from *taxe d'habitation:*

- buildings subject to the *taxe professionnelle*
- farm buildings
- student accommodation
- government offices.

The tax is calculated by the local authorities on the basis of the *cadastral* value on 1st January, *cadastral* value being the nominal rental value of the property. If you own an empty habitable rental property, then you pay the *taxe d'habitation*, otherwise the tenant pays. If the owner can prove that the property is uninhabitable, i.e. has no furniture in it, or is being renovated, then he or she can qualify for a temporary exemption. This should be negotiated with the *Trésor Public*. A person who rents a property short term cannot be made to pay the *taxe d'habitation*. Otherwise, the tenant pays the *taxe d'habitation*. Unoccupied, but habitable, holiday homes are liable for *taxe d'habitation*.

### Exemptions

Those on very low incomes are exempt. Also exempt is anyone who is over 60 years old, widowed, or disabled and unable to work. Anyone subject to Wealth Tax (ISF) cannot claim exemption. If you inherit a house which you intend to sell, and clear all the furniture out of it by 1st January (i.e. make it uninhabitable) you can escape the *taxe d'habitation* for a year. Caravans and mobile homes are exempt, as long as they have an engine or vehicle attached to them.

## Reductions

There are reductions for persons with children or elderly or infirm dependants. The *commune* can apply reductions of 5%, 10% or 15% depending on whether the house is your primary or secondary residence. If the taxable income for the first family part does not exceed €7,286, increased by €1,946 per half part there are reductions of 5%, 10% or 15% decided by the *commune*. Many persons coming into this category are completely exempted from paying *taxe d'habitation* on their principal residence.

The television licence fee, or *redevance,* is now levied as part of the *taxe d'habitation*. It is necessary to opt out of paying it, either because you do not have a television or because you are exempt for other reasons.

# Taxes foncières

There are two land taxes, or *taxes foncières*: tax on unbuilt land and tax on built-up land.

## Unbuilt land

Agricultural land is subject to the element of the tax that goes to the *commune*, but not those parts that go to the *département* and *région*. There are exemptions for certain kinds of forests and tree plantations for fixed periods of time.

## Built-up land

Types of buildings and constructions subject to the *taxe foncière* include:

- anything that has the character of a permanent construction
- warehouses
- private roads
- hard standings
- boats with permanent moorings
- grounds used for industry or commerce
- land with advertising hoardings.

Buildings used for farming or not-for-profit public services, are exempt. New buildings, or converted buildings, or extensions to buildings, are exempt from the tax for two years from the date of completion, as regards the regional and *département* element of the tax. As far as the *commune*'s part of the tax goes, there may be a two-year exemption for new residential property, or the *commune* may collect the tax.

The owner of the property pays the *taxe foncière*. If the property remains empty through circumstances outside your control for more than three months, you may obtain a rebate of the tax proportional to the time it has stood empty. If you buy a property you can agree to divide the *taxe foncière* for the year *pro rata temporis* with the vendor, unlike the *taxe d'habitation*.

Built-up land is assessed on the basis of 50% of the nominal rental value, the *valeur locative cadastrale*. Unbuilt land is assessed at 80% of the *cadastral* value. There are exemptions for those over 75 years old and the disabled, subject to certain conditions.

## Taxe professionnelle

The *taxe professionnelle* is by far the most lucrative for the local authorities, and accounts for about half their income. The tax is levied on individuals (*personnes physiques*) and companies (*personnes morales*) that regularly carry on a non-salaried business. Members of partnerships and so-called fiscally transparent companies (whose members are assessed individually for income tax), are assessed in their own names.

There is a long list of persons exempt from the tax of which a few are relevant to foreign residents:

- writers, artists and teachers
- recognised private schools
- artisans working alone, or in a cooperative
- correspondents on local newspapers.

There are temporary exemptions for new businesses in some areas of the country. The most significant exemptions (if they are granted) are for people who rent out *chambres d'hôtes* and *gîtes*, who fall under the category of *loueur en meublés*. Rooms rented out in your principal dwelling to another person who uses them as their own principal dwelling are always exempt from the *taxe professionnelle*. The tax is calculated on the basis of the *cadastral* rental value of the premises, with some additions for larger business. There are reductions for artisans who employ no more than three salaried workers.

## Taxe locale d'équipement

This is a tax payable on the completion of new buildings, and also on extensions and reconstructions. It is levied by *communes* with more than 10,000 inhabitants. Other *communes* may or may not levy it. The *Certificat d'Urbanisme* or outline planning permission will tell you whether you have to pay this tax, and what the amount is.

The tax is assessed at between 1% and 5% of the surface area of the building calculated on a fixed scale per square metre. One half of the tax is payable within 18 months of delivery of the building permit, and the second half within 36 months.

The main exemptions from this tax relate to building work done with certain state-approved loans, and buildings in certain zones earmarked for industrial development. The only exemption likely to apply to foreign residents or non-residents is for rebuilding a house destroyed by a natural disaster. The local *Division Départementale de l'Equipement* can let you know if you are eligible for any reduction.

## Taxe d'enlèvement des ordures ménagères

This is a rubbish collection tax, and can only be charged to tenants if it forms a separate item on the local tax bill. There is also the *taxe balayage* or local road-cleaning tax, which can be charged to tenants.

## Non-residents and local taxes

Non-residents who own property in France are liable for the *taxe d'habitation* and *taxe foncière* unless they qualify for an exemption. They would not normally have to pay the *taxe professionnelle*. As regards taxes on the letting of property, these are dealt with in chapter 18.

## Taxation of real estate owned by foreign companies

The French authorities have instituted an annual tax of 3% of the market value of real estate in France owned by non-French companies, more than 50% of whose assets consist of property, as a measure against tax evasion, and to discover the identities of the owners of the real estate. Since the UK has an agreement with France to combat tax fraud, this tax may not actually be applied in practice. It is, however, a serious disincentive to buying real estate in France through a UK company.

# Capital Gains Tax (CGT)

In French CGT is known as *Impôt sur les Plus Values* or IPV. The tax is levied on the sale of:

- buildings
- land
- shares
- furniture and other movable goods
- antiques and works of art
- precious stones and precious metals.

A distinction is made between short-term gains – *plus values à court terme* – made within two years of acquiring the assets, and long-term gains – *plus values à long terme*. In the following text, only the taxation of land and buildings will be dealt with. Companies with assets consisting of more than 50% property are treated as properties.

## Method of calculation

If you sell your French property within 15 years of acquisition, then you will be liable to pay French capital gains tax or *Impôts sur les Plus Values* (IPV) on a graduated scale. If you are selling your principal residence then there is no liability for IPV. A non-resident who owns a second home in France will be liable for IPV. The *plus value* on your property sale is worked out by deducting the original purchase price – *prix d'achat* – from the selling price – *prix de cession*. The costs associated with buying the property are added on to the original purchase price, thus reducing your liability. You can opt for a lump sum of 7.5% to cover such costs. Also added on is the cost of building work, extensions, renovations, etc., if you have owned the building for more than five years. It is advisable to have all the original receipts and invoices from when the work was done. If this is not possible, a state-appointed expert may produce a valuation of the work, or you may opt for a flat rate of 15%. If you or your family did the work yourselves this can also be taken into account, either using a valuation by an expert, or by multiplying the price of the materials you used by three.

## Insider Tip

It is advisable to make enquiries about possible ways of avoiding IPV, or whether you are even liable, before you try to sell the property. If you can show that the sale of the property was forced on you by family circumstances or because you had to move to another part of the country, you can claim exemption. No IPV is payable if you receive the property as an inheritance, as a gift, or through a divorce settlement.

Your capital gain is taxed as income at 16%, with a further 11% in social security taxes also payable. If you sell the property within five years of acquiring it, or it is repossessed, the gain from the sale of the property is added directly to your income tax liability, and the tax has to be paid immediately. Since 2004, where there is a long-term gain, the capital gains tax is payable at the time of signing the final deed of transfer (acte de vente). The notaire will take the amount of IPV out of the sale proceeds. Sellers are not required to enter a special declaration for IPV. The tax cannot be deferred.

There are two main methods of reducing IPV. In the first place, the gain is reduced by 10% for every full year after five years since the purchase of the property. Thus after 15 years there is no more IPV to pay. Secondly, there is a flat rate deduction of €1,000 from your gross capital gain (but only on one transaction per year). There are also deductions for holiday homes that have been owned for more than five years, which you have always had at your disposal.

Residents of other EU countries who are not tax resident in France are exempted from the social security tax element of 11%. Those who are neither residents in France or another EU country will pay IPV at 33.3%. If a non-resident is considered to have been trading in property then IPV is payable at 50% on the capital gain. The provisions of France's double taxation agreement with your home country may apply.

Non-residents can be exempted from IPV if they can meet the following conditions:

■ you were tax resident in France for at least two years at some time before the sale of the property
■ you are a resident of another EU country – this exemption only applies once.

This does not mean you escape capital gains tax altogether – you will still be liable for it wherever you are tax resident.

French residents can be exempted from IPV in some situations, for example:

■ you are a pensioner or officially incapacitated and not liable for income tax
■ the property has been your habitual principal residence since you bought it, or for at least five years in the past (even if owned through a SCI).

If you originally received the property free of charge, the fair market value at the time you acquired it is taken as the purchase price; there are no deductions for any taxes paid at the time on the transfer of the property.

# Wills and Inheritance Tax

The subject of succession tax (*droits de succession*) and gift tax (*droits de donation*) needs to be carefully considered before you buy a property in France. Failure to take the right steps before signing an *acte de vente* can have serious consequences for your heirs; it is difficult to make changes to the *acte de vente* once it has been registered. If your family situation is at all complicated – many foreign property buyers have been married more than once – then legal advice is a necessity, and highly desirable even in straightforward situations. This means dealing with an English-speaking lawyer who understands French and UK law, which generally implies a UK-based lawyer.

The French system of inheritance tax – strictly speaking 'succession rights' or 'succession taxes' (*droits de succession*) – is very different from the British one you are not free to leave your assets to anyone you please. Blood relatives always come first, while your spouse or partner is treated almost as though they were strangers. The logic behind this is simple. Napoleon saw that too many men were leaving their properties to their mistresses or their wives, so he instituted a system that would ensure that property remained with the blood family.

The first issue to consider is that of domicile, a concept that is not defined in UK tax law, but which rests on legal precedent. Domicile is something like nationality, but harder to lose. Generally speaking, your country of domicile is the one where you have had the longest lasting ties during your lifetime, or the country you intend to return to after living abroad. If you were resident in France on your decease, the French tax authorities will claim that your heirs should pay French succession taxes on your worldwide

*'the French system of inheritance tax is very different: you are not free to leave your assets to anyone you please'*

assets, subject to double tax treaties – for example regarding UK-based immovable property, i.e. land. The British tax authorities are also very reluctant to concede that a British citizen is no longer domiciled in the UK. Foreign domicile can only be established after 'exhaustive enquiries'.

There are potential advantages to being taxed in France if the inheritance exceeds the UK inheritance tax threshold. The top rate in France of 40% only kicks in on inheritances over €1.7 million (£1.2 million) in assets passing between spouses, while in the UK it starts at £300,000 (in 2007). (In the UK there is no inheritance tax between spouses if both are domiciled in the

# In the know

**Gill Bethell ran La Châtaignerie, a luxury bed and breakfast in Céret, located 900 m up in Roussillon or French Catalonia. Her experience provides a salutary warning to women coming to a new life in France with her husband or partner:**

My late husband and I looked forward to a long and happy retirement in the sunniest and most southern corner of France. Our eldest daughter, Kim, not wanting to be left in Scotland persuaded us to buy a bigger house than we planned so that she could run a B&B with us, her parents, helping her.

It sounded like a great idea at the time! We searched all of southern France until we reached the delightful town of Ceret and the lovely house we were to buy called La Chataigneriae (which means 'chestnut grove'), perched on the hill above the town with the most breathtaking views of Mt Canigou to the west and across the Roussillon Plain to the Mediterranean Sea to the east. It was love at first sight for both the town and the house. There seemed to be everything nearby; snow-capped mountains, sea, nearby international airports, three great cultural cities, and an excellent medical system with no waiting lists and of course the sunshine! Life was good. To wake up in paradise each day surrounded by such beauty and birdsong was a dream come true and to think that we actually called what we were doing 'work'!

My husband was in the process of switching the business from the UK to France, when he fell ill and passed away five months later.

Not only was it a shocking end to our dream but that was when I discovered how restrictive the French inheritance laws are and how unprepared and ignorant I was on the subject, having always left that side of things to my husband. I also learnt that our matching Scottish wills were worthless in France and that wills must be written, from start to finish, in your own handwriting, a copy lodged with the *notaire* and a second copy kept at home.

Under French law if you have not made alternative arrangements with a *notaire* before you sign for a house and your husband subsequently dies, the Napoleonic laws of France will take over and widows will find that they do not own all of their house as they thought – but that their children do. If there are children by previous marriages including on the husband's side, they too have a claim on the house.

I strongly recommend that women coming to France take responsibility for yourselves and go to a *notaire* with your husband, before you sign for a house to sort out exactly who you want your husband's estate (including your house) to go to should your husband die before you. You can then relax knowing that your estate will be left to the people of your choice.

UK and new rules permit a spouse to take on their dead spouse's allowance too.) Starting from 2005, succession tax was abolished on estates below €100,000, if the deceased has one child only, with no spouse. In France the tax is owed per beneficiary, not on the estate, so there are no general thresholds. If you are relatively wealthy, you will want to disperse your assets in good time, leaving as little as possible for the taxman. The good news is that there is a double taxation agreement between France and the UK concerning inheritances, so as long as you are open and honest about matters you will not have to pay inheritance taxes twice. There is also a general principle, however, that you pay inheritance tax in the country which has the higher rate.

# French Succession Taxes

Under French law, one part of your assets *has* to be left to specified members of your family (*la réserve légale*), while the rest is yours to do with as you please (*la quotité disponible*). Blood relatives are entitled to inherit in descending order.

1. Children: 50% for the first child; 66.6% between two children; 75% between three and above. No distinction is made between children from a first and subsequent marriage.
2. Parents: Since a law change in January 2007 parents of the deceased are no longer 'reserved' heirs. This means they do not automatically inherit a share if the deceased had no children – i.e. parents can be disinherited. However if there is no will and the person has died intestate and there are no children, then the parents would receive 25 % each. A single surviving parent can only receive 25%.
3. Spouses: Only become reserved heirs if there are no direct descendants.

Grandchildren become reserved heirs if the children are no longer living. Brothers and sisters can be disinherited. They only inherit automatically if there are no descendants, ascendants or spouse. If the former are deceased, nephews and nieces can inherit in their place. Children of the current marriage are treated equally with children of previous marriages, and children born outside marriage, including half-siblings of the deceased's children. The principle that children born out of 'adultery' have equal rights with their half-siblings has only recently been accepted in France. In the absence of the above then relatives take precedence over strangers, depending on their relationship to the deceased, up to the sixth degree. Relatives beyond the fourth degree, meanwhile, are considered to be unrelated for the purpose of inheritance tax.

The 2005 French Finance Act changed succession tax rates to favour the children of the deceased. Children now benefit from an abatement of €50,000 each (increased from €46,000). The surviving spouse benefits from a tax-free amount of €76,000 as previously. In addition, from 1st January 2005, there is an additional €50,000 nil-rate band (NRB) against the deceased's estate for the benefit of the surviving spouse and the children. Note that 'spouse' only refers to your marriage partner; other rules apply to common-law partners.

The table below lists French inheritance and gift tax rates. Brothers and sisters pay at rates of 35% (€0–€23,000) and 45% on the excess. More distant relatives up to the fourth degree pay at 55%. Anyone else pays at 60%.

| Inheritance and gift tax rates | | |
|---|---|---|
| Tax (%) | Spouse (€) | Children/grandchildren/parents (€) |
| 5 | the first 7,600 | the first 7,600 |
| 10 | 7,600–15,000 | 7600–11,400 |
| 15 | 15,000–30,000 | 11,400–15,000 |
| 20 | 30,000–520,000 | 15,000–520,000 |
| 30 | 520,000–850,000 | 520,000–850,000 |
| 35 | 850,000–1,700,000 | 850,000–1,700,000 |
| 40 | 1,700,000 and over | 1,700,000 and over |

# Matrimonial regimes and succession

French law is far less favourable to partners than British law; to improve the partner's situation the law was changed in 2002, the main change being that the surviving married partner has the option of remaining in the marital home for the rest of their lives. The partner can also choose to move out of the property, and receive their part of the assets of the deceased. This is often the best solution where several children jointly inherit a property and want to dispose of it. It can be too much of a headache staying on in a property which is owned by children of your partner's previous marriage with whom you do not get on.

The law distinguishes between three types of partner: a marriage partner; a *concubin* with whom you live without entering into a legally recognised partnership, known as a *union libre* (roughly equivalent to a 'common-law partner'); and a partner with whom you have entered into an official civil contract, the PACS (*Pacte Civil de Solidarité*). This can be a private agreement drawn up by *avocats*. This type of contract was instituted in 1999 to improve the lot of gay couples but is open to heterosexuals as well; the contractants make themselves liable for each other's debts and agree to support each other; they can file joint tax returns from the time that they enter into their civil contract in the same way as married partners (previously they had to wait three years). The two people must be a couple in the sense of having sexual relations together and living together. The PACS can be dissolved as well. The basic tax-free sum for PACS partners is €57,000, and the rate of tax is 40% for the first €15,000 above that and then 50% on amounts above that – as against 60% for a complete stranger. If you simply live with another person in a *union libre* then your partner is treated as unrelated, and pays the full 60% rate.

## Marriage regime change

An important means to improve your partner's situation is to change your marriage regime. You can do this even if you are not resident in France but have a second home there – in which case the contract covers only your property (or land) in France. If you are French resident it covers all your worldwide assets.

## In the know

British people are surprised to learn that they are not free to leave their French assets to their partner under French law. One solution may be to change the marriage regime to a communauté regime under French law and provide that the community assets will remain the surviving spouse's property. This inheritance through marital contract is free of tax. Otherwise under French law, most British citizens are presumed to have been married under the separate estates regime (séparation de biens), which means that the assets of the deceased spouse will go to his/her children (if any). The partner can only claim for 25% of the whole property or opt for its usufruit (lifetime use). In France a change of marital contract has to be witnessed by a notaire and validated by a court. However, The Hague Convention dated 14th March 1978 allows non-French citizens to change their marriage regime so far as it applies to their immovable property in France by executing a deed which is witnessed by a notaire. We have qualified experts in my office who can assist to carry this out. It is not, however, advisable in practice to change your marriage regime if there are children from a first marriage, because they have the right to oppose the change, in so far as it would reduce their inheritance. Of course if you change your marriage regime to a communauté regime and you then get divorced, you will have to go through the process of valuing the assets so as to share them out between the couple.

Patrick Delas, a French *avocat* presently practising in London with Russell-Cooke Solicitors, has some advice on changing your regime:

In all there are five different marriage regimes, making the system very complex. Changing marriage regime can be costly as you need to take professional advice. However, if this is done before the purchase of the French property, it costs only the solicitor's or *notaire's* fees to draft it. With a UK-based firm such as Blake Lapthorn Tarlo Lyons, for example, this works out at £450 plus VAT. It is more expensive if this is done after the purchase, as in addition to the previous amount, you need to consider the *notaire's* fees and in some cases the costs of registration at the land registry. Be aware that some *notaires* are not used to the Hague Convention which governs this area, so they may apply taxes or duties or disbursements not necessary for the marriage contract to be binding for tax purposes in France. If you go for the *communauté universelle avec clause d'attribution intégrale* your partner acquires all your assets on your death without any succession tax being paid; only 1% registration duty is payable. No declaration has to be made for succession purposes. Your children and other heirs then have to wait for the second partner's decease before they can inherit their rightful share. This solution cannot be used to disinherit children from the deceased's previous marriages. This is the option that was chosen by most French married couples in the past.

There are several disadvantages with this regime. Firstly, the children of the marriage will pay a higher rate of succession tax than they would have if they had received their inheritance directly. Secondly, each partner is liable for the debts of the other. Thirdly, the surviving partner can do what he or she wants with the assets (subject to the reserved heirs' rights), and may use them to benefit his or her new partner.

Another possibility is the *communauté légale réduite aux acquêts* – where only the assets acquired during the course of the marriage are common property. In this case the surviving partner pays succession tax on half of the deceased's part of the common property. A simpler solution is the *régime de séparation des biens* – separate estates – where the marriage partners' assets before and during the marriage remain completely separate. The French authorities assume that you are married under the *régime de séparation des biens* if your marriage was contracted in the UK, and for most marriages in the USA (a few states influenced by French law have a different system).

A common way to improve the marriage partner's lot is to make a *donation entre époux* (gift between spouses), an act which can be registered with a notary for a minimal cost.

# Buying *en tontine*

The *tontine* was thought up by an Italian banker, Lorenzo Tonti, in the 18th century. In France it is more correctly called a *clause d'accroissement*. This is where two or more people whether married or not, acquire assets, on the understanding that the one who lives the longest acquires the whole, thus entirely cutting out the inheritors of the other members of the *tontine*. For legal purposes deceased members of a *tontine* – and, by extension, their inheritors – are treated as though they never had any share in the assets. The survivor is treated as though they owned the property from the day that it was bought. Where the partners are unrelated, or concubins, the 'winner' of the *tontine* is subject to succession tax at 60% on half the value of the property, unless the property is worth less than €76,000 and it is their principal residence, in which case the survivor only pays 4.89% transfer taxes. If there is a PACS between them, the succession tax is 50%. Married partners pay the usual succession tax applicable to them.

Partners can enter into a *tontine* if they have roughly the same life expectancy and can therefore profit equally from the *tontine*. They should also contribute equal amounts to the purchase. It is not allowed to buy *en tontine* with your children as partners, or with someone who is likely to die soon. A disadvantage of a *tontine* is that it is impossible to sell your part of the *tontine* since the buyer will lose everything if the person they bought their share from dies before the other members. If your partner in the *tontine* is also your spouse, then any dispute becomes very unpleasant. All the members have to agree to dissolve a *tontine* and it is still a costly and slow process.

Spouses married under the separate estates regime – which means everyone married in the UK, and most couples married in the USA – can enter a *tontine* and could benefit from this arrangement. The main advantage is that it allows you to decide who will inherit your property. It is very effective in cutting the family of the partner who dies first out of the will. It is not actually tax efficient (except for very cheap properties), since there is only one heir in this situation, and no flexibility as to who inherits. The *tontine* clause has to be put into the *acte de vente* before it is signed; afterwards is too late.

## Setting up a *société civile immobilière* (SCI)

A potentially useful way of minimising succession taxes is to buy your property through an SCI which you have set up yourself. You are then the owner of the shares which you can give to your children during your lifetime. This is best done at the start, otherwise you will have to pay transfer taxes if you sell the property to the SCI later. Note that inheriting shares of an SCI or receiving a direct share in a house is taxed in France in exactly the same way regarding inheritance tax, CGT, gift tax and so on. The advantage of the SCI is to give you flexibility in transferring shares during the *lifetime* of the shareholders – as the land registry records do not need to be amended every time the shareholders change.

> ### Insider Tip
>
> There can be considerable costs involved; setting up the SCI in France may cost on average €2,500. It is worth shopping around. Some UK law firms who specialise in French law will charge £1,000 + VAT for a straightforward SCI, for which the client will also receive a full English translation.

If you already own a property and want to set up an SCI, the most effective method is to transfer only the *nue propriété* (ownership without lifetime interest or *usufruit*) of the property to the SCI, which has a far lower value than the *pleine propriéte,* while retaining the *usufruit* for your lifetime. You would then give your child(ren) the shares in the company that correspond to the *nue propriété,* and pay a small amount of gift tax on the amount. Your children already have a minimum tax-free sum, and the tax on gifts made during your lifetime is far less than the usual inheritance tax. In the case of *nue propriété* it is a reduction of either 35% if the donor is below 70 years old, or 10% if the donor is older but below 90 years old. The reduction is 50% if you give the *pleine propriete* and the donor is under 70 years old.

The main requirement of the SCI is the holding of an annual general meeting. Decisions about the running of the company can be made by majority shareholder voting, thus avoiding the problems of the *indivision* where unanimity is required between all the partners. The SCI is not ideal if you are planning to run *gîtes,* or *chambres d'hôtes.* By definition an SCI is meant to be non-trading, and it only owns property, not furniture. The solution is to rent the property out to another business structure, a *SARL* (société á responsabilite limitee). There are also certain implications from the point of view of UK tax authorities, which concern directors' benefits-in-kind. If the authorities are aware that as a director you have the free use of a property in France for holidays then you can become liable for income tax on the assessed benefits-in-kind. The way around this is to ensure that shareholders are not directors – *gérants* – of the company.

You should seek expert legal advice if you are thinking of setting up an SCI. While it is not that difficult to set one up, the terms under which it is set up must be carefully considered. The SCI is useful for expensive properties. It is also very useful where unrelated people wish to buy a property together, such as in the case of co-ownership.

## Buying *en indivision*

The concept of *indivision* is fundamental in French law. Where two or more people buy a property jointly they automatically enter into an *indivision,* unless they opt for another regime, such as the *tontine* or the SCI. The term *indivision* came about because, while the members of the *indivision* have separate shares, the assets themselves are not divided up. Members of the *indivision* can leave if they wish, or ask to have the *indivision* dissolved through a court of law. Couples married under the regime of common property – *communauté des biens* – automatically have equal shares in a property, given that their names are on the *acte de vente*. There is also the possibility that only property that is acquired during the marriage is commonly owned. Under the regime of separate estates – *séparation des biens* – the property can be divided up unequally, or only one partner may own it.

Where two or more heirs inherit a property, they automatically enter an *indivision* and become *indivisaires*, until such time as the members decide to end the *indivision*. If you go to a *notaire* and ask to see their portfolio of properties, you may see a file of 'problem' properties, where the owners are *indivisaires* or several people have some claim to a property. Often it is more convenient to rent the property out and leave matters alone. The *indivisaires* can decide to prolong the *indivision* for a certain length of time, and make up a *convention d'indivision,* a written contract. Once the members fall out with each other the only solution is to break up the *indivision*. Serious problems can arise if one member dies. The positive side of the *indivision* is that it is easy to enter into; no written agreement is required. Each member retains their share of the property and benefits proportionately from the income generated.

## Using gifts to favour your heirs

Depending on your age, you can lighten the tax burden by giving away assets in good time. Gift tax – *droits de donation* – is payable at the same rates as inheritance tax. It has to be paid immediately, but the donor can pay the tax on behalf of the donee. Every six years a French taxpayer can give – free of tax – the equivalent of the relevant tax allowance. For example, a parent can give up to €50,000 to each of his/her children free of tax every six years. Or a spouse can give to the other spouse up to €76,000 free of tax. This is unlike the system in the UK where the donor has to survive a certain number of years – currently seven years – to make the gift exempt from tax. In France an additional tax-free amount of €20,000 was allowed for gifts to children and grandchildren over 18 years old between 25th September 2003 and 30th June 2005 but this concession has not been available since.

Grandparents can give grandchildren €30,000 tax-free every six years. Gifts that are not revealed to the tax office will not be subject to gift tax, but if their existence becomes known after the donor's decease then they will be treated as part of the inheritance and will be subject to full succession tax. The gift can be witnessed by the *notaire*, who will make up an *acte authentique,* a document which has legal force and which is recognised by third parties. The *notaire* can put certain advantageous clauses into the gift act, and there is then no risk of being penalised later when succession tax has to be paid.

## *Donation entre époux/donation au dernier vivant*

These are two names for one type of gift. The gift can be written into the marriage contract in which case it is irrevocable; otherwise it can be revoked without informing the partner. The *donation au dernier vivant* means 'gift to the survivor'. The survivor only receives the assets on the death of their partner. Succession tax is payable above the basic allowance of €76,000. If the partners are married under the *communauté des biens* regime, then any personal assets are also subject to succession tax.

The *donation entre époux* is of benefit to the spouse when the deceased leaves family members who are reserved heirs. Without the *donation entre époux* the surviving partner will receive less than they would have if their partner had made the donation. On the death of the partner the survivor can opt to continue to have the *usufruit* or benefits of the spouse's entire assets for the rest of their lives, while the children have the *nue propriété*, i.e. they own the assets without having the use or profit of them. The surviving partner can manage the deceased's portfolio of investments, but they can be challenged by the deceased's blood relatives if they appear to be mismanaging the assets. The survivor can also opt to receive the part of the inheritance that they are allowed as *pleine propriété*, without the *usufruit*, or to have 25% *pleine propriété* and 75% *usufruit*. Where there are children from a previous marriage (including those born out of wedlock, or adopted) the situation becomes more complex. The law is such as to ensure that children of the first spouse are not disadvantaged by the donation nor should the second spouse receive more than her fair share.

> ## Insider Tip
>
>
>
> The *donation entre époux* may not be the best method of reducing succession taxes; it is simpler and cheaper to put the provisions you want in your will. It is advisable to take legal advice before making a gift to ensure that this is best for you. This type of gift must be registered with a *notaire*.

It would appear that non-residents cannot enter into a *donation entre époux*.

## *Donation-partage*

One or both parents can make a gift to their children during their lifetime, and thus reduce the amount of taxes payable on transferring assets to their children or grandchildren. This is a method of dividing up and giving away your assets early. If the parents make the gift jointly – the *donation-partage conjonctive* – it is assumed for fiscal purposes that half the gift came from the father and the other half from the mother. Gift tax (*droits de donation*) is payable on the *donation partage*. The amount of tax reduction depends on the age of the donor, and the amount of time that elapses before the donor's death. If both parents make a gift jointly to their children, the children are allowed up to €50,000 per parent – i.e. €100,000 in total – free of tax.

Gifts made under *donation partage* still form part of the inheritance. Ordinary gifts – *donations simples* – are reabsorbed into the inheritance and evaluated for succession tax. The parents do not have to divide up their gifts equally between the children; normally the children agree that the gifts should be apportioned in a certain way. Children are not legally obliged to accept a gift, and this has no effect on their legal rights. They can challenge the distribution of the gifts after the parent's decease, if they believe that the gift has reduced their inheritance, e.g. they were not born when the gift was made.

## Disinheriting a partner

Since 2002, it has become much more difficult to disinherit a partner entirely. However, you can still disinherit the surviving spouse – unless you have no children. In that case, the surviving spouse is a reserved heir and must receive a compulsory share of 25%. The surviving partner has an absolute right to remain in the marital home for a year after the death, even when the home is rented. Although various provisions can be put into a *testament authentique* to try to prevent the surviving partner from continuing to occupy the conjugal home, these are not likely to stand up in a French court. A great deal depends on how many reserved heirs there are.

## Disinheriting other family

If you want to favour your partner and provide them with an income for life, the simplest thing to do is to sell your property for a *rente viagère*, a pension annuity on a reversion property. The buyer often pays an initial 20%–30% of the price, and then an agreed annual sum to you and your partner, until your death. The contract includes a clause that your partner then receives the annuity until they die. The property then passes to the buyer. Your family cannot make any objections. The main inconvenience is that there are fewer and fewer buyers willing to enter this kind of arrangement, given the increasing life expectancy of sellers.

## *Legs résiduel*

This is a new possibility, which became law on 1st January 2007 for couples with children from previous relationships. It allows one spouse to leave assets to the surviving spouse, with the freedom to do with whatever the survivor wants, but instructs that any remaining value should be returned to the deceased's reserved heirs. The advantage of this is that, when the reserved heirs eventually inherit from the second death, they are considered to be inheriting from their direct ascendant, and will therefore pay tax at the rates applicable between parents and children rather than at 60% on assets passing to unrelated individuals.

## Types of will

There are three types of will, as follows.

- ■ Holographic (*testament olographe*): entirely in the person's handwriting, it is best done in French, and is generally not witnessed. If you choose, you can register it with the central register of testaments, the *Fichier de Dernières Volontés*. Most wills in France are in this form.
- ■ Authentic (*testament authentique*): can be printed or written and has to be witnessed by two notaries or one notary and two other persons. Automatically registered with the *Fichier de Dernières Volontés*.

■ Secret (*testament mystique*): a will made up or dictated by a person who then hands it over in a sealed and signed envelope to a notary in the presence of two witnesses. The notary writes on it 'sealed document' or other comments. The testator either leaves it with the notary or keeps it themselves.

The holographic testament is generally the best, with the proviso that someone needs to know where it is kept. The secret testament has virtually fallen out of use.

# Inheritance procedures

Once someone has passed away, the family and/or partner need to advise a *notaire* as soon as is practically possible after registering the death at the town hall. The surviving partner, potential inheritors, the executor or creditors can request a *greffier en chef* (chief clerk) from the local civil court to put seals on the deceased's property (*pose de scellés*) if they believe there is a risk of theft or fraud. The *greffier* can make up a list of the goods and conduct a search for a will.

Legally, the reserved heirs, and anyone with a power of attorney, has the right and duty – known as *saisine* – to use the deceased's assets from the moment of death, and to pay debts or bills as they arise. The deceased's bank account is automatically blocked, but money can still be taken out for bills, the funeral, and standing orders.

The names of the heirs are listed on the *acte de notoriété*, a legal document made up by the *notaire* or by a chief clerk of the court. This does not mean that heirs can immediately take their part of the inheritance, or that they are bound to accept an inheritance encumbered with debts. An heir can register the deceased's car in their name, with the right documents, and the agreement of the other heirs, before the estate is finally divided up.

A number of documents are required to start the inheritance process:

■ the death certificate
■ a copy of the French will
■ a copy of the British will, translated into French
■ the names of all the potential inheritors
■ marriage/divorce certificates
■ death certificates of deceased former inheritors still mentioned in the will, if any.

In the course of time, you will need to produce documents relating to all of the deceased's bank accounts, investments and properties. The inheritors, and anyone who has received gifts from the deceased subject to gift tax, are required to file a *déclaration de succession* within a year. Interest is payable on the succession tax after 6 months if the deceased died in France, or 12 months if abroad. The *déclaration* is a form obtained from the French tax office, to be filled in in duplicate if the assets are over €15,000. Foreigners will find it convenient to mandate a notary to make the *déclaration*. The succession tax has to be worked out by the person filling in the *déclaration*. The tax authorities can challenge the value you place on a property, by comparing it with similar properties in the area. A small undervaluation is acceptable, but you can't go too far.

The tax does not come out of the inheritance; the inheritors are required to pay it together before they can receive the inheritance. It is possible to ask for a delay in payment of up to 10 years; you can also ask to pay in instalments.

It is possible to use an executor (*exécuteur testamentaire*) named in your will in France, but this is probably best avoided, unless you have reason to believe that your next of kin are untrustworthy or incompetent. The executor is charged with filing the *déclaration de succession* correctly. They are entitled to payment for the work they do, which can come to a substantial sum – one reason to avoid using them.

## Further reading

For a detailed study of French succession law, see Henry Dyson's *French Property and Inheritance Law*, published by Oxford University Press. This is a technical work written for lawyers. If you read French, then you can find the latest information on the website www.lesechos.fr or the government website, www.service-public.gouv.fr.

# Wealth Tax (ISF)

ISF or *impôt de solidarité sur la fortune* only affects those with net assets over €760,000 if they are resident or have assets in France on 1st January of any tax year. The tax is levied on the *foyer fiscal* (fiscal household) defined as:

- single persons, divorced, widowed, unmarried or separated from their partners
- married persons, including dependent children under 18 years old
- persons who are known to be living together (*concubinage notoire*), and children
- those who have entered a PACS (partnership contract) and children.

The household's net assets as of 1st January are calculated by the householder himself or herself; they include the assets of everyone in the household, including children under 18 years old. The declaration, accompanied by payment in full, is due by 15th July for EU citizens, and 15th June for French citizens. Other foreigners (e.g. US citizens) have until 31st August to pay. Variations in the value of your assets during the year cannot be taken account when calculating your liability.

All your assets, including cars, yachts, furniture, etc. must be taken into account. You will need to produce receipts and insurance policies if you are asked to justify your valuations. You are expected to calculate the 'fair market value' (*valeur vénale réelle*) of your property on the basis of prices in your area. The tax authorities have their own ways of assessing your net worth.

There are a number of items exempt from wealth tax, of which a few are given here in a simplified form:

- antiques over 100 years old
- copyrights on works of art, literature and music

- personal injury compensation
- goods that you require to carry on your profession
- shares in companies of which you are a director, with more than 25% voting rights.

It may be possible to have assets that you need to run *gîtes* or *chambres d'hôte* exempted from wealth tax. You are allowed a 20% reduction on the household's principal residence (not more than one house). You are not exempt from paying wealth tax on shares in French companies, or foreign companies owning property in France.

Since the basis on which ISF is calculated is your net worth, any debts can be deducted from the total. This includes any property loans. Any money you owe to builders or other tradesmen can be deducted, as can the taxes you owe for the previous year (including the ISF itself). Money that is owed to you is added to the total.

| Wealth tax tariffs (as of 2007) | |
|---|---|
| Net taxable assets | Tariff |
| Less than €760,000 | 0% |
| €760,001 to €1,220,000 | 0.55% |
| €1,220,001 to €2,420,000 | 0.75% |
| €2,420,001 to €3,800,000 | 1% |
| €3,800,001 to €7,270,000 | 1.3% |
| €7,270,001 to €15,810,000 | 1.65% |
| Above €15,810,000 | 1.8% |

There is a further limitation on wealth tax, inasmuch as your total tax liability (including income tax) cannot exceed 60% of your net taxable income. This is known as the *bouclier fiscal* or tax shield. This does not however include taxes on second homes, the TV licence, social charges or taxes paid abroad. Taxpayers who want to claim a refund under the tax shield rules need to file form 2041 before 31st December 2007 for excess taxes paid in 2006.

# Payment and penalties

Your wealth tax return and payment have to be made to the local Recette des Impôts by 15th July. If you are not resident in France payment is made to the Recette des Impôts des Non-Résidents, 9 rue d'Uzès, 75094 Paris Cedex 02. If you reside in Monaco it is made to the Recette des Impôts in Menton.

In the unlikely event that you cannot pay the tax, you may give works of art instead. The penalties for submitting a false return, or late payment, are very high. Any assets that are not declared will be taxed under the inheritance laws as though they were gifts, and interest and other penalties will be levied. Since the wealth tax is not that onerous, it would be stupid not to pay it. From the point of view of the French state, it is useful as a way of keeping tabs on taxpayers' assets as much as a source of revenue.

# Tax and Investment Advice

The law firms listed in The Directory will give advice on how to plan ahead to benefit your heirs. There are several UK firms that specialise in giving advice to UK citizens who are buying or already own property in France. Some hold seminars in different locations in France. These are publicised in French property magazines and the monthly *French News* published from Périgueux.

## Useful financial websites

www.impots.gouv.fr. Government site, with tax simulation programme.

www.lesechos.fr/patrimoine/index.htm. Finance website.

www.frenchentree.com/fe-legal.

# Insurance (*assurances*)

The French insurance market is very high profile. AXA and the state-owned GAN are household names in Britain. You can also add your French property to your UK insurance, as long as it fulfils French legal requirements. It is in any case always easier to insure with a company that can handle claims in English, so that you get a quick response in case of problems. Having your claim translated into French is expensive and time consuming. There are English-speaking agents in many parts of France who can arrange insurance for you. There are agents who only sell policies for one company (*agents généraux*), and those who deal with several (*courtier d'assurances*).

## House and contents insurance

The basic house and contents insurance is the *assurance multirisques habitation,* also often called *assurance multirisques vie privée* or *la multirisque.* This will include cover against natural disasters as a matter of course. Civil liability insurance – *responsabilité civile propriétaire* – is essential, in case an event on your property affects your neighbours. Your possessions also need to be insured. This kind of policy does not insure you against personal accidents, unless you ask for it. There are numerous formulas for the *assurance multirisques*, depending on your requirements.

*'it is always easier to insure with a company that can handle claims in English, so you get a quick response'*

If you are planning to build on a piece of land, an *assurance dommages-ouvrage* is compulsory. It is possible to take over the existing insurance from the previous owner of the property you are buying; if you say nothing then it is assumed. If you do not wish to continue the same insurance policy – generally the wisest course of action for foreign buyers – you are required to present another policy to the *notaire* before you can sign the final *acte de vente*.

It is normal to insure the contents of your property as well. The current market value or *valeur vénale* of the items is used to work out the amount of cover; depreciation is taken into account. The insurers can insist on shutters being fitted to windows and bars on doors, and other security measures. You need to keep receipts, guarantees, photographs etc. of your possessions in a safe place for any claims. Read the small print in the policy, and watch out that you are not underinsured.

If there is nothing of value in your property you can take out basic insurance against damage from natural causes, vandalism, terrorist acts, etc., known as an *assurance multirisques d'immeuble*. This is used by *copropriétés* and some owners of blocks of flats. This will be calculated by the square metre. There should be a clause in which the insurer agrees to rebuild or restore the property to its original state within two years in the same style.

## Insurance and tenants/*copropriétés*

If you rent a property for a long period the owner will ask you to take out an *assurance multirisques habitation* to cover the building and any risks that could affect neighbours, e.g. floods, fire, explosions, etc. According to the laws governing tenancy, the *Loi Quillot* and *Loi Méhaignerie*, the proprietor can insert a clause in the tenancy agreement allowing him or her to cancel your tenancy immediately if you don't have adequate insurance. You should ask the owner whether you need insurance well before you sign a tenancy agreement. You are free to choose any insurance company you want.

In the case of a *copropriété* the building insurance will be taken care of by the manager of the property, and your share of the premiums will appear on the monthly charges. You are responsible for insuring your own possessions, and third party insurance for anyone visiting your premises.

## Holiday homes

Burglaries of holiday homes are common, especially on the Riviera, or any isolated area. An insurance policy for a principal residence is not suitable for a holiday home; there are usually clauses making the policy void if the house is left empty for more than 30 days. In order to get insurance cover, you will be expected to put in additional locks, shutters, burglar alarms and grills. Some owners go so far as to install webcams so they can watch their property being broken into. The longer you are away from the property, the higher your premiums will be, and the less likely the insurers are to cover valuables. Your premiums will be reduced if you install burglar alarms, electronic surveillance systems, and so on. Premiums vary widely around the country; they are highest in the south-east where there are more fires than in the rest of France. To give a rough idea: a €150,000 property in the Landes could cost €700 per year to insure, while in Aix-en-Provence it would be €1,400. The website www.intasure.com has a very useful calculator to help you work out how much insurance will cost in different parts of France. Mike Farley of Intasure says: 'In today's market, flexibility is central to the cover. A comprehensive buildings and contents insurance policy should allow you to live in, leave your property unoccupied or let it, whether short or long term, to be of any real use to the policy holder.'

There is a particular risk of blocked or frozen pipes causing flooding, and every possible measure has to be taken to prevent this. You need to take sensible precautions: there has recently been a high-profile case of a woman who kept containers of kerosene in her flat, and received nothing when the place burned down. Insurers will take into account the condition of the property when they pay for repairs. If the original plaster or roofing was not that good then they will pay proportionately less to have it replaced.

## Thefts

It is a condition of insurance policies that you report thefts within 24 hours to the police, or as soon as possible, if you want your claim to be taken seriously. The police will give you a form – *déclaration de vol* – with the details of what you have lost. You need to inform the insurers within two working days of the theft and send the receipt of the *déclaration* by registered post (*recommandée*), with an *avis de réception* (AR) or receipt. It is advisable to telephone the insurer immediately and they will send you a confirmation. You then draw up a list of the stolen goods and send it by registered post.

## Natural disasters

There is a whole raft of regulations about which natural events count as disasters or *catastrophes naturelles*. The amount of time you have to report a disaster ranges from four days for hail to 10 days after a storm, if this has been declared a *catastrophe naturelle* in the official journal. Your house insurance should cover not only *catastrophes naturelles* but all kinds of other natural risks. You do not have to pay for cover against snow, unless you think it is necessary. Check that the policy covers damage to electrical items as well.

## Checking the small print

Look carefully at the small print in the policy to see what conditions are set for reporting damage, thefts, etc., and any exclusions. Check for the *franchise* or excess, i.e. the first part of the claim that is not paid. Taking videos and photographs of property is an eminently sensible precaution to make sure you are paid in full. You can use a court bailiff – *huissier* – or an insurance expert, to prepare a report on damage to your property (for a fee). The insurance company will normally send their own expert to draw up a report on your loss.

Policies are renewed automatically (*tacite reconduction*); you are given a period of time before the renewal date when you can cancel the policy. Though the insurance market in France is gradually opening to greater competition, it is still much harder to switch insurance contracts as you can in other countries such as Britain. And once that renewal date has passed it is too late to cancel. You can't simply pick up a telephone and switch insurers when you find a better deal. Premiums should be paid by standing order, within 10 days of the set date. You will receive a warning (*mise en demeure*) from the insurer. If you haven't paid within 30 days your policy will be cancelled, but you will still be liable for the outstanding amount and the insurer's costs.

Insurers may not take you on if your insurance has been cancelled for non-payment. Recent claims for damage through floods, avalanches and other major disasters make it difficult to get insurance.

## Insurance of schoolchildren

The state school system obliges parents to insure their children when they undertake voluntary activities. Private schools set their own rules. If one of your children goes to a state school and another to a private school you may be able to put them both on one policy. The *assurance scolarité* should cover not only harm that a child could occasion to third parties, but also any harm that could come to him or her (*garantie individuelle accidents*) which is not included in your usual house insurance. Without this insurance, your child will not be allowed to go on excursions. You can go further and insure your child's belongings, or against all sorts of diseases; the sky is the limit.

## Where to find insurance

Insurance companies are listed in the French yellow pages under *assurances;* some agents advertise in the French property magazines, such as *French Property News.*

Insurance companies specialising in foreign homes, as well as other types of insurance, are listed in The Directory.

# 16 Services

## Utilities

### Gas

IN URBAN AREAS YOU MAY HAVE ACCESS TO *GAZ DE VILLE* – mains gas – supplied by Gaz de France (GDF), which shares offices with Électricité de France. There is a similar payment system in place to electricity, with four different tariffs depending on how much gas you use. Bills are sent every two months. For more information see the website www.gazdefrance.com/particuliers.

Elsewhere it is usual to rely on bottled gas; it is easy to have it delivered to your home, or you can fetch it yourself. There is a choice between propane and butane. Propane is reckoned to be more suitable for properties where the temperature goes below freezing in winter. You may find yourself unable to cook in the winter if you rely on butane. Alternatively you can have a *citerne* or metal container of about two cubic metres installed on your property, which is periodically filled by a tanker with liquefied gas. If you just use this gas for cooking it will last you a long time and works out cheaper than using bottled gas after the initial expense of installing the tank. The *citerne* should have a meter to show how much gas is left. New gas installations must be checked by a representative of the national organisation, Qualigaz. See www.qualigaz. fr for more information. New legislation in the future will require property sellers to show that their gas heating is in good working condition. The law has also now broken GDF and EDF's monopoly on energy supplies, but very few people are opting to choose private suppliers.

### Electricity

Most foreign property buyers take little notice of the state of the wiring in the property that they are thinking of buying, something that can prove to be an expensive mistake. While they think nothing of spending thousands of euros on a bathroom suite, they find it hard to bear the prospect of spending €5,000 or more on bringing the wiring of the house up to standard. One survey of French housing built before 1974 estimated that 96% of units had some deficiencies in the wiring. Promotelec, the organisation that promotes higher standards of electrical equipment, estimates that there are 7 million dangerous electrical appliances in France. The main problems are lack of, or insufficient, earthing, corroded wiring and unsuitable circuit-breakers. In older properties you can still find pre-world war 1-style cotton-covered wiring. Old plastic plugs can literally fall to pieces in your hands. Apart from any risk of electrocution, if you are taking *'most foreign property buyers take little notice of the state of the wiring in the property, something that can prove to be an expensive mistake'*

over an older property it is essential to find out whether the wiring can handle heavy-amperage equipment such as washing machines and electric cookers. If you need to run electric heating at the same time as other heavy equipment like an electric cooker, water heater, washing machine etc., then you will require a supply of at least 12 KvA (kilovolt amperes or kilowatts), for which heavier wiring is needed to the electricity meter.

The British system is inherently safer because there are fuses in the plugs themselves. In your French house you will find two types of socket: two-pin sockets for low-amperage equipment, and two-pin sockets with an earth pin (*prise de terre*) for heavier appliances. In France you will find ordinary light switches being used in bathrooms, something that is illegal in the UK. On the other hand, wiring in the UK can be directly installed into the plaster, whereas in France all wiring in the wall has to be enclosed in a plastic tube, or *goulotte*.

If you buy a house without an electricity supply, the French state firm, Électricité de France (EDF), will connect you to the grid. There is a basic charge of €600 for a new connection, plus €1,500 for every new electricity pole that has to be erected. If you cannot see an electricity pylon nearby then your connection could cost more than the property itself. If on the other hand your electricity has been cut off while you rebuild the property then you will receive a basic 3 kW *chantier* supply, charged at an extortionate €200 per month. If the electricity has been cut off for work to be done, then you will require a *certificat de conformité* or CC from the safety organisation Consuel to certify that the system is safe before EDF will reconnect your supply. Consuel does not inspect an electrician's work unless there is a good reason, neither does it certify that your system conforms to a certain level. They will only test the earthing and the consumer unit (*tableau principal*).

If you are intending to buy a property in France, then it is in your interest to ask the seller to allow a *Diagnostic Confiance Sécurité* to be carried out. This is a 40 minute inspection covering a list of 53 points resulting in an objective assessment of the state of the wiring of your house. Once the inspection has been carried out, you can call in an electrician to give an estimate (*devis*)

## Insider Tip

*(i)*

The basic system of wiring in French houses is a spur system rather than the ring main system used in the UK. A ring main is a way of connecting a series of power sockets. The cabling starts and ends at the fuse box, having gone through each socket on the circuit so creating a ring. The spur system used in France starts at the fuse box and can either daisy chain on from one socket to the next or can branch out from a junction box. Consequently there are more fuses that can blow if you overload the system.

of the cost of any work needed. The DCS only costs €80 including taxes. Needless to say, if your prospective seller refuses to allow a DCS then you should be suspicious. A DCS can be arranged by calling an EDF advisor on 0801 126 126, or through Promotelec who carry out the DCS, on 0825 046 770 or through their website www.promotelec.com.

Having the house rewired can be very disruptive as well as expensive, because of the necessity of taking out at least some of the plaster. There are therefore grounds for asking for a reduction in the price of the property to cover the costs. At the same time you can take the opportunity of installing the most up-to-date energy-efficient system.

## Electricity tariffs

EDF has three different tariffs for electricity: the *Tarif de Base*, the *Tarif Heures Creuses*, and the *Tarif Tempo*. Which one is suitable for you depends on how much electricity you use.

- *Base:* basic tariff for 3–18 kW use.
- *Heures Creuses/Heures Pleines:* allows you to benefit from cheaper electricity at periods of low demand. For 6–36 kW use.
- *Tempo:* for heavy users, above 9 kW. The price varies according to three tariffs, with 300 white days, 43 blue days, and 22 red days, when the price is very high. This requires installation of a system to let you know what tariff is in force at any particular time.

Electricity meters are read every 6 months; bills are sent every 2 months, the intervening readings are estimated. If you are never in when the meter reader calls you can arrange to send readings yourself, at a stipulated time. For further information see the websites: http://monagence.edf.fr and www.mamaison.edf.fr, which has helpful tips on saving on electricity and all the tariffs.

EDF supplies electricity at different KvA or kilovolt amperes (colloquially kilowatts or kW) depending on customer requirements. The following will give you an idea of how many kilowatts you might require.

| | |
|---|---|
| 3 kW | Lighting, fridge, TV, computer, vacuum cleaner. |
| 6 kW | Washing machine, dishwasher, electric cooker, water heater. |
| 9 kW | Allows you to run two of the above simultaneously, along with the lighter appliances. |
| 12–36 kW | Makes it possible to run heavy equipment simultaneously, andelectric heating as well. |

The above are charged at different monthly rates. If you use very little electricity and only require 3 kW then you can get a very low monthly standing charge. If you can remember not to run more than one heavy amperage appliance at a time then you may manage with 6 kW; 9 kW will give you more of a margin for error. If you increase the kilowattage higher than 12 kW you may have to install heavier wiring to the electricity meter.

# Water

The mains water supply is safe to drink, if not always that tasty. The French consume a lot of bottled mineral water, on average 100 litres per person per year.

Mains water is supplied by Générale des Eaux and other local companies around France. Lyonnaise des Eaux is well known and owns some UK water suppliers. There have been water shortages in central and southern France in recent years during hot weather. You'll need to keep an eye out for local water restrictions. The water supply is metered and can cost twice as much as in the UK. There will be a meter outside the property. It is essential to check the reliability of the supply if you are buying property. Water leaks should be reported quickly.

In the case of an apartment without a water supply the situation can be difficult, since the local water company will only make one connection to a property.

On average, mains water costs €2.8 per cubic metre. The average person in the north of France uses 43 cubic metres a year, while on the Côte d'Azur the figure is 74 cubic metres. In Paris it is 66 cubic metres. Evidently, it is worth investing in water-saving measures if possible. To find out the local price of water, and the nearest supplier look at the website www.generale-des-eaux.com.

# Heating

The subject of heating is often overlooked by foreigners looking at a property when the weather is sunny. Northern France is as cold as southern England in winter. Areas such as the Limousin, Poitou-Charentes and even parts of the Dordogne can be just as cold too. You may get away without central heating – *chauffage central* – in the south of France, but you will still need some kind of heating. Upland areas, such as the Massif Central, can be bitterly cold in winter. You also need to consider whether your property is in a 'frost-hollow', which can lower the temperature by up to 5°C in winter.

Gas central heating is not common outside the cities; in much of France there is no mains gas supply. Although one can run gas central heating from a *citerne* in one's garden, the experience of foreign property owners has been that this is not a good solution. You are then left with a choice between using cheap-rate electricity or heating oil – *mazout* or *fioul* (which is the English word 'fuel'). The downside of oil is that the price can fluctuate a lot. One solution is to combine electricity and oil in a system called Bi-Énergie, which you can switch over to oil when electricity is at peak rate.

If the property is to be left unoccupied during the winter then central heating may be unnecessary. Wood-burning stoves are a good solution, with some portable heaters or oil-filled radiators as a back-up. If you are interested in using solar panels or heat exchangers, contact the energy efficiency organisation ADEME: see www.ademe.fr. They are not cheap to install but may be economical in the long run and attract some tax breaks available for installing environmentally friendly heating. You also need to consider the benefits of getting your house properly insulated; this will save you as much money as getting an efficient heating system.

## Water heaters

You will find the same kinds of water heaters in many houses France as are found in the UK. One type that is not found in the UK is the *chauffe-eau* (short for *chauffe-eau à accumulation*) a tank with a double skin that heats water using cheap-tariff electricity or gas. The advantage of the *chauffe-eau* is not only the good insulation, but also the fact that it can be located anywhere in a building as it works from mains pressure. The main consideration is to make sure that the capacity is large enough to fill a bath. A *chauffe-eau direct/à faible capacité* heats water at the point of delivery, i.e. by gas. Good ventilation is essential.

## Septic tanks/*fosses septiques*

The state of one's septic tank is a favourite subject of conversation with foreign residents in France. Septic tanks are common in France, where many properties are far from the local sewage system. There is a trend in France to connect more properties to the main sewage system, known as *tout à l'égout*. There are some costs involved for the owner. Cess pits – *puisards* – where all the waste simply goes into a hole in the ground are being phased out, and it is no longer legal to build one.

The idea of the septic tank is to process the waste from toilets, and other used water, through the natural action of bacteria, so that eventually only fairly harmless water is left. All the waste runs into the first settling tank, or septic tank, where the solid matter sinks to the bottom, while scum forms on the surface. The naturally present bacteria break the waste matter down, releasing methane; so no naked flames! The remainder goes into a second settling tank, which should be half the length of the first tank, and then into a 'drain field' or system of soakaways, with a series of drain pipes or drain tiles laid on gravel. The drain pipes or tiles are perforated so that the effluent filters away into the ground. Before the effluent reaches the soakaways, there has to be an inspection chamber, or *regard de visite*. The solid matter in the septic tank has to be emptied once in a while, the so-called *vidange*. The interval depends very much on

### Insider Tip

If you are looking at country properties, make sure to find out whether there is a fosse septique. If there is none you will be required to install one. Since the whole contraption extends at least 70 ft from the house, it is essential to have enough land to build one. The larger your fosse septique the less trouble it will give you. You cannot construct anything over the fosse septique, and there should be a minimum of trees around it, none of which should be closer than 3 m to the fosse septique. You should also look at the slope of the land, and make sure that the water table is not too close to the surface.

---

☑ *Been there, done it...*

**Richard Coman had troubles with his main drainage system.**

For about 10 years we were fine with our *fosse septique* but then we were told by the *commune* that we had to be on the main drainage system, the *tout à l'égout*. The contractors had to use dynamite because the ground was solid granite under three inches of soil. Then the next-door neighbour found cracks in his walls and accused us of having planted trees too close to his house. I had got a *pépiniériste* (nurseryman) to plant some trees along our boundary 14 years earlier, but he had failed to observe the regulation that says you can't plant trees within three m of an adjoining property, so I had to ask him to come and dig the trees up. On top of that the contractors who dug the sewage trenches left a huge mound of granite chippings on my land. I went to see the *maire* and got a London firm of translators to write a business letter in French, at great expense, but to no effect. Finally I had the *notaire* threaten legal action, which did the trick, but of course I had to pay the legal fees.

---

how well the tank is maintained. The local municipality will recommend at what intervals the tank should be emptied. Anywhere between two and 10 years is possible.

Generally, *fosses septiques* work better in hotter climates, which favour the breakdown of the wastes. The price of new *fosses septiques* is going up rapidly because of ever more stringent regulations. A new one can cost €5,000, including installation. For suppliers look at French property magazines, or the website www.profosse.com. New installations have to be approved, inspected and finally certified by the local drainage department, as new legislation is gradually being introduced. Each *commune* has a team of experts who check the conformity of the *fosse septique* and you can be asked to change one that does not conform. When selling, the *notaire* will check whether you have your *certificat de conformité*: at the moment, most people don't, so the *notaire* simply states that the *fosse* is working.

## Security and Housesitters

For second-home owners, burglary is a major concern. If a property is left empty for long periods of time then there is a likelihood that professional burglars will notice. These will generally be outsiders, who cruise around looking to see whether properties are empty. The classic tactic is to come along in a white van and remove the entire contents of the house, down to the fitted cupboards.

Your insurers will advise you on what measures to take; they may not insure you unless you add more locks, bars and shutters to the property. The most effective method is to fit heavy shutters to all doors and windows. Even then burglars have been known to smash down doors.

You are much safer if you have close neighbours, or if your property is in a terrace. Otherwise you could consider using housesitters, or professional watchmen.

## Housesitters

If one of the main problems for an owner whose property is in a remote area is burglary, others include possible damage from blocked gutters, burst pipes or fire, which can be avoided or at least dealt with if there is someone on the spot to attend to them.

Prospective housesitters advertise their services in the local English-language magazines, such as *French News, FUSAC* or *Riviera Times*. It would be advisable to insist on references. Your housesitter should have their own transport. From the housesitter's point of view the main drawback is isolation – this is something best done in pairs – and also the lack of income. According to French regulations, housesitters are entitled to payment. Housesitters also advertise in French property magazines.

# Employing Staff

As with most things in France there are complex regulations governing the employment of domestic staff, gardeners, handymen, etc. The rules require domestic employees to enjoy the same rights as other workers. You are expected to draw up a written contract, specifying the number of hours and nature of the worker's duties. The minimum level of remuneration is determined by a *Convention Collective Nationale* for all workers employed in the home, covering cooks, cleaners, nurses, handymen/women, nannies, babysitters, governesses, butlers and chauffeurs, amongst others, but not gardeners and caretakers.

Often the person working for you will be working for other people as well, but this makes no difference to the amount of social security charges you have to pay. To take a simple example: if you pay a babysitter €100, you may pay €70 in social security charges. For anyone on an average income, half the charges, the employer's part, are refunded by the *Caisse d'Allocations Familiales*. Half the rest is refunded as tax credits: effectively you pay €17.50 of the total. The employer is not liable for payroll tax if they pay no more than €15,000 to domestic employees in total (this amount may change).

Domestic workers enjoy the same protection as every other worker: they cannot be dismissed without a good reason. The law regarding workers who are paid in kind or partly in kind is less specific. In principle the remuneration should reflect the value of the work, but cannot fall below the minimum wage. If you help out your neighbour or a relative then this is not regarded as paid employment and there is no obligation to declare the work to the taxman. You should not underestimate the zealousness of the tax inspectors in tracking down cash-in-hand workers; there is a general culture of informing on your neighbours in France, and the person you employ may inform the authorities if you do not pay their social security contributions.

In order to ensure that domestic employees are correctly paid, town halls will provide a ready-made cheque-book, the *chèque emploi-service*, specifically for domestic employees. The cheques have two parts: one section is to pay the employee; the other is a declaration to send to URSSAF, the authority that collects social security contributions. By using the cheques you can meet your obligations as regards social security payments and avoid breaking any laws.

As a rule, you should be cautious about whom you employ to do work around your property, especially on the Riviera. References should be taken up. There are English-speaking foreigners who will take advantage of the fact that they speak the same language as you to try to gain entry into your property for nefarious purposes.

# 17 Renovating A Property

FOR SOME FOREIGNERS, THE WHOLE POINT OF BUYING IN FRANCE IS TO FIND A DERELICT BUILDING and turn it into a bijou residence they can sell on. Some properties in remoter areas are put on the market by the French in the full knowledge that only a foreigner would buy them.

One should be wary of getting sucked into a project which could eat up huge sums of money for little return. Doing up a derelict property can cost as much as building a house from scratch. The French may admire your determination, but you should be careful not to let them 'take you for an Englishman' or 'a *pigeon*', another expression for taking someone for a ride. The fact that the British tend to pay over the odds for building work might have something to do with it.

The details of property renovation are beyond the scope of this book. There are several books on the market that deal with renovation; the best is David Everett's *Buying and Restoring Old Property in France*, which is mainly concerned with restoring rather than buying. If you read French, it is worth getting *Architecture Rurale et Bourgeoise en France*, by Georges Doyon and Robert Hubrecht, a fascinating survey of traditional building techniques and terminology covering the whole of France, through www.amazon.fr. This also gives advice on how to restore properties in an authentic style. For more information, on the planning process and using artisans see chapter 9.

## Grants

It is worth enquiring about grants – *subventions* – for restoration. The ANAH – *Association Nationale pour l'Amélioration de l'Habitat* – has offices in every DDE – *Division Départementale de l'Équipement*. There are more generous grants available for listed buildings and buildings considered to be noteworthy because some famous person lived there. See the website: www.anah.fr. There are more possibilities if you are planning to start a business or run *gîtes*, which are listed in chapter 19. Some *communes* may offer grants towards the cost of being connected up to the electricity or water supply. The *mairie* will let you know what is available.

✓ *Been there, done it...*

**Tim Weir bought a traditional farmhouse in Deux-Sèvres with the intention of renovating and starting *gîtes*. His website is www.leshiboux.com.**

If you are lucky enough to find the 'ideal" property for restoration, the project is at least a year away from the real start. All sorts of rules and regulations need to be adhered to, e.g., architects plans are obligatory if the build size is greater than 170 sq m. Engaging an architect is a good idea. He will either charge a set fee for the drawings – including submission to the local *mairie* – or he will act as a project manager and charge a percentage of the final build. Either way a good architect is a valuable friend and best found by recommendation (the local *mairie* is a good starting point!).

Having got your *permis de construire*, you then have to look for artisans. Again we found that recommendations are the best route and a trip back to the local *mairie* is essential. It is quite usual to obtain at least three *devis* (estimates) for all jobs and to take your pick. Keeping a good flow of artisans along with all their materials is a juggling act, as it would be in the UK. We have found that it is almost impossible to find a 'Jack of all trades' and artisans are usually unprepared to do another artisan's work, i.e. a plumber will be unwilling to cut wood. Perhaps this originates from the 10 year guarantee supplied on all work carried out by registered artisans and therefore they don't wish to be held responsible for work outside their own trade. We have found that any artisan worth his salt will have at least a three-month waiting time and this is the minimum time that should be allotted prior to commencing work. But once you start getting to know the locals, and in particular artisans, two things seem to happen: they are very often prepared to do 'Saturday' work for cash with almost no delay, or the time period of availability is reduced in proportion to the length of time you've known an artisan – perhaps they deliberately leave spaces in their work diaries to help out friends in need?

We were lucky enough to find a fantastic local bloke with a digger and who helped with digging out the barns ready for internal foundations and putting in the trampoline pit whilst digging trenches for the above cables. A lot of the other 'big' works, e.g. laying of concrete slabs and building limestone external walls, were carried out by a local building company, with the remaining works e.g. building internal walls and insulation, carried out by ourselves, often with guidance from friends and local artisans.

It is advisable to spend time doing some background research on tradesmen. Unfortunately there are increasing numbers of unscrupulous unregistered English tradesmen who are prepared to work in your own language, but often at a cost to you financially and otherwise later on. Local regulations are very different from those in the UK, and there are also practical considerations, for example, local stone has been used for hundreds of years to keep out the heat in the summer and keep it in during the winter, so carry on using it, because usually it's cheaper, more readily available and your London brick house will look out of place amongst the local Charantaise limestone!

# Builder's Suppliers

There are plenty of do-it-yourself shops, just as in Britain. The best-known include Castorama, Leroy-Merlin, Bricomarché, Brico Dépôt and Mr Bricolage. The main drawback is the terminology, which can make it a laborious task getting what you want.

Islay Currie, of Currie French Property Services, has the following story:

> I was fairly new to building in France. I went into a builder's shop and spent an hour and a half explaining all the different stuff I needed, like left- and right-threaded joins and so on. The assistant patiently went back and forth showing me everything they had. As I was leaving, he said 'Have a nice day.' 'So you speak English, then', I said. 'Of course', came the reply, 'I lived in New York for 14 years. But, you know, this is France, so you have to learn to ask for things in French.'

# Swimming Pools

A swimming pool (*piscine*) is not just a luxury in France: if you are buying a property of a substantial size to rent out to an up market clientele then it is virtually a necessity, whether you are on the French Riviera or in Normandy. The presence of a swimming pool is the most crucial factor in determining the pulling power of your property, and installing one is an investment well worth making. It is important to bear in mind that a swimming pool entails substantial running costs; £1,500 annually for a minimum £15,000 pool is a fair average.

Deciding on what kind of swimming pool to install is not an easy decision. The three main possibilities are the prefabricated fibre-glass pool, a galvanised steel construction with a vinyl liner, or reinforced concrete. The first crucial point is to determine the water table of the land. If the pool bottom is below the water table then you will first have to install pumps to drain the land before you can install the pool. Should it rain heavily you will need to pump out again, otherwise your pool could literally float away, or, if it is made of concrete, it could break up. In any case, it would be unwise to empty your pool in this kind of situation without expert assistance, since the weight of the water could be keeping it anchored to the ground. In some areas the problem may be earth tremors or porous rock. Take advice from qualified experts, rather than from a French swimming pool franchisee.

A concrete construction consists of a double layer of blocks with steel reinforced concrete inside. Another possibility is a prefabricated fibre-glass pool which is then back-filled with pea-shingle. The Oxford-based company, Bakewell Pools, can arrange for the pools to be delivered anywhere in France (they are manufactured in Dijon), for a uniform price; the installation is then DIY or with the help of local contractors. Another possibility is to bring over a pool from the

'the French may admire your determination, but you should be careful not to let them 'take you for an Englishman' or 'a pigeon', another expression for taking someone for a ride'

UK, in the form of metal sheets with a vinyl liner. The pool can be flat-packed and loaded onto a trailer. The advantage in this case is that the pool can be erected above ground, or even on top of a building, avoiding the water table problem. This is less desirable if you plan to rent out your property, as holidaymakers tend to dislike above-ground pools. There is also the possibility of a smaller plastic pool of which there are plenty available in France.

France has numerous swimming pool companies; it is a matter of whether you feel comfortable dealing with French contractors, or would rather deal with an English-speaking company. It is best to avoid national franchises; rather go for local companies. If you want to know more about French pools, there is a dedicated magazine: *Techniques Piscines* (www. techniques-piscines.fr).

In theory you are not allowed to build a swimming pool within view of a road, as the sight of scantily clad swimmers could cause a traffic accident. There is also a rule that you cannot build anything closer than 3 m to someone else's property or boundary, or half the height of the adjoining wall if this exceeds 6 m.

## Insider Tip

Construction of swimming pools up to 20 sq. m does not require a permis de construire but you may need to apply for a déclaration de travaux exemptés de permis (see chapter 9). The local mayor or town planning authority may raise objections, so it is essential to find out first what you can do. In principle, the authorities are not allowed to stop you from building your pool. An experienced swimming pool contractor will be able to advise you on the procedures.

Strict new regulations came into force in May 2004, making it compulsory for safety devices to be installed to prevent young children from drowning. Owners of rental properties have to install safety devices. There are several means of childproofing pools. One is to install fencing, which has to be at least 110 cm high, with a maximum 12 cm gap at the base, making 122 cm in all. The gate must be self-closing and self-locking. If the lock is of the plunger type it must be at 150 cm high. The fence must be a minimum of 1 m from the edge of the pool and not too far away to lose its effectiveness. There is no requirement to install for an alarm to detect attempts to climb over. A living fence, e.g. a hedge, will not conform. The fence must carry an official certificate of conformity to say that it has passed the AFNOR standard.

Another solution is to install a cover, either electrically or manually operated, which cannot be removed by a child under five years old. You could also install a dome (abri) to cover the pool completely; this has the advantage of also keeping the water temperature higher. The cheapest and least intrusive option is an alarm that is set off if someone falls into the water; this can be an immersion alarm or an infra-red area alarm. These may not be the most effective solutions. There is a €45,000 fine for failing to install safety devices. Insurers will make it obligatory for you to comply with the law. These solutions must meet AFNOR standards NF P90 306, 307, 308 and 309.

## Swimming pool campanies

**Bakewell Pools:** ☎ 01865 735205; email bob@bakewellpools.co.uk; www.bakewellpools.co.uk.
**Christal Pools:** ☎ 01384 440990; email sales@christalpools.com; www.christalpools.com.
**Eausparke:** ☎ 05 53 82 06 39 or mobile 06 07 50 37 16; email eausparke@wanadoo.fr; www.eausparke.com. Contact Alan Sparke.
**Installapool:** ☎ 05 49 39 67 12; email terry@installapool.com; www.installapool.com.

# Gardening

Daffodils are not the only flowers. France is known for its formal gardens, with lots of bushes and geometrical pathways. The flower gardens that are popular in the UK are much less common, even in the north of the country, where the climate is more suitable for this kind of gardening. This is partly a reflection of the formalist tradition in France, as opposed to the British Romantic tradition of William Wordsworth which favours the natural garden. The basic garden is the *jardin potager* or vegetable garden. North-western France has

*'Gardening for pleasure is taking off in France, as more city-dwellers move out of town and find that they have to look after their gardens'*

rainfall comparable to the UK, so there is no problem with having a green lawn all the year round, but even Paris is not that good for lawns. Maintaining a garden in the southern half of France is a rather different experience. South of Limoges-Clermont-Ferrand the climate is dry and hot in summer; the rain falls in spring and autumn, so your lawn is not going to prosper. Lack of regular rain is a major problem in the south of France; the Vendée and Deux-Sèvres are also low rainfall areas, and not suitable for an English garden. There are few parts of southern France where you can grow the thirsty annuals and herbaceous plants we see in England. But the British can at least thank the French for their pansies; the word comes from the French *pensée* meaning 'thought'. Flowers should be planted where they receive morning sun and are protected from afternoon sun.

Pot plants are often the best solution; geraniums are very hardy and do well everywhere. The south-west, especially the Ariège, is famous for its roses. Indeed, roses do well over all over France, except for the Bourbon type. Hotter areas are ideal for wisteria (*glycines*). Around

*'France is known for its formal gardens, with lots of bushes and geometrical pathways'*

Paris one will find all the kinds of bushes and trees that one would expect in south-west England. In the south-east one is looking at a classic Mediterranean garden, with low-maintenance plants such as oleander, hibiscus and creepers, as well as herbs and lavender. Yuccas, palm trees, apricots, olive and cherry trees are obvious plants to keep in the south. There are restrictions on watering during the summer, and it is a requirement to *débroussailler*, that is remove bushes and trees around your house for a distance of 50 m (in some cases) in the south-east, where there have been recently been major bushfires.

You can see from the plants your neighbours have and the region in general what will grow: on rocky ground, such as in Brittany, the soil layer is thin and not suitable for a luxuriant garden. Grass, creepers, ground cover and bushes in pots are often the best solution here. In wine-growing regions there is a lot of clay with limestone. Clay is difficult to work with: muddy and sticky when it rains, but like concrete in summer. However, you can improve it by adding organic material. You may have to remove a lot of small stones if you are taking over a piece of land that has only been used for agriculture in the past. In Normandy there are a lot of flints in the soil. You can improve small sections of gardens (borders and kitchen gardens) by adding a lot of humus (self-made compost) or vermiculite to break up the soil. Mulches such as grass cuttings and straw retain water and prevent weeds from getting out of control. Regularly working the soil by hoeing or rotavating helps to create crumbly, workable soil.

## Garden centres

Gardening for pleasure is taking off in France, as more city-dwellers move out of town and find that they have to look after their gardens. There has also been an increase in garden centres. The range of plants is more limited than in the UK, but at least what you buy is suitable for the prevailing conditions. Many French people buy seeds and plants by mail order, though sometimes the quality is less good than in garden centres, even if the choice is wider. There is little point in bringing gardening equipment over from the UK. The range in France is perfectly adequate. If you need to buy trees and bushes, go to a local nursery or *pépinière*. Useful information about plants and soil types can be found on a website such as www.aujardin.info.

## Gardening reading list

Barbara Abbs, *French Gardens: a region by region guide.*
William Robinson, *Gleanings from French Gardens.*
Louisa Jones, *Gardens of the French Riviera.*
Natasha Spender, *An English Garden in Provence.*
Geraldene Holt, *Diary of a French Herb Garden.*

# My House in France
## Ellie Jones

Ellie, 25 years old, and husband Nicholas have moved from Leicestershire to the Auvergne.

### How did you find the buying process? Can you describe what you went through?

The buying process was straightforward and it was made easier because the estate agent spoke English and they had a translator for the actual signing. The first set of papers were sent to us in the UK so we only actually had to come out once to sign. For the final signing the *notaire* went on holiday which held it up for a week but the owner allowed us to have the key and start moving in before we had completed – with a short contract drawn up in case we did any work on the place in that time.

### What would your advice be to anyone else buying in France?

Try to find someone who speaks the language well if you don't, to go through the paperwork and legal issues. Don't be afraid to haggle on the price. Be aware that the properties on the internet tend to be a lot more expensive than ones in agencies. Visit the area before you decide to move there. Speak to the neighbours about the property you are interested in as they tend to know a lot more than the estate agents.

### What was the move like?

It was very complicated because of all the things we were bringing with us and the fact that we hadn't completed when we moved. We had animals, two horses and a dog, to bring and all our worldly possessions. We had also been living on a narrow boat for the 8 weeks after selling our house in the UK before we moved – so our belongings were all in different places. We had a lot of loose ends to try and tie up, jobs to finish, paperwork and export licences for the horses to organise and transport to find. It was difficult but we managed it.

### Did you have to do any work on the house?

The first thing we did was to replace the roof. Getting permission merely involved a quick chat with the *mairie*. Many of the materials were readily available at the *Bricolages*. We didn't have the money to get someone to do it for us so between Nick and I, and various family members, we stripped the roof and rebuilt it ourselves. We were well prepared for the work but not for the weather, which alternated between roasting hot and howling gales!

We have had to plumb and rewire the whole house as well, again it's being done by ourselves after plenty of reading and researching. Luckily Nick is very clever and good at DIY and I have no problem with heights and labouring, so between us we are doing well. We still have a lot of work ahead of us, but so far, fingers crossed, it is going well.

**What are the main advantages of living in France as far as you are concerned?**

The lifestyle is much better. Although we have had problems with money and the house we still feel more relaxed and happy. Our home is our own outright so we have no mortgage to pay and a huge property to show for it. The French are very laidback and friendly people, and life is a lot quieter.

Living in France has meant meeting some very wonderful friends and embarking on a lifestyle that, although it will be hard for a while, will reward us in the end. We have an active social life, a wonderful home and live in a beautiful country, what more could we want?

**What advice would you give to anyone reading this book who is thinking of moving to France or buying a property there? How would you do things differently?**

I would recommend spending as much time as you can afford in the area where you want to buy. Don't settle for finding property on large websites, look for local agents websites and in *notaires* offices.

Learn the language in any way possible and when you get here, do not sit alone at home and not speak to the French. Everyone knows everyone, especially in rural France so integration is paramount.

Don't be afraid to do renovations yourself, as long as you have the correct planning permission and are confident.

Finally, remember that moving to France is not mad, stupid or brave; it's an adventure, you only live once and I wouldn't change it for the world.

# PART SIX
## Making Money From Your Property

# 18 Letting Your Property

IF YOU ARE HOPING TO MAKE MONEY OUT OF YOUR PROPERTY IN FRANCE then letting it out is probably the most likely solution. This is a growing trend among owners who see property in France as much as an investment as a place to live or to go on holiday. However, as with any investment you need to think it through carefully when buying a place to rent out. Location, as ever, is the key. But there are also a number of more mundane but important technical and legal issues you will need to know, depending on what type of letting you go for.

## Maximising your Income

If you are buying purely to let out your property then the first issue to consider is where to buy. Where you buy and the type of property you purchase will naturally determine what kind of clients you can expect – and how much you will be able to charge. If you buy further south where the weather is warmer and the seasons are longer then you will have a greater chance of higher occupancy rates for short-term lets. On the other hand you will probably be paying far more for the property in the first place so you'll need to make more money to get a decent return on your investment. First, you need to work out who your likely tenants will be and why they would want to rent your place. Will they be foreign, French from another area or locals? You also need to consider the facilities that are near by. How good are the roads, airports, schools, shops and leisure facilities? If you are going for long-term lets you will have to consider whether this is a desirable place to live in all year round. What are the winters like? Another important consideration is the age of the property. Older, character properties can be charming and may appeal to a particular market, perhaps people from overseas wanting to sample 'traditional' French life. But is that the kind of place that local people want to rent? They may prefer a

*'older, character properties can be charming and may appeal to a particular market, perhaps people from overseas wanting to sample 'traditional' French life'*

modern property close to facilities and transport rather than a quaint cottage a kilometre down a remote lane in the countryside. There is also the issue of maintenance and wear and tear. Generally speaking, new properties are easier to maintain than older ones, and thus cheaper as a result. You will also want to be sure that your property has the facilities that people are looking for, for example internet connections and a room they can use as a study/office if necessary. A modern kitchen and a garden will also be good selling points, as will a garage. Under the cost of the project you will have to consider the expense of furnishing the property to a level and quality that will attract tenants. There is little point in furnishing too cheaply, as not only will items need replacing more often, but this will not be attractive to potential tenants. On the other hand, unless you are renting to the luxury end of the market you may not want to pay a fortune for items that will soon get worn and broken under constant use.

## Where?

### Insider Tip

*The obvious benefit of letting out yourself is that you don't have to pay any agency fees to anyone else and so your profit margin should be higher. Managing the let yourself can also give you more flexibility over your own use of the property. And if you live close to the property meeting, greeting and looking after tenants can sometimes have a social benefit too. However, marketing and managing the let will take up more of your time and energy and could cost money too if you need to travel to the property more, especially for short-term lets.*

On the whole the best places for rental purposes will be the south of France, especially along the Mediterranean coast, and the Alps – for short-term winter lets and probably summer lets too. Similarly the Atlantic coast and the Pyrenees are worth considering, as are large prosperous or up-and-coming cities such as Paris, Bordeaux and Marseille. You need to be more careful if thinking about buying to let in the centre of France in places such as the Auvergne, the Centre or the Limousin. Will these properties be in strong demand all year round and will people be willing to pay good money to rent them?

## How Much?

When it comes to pricing, the amount you can charge will obviously depend on where you are in France, the time of year (for holiday or short-term lets) and the type of property and its facilities. You'll need to investigate prices in your area. Some people choose the top end of the local rates, accepting that they may not be full all the time. Others prefer to set the most competitive rates they can to ensure the property is fully occupied.

## Deciding whether to use a letting agent

Should you use a letting agent? Or should you try to market it and let it yourself? There is also an element of security and peace of mind in knowing that someone on hand is responsible for the place. Marketing your property on your own can be tough, even if you have a good personal website. If you do manage the letting yourself, you may want to consider advertising the property on one of the larger websites that attract heavy traffic. To find letting agencies it's

## In the know

**Ross Husband of Rent a Place in France (www.RentaplaceinFrance.com) outlines some rental charges in France:**

Prices obviously vary widely depending on the type of property, location, length of rental and time of year. A cottage sleeping six in Brittany can charge around £350 per week in summer whereas a small village house in Provence sleeping two or four can be £400 per week. If you have a pool you can normally expect about 50% extra for summer holiday lets. As a guideline monthly winter lets can be around the same price as a week peak season holiday rental. A house in Dordogne sleeping six can charge around £500 per month for winter rentals. It's always advisable to check the internet to see what similar properties charge to help gauge your price.

a good idea to contact local estate agents. They will either manage lets themselves, or know someone who does.

## Holiday let versus long-term let

Whether you opt for long-term rental will depend on a number of factors, including the type of facilities near your property, the local climate, the yield you are looking for and the amount of work you are prepared to do or pay for. Holiday lets in good holiday locations can generate the most income, but usually mean more work as there is a quick turn around of tenants. One option is to use short-term lets in the summer to maximise your income but look for longer lets in the off-season. The traditional summer holiday season in France can be quite short, sometimes only stretching to 10 weeks or so. Providing longer lets of a month plus during the rest of the year can be a sensible combination.

# Short-term Letting

Many foreigners only rent out their second home occasionally to people they know, or privately through placing small ads in the UK. Short-term lets of holiday homes come under the *location libre* regime, which protects the owner as long as they observe certain conditions. If the right conditions are not observed, and the tenants refuse to leave the property, there will be major legal costs involved in evicting them. To be able to let your property under the *location libre* regime, the following conditions need to be met (amongst others):

- the property should be fully furnished
- the rental is for no more than three months

- the tenants have a principal residence elsewhere
- the property is only to be used for holidays.

It is advisable to draw up a written contract – *contrat de location* – which includes an inventory of the contents of the property, the *état des lieux*.

## In the know

**Courtney Wylie of www.Holiday-Rentals. co.uk talks about the things to consider when renting out your property:**

If you are depending on income from holiday rentals to make a significant contribution to your dream holiday home in France, it is important that you buy with your head, not your heart. While this may seem obvious, many people investing in property abroad still make the mistake of being led by their personal feelings, rather than by business sense. Any investment should be thoroughly analysed, and a holiday home is no exception!

Travellers to France already have a huge choice of accommodation so you can no longer expect to just buy a property and have a pool of holidaymakers eager and waiting to rent it out. Recent research has shown that French properties rent on average 17 weeks per year, the average weekly rental rate is £945, and the average purchase price is around £320,000.

Bearing in mind these figures, average annual rental income would be £16,065. Despite the competitive market, this shows it is still possible for holiday-home owners in France to achieve a level of rental income that makes a significant contribution towards the total cost of the property each year.

When buying a holiday home, the four criteria people look for are price, size, location and view and the last three should be very carefully considered when buying to rent. These three factors will influence the type of travellers you can rent to, the rates you can charge, and the number of weeks you will be able to rent the property each year. Industry research has also shown that access to a swimming pool is a key factor. So, if your dream property does not have access to a pool, you may need to consider the cost of installing one.

Finally, you need to decide how you will market your property and manage rentals. There are two methods: you can either self-manage your rentals, or employ a rental management agency. An agency will deal with everything for you, but you must remember to factor in commission and fees, which can take up to 30% of your rental income.

(Continued)

The alternative is to manage the process yourself and thanks to the internet, this is actually very simple. With over 50% of travellers now starting their holiday research online, the internet is the best place to advertise, and the most cost effective. With websites such as www.Holiday-Rentals.co.uk, you pay an annual subscription for a full page property listing and travellers can email you via the site. A standard advert includes four colour photographs, text fields to describe the property and location, a full list of facilities, a table for displaying rates and a 12 month availability calendar to help you keep track of bookings. When advertising on a holiday rental site, you will also benefit from their marketing efforts.

If you do choose to self-manage your rentals, make sure you have considered the time it will take, and whichever method you choose, just make sure you've done the maths!

You may prefer to engage a local agent to handle the rental of your property. They will charge a fee of about 15% for managing the rentals. The main consideration is to make sure that the agent is actually handing over the money to you from rentals. It is a good idea to install a telephone in the property that will only take incoming calls, so you can check up if there is someone actually staying there. There are other drawbacks in terms of undesirable tenants trashing your place or upsetting the neighbours. All these aspects have to be covered in letting contracts.

The holiday-let market is very competitive and so you'll need top-quality facilities or some great local attractions. This is why location is so important when choosing a place to buy – esepcialy if you plan to rent it out for significant periods.

## Taxation

If you are not tax resident in France, letting income from French property still has to be declared to the French tax authorities by 30th April each year, on the usual income tax forms: No. 2042, and No. 2042C (specifically for rental income). These are sent to the Recette des Impôts des Non-Résidents, 9 rue d'U'zès, 75094 Paris Cedex 02. You can choose to be taxed under the *Micro-BIC* regime, in which case you will receive a flat-rate deduction of 72% from your gross letting income, which also includes an amount calculated on the basis of how much you have used the property yourself. The net letting income is taxed at a flat rate of 25%, unless the income is very

### Insider Tip

The number of weeks you can expect to rent out a property depends on the climate, and the presence of a swimming pool. The core letting season is only July and August; most French take their holidays in August. The months of June and September are known as 'shoulder months' and have less trade. This should be taken into account when you buy a property where the income is a significant factor in your decision. Outside of the key months you will probably need something special or different to attract visitors, who will have plenty of accommodation to choose from.

small. You should declare your rental income to the UK taxman, and you will have to pay the difference between the 25% tax in France, and higher rate tax in the UK if it applies to you. You may be able to obtain tax relief on the mortgage interest from the UK taxman.

You can also opt to be taxed under the *régime réel* in which case you deduct your expenses, mortgage interest, and 4% annual depreciation from your gross income – *pro rata temporis* – to arrive at your taxable income. The *régime réel* requires you to present a lot more paperwork, but may be advantageous in the end.

There are considerable risks involved in not declaring letting income to the French authorities. If they discover that the property has been let, they can choose to tax you on 52 weeks' letting income, and you will lose the right to tax deductions. While you may get away with not declaring the odd week or two, it is not worth risking a much higher tax bill by not declaring.

> 'there are considerable risks involved in not declaring letting income to the French authorities'

Similarly if you are tax resident outside France you must declare all your income from letting the property to your tax authority. The UK authorities in particular have become aware that a significant number of people tax resident in Britain have not been declaring overseas earnings – including from rental properties in countries such as France. During 2007 the British tax authorities gave a limited form of 'amnesty' in which they allowed people to declare previously undeclared income without facing the usual full penalties for non-declaration.

Whether resident or non-resident, if you let your French property unfurnished, you become liable to the *taxe sur les revenus fonciers*. For this you fill in blue form No. 2044. If your income is under €15,000 you can be taxed under the *micro foncier* regime; otherwise it is the *foncier normal*. There are numerous deductions. The tax is charged on unbuilt land, lakes, factories, and everything that stands on land.

# Long-term Letting

Tenancy agreements (*bail* or *baux* in the plural) can come under one of four possible legal regimes, of which only one is relevant to holiday properties. This is the so-called *location libre* (free tenancy), which is subject only to the articles 1708 to 1762 of the *Code Civil*. The rental agreement can be for a defined or indeterminate period of time, and can be verbal or written. Because the provisions of the *Code Civil* are in the lessor's favour, the state has imposed certain conditions to prevent abuses. In the first place, it is only applicable to fully furnished premises (fully furnished meaning that the tenant has everything they need to be able to live on the premises), or to second homes or holiday homes. Where the lessor rents out more than four properties of this type, the rental contract is always for a year, and is automatically renewed, unless one of the parties gives notice, which is three months from the side of the lessor, and a month from the side of the lessee.

French law has recently changed for some furnished rentals. Previously, there was no legal requirement to use a lease for a furnished rental and it was possible to agree any duration. As from 2005, except for holiday lets, a contract of at least a year is legally required if renting furnished property to a tenant who owns no other property or has no other tenancy agreement as his main residence. If the tenant has other accommodation as his main residence then there is still no legal requirement for a lease (it can be of any duration). The parties are free to agree their own terms and contracts can vary. The problem lies where the tenant is effectively of no fixed abode, perhaps when the tenant has sold his home in the UK or elsewhere, and the French rental property will be his main residence for a time.

So, if a year's lease is legally required, how can you amend its duration so both tenant and owner are happy signing it? Many furnished rentals are for periods of considerably less than a year and rentals of several months are common. In these cases both owner and tenant are unlikely to feel happy signing a year's lease. It is true the tenant can end the rental by giving a month's notice. But many will still feel uncomfortable signing a year's lease for perhaps a six-month rental. One solution is for the tenant to supply written notice several days after signing the lease and prior to the date of entry. By signing a notice

> *'So, if a year's lease is legally required, how can you amend its duration so both tenant and owner are happy signing it?'*

to quit at the outset for a given date, say six months from date of entry, the year's lease is effectively transformed into a six-month lease. Both tenant and owner know where they stand, and the owner is then free to take on further lets after the notice period ends.

# Evictions

Most long-term rental agreements now come under the law of July 1989, which gives tenants considerable protection against eviction, but proprietors can still eject tenants who behave unreasonably, after obtaining an injunction from a civil magistrate (*juge d'instance*). Eviction is a long-winded process. If tenants cannot pay their rent then social services will be called in. It can take years – though in reality it is often a matter of months – to get to the point of forcible eviction; the police are generally very reluctant to get involved.

The only situation where a tenant can stop paying the rent is when the property has become uninhabitable. If the proprietor persistently refuses to make repairs, the tenant can first call in a bailiff (*huissier*) to make a report on the nature of the problem, and then obtain an injunction from a magistrate to carry out the repairs him or herself. The tenant can then legally withhold a part of the rent to pay the costs.

Tenants are given considerable leeway to make necessary improvements to a property, but any permanent additions become the property of the owner when they leave. They cannot, however, replace permanent appliances or equipment such as baths or heaters without the owner's permission. If they want to install a satellite dish or new aerial on the outside of the property, they are required to ask the owner's permission. If the owner doesn't respond within three months to a request, then it is assumed that permission has been given. Proprietors may

## In the Know

**Ross Husband runs a company called Rent a Place in France (www. RentaplaceinFrance.com), and is based in the Haute-Garonne. He has the following advice if you are considering long-term letting:**

There is a lot of competition for summer holiday rentals and the season can be quite short. Another option would be to take on longer furnished lets of a month or more. These can run at any time of the year but are particularly popular in the off-season when rentals are more affordable.

If you are considering longer lets ensure your property is suitably heated and furnished for winter and you can offer good unbroken periods of availability. Make it clear what the tenant needs to pay for and when. Some owners offer an attractive 'all inclusive' price but it is more common to charge extra for such things as utilities and firewood,

> 'There is a lot of competition for summer holiday rentals'

especially so in the winter months. Ideally, the prospective tenant should visit the property before committing, to it – this is particularly important for longer lets of six months or so. It is advisable to ask for references and to use a lease for longer rentals. These can easily be obtained from paper shops or your *notaire* should be able to help. Guides to renting and leases can also be downloaded from www.pap.fr.

Effective advertising where your property is accurately and well presented for your market is crucial. Try an appropriate Google search such as 'long lets in France' to help here. Remember most of your potential tenants will be conducting similar searches.

An attractive option for many owners is to rent out weekly in the summer to holidaymakers and then take on longer lets during the winter months. Many of these longer lets are sought by house hunters, but they are also in demand among artists, writers, people on sabbaticals and extended holidaymakers.

It can also be worthwhile offering some value-added services. Think of your skills and your market. A combination of some of the following might be worth considering: airport runs, guided walks, arranging transportation and picnics for clients own self-guided days out, hiring out bikes and sports equipment, painting or photography courses, baking and cooking classes, property search and general advice on purchasing.

be held liable for losses caused by theft if it can be shown that the construction of the house makes it easy for burglars to enter.

# Working at a rental

It is normal to carry on a profession in a rented property, such as working as an architect or doctor, while also living there. Since 2003, you have an absolute right to register a business at your home address for five years; you are only required to inform the landlord. Tenants are permitted to run their business from home, on condition that:

- they do not receive customers at home
- there are no deliveries
- they are working from their principal residence.

# Rental payment

Payment intervals can be set by agreement with the owner of the property, but the prospective tenant can legally insist that payment should occur monthly. The tenant can ask the owner to come to the property once a month to collect the rent in cash; owners cannot compel tenants to agree to pay by bank transfer, or other non-cash form of payment. In practice, payment will most likely be by standing order but this does not follow automatically.

As in the UK, rental payments may not be used in lieu of notice. The repayment of the rental deposit (*dépôt de garantie*) will only take place after the tenant has vacated the premises.

# Increases in rent

The rental contract should spell out on what grounds rent can be increased. Improvements to the property can be used as a justification for an increase, but the general practice is to limit increases to reflect the rise in the index of building costs (*indice de la coût de la construction*), or where the rent is manifestly too low. A cost-of-living index, or other indexes showing rises in average rents cannot be used to justify rent increases, on the principle that like must be compared with like. The proprietor will have to show that the rent is too low by giving examples of average rents in the area; in the Paris, Lyon and Marseille regions rents of six different properties comparable to the one in question will be listed, in the rest of the country only three. In the Paris area the rent can only be raised by half the difference between the average rent in the area and the rent in the contract. In the same region, where the owner has spent the equivalent of at least a year's rent on improvements, the rent can be raised by 15% per year.

# Conciliation services

Where a dispute has arisen, one or both parties can apply for the mediation of a *conciliateur de justice*, a professional conciliator; the departmental prefecture will give you the name and address. The services of the conciliator are free of charge. Neither party is obliged to act on the conciliator's recommendations. These are deposited with the local civil magistrate, and will be taken into account if the case is heard in court.

## Rights and duties of owners

The principal duties of owners are to supply the dwelling as agreed, to keep it in a good state of repair, and not to interfere with the tenant's use of the dwelling. As a bare minimum owners have to ensure that there is running water, although even this condition can be got around with the agreement of the tenant. Owners have to give warning if they plan to carry out major repairs. If the repairs go on for more than 40 days then the tenant is entitled to a reduction in rent.

Damage caused by defects in the construction of the house, e.g. water seeping through the walls, is the owner's liability. If a tenant is affected by 'hidden defects' (*vices cachés*) they can gain legal redress, similarly to when one buys a property. If the owner shows someone around a property and it subsequently comes to light that defects, such as damp patches or mould, were covered up, then tenants may ask for repairs to be carried out. If the defects in a property actually limit the tenant's ability to enjoy its use, then they may request a lower rent.

## Who pays for what?

The issue of who has to pay for what is regulated by decree No. 87-713 passed in 1987, but this only covers a part of the possible items that could become a subject of dispute. In other cases, legal precedent will influence the judge to decide one way or the other. Rental agreements drawn up under the 1989 law do not allow owners to make tenants responsible for all repairs to the property. Under the *location libre* rules, which derive from the *Code Civil*, tenants can in theory be made liable for all repairs, even including major ones, but the courts are likely to decide in the tenant's favour if the amount of money involved is excessive.

Certain general principles apply in disputes. Firstly, tenants are not expected to pay for repairs to any items that are not mentioned in the rental agreement, but the owner can always point to legal precedent to show that the law is on his or her side. Tenants are not required to pay for the maintenance of any item that they never actually use. If you live on the ground floor you do not have not pay for the lift.

As a guiding principle, tenants have to pay for 'running repairs' (*entretien courant*) which arise out of their use of the property, on the basis that the item should still be in working order when they leave the property. This does not mean, however, that they have to restore everything to its original condition. The owner is expected to pay for 'normal repairs' (*entretien normal*), which is interpreted as meaning major repairs to the premises, or replacement of the larger working parts of machinery. Tenants are not required to pay for the repair of equipment if it stops working because of old age. The tenant can obtain a statement from a repair person that the equipment is worn out. If the owner refuses to have the item repaired, then the tenant can go to a lower civil court – *tribunal d'instance* – and compel the owner to pay up.

Under normal circumstances an inspection report *(état des lieux contradictoire)* will be drawn up in the presence of both parties before the start of the tenancy, listing all defects to the property. The tenants are then protected from malicious demands by the landlord when they leave.

## Taxation and rental agreements

The taxation of rental income has been dealt with above. Certain taxes related to rented property are considered to be *charges récuperables* (charges to be paid for by the tenant). Owners are required to pay what is known as *la contribution sur les revenus locatifs* (CRL) or letting right tax to the central government. This works out at 2.5% of income from rental above €1,830 on properties older than 15 years.

Tenants are liable for a *taxe d'habitation* as from 1st January. The rental agreement can require them to pay from the time they move in. The land tax – *taxe foncière* – is the owner's responsibility. The tenant will be required to pay the local *taxe d'enlèvement des ordures menagères* – domestic rubbish collection tax – and then can send the bill through to the owner. Taxes for road cleaning or snow clearing are also the responsibility of the tenant. Where the precise amount of the rubbish collection tax is not stated by the municipality in its tax demand, the tenant cannot be made to pay it.

# Leaseback

A popular way among the French of buying investment property is by using a system called leaseback, which we have covered in chapter 8. Many overseas buyers like to take the option where they can stay at the property for a few weeks a year – the management company to whom you have leased it then rents it out for the rest of the time. In such cases you obviously need to buy somewhere where you want to go on holiday. Of course, if you take this option you will get a lower return on your investment than if it is let out all the time. If you are planning to buy a leaseback property purely as an investment and not to stay there yourself, then you must think with your head and not your heart. It doesn't matter if the property is not in an area where you want to go on holiday – what matters is the likely return you'll get on your investment. So you might want to consider leaseback options in large cities such as Bordeaux, Marseille and Paris, as well as in rural areas. Once again, think about where most people in France want to go on holiday or to live – big thriving cities, the coast, the south – when making this kind of investment.

☑ *Been there, done it...*

**Ian and Sheralee Hayes-Fry from Les Perdigots in the Haute Garonne share their experience of letting out property in France.**

We moved to L'Isle-en-Dodon in 2002 with the idea of letting *gîtes* while renovating our 17th-century farmhouse, and since then we have successfully let 'The Villa' and 'The Bakehouse' for both summer holiday and long-term off-season rentals.

We'd always intended to offer something more than the 'indoor camping' we remembered from *gîtes* of old, and we've tried to provide a real 'home from home' with fully equipped kitchens, comfortable furnishings, satellite TV and internet access.

Having invested in our *gîtes*, we were keen to maximise our rentals as we'd been advised that 12 weeks occupancy was good, and anything approaching 20 was optimistic.

We felt there were more possibilities than this, with people looking for reasonably priced, long-term rentals – and this would increase our income opportunities, and keep our properties occupied through the winter months.

We already had a good marketing base for summer lets, and decided to advertise on the internet for long-term tenants out of season. By chance, one of our first winter guests was in the process of setting up a specialist website for this very purpose, and www. RentaplaceinFrance.com has since provided most of our long-term bookings!

People have stayed here for house hunting, to learn French, for academic research in nearby Toulouse, or to simply unwind for a few months. We've found that these guests are generally more self-contained and independant than summer holidaymakers, and become more like neighbours. This works well for everyone, on a practical and personal level, as we can all enjoy our own space, while our guests always know that a helping hand or a glass of wine is never very far away.

# 19 Running A Business From Your Property

**M**OVING TO FRANCE COULD PROVIDE THE OPPORTUNITY, or necessity, of starting up a business. A surprising number of people buy a house and move to France and only *then* consider how they will earn their living. There are all sorts of possibilities, such as starting up an art gallery, a dogs' beauty parlour, taking over a café, or running cultural holidays.

A good deal of imagination may be needed to find an idea that will sell. One of the more original ones was the Camembert heritage centre started up by Rosemary Rudland in the heart of the village of Camembert, which became something of a *cause célèbre*. Whatever you do, make sure you plan well in advance and, above all, be realistic about your likely income and profits. If you're new to running a business then expect to make mistakes – they key thing is to learn from them as quickly as possible.

If you are starting up as a self-employed person – perhaps a professional such as an IT consultant – then you should register immediately with your local branch of URSSAF–*Unions de Recouvrement des Cotisations de Sécurité Sociale et d'Allocations Familiales* – who will handle such issues as the payment of your social charges. To find your local branch visit: www.urssaf.fr. Remember that in France only about half of working people pay income tax. Unless you are a medium to high earner in France by far your biggest tax will be what are called social charges. In effect they are the French equivalent of National Insurance in the UK, only higher.

As far as taxation goes, you can be considered a *micro-entreprise*. The ceiling on turnover is €76,300 if you are selling goods, or food; otherwise it is only €27,000. Above this, you have to register for TVA and

## Insider Tip

Before you can do anything, you will have to register with the local chambre de commerce, who will send you on a business management course to make sure that you are a fit person to run a business. You may not understand everything that you are being taught, but the bookkeeping advice will be useful.

☑ *Been there, done it...*

**Anne Pilling has worked as a self-employed Certified Counsellor in Nice since 2003, via a UK-registered company, Calmcare Ltd.**

I qualified as a State Registered Nurse in 1971, and then went into counselling in 1986 with two internationally known treatment centres. I have also trained in massage and Reiki (Japanese spiritual healing) and bereavement counselling. In 2001 I started to think about what I had not done in my life, and one of them was to start a company, so I registered Calmcare in the UK. Here I am registered under my own name. I came to Nice knowing one person, and he was able to help me over the first hurdles in getting started as a self-employed therapist. I obtained my SIRET and SIREN numbers, and went along to URSSAF (the social security agency), who passed on my details to various other agencies, who in turn sent me forms to sign for various payments. My social security payments are very substantial, but there is no way of avoiding them. I pay pension contributions to CIPAV, a national organisation for professionals such as myself.

I also use the services of a business adviser, which removes a lot of my day-to-day concerns with bureaucracy. I am a *micro-entreprise* for tax purposes, which means that I deduct a fixed percentage of my income to cover all expenses. I still pay National Insurance contributions in the UK in order to receive a full UK pension.

Although I offer a number of services, my clients mostly request counselling, and come from a range of backgrounds, from boat captains to stewardesses to villa managers from Monaco and other Côte d'Azur residents. I offer help with eating disorders of anorexia, bulimia and compulsive overeating, codependency issues, family and relationship problems and grief therapy.

keep full accounts. If you use premises that can be visited by the public you are liable for the *taxe professionnelle,* rather than the *taxe d'habitation.*

Further details can be found in the forthcoming *Starting a Business in France,* published by Vacation Work. You can also find guidance on setting up a business or becoming self-employed in France at www.frenchentree.com.

# Bed and Breakfast/*Gîtes*

For many Britons the best, or only, way to make a living in France is to rent out rooms in their property, either as *chambres d'hôtes* (bed and breakfast) or as *gîtes* (basic self-catering accommodation). French rules state that if you rent out more than five rooms or *chambres d'hôtes* in your property, then you are actually running a hotel and will therefore be liable for VAT and other paperwork. The alternative to bed and breakfast are *gîtes:* the word originally meant a basic dwelling, but is now applied to any kind of self-catering lodgings. *Gîtes* are less lucrative than bed and breakfast, and it is reckoned that you need space for at least 15 people to make a living from them. There has been a downturn in the *gîtes* market in recent years, and many owners are struggling to make

> 'the alternative to bed and breakfast are gîtes: the word originally meant a basic dwelling, but is now applied to any kind of self-catering lodgings.'

ends meet. This is partly to do with the proliferation of such places, but also with the general downturn in the tourist trade in France following 9/11. Statistically, only 6,000 households make a full-time living out of *gîtes* in France. In general terms those *gîtes* that do well have something special or different to offer. This might be stunning views, large swimming pools, top-of-the-range furniture and fittings or a range of activities and leisure facilities on hand. At least one has started to offer 'carbon neutral' holidays to cater for people worried about the effect of their holiday on global warming. It's also true that – to a certain extent – the *gîtes* market has 'eaten itself'. Many people holidaying in such places throughout France were so attracted by the lifestyle that they decided to have a go themselves. The result was that in some areas supply rose and demand fell. This doesn't mean you can't make a living by owning *gîtes*, simply that you need to do your homework in advance, study the market and be realistic.

The buying process for *gîtes* is slightly more complex because the *Société d'Aménagement Foncier et d'Etablissement Rural* (SAFER) has a right to make an offer on the property. It is up to the *notaire* to contact anyone who has pre-emptive rights to make sure that they do not intend to exercise them.

Before you even consider buying property to let out furnished, you must be aware that it is not possible to rent out furnished property in *communes* with over 10,000 inhabitants if you are classed as a professional landlord, i.e. over 50% of your income comes from rentals, or where rental income exceeds €23,000 a year. This restriction can be waived where a property is regularly let in a tourist area. Before you do anything else you should make sure that you do not fall foul of this rule.

Before buying a property with a view to renting it to holidaymakers, you need to make a hard-headed analysis about the attractions of the place.

- Is the place easy to get to?
- Are there any cultural attractions nearby?

## Insider Tip

It is important to note that chambres d'hôte and gîtes come under a legal regime relating to farms: the original concept involved farmers letting people stay with them to make a bit of extra money. Before you can buy a farmhouse to make it into chambres d'hôte or gîtes the local farmers' cooperatives or SAFER have a right to make an offer on the property (though they tend to be more interested in properties with lots of land); this makes the buying process a little more uncertain.

- How far is it from the sea/mountains/lakes?
- How will it look in a photograph?
- How much income do I need to make it viable?
- How many weeks of the year do I want to use it myself?
- Can I get a grant to renovate the place?
- How much will it cost to furnish?
- Can I install a swimming pool?
- Are there any shops nearby?
- How long is the potential letting season?
- What is the weather like in spring and autumn?
- Can you extend the season e.g. by offering long winter lets?
- What are local competitors offering?

Making a success of chambres d'hôte requires a willingness to open your home to outsiders, and to be genuinely hospitable at all hours. There is no requirement to supply evening meals, although it is a plus point in country areas, where your guests may have to go a long way to find a restaurant. If cooking is not your forte, you might be best advised to have your chambres d'hôte near some restaurants. Not supplying dinner will cut down on your potential profit. Installing a swimming pool is the easiest way to maximise your takings, but not every property is big enough or suitable for one. Remember to take into account not only the cost of installation but also ongoing maintenance. One potential downside with a pool is that it may tempt your guests to linger – for a B&B operation this could lead to some guests outstaying their welcome.

> 'making a success of chambres d'hôte requires a willingness to open your home to outsiders, and to be genuinely hospitable at all hours'

The gîtes business is rather different from chambres d'hôte. All that is needed is someone to handle the changeover between guests, and to see that they have everything that they require. There is also cleaning, of course. There are many agencies who will deal with the whole process, but you will need to pay them up to around 15% of your letting income. The organisation Chez Nous is well known in the UK, but it is not universally popular with foreign owners in France, who consider that it attracts too many undesirable customers. It is never that easy to accept complete strangers staying in your house and maybe doing damage to it.

Furniture and equipment for holiday rental property or gîtes needs to be adequate but not too expensive, since there will inevitably be breakages. It is best to buy plain IKEA-type furniture that fits in with the surroundings. Older French houses tend to be dark and badly lit by British standards; holidaymakers prefer bright, light colours. Attention to detail is important. It is often the little things that can help make – or sometimes ruin – someone's stay. Remember too that guests' expectations are constantly rising and you will need to update and refresh your facilities.

# ✓ Been there, done it...

**Jane and John Edwards'** *chambres d'hôtes* **at Pauliac near Verteillac, Dordogne, have the reputation of being some of the finest in France (see www.pauliac.fr). They are listed in Alastair Sawday's** *Special Places to Stay.*

My father had bought the larger of the two houses in 1983 and was having it done up with a view to doing B&B with his wife but she died in 1985. The house was empty for 4 years and in the meantime the house next door came up for sale, so we bought it and did it up for us to live in. Both buildings are of limestone; we created bedrooms for B&B with stud partitions, and put in new floors. Because we liked bare stone at the time, we removed a lot of plaster and jointed between the stones. There was an existing *citerne* in the garden used to collect water from the roofs, which is now the plunge pool, and my husband dug out a smaller children's pool. We did most of the conversion work ourselves, and called in friends with more expert knowledge when we needed to.

My husband got a job early on, a government-sponsored job for the unemployed. The business was in my name and he had no 'status' and we didn't know that he could be a *conjoint collaborateur* (business partner spouse) at that stage. Training courses weren't compulsory in the olden days, but I now receive training as I pay an annual fee to URSSAF (the social security organisation) entitling me to €1,500 worth of training per annum. The money for the training is paid through the *chambre de commmerce* and AGEFICE, an organisation for non-salaried directors of small companies.

One of the main differences between the UK and France is that it is very difficult to obtain an overdraft or credit. Generally I don't think it is France that makes it difficult to run a business; it is to do with oneself. If you're good at jumping through the hoops and diligent and attend to the details then it's just a system to be mastered like any other bureaucracy. It would have been helpful if we had known how much social security contributions were going to be, and how to reclaim them. We never approached *Gîtes de France* for a grant. Try to get in a guide if you do B&B. We did much better once we had done this. Newspapers are a waste of time and money. We were very naive in retrospect; we thought 'if it doesn't work out we can just go back.' Our children were young then and we weren't too worried that they couldn't cope with a new country.

Running *gîtes* is a very seasonal business: the core months are July and August. Often the rooms will be unsuitable for use in cold weather.

## Grants

Before you do any work on a property, or even buy it, look into the possibility of applying for grants for the building work. Grants for *gîtes* are distributed by the local *Conseil Général* – the departmental government – through *Gîtes de France*, which is organised on a regional basis.

## Insider Tip

*It is a good idea to consider supplying some added services, such as sport facilities, rented bicycles or internet access. Linking your gîtes with courses in painting, yoga, or whatever, may be the only way to bring in enough customers. If you choose to do cooking for your guests, Gîtes de France attaches conditions to the type of food you can serve in a chambres d'hôtes: it has to be sourced locally and be typical of the region. It should also be given a French name; the British will turn up their noses at Stewed Rabbit, but they will love Civet de Lapin.*

The amounts available vary considerably. If you are lucky *Gîtes de France* may match the amount you spend. One British owner in Normandy who had spent €3,600 on conversion work was told by *Gîtes de France* that the work couldn't possibly have cost that little and was given €4,500 in matching funds. In other areas, the *département* may have little money to hand out.

There are conditions attached: you have to agree to allow *Gîtes de France* to handle the lettings and publicity for 10 years during the summer in return for a cut of your takings of 12%–15%. They have the final say in what kind of facilities your *gîtes* will have, and grades your premises in its catalogue with one to three *épis* or wheatears. If you sell the property within 10 years then the grant must be returned.

There are plenty of other organisations that can hand out grants, starting with the EU. The most important person to talk to is the local mayor, who not only knows about possible grants, but also has the power to approve building permits. Some grants are handled by the local *chambre de commerce*, who will be very pleased to help you. Because of the very high unemployment in country areas, any kind of business initiative is viewed very favourably, but you should have the right people on your side first. You should also contact the local *Office du Tourisme* or the *Syndicat d'Initiative*, whose function is to promote all kinds of small businesses and investments as well as tourism. If you are buying a listed building or one with special historical associations, there will be more generous grants available, but any renovations will be subject to more stringent requirements. Whatever kind of renovation you plan to do, all the plans and estimates must be approved first before any work is started, otherwise you will not receive the grant.

## Publicity

'some foreign owners find the demands of Gîtes de France intolerable and try to find other ways of publicising their gîtes or chambres d'hôte'

Some foreign owners find the demands of *Gîtes de France* intolerable and try to find other ways of publicising their *gîtes* or *chambres d'hôte*. There are other organisations that will handle your publicity, notably Chez Nous in the UK, but whoever you deal with, it will cost you money. Chez Nous charge a flat fee as do most websites. The alternative is to sign up with a website or advertise in UK magazines and newspapers, or even in local shops. If your *chambres d'hôte* are outstanding then you might be taken up by a specialised catalogue, such as Alastair Sawday's *Special Places to Stay in France*, but few qualify for this kind of honour. You should of course create your own website to publicise your business. It's worth taking some time to learn about search engine optimisation – SEO in the jargon. This is the process by which you make your own site more visible to search engines and thus more visible to potential customers. Try a Google search for 'SEO' and you'll find plenty of websites and companies offering advice on this technical but important subject.

## Publicity organisations

www.abritel.fr (a French site)
www.chateauxandcountry.com (specialises in châteaux)
www.cheznous.com
www.dordogne-vacances.com
www.holiday-rentals.co.uk
www.francedirect.com
www.frenchentree.com
www.quality-villas.co.uk
www.renting-abroad.com
www.villarama.com
www.villas-gites-cottages-france.com

## Taxation and bed and breakfast

If running *chambres d'hôte/gîtes* is your full-time occupation, and your turnover is under €76,300 annually, then you can qualify as a *micro-entreprise*. Capital gains are not included in the above figure. You do not have to set up a business structure or pay TVA. The simple solution is to be taxed under the *Micro-BIC* regime. Your taxable income is your turnover minus 72%, so you are taxed on the remaining 28% (on 2004 income). This regime is not obligatory – you can choose to be taxed on your real income (*régime réel*) – and it is not necessarily favourable to the taxpayer. You will need to keep separate records of all your expenses and income, in a standard daybook, but you do not have to present full accounts at the end of each year. On the tax return No. 2042C you simply enter your total turnover, and the type of services supplied at different locations.

If the net income from rentals exceeds €23,000, or constitutes more than 50% of your household income, then you are considered a professional landlord; you will be required to register as a business and you will pay higher social security taxes on the income. If the property is sold the capital gains will be treated as business rather than private gains. Non-residents can be taxed under the *Micro-BIC* regime, and are then taxed at a flat rate 25% on the net rental income.

It is a moot point whether you will be liable for the *taxe professionnelle* if you rent out *gîtes* and *chambres d'hôtes*. There are three cases where exemption may be granted by the local administration, namely:

- the renting out of *gîtes* for 6 months or less per year in a principal or secondary dwelling
- premises classed as 'furnished premises for tourists' which form part of your principal dwelling
- the renting out of any part of a dwelling, not covered by the former.

There is no certainty that you will receive this exemption; it depends on local practice.

If your household's net assets exceed €760,000 then you will be liable for wealth tax: ISF. It may be possible to have items that you need to run *gîtes* or *chambres d'hôte* exempted from wealth tax.

If you rent out furnished property then you are considered a *loueur en meublés* by the taxman. Your guests are considered tenants, and you become liable for a tax that was once known as the *droit de bail* (letting tax), but is now called the *contribution sur les revenus locatifs* (CRL). The name has changed several times recently, and many still call it the *droit de bail*. If you come under the *Micro-BIC* regime, the basis of calculation is the net income exceeding €1,830 attributable to rentals. The tax is only levied on properties over 15 years old.

You should consider all the possibilities for tax deductions. If you have taken out a loan, the interest may be tax-deductible. The local tax office or an accountant will advise you. For further information on running *gîtes* see *Starting a Business in France* published by Vacation Work. Also see *Letting French Property Successfully*, by Stephen Smith and Charles Parkinson, published by PKF Guernsey.

# 20 Selling On

WHEN YOU BUY YOUR PROPERTY, it is well worth thinking about how easy it will be to sell on. There are parts of France where prices of old property are not likely to increase much in the future, namely Alsace-Lorraine and all of central France, especially Auvergne. On the other hand, Provence and the west coast are generally a very safe bet. More and more people are moving to western France, so Brittany and Normandy should see some price rises. In fact buying anywhere along the French coast – the west or the Mediterranean – is probably a reasonably secure option. This is where the French themselves want to live so demand should remain high.

Paris is perhaps more uncertain, as the population is going to get younger according to the projections of the French Institute of Statistics. On the whole, though, Parisian property is far more likely to appreciate in value than, say, a remote home in the Auvergne, however beautiful it may be. The old saying about location applies just as much in France as anywhere else. Just because you like an area – perhaps for its wildness or remoteness – doesn't mean many others will necessarily share your feelings. If you are selling on to other foreigners, then prices may depend on what happens to the UK property market. As we stated at the beginning of this book, buying property in France as an investment does not make much sense unless you know exactly what you are doing and know the right areas.

## Decision to Sell

We can't always choose when to sell our property – sometimes the decision is forced upon us. A change of job, family bereavement or a change in financial circumstances may be the trigger. The problem is that this can mean you are putting your property on the market at a bad time or when the house itself is not at its best.

If you can choose the time of your selling then this should put you in a stronger position. Naturally you want to sell on a rising market not a falling one, so make sure that you keep in touch with local price trends as well as national ones. You might, for example, be able to wait until a new low-cost air service has been brought to your area, or a new TGV route – these are factors that could

> '*naturally you want to sell on a rising market not a falling one*'

boost your home's value. Choosing the time you sell also gives you time to put right any obvious and easy-to-fix problems with the property, especially those that might prove an obstacle to getting a sale. Simple cosmetic improvements such as mowing the lawn, tidying borders, painting windows and doors and clearing up yards can make a huge difference. But don't be tempted to pay a small fortune on improvements if you have no hope of recovering this money in the selling price. Having time on your side will also enable you to do some research and find out which is the best way of selling property in your area – be it privately or through an agency.

## Using an Agent

It is usual to place the property with an estate agent or a *notaire*, who will add their commission to the selling price. There are British estate agents in many areas who may do a better job of marketing your property than a French one would. They will certainly be more likely to be able to reach more easily he market you are aiming at if you are looking to sell to a foreign buyer. On the other hand if your property might be more attractive to someone from Paris or a local then you may want to consider a French agent who is plugged into that particular market. The principal disadvantage if you sell through an estate agent is that you will – in most cases – have to pay their fees. It is quite common now for the seller to pay an agent's fees. You must check on the fees in advance, before you sign any contract with an agency. You should also decide on whether you sign an exclusive contract with an agency or a non-exclusive one. The latter would allow you to sell the house privately if you were able to. Agency fees are lower for exclusive contracts, however. There are obviously some key advantages in using an agency; you are using people who are experienced and

### Insider Tip

*If you need to sell quickly you simply have to accept that you may be at a disadvantage. You may have to accept an offer on your property that is well under your asking price. There is little point in inflating the asking price in the first place to allow for this, as this will simply reduce the number of people who come to see it.*

hopefully good at selling, who know the local market and who, crucially, are likely to know where they can find buyers. A key point is to have a good photograph of your property; this is not as easy as it sounds, and you may be best advised to use a professional photographer. Unless the photograph is taken in the right way, the lines of the house tend to look distorted on websites and this certainly won't help you sell it.

## Selling Privately

You can try to advertise it privately, or put your house on an English website featuring private sellers, such as www.1st-for-french-property.co.uk or www.frenchentree.com. Most British sellers try to sell to other foreigners, on the basis that they can expect to obtain a better price. It used to be the case that the British were more likely to pay a little over the odds, while the poverty-stricken Germans paid less. However, the British have begun to be a little more prudent in their buying habits, while the recovery of the German economy has sparked new interest in buying property in France. It's also worth considering how you can sell your property to Parisians, many of whom are looking for second homes away from the capital. Ask around and you will found out which agents are best at reaching the Parisian market. You also need to watch out for scams, especially from buyers who urge you to make the sale a part cash transaction to reduce fees.

The regulations governing French estate agents have already been explained. From the seller's point of view, you can choose to give the agent a *mandat simple* or a *mandat exclusif.* In the first case, you can place the property with as many estate agents as you like, or find a buyer yourself. The agent is paid a commission if they introduce a successful buyer to you. With a *mandat exclusif* only one estate agent will look for buyers. You have to specify whether you wish to retain the right to look for buyers yourself – a *mandat exclusif simple* – or whether you give up that right – the *mandat exclusif absolu.* In the first case, the agent's commission is reduced if you find a buyer yourself; in the second, you would have to pay the agent an indemnity if you found a buyer yourself.

A *mandat* is for a limited time period. The seller can withdraw from the *mandat,* subject to certain conditions. After three months, a *mandat exclusif* can, in all cases, be cancelled through a registered letter. It is normal these days for the seller to pay the agent's commission.

## Insider Tip

When selling it is normal to emphasise the amount of attic space that could be converted, and to mention the proximity of railway stations and airports. According to some reports, Britons may pay up to 10% more for a property that is within easy reach of an airport with a low-cost service to the UK.

## Sharp practices

At one time the Masheder family owned a house in a village near Uzès in the Gard. In 1992, when the property market was very sluggish, they let a local agent know that they wanted to sell the property. What happened next took them by surprise:

We received a telephone call from a local Frenchman who was very excited about buying the property from us and asked us to come down to meet him as soon as we could. We got on the first plane and rushed down there, but were amazed to find that the supposed buyer had put up his own For Sale sign at a higher price than he was offering us. He was obviously hoping to find another buyer and pocket the difference. He used the excuse that he hadn't found a mortgage to get out of the contract. We never met the so-called buyer, and he removed the For Sale sign while our backs were turned. In the meantime, of course, we had lost a lot of time, and we couldn't sell the property until the following year. In the end we sold it to some Swiss people.

# Defects in the Property

As we have seen in chapter 11, owners are required to have reports drawn up on the possible presence of asbestos, termites and lead paint. As a general rule, the seller cannot be held liable for *vices apparents*, or visible defects in the property. The issue of *vices cachés*, or latent defects, is more complicated. It is normal to insert a clause into the final contract freeing the seller of responsibility if the buyer subsequently discovers latent defects, but this does not protect the seller from claims for compensation if it can be shown that the seller could reasonably have been expected to know about the defect.

> *'owners are required to have reports drawn up on the possible presence of asbestos, termites and lead paint'*

# Taxation on Property Sales

If you sell your French property within 15 years of having acquired it, then you will be liable to French capital gains tax, unless it is your principal residence. There are potential ways around paying French CGT, which are explained in chapter 15. You are not subject to French taxes on proceeds if you sell a property outside France.

# The Property Glossary

## General

| | |
|---|---|
| à débattre | negotiable |
| à rénover | to be renovated |
| aménageable | can be put to use |
| un appentis | lean-to |
| attenant | adjoining |
| BE/bon état/bien entretenu | good condition; well-maintained |
| un/les bien(s) | goods, property, estate, assets |
| le bornage | boundary marking |
| les bornes | boundary markers |
| la buanderie | washhouse |
| le carrelage | tiling |
| carrelé tiled | tiled |
| la cave | cellar |
| la cazelle | dry-stone shepherd's shelter; micro-gîte |
| CC/commission comprise | estate agent's commission included |
| le cellier | storeroom, pantry |
| le chai | wine/spirit storehouse |
| le chauffage fuel | oil heating |
| la clôture | fencing, paling, hedge or other enclosure |
| les combles aménageables | loft conversion possible |
| le crépi | roughcast |
| le débarras | junk-room |
| les dépendances | outhouses |
| un double séjour | large living room |
| une écurie | stables |
| en étage | on the same floor |
| en exclusivité | only one estate agent is handling the sale |
| F1 | one room + kitchen/bathroom |
| FAC/frais agence compris | agency's commission included |
| le galetas | garret; hovel |
| le grenier | attic |
| HNC/honoraires agence non compris | agent's commission not included |
| HT/hors taxes | not including taxes |

| | |
|---|---|
| un immeuble | apartment block, or commercial property |
| le madrier | beam |
| la maison de caractère | dilapidated or unusual |
| la maison mitoyenne | semi-detached; terrace house |
| mitoyenne d'un coté | end of terrace; semi-detached |
| n.c./non compris | not included |
| la penderie | wardrobe |
| le piano | cooking range |
| le plain pied | one storey |
| les poutres apparentes | exposed beams |
| les prestations | features |
| le ravalement | rendering |
| refait à neuf | completely renovated |
| le rez/rez de chaussé | RDC ground floor |
| la salle | living room |
| sans mitoyenneté | no commonly owned boundary walls or structures |
| sans vis-à-vis | no houses opposite |
| SdB/salle de bain | bathroom |
| SdE/salle d'eau | washroom |
| séj/séjour | living room |
| le séjour cathédrale | open-plan living room on two floors |
| le sous-sol | below ground-level |
| TI | Type 1; same as FI |
| TBE/très bon état | very good condition |
| les tommettes | hexagonal floor tiles in Provence |
| TTC/toutes taxes comprises | all taxes included |
| le verger | orchard |
| une vue imprenable | unrestricted view |

## Mortgage glossary

| | |
|---|---|
| apport personnel | buyer's percentage payment |
| assurance décès/invalidité | death/invalidity insurance |
| assurance perte d'emploi | unemployment insurance |
| échéance fixe | fixed redemption date |
| échéance modulable | variable redemption date |
| échéancier | repayment schedule |
| frais de mainlevée d'hypothèque | fee for removing mortgage charge from registry |
| indemnité de résiliation | early repayment penalty |
| mensualités | monthly repayments |
| prêt à taux capé | capped-rate loan |
| prêt à taux fixe | fixed-rate loan |
| prêt à taux révisable/variable | variable-rate loan |
| prêt relais | bridging loan |

| | |
|---|---|
| *remboursement* | repayment; reimbursement |
| *remboursement anticipé sans frais* | penalty-free early repayment |
| *résiliation* | cancellation |
| *TEG/taux effectif global* | APR; effective interest rate |

## Insurance glossary

| | |
|---|---|
| *l'assurance multirisques habitation* | house and contents insurance |
| *le bris de glaces* | window breakage |
| *le cambriolage* | burglary; housebreaking |
| *le certificat de perte* | police statement listing your losses |
| *l'effraction* | breaking and entering |
| *l'espagnolette* | window catch |
| *la franchise* | excess (UK); deductible (USA) |
| *la grêle* | hail |
| *l'incendie* | fire |
| *la police* | policy |
| *la protection juridique* | legal protection |
| *la résiliation* | cancellation |
| *la responsabilité civile* | civil liability |
| *les risques locatifs* | tenant's liability |
| *le store* | heavy shutters |
| *le vol* | theft |
| *le volet* | shutters |

## Glossary of French building terms

Building has its own terminology which is generally ignored in the big French–English dictionaries. The best, and very extensive, work is Don Montague's *Dictionary of Building and Civil Engineering*, published by Spon, which is both French–English and English–French. Hadley Pager Info (☎01372 458550) also publish a range of French/English technical glossaries. Listed below are some of the main terms you will come across.

| | |
|---|---|
| *un abri* | shelter |
| *un accès* | access |
| *un accotement* | roadside verge |
| *adossé* | backing onto |
| *un affaissement* | subsidence, collapse, sinking |
| *affaisser* | subside |
| *l'aggloméré* | agglomerate, or chipboard |
| *l'agrafe* | staple, wall tie, retaining clip |
| *l'aiguisoir* | sharpener, whetstone |
| *l'aménagement* | conversion; fitting out |
| *l'antigel* | frost protection; anti-freeze |
| *l'appui* | abutment, support, window sill |

| | |
|---|---|
| *un are* | 100 sq m |
| *l'ardoise* | slate tile used in Anjou, Brittany |
| *l'argile* | clay |
| *l'arpent* | 4221 sq m; 1.043 acres |

### Ardennes, parts of Alps and Auvergne, etc.

| | |
|---|---|
| *l'arrhes* | non-returnable deposit |
| *l'âtre* | fireplace, hearth |
| *le badigeon blanc (de chaux)* | (lime) whitewash |
| *badigeonner* | to whitewash |
| *la bande de calfeutrement* | draught excluder strip |
| *la bauge* | clay and straw daub |
| *le béton armé* | reinforced concrete |
| *le béton préparé* | ready-mixed concrete |
| *le bloc à poncer* | sandpaper block |
| *le boulon* | threaded bolt, pin |
| *le branchement* | connection, electrical lead, junction |
| *le cailloutage* | pebbledash |
| *la canalisation* | ducting, pipework |
| *le caniveau* | road drain |
| *la chaux hydratée/éteinte* | slaked lime |
| *la chaux vive* | quicklime |
| *cintré/cinglé* | arched, vaulted (also slang for 'crazy') |
| *cloqué* | blistered (paint) |
| *cloquer* | to set (e.g. of glue); to blister |
| *le coffrage* | casing, formwork, shuttering |
| *le couvreur* | roofer |
| *le crépi* | roughcast rendering |
| *la cuvette* | toilet basin, bowl |
| *le débit* | discharge, yield, debit |
| *le déblayage* | excavation |
| *le disjoncteur* | circuit-breaker |
| *l'écrou* | nut |
| *l'écrou à oreilles* | wing nut |
| *encastré* | embedded, flush, built-in (e.g. cupboard) |
| *l'enduit* | rendering, coating |
| *l'entretien* | maintenance |
| *l'équerre* | set-square, angle-bracket |
| *l'espagnolette* | shutter bar, shutter bolt |
| *l'essente* | wooden shingle, used in Alps, Vosges |
| *l'étagère* | shelving |
| *l'éverit* | Everite; white asbestos |
| *la fibre de verre* | fibreglass |

| | |
|---|---|
| *le flotteur* | ballcock |
| *la foreuse* | electric drill |
| *le fossé* | ditch |
| *le galet* | pebble, cobble |
| *le gazon* | turf |
| *le gond* | hinge |
| *la gouttière* | gutter |
| *le gravier concassé* | gravel |
| *la haie* | hedge |
| *le hectare* | 2.471 acres; 10,000 sq m |
| *l'installateur* | fitter |
| *l'isolation* | insulation |
| *le lambrissage* | wainscoting, pannelling |
| *la latte* | batten, lath |
| *la lauze/la lave/le platin* | thick stone slate, used in Auvergne |

### Alps, Burgundy, Manche, Anjou

| | |
|---|---|
| *le lavabo* | wash basin |
| *la lime* | file |
| *la lucarne* | dormer window |
| *le madrier* | massive beam |
| *le mastic* | mastic |
| *le mazout* | heating oil |
| *le menuisier* | joiner, carpenter |
| *le moellon* | quarried stone |
| *le moellon brut* | rough stone |
| *la moquette* | fitted carpet |
| *la moulure* | moulding |
| *la nappe phréatique* | water table |
| *la nivelle* | spirit level |
| *le nivellement* | levelling |
| *la norme française* | French standard |
| *l'ossature* | framework |
| *la panne* | pantile; also mechanical breakdown |
| *le panneau de plâtre* | plasterboard |
| *le parpaing* | breeze block; block exposed at both faces of a wall |
| *le pignon* | gable |
| *le pignon à gradins* | Flemish-style stepped gable |
| *le placoplâtre* | plasterboard |
| *le plafond suspendu* | suspended ceiling |
| *le plafonneur* | plasterer |
| *le plâtrier* | plasterer |
| *le plombier* | plumber |

| | |
|---|---|
| *la ponceuse* | sander |
| *le poteau* | post |
| *la poutre* | roof beam |
| *la poutre apparente* | exposed beam |
| *la poutrelle* | smaller roof beam |
| *le rabot* | plane |
| *ramoner* | to sweep a chimney |
| *ravalé* | resurfaced; newly rendered |
| *le ravalement* | resurfacing; rendering |
| *le remblai* | embankment; hardcore |
| *la remise* | storeroom |
| *la rive* | edge of roof or panel; riverbank |
| *le sable* | sand |
| *la scie* | saw |
| *la serrure* | lock |
| *la souche* | chimney stack (visible part) |
| *le stère* | a cubic metre |
| *le tamis* | sieve |
| *tapisser* | to wallpaper; to upholster |
| *la tapisserie* | wallpaper, wall-covering; tapestry, upholstery |
| *la tôle ondulée* | corrugated steel sheet |
| *la tôle zinguée* | galvanised steel sheet |
| *la tondeuse* | lawnmower |
| *le torchis* | cob, wattle and daub |
| *le tournevis* | screwdriver |
| *la trappe de visite* | inspection hatch |
| *le trop-plein* | overflow pipe |
| *la tuile* | flat tile in baked clay, used in Burgundy |

## Ile-de-France, Normandy, Nièvre, Dordogne, Champagne, Loiret

| | |
|---|---|
| *la tuile canal* | Spanish-style pipe tile |
| *la tuile faîtière* | ridge tile |
| *la tuile flamande (panne du nord)* | S-shaped Flemish pantile |
| *le tuyau* | pipe, tube |
| *la vanne* | valve |
| *le vernis* | varnish |
| *le vilebrequin* | brace and bit |
| *le voyant* | inspection window |
| *zingué(e)* | galvanised |

# The Directory

## TRAVEL AND TRANSPORT

### Ferry companies

**Brittany Ferries:** ☎08703 66533; www.brittany-ferries.com. Portsmouth to St Malo/Caen/Cherbourg; Poole to Cherbourg; Plymouth to Roscoff.

**Condor Ferries:** ☎01202 207207; reservations 0845 345 2000; www.condorferries.co.uk. Poole/Weymouth to St. Malo via the Channel Islands. May to September only.

**LD Lines:** ☎0870 428 4336; www.ldlines.co.uk. Nehaven to Le Havre/Dieppe; Portsmouth to Le Havre.

**Norfolkline:** ☎0870 870 1020; www.norfolkline.com. Dover to Dunkerque.

**P&O Ferries:** ☎0870 5 98 0 333; www.poferries.com. Dover to Calais; Hull to Zeebrugge (Belgium).

**Sea France:** ☎0870 571 1711; www.seafrance.com. Dover to Calais. Conventional ferry.

**SpeedFerries:** ☎0870 220 0570; www.speedferries.com. Dover to Boulogne.

**Transmanche Ferries:** ☎0800 917 1201; www.transmancheferries.co.uk. Newhaven to Le Havre/Dieppe; Portsmouth to Le Havre.

### Airlines

**Air France** flies from 16 UK airports: ☎0870 142 1000 (UK); 0820 820 820 (FR); www.airfrance.co.uk.

**bmi British Midland** flies from Edinburgh, Leeds and London Heathrow: ☎0870 607 0555; www.flybmi.com.

**bmibaby.com** flies from Cardiff, Durham, Manchester and Nottingham–East Midlands: ☎0870 264 2229; www.bmibaby.com.

**British Airways** flies from 16 airports in the UK: ☎0845 773 3377; www.britishairways.com. Also operates GB Airways: www.gbairways.com.

**Easyjet** flies from Belfast, Bristol, London Gatwick, London Luton and Stansted: ☎0870 600 0000; www.easyjet.com.

**Euroglobe Travel:** offers charters and business travel: ☎020 8677 5124.

**European Executive Ltd** flies from Brighton (Shoreham Airport); approx. 12 flights per week: ☎02173 446447; www.euroexec.com.

**Flybe** flies from Belfast, Birmingham, Bristol, Edinburgh, Glasgow, Glasgow, Jersey, Manchester and Southampton: ☎0871 700 0535; www.flybe.com.

**Flyglobespan.com** offers cheap flights from Glasgow and Edinburgh: ☎0870 556 1522; www.flyglobespan.com.

**Jet2.com** operates from Manchester and Leeds/Bradford: ☎020 7291 8112; www.jet2.com.

**Lyddair** flies from Lydd (Kent) to Le Touquet: ☎01797 322207; www.lyddair.com.

**Ryanair** flies from Dublin, Cork, Glasgow, Liverpool, London Stansted and Luton: ☎0870 333 1244; www.ryanair.com.

**SkyBargains.co.uk:** ☎0800 195 1300 or book online at www.skybargains.co.uk. ABTA members.

**Thomsonfly** operates from Bournemouth, Coventry and Doncaster-Sheffield: ☎0870 190 0737; www.thomsonfly.com.
Note that some flights are only seasonal and that schedules and destinations frequently change.

## FINANCE

### Mortgage brokers/advisors

**Axa-Baud:** ☎02 97 51 01 45; email agence.herrmann@axa.fr. Mortgages, loans and insurance. Based in Brittany.

**Banque Transatlantique Representative Office:** A French bank for newcomers to France. Bank accounts, mortgages (upmarket properties in Paris and selected provincial areas), legal and tax information. www.transat.tm.fr.

**Barclays:** ☎0845 675 0555; www.barclays.co.uk/buyingabroad/france/index.html.

**BNP Paribas:** www.bnpparibas.com/en/home.

**Conti Financial Services:** ☎01273 772811; email benedict@mortgagesoverseas.com; www.mortgagesoverseas.com. Well-established independent mortgage brokers.

**Crédit Agricole du Calvados:** offers a dedicated 'Britline' ☎02 31 55 67 89; email britline@ca-calvados.fr. Specialist branch for English-speaking customers offering a global banking service in English including property finance and insurance.

**Cred'Immo:** Crédit Mutuel de Bretagne; ☎0821 011011; www.cmb.fr.

**Credit Immobilier de France:** ☎0821 80 20 10; www.creditimmobilierdefrance.fr.

**France Home Finance:** Independent mortgage advice for non-resident buyers in France. 23 rue Charlot, 75003 Paris, France; ☎01 72 33 94 33 and 0820 20 23 26; email info@francehomefinance.com; www.francehomefinance.com.

**MFS Partners:** Specialising in French mortgages for 18 years, with 21 independent advisers. ☎01752 664777; email marcusconnell@zetnet.co.uk; www.mfspartners.co.uk.

**Michael Hackney:** Independent mortgage broker who was MD of Abbey National France for 4 years. ☎01869 278181; www.french-mortgage.com.

**Mortgage France:** Based in Alpes Maritimes; arranges mortgages all over France at no cost to applicant. ☎04 93 32 13 95; email info@mortgagefrance.com; www.mortgagefrance.com. Useful website.

### Expatriate financial planning

**Axis Strategy Consultants:** ☎01 39 21 74 61; email dcooney@axis-stratefy.com; www.axis-strategy.com; www.axis-strategy.com/personal–finance.htm. Specialises in financial advice for expats living in France.

**Blevins Franks:** Specialists in the expat financial sector. ☎020 7336 1000; www.blevinsfranks.com. Publishers of the book *Living in France* available from Blevins Franks partners.

**Brewin Dolphin Securities:** ☎01672 519600; email info@brewindolphin.co.uk; www.brewindolphin.co.uk. Services include international portfolio management with off-shore facility for those domiciled or resident outside the UK.

**Dixon Wilson:** Paris: ☎01 47 03 12 90; email dw@dixonwilson.fr. London: ☎020 7680 8100; email markwaterman@ dixonwilson.co.uk. Chartered accountants.

**Hansard Europe Ltd:** Dublin: ☎01 278 1488; email victoria.westhead@hansard. com; www.hansard.com. Products aimed at the French market and designed to be tax efficient with regard to French tax and life assurance regulations.

**John Siddall Financial Service Ltd:** ☎01329 288641; email france@ johnsiddalls.co.uk; www.siddalls. net. Independent financial advisers providing expertise across a spectrum of investments, retirement and tax planning for private clients at home and abroad.

**John Siddall International Ltd:** ☎05 56 34 75 51; email france@ johnsiddalls.co.uk; www.siddalls.net. French office of John Siddall Financial Services (above).

**PKF (Guernsey) Ltd:** Guernsey: ☎01481 727927; email french.tax@ pkfguernsey.com; www.pkfguernsey.com. Chartered accountants and French tax specialists. Also publishers of the excellent *Taxation in France, A Foreign Perspective* by Charles Parkinson. Updated annually.

## PROPERTY

The following agents are listed with the areas that they cover. Unless otherwise stated, they will mainly deal with properties in the western half of France, where most English are located, outside of the big towns. You should check to see if they belong to a professional organisation such as the NAEA or FOPDAC.

## UK-based estate agents

**1st for French Property:** ☎0870 720 2966; email info@1st-for-french-property. co.uk; www.1st-for-french-property.co.uk. Premier internet portal for potential buyers and sellers.

**A Home in France:** ☎0870 748 6161; email info@ahomeinfrance.com; ahomeinfrance@wanadoo.fr. All areas.

**A House in France Ltd:** ☎020 8959 5182; email john.hart@virgin.net; www. french-property-news.com/ahif.htm.

**All France Properties:** ☎020 8891 1750; email sales@all-france-properties. com; www.all-france-properties.com.

**Beaches International Property Ltd:** ☎01562 885181; email info@beachesint. com; www.beachesint.com. French Alps.

**Capital Mover Ltd:** ☎020 8746 0857; email enquiries@capitalmover.com; www. capitalmover.com. Individually designed new-builds throughout France.

**Currie French Properties:** ☎01223 576084; email info@curriefrenchproperties. com; www.curriefrenchproperties.com.

**David King Associates:** ☎020 8673 6800; www.dkassociates.co.uk. Paris, SW France; over £150,000.

**Domus Abroad:** ☎020 7431 4692; www.domusabroad.com. Services for both buyers and sellers.

**Dordogne & Lot Properties:** ☎01865 558659 or 513143; www.dorlotproperties. net.

**Eclipse Overseas:** ☎01425 275984; www.french-property.com/eclipse. Normandy, Charente, Loire, Vendée, Brittany.

**Francophiles Ltd:** ☎01622 688165; email sales@francophiles.co.uk; www. francophiles.co.uk.

**The French Property Shop:** ☎01233 666902; email info@frenchpropertyshop. com; www.frenchpropertyshop.com.

**Gascony Property:** ☎01702 390382; email info@gasconyproperty.com; www. gascony-property.com. SW France.

**Hamptons International**: ☎020 7589 8844; email international@hamptons-int. com; www.hamptons-int.com. Côte d'Azur. Branch in Nice.

**Hexagone France Ltd:** ☎01303 221077; email info@hexagonefrance.com; www.hexagonefrance.com. Normandy, Picardy, Brittany.

**Latitudes:** Penny Zoldan, ☎020 8951 5155; www.latitudes.co.uk.

**Leisure & Land**: ☎020 8951 5152; email sales@leisureandland.co.uk; www. leisureandland.co.uk. Specialises in income-producing properties.

**Maison France:** ☎01427 628537; email info@maisonfrance.com; www.agence-maisonfrance.com.

**Mistral Estate Services:** ☎1 516 620 0298 (USA); mistral@polaris.net; www. real-estate-in-france.com. US-based agent with a French network of real estate agents and property owners and able to provide a listing of all kinds of real estate including vineyards, villas, châteaux, and farmhouses for leisure, work, retirement, business etc.

**Propriétés Roussillon:** ☎021 459 9058; email sales@proprietes-roussillon.com; www.proprietes-roussillon.com. All areas.

**La Résidence:** ☎01491 838485; email sales@laresidence.co.uk; www.laresidence. co.uk.

**Sifex Ltd:** ☎20 7384 1200; email info@ sifex.co.uk; www.sifex.co.uk. Exclusive properties in Southern France. Châteaux in all regions of France.

**Sinclair Overseas Property Network:** ☎01525 375319; www. sinclair-frenchprops.com. Associate offices throughout France.

**VEF (Vivre en France) UK:** email www.vefuk.com. New-builds.

**Villas Abroad Ltd:** ☎020 8941 4499; email villasabroad@fopdac.com; www. villasabroadproperties.com. Côte d'Azur. Mostly new-builds.

**World Class Homes Ltd:** ☎01582 832001; FREEPHONE UK ☎0800 731 4713; email info@worldclasshomes.co.uk; www.worldclasshomes.co.uk. Languedoc Roussillon. New-builds.

## France-based estate agents

**ABC Immobilier:** Béziers: ☎04 67 49 20 10; 92; email beziers@abc-immo.fr; www.abc-immo.fr. Hérault.

**L'Affaire Française:** ☎020 8570 9844 (UK); ☎05 45 81 76 79 (FR); www. French-Property-Net.com. Charente, Dordogne, Limousin.

**Agence Christol:** Clermont-L'Hérault: ☎04 67 96 00 60; email christol34@ aol.com; www.openmedia.fr/christol. Specialises in the Languedoc around Montpellier.

**Agence Hamilton:** Carcassonne: ☎04 68 72 48 38; email info@agence-hamilton.com; www.agence-hamilton.com. Languedoc, Midi-Pyrénées.

**Agence Hermann de Graaf:** St Jean de Côle: ☎05 53 62 38 03; email agence@immobilier-dordogne.com; www. immobilier-dordogne.com. Dordogne.

**Agence L'Union:** St Antonin-Noble-Val: ☎05 63 30 60 24; email info@ agencelunion.com; www.agencelunion.com. Tarn, Tarn-et-Garonne, Lot, Aveyron.

**Agence Vallée des Rois Sarl:**
Beaufort-en-Vallee: ☎02 41 45 22 22;
www.loireproperty.com. French agency
with British staff. Loire Valley between
Angers and Saumur.

**Balagne Immobilier:** Corsica: ☎04
95 60 70 22; www.corse-immobilier.com.
Corsica, especially the northern half of the
island.

**Breton Homes:** 5 Place du Général de
Gaulle, 22210 Plemet: ☎07005 981 221
(UK) ☎02 96 50 19 97 (FR); www.breton-
homes.com. Brittany.

**Charles Loftie Immobilier:** Cazals: ☎
05 65 22 83 50; email info@charles-loftie-
immo.com.

**Coast & Country:** Mougins: ☎04 92
92 47 50; email info@coast-country.com;
http://coast-country.com.

**La Foncière Charentaise:** David and
Vanessa Leake, 14 bis, Grand Rue, Aigre,
16140 France; ☎05 45 21 78 38; www.
french-property.com/lafc. Poitou-Charentes
region.

**France Limousin Immobilier:**
Eymoutiers: ☎05 55 69 74 39; email
info@fralimo.com; www.fralimo.com.
Limousin.

**ImoCONSEIL:** L'Isle-Jourdain: ☎05
49 84 18 33; www.imoconseil.com. South
Vienne.

**Janssens Immobilier:** Bonnieux: ☎04
90 75 96 98; email janssens.immobilier@
wanadoo.fr; www.janssensimmobilier.com.
Luberon.

**Jon Coshall, Eymet Immobilier:**
Dordogne: ☎05 53 22 50 25; email info@
eymet-immobilier.com; www.eymet-
immobilier.com.

**Langlois Gordon Hay:** Angoulême:
☎05 45 95 08 51; email contact@
lghfrance.com; www.lghfrance.com.
Charente.

**Nowak Immobilier:** Civray: ☎05 49 87
39 85; email nowakimmobilier@wanadoo.
fr; www.nowakimmobilier.fr.

**Papillon Properties:** St. Gaudent: ☎05
49 87 45 47; www.papillon-properties.com.
In the UK contact Samantha Lear; ☎0870
800 1087. Offers properties in the Poitou-
Charentes.

**Properties 47 Ltd:** Bazens: ☎05 53
84 49 66; email intman@easynet.fr Lot-et
Garonne, Lot, Tarn and Gers. Also around
Beziers, Biarritz and Andorra.

**Properties in France Sarl PIF:**
Mouliherne: ☎02 41 52 02 18; email pif@
compuserve.com. Loire Valley.

**Purslows Gascony:** Mirande: ☎05 62
67 61 50; www.purslows-gascony.com. Sells
farmhouses, small châteaux and manoirs,
many already restored.

**S.A.R.L. Bacchus:** Cognac: ☎05 45 82
48 93; email props@charente-properties.
com; www.charente-properties.com.
Charente.

**Vialex International:** Beauville: ☎05 53
95 46 24; www.vialex.com. French/English
partnership specialising in SW France (Lot,
Lot-et-Garonne, Tarn and Atlantic, and
Andorra).

## Property consultants

While it is sometimes difficult to separate
them from property agents, some
consultants offer wide-ranging services
covering all aspects of property purchase.

**A Home in France:** Buckinghamshire,
UK: ☎0870 748 6161; email info@
ahomeinfrance.com; ahomeinfrance@
wanadoo.fr.

**Anglo-French Homes:**
Vimoutiers: ☎02 33 39 80 55; email
anglofrenchhomes@wanadoo.fr; www.
anglo-french-homes.co.uk. Normandy.

**Sam Crabb:** ☎01935 851155; www. samcrabb.com. Independent consultant since 1993.

**Homehunts:** Marseille; ☎04 92 28 05 42; email tim@home-hunts.com; www. home-hunts.com. PACA and Languedoc-Roussillon. Contact Tim Swannie.

**PWT NormandyLife:** Brighton, UK: ☎07880 501 116 or 01237 422 143; email info@normandylife.com; www. normandylife.com. Normandy.

## Property websites in English

www.1st-for-french-property.co.uk.

www.alps-property-finder.com.

www.angloinfo.com.

www.europropertysearch.com.

www.everythingFrance.co.uk.

www.frenchconnections.co.uk.

www.frenchentree.com.

www.french-property.com.

www.frenchpropertylinks.com.

www.french-property-news.com.

www.frenchways.com.

www.green-acre.com.

www.homesoverseas.co.uk.

www.houseweb.com.

www.livingfrance.com.

www.salut-france.com.

www.skiproperty.com.

www.snowandsea.com.

## Websites with private property adverts

www.appelimmo.fr.

www.bonjour.fr.

www.entreparticuliers.fr.

www.explorimmo.com.

www.frenchentree.com.

www.journaldesparticuliers.fr.

www.kitrouve.com.

www.lacentrale.fr.

www.lesiteimmobilier.com.

www.pap.fr.

## National property websites

www.123immo.fr.

www.abonim.com.

www.century21.fr.

www.eurofoncier.com.

www.europropertysearch.com.

www.fnaim.fr. National estate agents organisation.

www.immoneuf.com. New property.

www.lesiteimmobilier.com.

www.letuc.com.

www.logic-immo.com. One of the best French property websites.

www.nexdom.com.

www.orpi.com.

www.panorimmo.com.

www.partenaire-europeen.fr.

www.p-e.fr.

www.proprietesdefrance.com. Upmarket properties.

www.seloger.com.

www.snpi.com. National estate agents organisation.

## Property rental websites

www.alouer.fr.

www.appelimmo.fr.

www.bonjour.fr.

www.colocataire.fr. For those looking for a shared house or apartment.

www.entreparticuliers.fr.

www.foncia.fr.

www.journaldesparticuliers.fr.

www.kitrouve.com.

www.lacentrale.fr.

www.lesiteimmobilier.com.

www.locat.com.

www.pap.fr.

www.RentaplaceinFrance.com.

www.seloger.com.

## Law firms dealing with French property

**A Home in France:** ☎0870 748 6161; www.ahomeinfrance.com. Run by Danielle Seabrook, this company offers complete bilingual legal assistance to British residents to manage their risk when buying in a foreign jurisdiction. Also has an office in Chinon, Indre-et-Loire.

**Bennett & Co Solicitors:** Cheshire: ☎01625 586937; www.bennett-and-co.com.

**Blake Lapthorn Tarlo Lyons:** London: ☎020 781 46932 ; email frenchteam@bllaw.co.uk ; www.bllaw.co.uk. Has an in-house team of three French lawyers. Offices in Oxford, Fareham, Southampton and Portsmouth.

**Bright Jones:** Toulouse: ☎05 61 57 90 86; email brightjones@wanadoo.fr. British lawyers, qualified and based in France.

**Fox Hayes Solicitors:** Leeds: ☎01132 496496; www.foxhayes.co.uk. Contact France Legal: Susan Busby; Bury St. Edmunds; ☎01449 736644; email ssb@francelegal.co.uk; www.francelegal.co.uk.

**French Lawyer:** Isabelle Cès, London: ☎0845 644 3061; email info@french-lawyer.com; www.french-lawyer.com.

**John Howell & Co:** London and Leeds: ☎020 7061 6700 (London); 020 7061 6748 (Leeds); email info@LawOverseas.com; www.lawoverseas.com. As John Howell, the firm has been specialising in the law of other countries for over 20 years. From their London offices their 40+ staff pride themselves on finding cost effective solutions to their clients' international legal problems. Graham Platt, based in Leeds, is qualified both in Britain as a solicitor, and admitted to practise as an Avocat in France. Deals with property, company, litigation and probate.

**The International Property Law Centre:** Hessle: ☎0870 800 4565; email internationalproperty@maxgold.com; www.maxgold.com. Contact senior partner and solicitor Stefano Lucatello, an expert in the purchase and sale of property and businesses in Bulgaria, Cyprus, the Dominican Republic, Dubai, France, Florida, Goa, Italy, Malta, Portugal, Spain, the Cape Verde Islands and Turkey, and the formation of offshore tax vehicles and trusts.

**Howard Kennedy Solicitors:** ☎020 7636 1616; www.howard-kennedy.com. Large London firm dealing with the top end of the market. Ask for Anthony Slingsby.

**Kingsfords Solicitors:** Ashford: ☎01233 624544; email enquiries@kingsfords.net; www.kingsfords-solicitors.com. British lawyers with expertise in French conveyancing. Fixed-price property buyer's package and other services.

**Liliane Levasseur-Hills:** Godalming: ☎01483 424303. Fully qualified French *notaire* offering assistance with buying and selling French property, French inheritance law, and French wills.

**Sean O'Connor & Co:** Tonbridge: ☎01732 365378; email seanoconnorco@aol.com. Bilingual solicitors.

**Pannone & Partners:** Manchester: ☎0161 9091553; email lindsay.kinnealy @pannone.co.uk; www.pannone.com. Contact Lindsay Kinnealy.

**Penningtons Solicitors:** London: ☎020 7457 3000; www.penningtons. co.uk. Paris office: ☎01 44 51 59 70.

**Prettys Solicitors:** Ipswich: ☎01473 232121; www.prettys.co.uk. Prettys' French Property Group are multi-lingual and assist clients on the whole process of buying a property in France including; advising on obtaining finance and insurance, French income and capital gains tax, and issues with wills and future considerations.

**Riddell Croft & Co Solicitors:** Ipswich: ☎01473 384870; www.riddellcroft.com. Experienced, bilingual practitioners offering help with buying and selling property in France, rentals, tax and estate planning and wills. Can also help with property search.

**Russell-Cooke:** London: ☎020 8789 9111; email Aldersond@russell-cooke. co.uk; www.russell-cooke.co.uk. Large firm with French law and property department, headed by Dawn Alderson, qualified in both English and French law and member of the Bordeaux bar. Bordeaux office: ☎05 56 90 83 109

**Stephen Smith (France) Ltd:** Ipswich: ☎01473 437186; email StephenSmith@stephensmithfranceltd.com; www. stephensmithfranceltd.com. Stephen Smith is the author of *Letting Your French Property Successfully*, published by PKF Guernsey.

**Taylors Solicitors and Notaries Public:** Sheffield: ☎0114 2766767; www. taylorssolicitors.co.uk.

**Thrings and Townsend Solicitors:** Bath: ☎01225 340000; email solicitors@ttuk.com; www.ttuk.com. Advice on french property purchase, and setting up a French business. Offices in Newbury, Swindon and Frome.

**Turner and Co Solicitors:** Birmingham: ☎0121 2001612; email turneranco@aol. com; www.french-property-news.com/turnerandco.htm.

www.immonot.com.

www.min-immo.com.

www.notaire.fr.

Many *départements* have their own *notaire* websites. Try *chambre+des+notaires+* [name of *département*].

There is also a good list at: www.day-tripper.net/propertyxnotaires.html.

## Surveyors

**Nick Adams:** ☎05 49 64 42 96; email info@adamsgautier.com; www. adamsgautier.com. Mid-SW France.

**Andrew Bailey:** ☎08000 744 615 (UK); email abpswebsite@hotmail.com; www. surveylinkfrance.com. All areas.

**Mary Hall:** ☎05 65 24 66 46; maisonminders@aol.com; www.French-property-news.com/fpn/minders.htm. SW France.

**Brian Hersee:** ☎05 45 64 94 56; email cassiehersee@wanadoo.fr. Charente and neighbouring departments.

**Burrows Hutchison:** ☎02 97 39 45 53; email burrowhutch@aol.com; www. burrows-hutchison.com. Brittany, Loire Valley, Vendée and Charente.

**James Latter:** ☎02 31 90 17 70; www. surveyors-en-france.com. Normandy, Pays de Loire and Ile de France.

**Ian Morris:** ☎01684 576775 (UK); ☎04 67 89 43 46 (FR); www.surveyors-en-france.com. Languedoc-Roussillon, Midi-Pyrénées and Aquitaine.

**Nick Norrie:** ☎07979 771166/01869 346973; email office@subject2survey.fsnet. co.uk; www.subject2survey.com.

**Surveyfrance:** ☎01394 610227; email enquiries@surveyfrance.co.uk; www. surveyfrance.co.uk.

**Pierre Weingaertner:** ☎06 60 55 29 74; www.surveyors-en-france.com. PACA.

## Home insurance companies

**Agence Eaton:** Continent Assurances, Arradon, France: ☎02 97 40 80 20; email info@french-insurance.com; www.french-insurance.com. Bilingual insurance bureau.

**AXA Courtage:** Paris: ☎01 49 49 40 00; www.axa.fr. Large French insurer with branches in the UK.

**Azur Assurances:** ☎0820 01 4000 (only within France); www.azur-assurances. fr. House, car and health insurance.

**Bacchus Insurance:** ☎05 45 82 42 93; email insure@bacchus-insurance.com; www.bacchus-insurance.com. All types of insurance; based in Charente.

**Copeland Insurance:** ☎020 8656 2544; email info@acopeland.com; www. andrewcopeland.co.uk. Buildings and contents insurance for France and special scheme for UK-registered cars in France.

**Intasure:** ☎0845 111 0680; email enquiries@intasure.com; www.intasure. com. Intasure's property insurance policy is designed specifically to meet the needs of UK residents with holiday homes in France. Flexible buildings and contents insurance allows you to live in, leave your property unoccupied, or let short or long term. All documentation is written in English and supported by a UK-based team.

**O'Halloran & Co:** ☎01522 537491; email tpo@ohal.org; www.ohalloran. org.uk. Will arrange cover for holiday homes in Europe. Contact Linda O'Halloran.

**Towergate Holiday Homes Underwriting:** ☎0870 242 2470; email holidayhomes@towergate.co.uk; www. towergateholidayhomes.co.uk. Specialists in providing cover for holiday homes, chalets and caravans in Europe, with policy wording to meet local requirements, including the payment of insurance taxes.

## General information websites

www.ademe.fr. Agency promoting environmentally friendly building.

www.anah.fr. National association for housing improvement.

www.anil.org. State agency for housing information.

www.fnaim.fr. Estate agents organisation.

www.ideesmaison.com. Information on building new property.

www.immoprix.com. An excellent site comparing prices of property and land by region and town.

www.immostreet.com. General information.

www.infologement.fr. Mortgage advice.

www.juri-logement.org. Legal information.

www.logement.equipement.gouv.fr. Ministry of Housing and Urban Planning.

www.logement.org. General information.

ww.mon-immeuble.com. General information.

www.panoranet.com. Information on mortgages and insurance.

www.seloger.com. General information.

www.service-public.gouv.fr. Government information site.

www.snpi.fr. Estate agents organisation.

www.uncmi.org. National union of residential property builders.

www.unpi.org. Proprietors' union.

## REMOVALS

### Removal firms dealing with France

**Abels Moving Services:** ☎01842 816 600; enquiries@abels.co.uk; www.abels. co.uk. All areas of France.

**Allied Pickfords:** ☎0800 289 229; www.pickfords.co.uk; www.allied-pickfords.co.uk (UK) or www.alliedintl. com (USA).

**Crown Worldwide Movers:** Barking: ☎020 8591 3388; www.crownworldwide. com.

**Ede Brothers:** ☎01306 711293; www. edebros.co.uk. Family-run firm established in 1926. All areas of France.

**French & Spanish Connexion:** ☎020 8648 6686; email funnellsremovals@aol. com. Regular removals to and from France and throughout the UK; from single item to a complete house load.

**The Old House (Associated Moving Services):** ☎01323 892934; email enquiries@amsmoving.co.uk; www. amsmoving.co.uk. Established for over 45 years. Fully bonded members of BAR Overseas. Full and part loads; free quotations and advice.

**Robinsons International Moving Services:** ☎0800 833 638; email international@robinsons-intl.com; www. robinsons-intl.com.

### Exporting pets

**Airpets Oceanic:** ☎0800 371554 or 01753 685571; email info@airpets.com; www.airpets.com.

**Dogs Away:** ☎0870 201 2501 or 0209 8441 9311; email contact@dogsaway.co.uk; www.dogsaway.co.uk.

**Independent Pet and Animal Transport Association:** ☎001 903 769 2267; email inquiries@ipata.com; www. ipata.com.

**Par Air Services:** ☎01206 330332; email parair@btconnect.com; www.parair. co.uk.

**Pets Travel Scheme:** 1 Page St, London SWIP 4PQ; ☎0870 241 1710 or 01206 330 332; email pets.helpline@defra.gsi.gov. uk; www.defra.gov.uk.

## LIVING IN FRANCE

### Language course providers

**Alliance Française:** Paris: ☎01 42 84 90 00; email info@alliancefr.org; www. alliance.fr.org.

**Alliance Française de Londres:** ☎020 7224 1908; email network@ alliancefrancaise.org.uk; www.alliance francaise.org.uk.

**Inlingua School of Languages:** Cheltenham: ☎01242 250493; www. inlingua.com.

**Institut Français Londres:** ☎020 7073 1350; www.institut-francais.org.uk.

**Learn French At Home:** www. learnfrenchathome.com.

**Linguaphone:** www.linguaphone.co.uk, www.linguaphone.com/usa.

**MyLanguageExchange.com:** www.
mylanguageexchange.com.

**Parler Parlor:** email info@parlerparlor.
com; www.parlerparlor.com.

## Major French banks

**Barclays Bank SA:** www.barclays.fr.

**Banque Populaire:** www.
banquepopulaire.fr.

**BNP Paribas:** www.bnpparibas.net.

**Britline:** www.britline.com.

**Caixa Bank:** www.caixabank.fr.

**CCF:** www.ccf.com.

**Crédit Agricole:** www.credit-agricole.fr;
www.ca-[name of department].fr.

**Crédit du Nord:** www.credit-du-nord.fr.

**Crédit Lyonnais:** www.creditlyonnais.
com.

**Lloyds Bank SA:** www.lloydstsbiwm.
com.

**Société Générale:** www.socgen.com.

## INTERNATIONAL SCHOOLS

## Schools in Paris

**American School of Paris:** ☎01 41 12
82 45; www.asparis.org.

**British School of Paris:** ☎01 34 80 45
90; www.britishschool.fr.

**Collège International de
Fontainebleau:** ☎01 64 22 11 77;
www.anglosection.com.

**The International School of
Paris:** ☎01 42 24 09 54; www.isparis.
edu.

## Schools outside Paris

**American International School on
the Côte d'Azur:** Nice: ☎04 93 21
04 00.

**Bordeaux International School:** ☎05
57 87 02 11; www.bordeaux-school.com.

**Cité Scolaire Internationale:** Lyon:
☎04 78 69 60 06; www2.ac-lyon.fr/etab/
lycees/lyc-69/csi/index.html.

**CIV International School of Sophia
Antipolis:** Nice: ☎04 92 96 52 24; www.
issa.net.

**Collège-Lycée Cévenol
International:** Le Chambon-sur-Lignon:
☎04 71 59 72 52; www.lecevenol.org.

**Collège et Lycée de Sèvres:** Sèvres
92310: ☎1 72 77 70 40; www.sis-sevres.
net.

**Ecole Internationale Michelin:**
Clermont-Ferrand: ☎04 73 98 09 73;
email ecoleinternationale@yahoo.fr.

**International School of Nice:** Nice:
☎0493 21 04 40; www.isn-nice.org.

**International School of Toulouse:**
Colomiers: ☎05 62 74 26 74; www.intst.
net.

**Mougins School:** Mougins: ☎04 93 90
15 47; www.mougins-school.com.

**Strasbourg International School:**
67100 Strasbourg: ☎3 88 31 50 77; www.
strasbourgis.org.

**Information Sources**

**Centre National de Documentation
sur l'Enseignement Privé:** ☎01 47 05
32 68; www.fabert.com.

**Council of British Independent
Schools in the European Community
(COBISEC):** ☎01367 242655; www.
cobisec.org.

**ECIS North America:** New Jersey
USA: ☎908 903 0552; email malyecisna@
aol.com; www.ecis.org.

**English Language Schools
Association France (ELSA):** ☎01 45
04 48 52; email elsa.france@wanadoo.fr;
www.elsa-france.org.

**European Council of International
Schools:** ☎01730 268244; email ecis@
ecis.org; www.ecis.org.

**FrenchEntree.com:** www.frenchentree. com/fe-education.

**Ministère de l'Éducation Nationale et de la Culture:** Paris: ☎01 49 50 10 10; www.education.gouv.fr.

**Office National d'Information sur les Enseignements et les Professions (ONISEP):** ☎01 40 77 60 00; www. onisep.fr.

### Health insurers

**Agence Eaton:** Arradon: ☎02 97 40 80 20; www.french-insurance.com.

**British United Provident Association (BUPA):** Brighton: ☎01273 208181; www.bupa-intl.com.

**Expacare Insurance Services:** Berkshire: ☎01344 381650; email info@ expacare.net; www.expacare.net.

**Goodhealth Worldwide (Europe):** ☎0870 442 7376; www.goodhealth. co.uk.

**Groupama:** www.groupama.fr.

### Golf websites

www.backspin.com.
www.doucefrance.com/golf.
www.europegolftravel.com.
www.golfagora.com.
www.golflounge.com/fr.

### French property magazines' websites

www.appelimmo.fr.
www.ibneuf.com.
www.immobilierenfrance.com.
www.immoneuf.com.
www.indicateurbertrand.com.
www.residencessecondaires.com.

### Newspapers

**Alsace:** *L'Alsace* (www.alsapresse.com); *Dernières Nouvelles d'Alsace* (www.dna. fr/dna).

**Aquitaine:** *Sud Ouest* (www.sudouest. com); *Nouvelle République des Pyrénées* (www.nrpyrenees.com).

**Auvergne:** *Centre France-La Montagne* (www.centrefrance.com).

**Brittany:** *France Ouest* (www.france-ouest.tm.fr; www.ouestfrance-immobilier. com); *Télégramme de Brest* (www. letelegramme.com).

**Burgundy:** *Bien Public* (www.bienpublic. com); *Journal du Saône-et-Loire* (www.lejsl. com); *Journal du Centre* (www.centre-france.com).

**Centre:** *Berry Républicain* (www. centrefrance.com); *La Nouvelle République* (www.lanouvellerepublique.fr); *La République du Centre* (www.larep.com).

**Champagne-Ardennes:** *L'Union Reims* (http://lunion/presse.fr); *L'Ardennais* (http://lunion/presse.fr); *Journal de la Haute Marne* (www.journaldelahautemarne.com); *Libération Champagne.*

**Corsica:** *Corse Matin* (www.corse.info); *Journal de Corse* (www.jdcorse.com).

**Franche-Comté:** *Progrès de Lyon* (www. leprogres.fr); *Voix du Jura* (www.voixdujura. fr); *L'Est.*

**Languedoc-Roussillon:** *Midi Libre* (www.midilibre.fr); *Dépêche du Midi* (www. ladepeche.com); *L'Indépendant* (www. lindependant.com); *Lozère Nouvelle* (www. lozere-nouvelle.com).

**Limousin:** *Centre France-Le Populaire du Centre* (www.centrefrance.com).

**Lorraine:** *Est Républicain* (www. estrepublicain.fr); *Liberté de l'Est* (www. lalibertedelest.fr).

**Midi-Pyrénées:** *Nouvelle République des Pyrénées* (www.nrpyrenees.com); *Journal de Millau* (www.journaldemillau.com); *La Dépêche* (www.ladepeche.fr).

**Nord-Pas de Calais:** *La Voix du Nord* (www.lavoixdunord.fr).

**Normandy:** *France Ouest* (www.france-ouest.tm.fr); *Informations Dieppoises* (http://infos-dieppoises.fr); *La Manche Libre* (www.normandiepa.com).

**Paris-Ile-de-France:** *Le Parisien* (www.leparisien.fr); *Nouvel Observateur Paris-Ile-de-France* (www.parisobs.com).

**Pays de la Loire:** *France Ouest* (www.france-ouest.tm.fr); *Presse Océan*.

## EMBASSIES AND CONSULATES

### British consulates in france

**British Consulate:** 18bis rue d'Anjou, 75008 Paris: ☎01 44 51 31 00; fax 01 44 51 31 27; email consularemailpavis. consularemailpavis2@fco.gov.uk. Covers: Aube, Calvados, Cher, Côtes-Du-Nord, Eure, Eure-et-Loir, Finistère, Ille-et-Vilaine, Indre, Indre-et-Loire, Loir-et-Cher, Loire, Loire-Atlantique, Loiret, Maine-et-Loire, Manche, Marne, Haute-Marne, Mayenne, Meurthe-et-Moselle, Meuse, Morbihan, Moselle, Nièvre, Oise, Orne, Bas-Rhin, Haut-Rhin, Sarthe, Paris (Seine), Seine-Maritime, Seine-et-Marne, Yvelines, Vendée, Vosges, Yonne, Essonne, Hauts-de-Seine, Seine-St Denis, Val de Marne, Val d'Oise and DOM-TOM. Opening hours: Monday/Wednesday/Thursday/Friday, 9.30am–12.30pm and 2.30-5pm. On Tuesdays the consulate is open from 9.30am to 4.30pm without a break. Emergency number: 01 44 51 31 00.

**British Consulate:** 353 bvd du Président Wilson, 33073 Bordeaux: ☎05 57 22 21 10; fax 05 56 08 33 12; email postmaster. bordeaux@fco.gov.uk. Covers: Ariège, Aveyron, Charente, Charente-Maritime, Corrèze, Creuse, Dordogne, Haute-Garonne, Gers, Gironde, Landes, Lot, Lot-et-Garonne, Pyrenées-Atlantiques, Hautes-Pyrénées, Deux-Sèvres, Tarn, Tarn-et-Garonne, Vienne and Haute-Vienne. Opening hours: Monday to Friday, 9am–12 noon and 2–5pm. Emergency number: 06 85 06 38 32.

**British Consulate:** 11 Square Dutilleul, 59800 Lille: ☎03 20 12 82 72; fax 03 20 54 88 16; email consular.lille@fco.gov.uk. Covers: Nord, Pas-de-Calais, Somme, Aisne and Ardennes. Opening hours: Monday to Friday, 9.30am–12.30pm and 2–5pm. Emergency number: 03 20 54 79 82.

**British Consulate:** 24 rue Childebert, 69002 Lyon: ☎04 72 77 81 70; fax 04 72 77 81 79. Covers the regions of Auvergne, Bourgogne, Franche-Comté and Rhône-Alpes. Opening hours: Monday to Friday, 9am–12.30pm and 2–5pm. Emergency number: 04 72 77 81 78.

**British Consulate:** 24 ave du Prado, 13006 Marseille: ☎04 91 15 72 10; fax 04 91 37 47 06; email MarseilleConsular. marseille@fco.gov.uk. Covers: Pyrénées Orientales, Aude, Hérault, Lozère, Gard, Vaucluse, Bouches-du-Rhône, Var, Alpes-Maritimes, Alpes-de-Haute-Provence, Corsica and Monaco. Opening hours: Monday to Friday, 9am–12 noon and 2–5pm. Emergency number: 04 91 15 72 10. Useful Addresses

### French consulates abroad

**French Consulate:** Service des Visas (Long Stay Visas), 6A Cromwell Place, PO Box 57, London SW7 2EW: ☎020 7073 1200. Open 9–10am and 1.30–2.30pm for long stay visa applications only. Closed on UK bank holidays and French public holidays.

**French Consulate at Edinburgh and Glasgow:** 11 Randolph Crescent, Edinburgh, EH3 7TT: ☎0131 225 7954; visa info-line 0131 220 6324; fax 0131 220 6324; www.consulfrance.edimbourg.org/. Open daily 9.30–11.30am for visas.

**French Consulate General:** General Inquiries, 21 Cromwell Rd, London SW7 2EN: ☎020 7073 1200; www. consulfrance-londres.org. Open 8.45am–midday, Monday to Thursday; 8.45am–11.30pm Friday. To make an application it is essential to make an appointment first either through the website above or by calling 09065 540 700 (£1 per minute). Persons residing outside Greater London can submit applications by post. Those living outside Greater London or the Home Counties are allowed to make enquiries in person until 3.30pm from Monday to Thursday, and until 1pm on Fridays. Times are subject to change, so call first before going to the consulate. It is also possible to make enquiries by email visas. londres-fslt@diplomatie.gouv.fr.

**French Embassy:** Cultural Department, 23 Cromwell Rd, London SW7 2EL: ☎020 7073 1300.

**French Embassy and Consulate General:** 4101 Reservoir Rd NW, Washington DC 20007: ☎202 944 6195; www.ambafrance-us.org. For visas, look at www.consulfrance-washington.org/visas.htm or call 202 944 6200, 2–5pm Monday to Friday. There are 10 French consulates in the USA; consult www. ambafrance-us.org to find the one dealing with your state.

**French Embassy in London:** 58 Knightsbridge, London SW1X 7JT: ☎020 7073 1000; fax 020 7073 1256; www. ambafrance-uk.org.

## British embassy services in france

Documents are issued from Paris. The Consulates-General can issue forms, which you then send to the British Embassy in Paris. The Consulates-General can issue emergency passports valid for one journey. Addresses of Consulates-General are given above. The British Embassy advises all British citizens who remain in France for any length of time to register with the Embassy.

**British Consular Services Paris:** 18bis rue d'Anjou, 75008 Paris; ☎01 44 51 31 00; fax 01 44 51 31 27.

**British Embassy:** 35 rue du Faubourg St Honoré, 75008 Paris Cedex 08: ☎01 44 51 31 00; fax 01 44 51 32 34; www.amb-grandebretagne.fr.

## US embassy and consulates France

**United States Consulate:** 2 rue St Florentin, 75382 Paris Cedex: ☎as above.

**United States Consulate:** place Varian Fry, 13006 Marseille: ☎04 91 54 92 00; www.amb-usa.fr/marseille/default.htm.

**United States Consulate:** 15 ave d'Alsace, 67082 Strasbourg: ☎03 88 35 31 04; www.amb-usa.fr/marseille/default. htm. There are also American Presence Posts in Bordeaux, Lille, Lyon, Rennes and Toulouse, and a Consular Agency in Nice. See the embassy website for details.

**United States Embassy:** 2 ave Gabriel, 75008 Paris: ☎01 43 12 22 22; fax 01 42 66 97 83; www.amb-usa.fr.